Birds in the Yard

Month by Month

*To Karen —
Enjoy the birds!
Sharon Sorenson*

Birds in the *Yard*

Month by Month

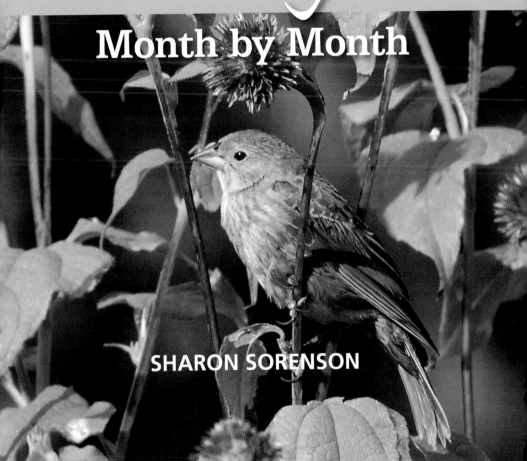

SHARON SORENSON

STACKPOLE
BOOKS

To the tireless men and women
whose largely thankless years of avian research and thoughtful reporting
help us better understand the conservation of birds
that share with us their world.

Published by
STACKPOLE BOOKS
5067 Ritter Road
Mechanicsburg, PA 17055
www.stackpolebooks.com

Printed in the United States of America

10 9 8 7 6 5 4 3

FIRST EDITION

Cover design by Caroline M. Stover
All photographs by Charles and Sharon Sorenson

Library of Congress Cataloging-in-Publication Data

Sorenson, Sharon.
    Birds in the yard month by month / Sharon Sorenson. — First edition.
        pages   cm
    Includes bibliographical references and index.
    ISBN 978-0-8117-1151-7 (paperback)
    1. Birds—East (U.S.)—Identification.   2. Bird watching—East (U.S.)—Handbooks, manuals, etc. 3. Bird attracting—East (U.S.)—Handbooks, manuals, etc. I. Title.
QL683.E27S78   2013
598.072'3474—dc23

                                            2013013522

CONTENTS

PREFACE

Like many other folks, I used to think that attracting birds to the backyard was all about birdfeeders and feed. Maybe add a pan of water, and I would have done all I could for our wonderful winged creatures. Now I know otherwise.

Even so, after a forty-five-year effort to become the perfect host for my yard's birds, I'm still learning. But I've made enough progress over time to understand one key principle: I will see in the yard only what the habitat attracts. For birds, habitat is everything. It's food, water, shelter, and places to raise young. And "food" includes far more than birdfeeders and feed.

As a country kid, I grew up loving birds, but only as an adult did I learn about intentionally adjusting habitat for their benefit. For me, it's been an education by trial and error, reading and listening to what others have said and then, fully inspired, launching a grand experiment, altering my three-acre southwestern Indiana setting accordingly. The result has been a surprising yard list of more than 160 species. Not a bad count, I think.

Last year, however, to further hone my understanding, I followed birds in the yard week by week, month by month, detailing the activity—a sort of Big Year in the Yard. For instance, who lived or visited the yard in October? What did they do here? Did they find what they needed and stay the winter? Or were they passing through? What did they eat? Where did they roost? What kept them safe and warm? How did they survive autumn storms?

That year, 114 species of birds joined the month-by-month action in my backyard habitat.

It would seem obvious that a Big Year in the Yard would verify that February differed from April, May differed from July, and August differed from October. The differences, though, were not merely in which birds were—or were not—here. Instead, the differences really revolved around *why* they were—or were not—here. Some birds arrived from the tropics to nest in summer. So they needed nesting habitat, security, and bugs beyond belief to feed nests full of babies. Some sailed in only to spend the winter. So they needed survival habitat, with protection from snow and ice, and vast resources for energy. Some zipped through in spring and idled back through in fall. So they needed stop-over habitat, particularly an abundance of bugs, safe roosts, and lots of water during fall's drought. And some, of course, remained faithfully year round, major characters in the full-length twelve-month backyard drama. So they needed it all—complete and supporting habitat for themselves and their young, day after day.

Last year did, indeed, enhance my education. Month by month, birds' needs changed. Month by month, my backyard habitat changed, sometimes for the better, sometimes for the worse. The tricky part was figuring out how to adjust ever-changing backyard habitats to meet birds' ever-changing needs.

Sharing a lifetime of learning is no simple task. But much of my education comes from others whose impressive yard-bird lists verify their successful backyard habitat management.

From them, I know that any size yard can be a bird magnet, from a high-rise apartment's lofty balcony to a condo's tiny plot, from a subdivision's modest yard to a rural home's acreage.

Thus, I've put my very heart into this project, preparing a handy guide that I hope is educational, benefiting you, my readers, but above all benefiting the birds.

What's happening—or should be happening—each month in your backyard habitat? Which birds likely arrive when? Why are they there? What do they need? How do you lure more birds to your yard? If attracting birds demands more than feeders and feed, what's the draw?

Rooted in the principles of conservation, this guide aims to answer these questions. Month by month, we'll trace the birds' annual cycles and their regular comings and goings, relating timely topics and smile-making memories.

Over the twelve monthly chapters, I'll also profile fifty-five of my avian friends during the season in which I most enjoy them, sharing insights into how they live and work and what makes each spectacular. A tie-it-all-together identification checklist and accompanying photographs help differentiate each species. And you'll meet others, more casually, throughout the year—about one hundred altogether.

A note on capitalization: Throughout this book, a bird's full proper name, like Northern Cardinal, is capitalized. The name's shortened form, like cardinal, is lowercase.

Content, however, moves well beyond narrative and profiles. Every chapter includes more than a dozen sidebar topics:

- "Biology Bits" share insights into what makes a bird a bird.
- Quirky behaviors gain attention—and explanation—in "Why Do Birds Do That?"
- "Habitats—Yours and Theirs" is filled with hints for making your personal habitat more bird friendly.
- "How Does Your Garden Grow?" suggests plants and practices that make your garden and yard attractive to birds.
- "Botany for Birds" sorts out the connections between birds and the plant life on which they irrevocably depend.
- "Notable Behavior" sheds insight on the idiosyncrasies of routine avian life.
- Food and water, essentials to good habitat, are addressed in "Feeder Focus" and "Water Ways," detailing what tends to work and what doesn't.
- "Problem Solver" addresses the most common hair-pullers backyard bird hosts face.
- To expand bird watching beyond the confines of the backyard, "Conservation Corner" peeks at what national and international organizations suggest to protect birds.
- Each monthly chapter wraps up the narrative with a "Things to Do" list, timely suggestions for good habitat practices, and a list of birds I typically see in my yard that month. Depending on where you live, timing may vary slightly, but the seasonal progressions north and south follow a consistent cycle.

The illustrations of both flora and fauna were photographed almost entirely in my own yard and help put a reality stamp on the suggestions you find here.

Finally, there's no magic starting point for reading this book. Some folks will, out of habit, begin at the beginning and march right through. Others may choose to begin in the present, whichever month it is. Others may peruse the pages, plucking sidebars, one set for this reading and other sets for later. So while no fast and firm rules dictate how to best read this guide, I sincerely hope you'll return to it time after time to answer questions, check IDs, plan habitat improvements, or note the annual cycle's progress.

Ultimately, of course, birds forage everywhere, always on the search for habitat, their short life-long dramas built on their ongoing struggle to survive. May your habitat become a part of their search, their very presence reward enough, adding joy to your life.

Follow the author on www.birdsintheyard.com and on Facebook: Sharon Sorenson (Bird Lady).

January

*You can know the name of a bird
in all the languages of the world,
but when you're finished,
you'll know absolutely nothing whatever
about the bird.*

RICHARD P. FEYNMAN

now swirls outside my window; meteorologists predict biting cold tonight; and birds swarm the feeders. I'm compelled to watch. Northern Cardinals feast on safflower seed, American Goldfinches line long thistle-filled tube feeders, and Tufted Titmice zip from peanut feeder to tree branch on one-peanut-at-a-time trips. Carolina Chickadees gorge on sunflower hearts, Carolina Wrens pick at peanut butter, White-throated Sparrows forage in the weed patch, and American Robins flip though leaf litter. Dark-eyed Juncos circle the bubbling rock, drinking, and Downy Woodpeckers cling to clumps of suet, stuffing away the fat-rich morsels.

Why Watch Birds?

With a long to-do list on my desk, why fritter away precious hours watching birds? For me, watching birds puts life in perspective, puts me in touch with the real world—the natural world, the one that was here before we were, the one we're borrowing from our grandchildren, the one we need to conserve for their children. In short, watching birds soothes my soul.

NOTABLE BEHAVIOR   **How Birds Affect Our Lives**

Birds affect our lives in more ways than most folks realize. For instance, if we didn't have birds, we'd be inundated by bugs. Most birds eat bugs, and 98 percent feed their babies bugs. Thus, birds choose nest sites based on the availability of the high-protein morsels. A single pair of Grasshopper Sparrows feeding babies will snag more than a bushel of their namesake bugs in one breeding season.

In addition, if we didn't have birds, we'd be overwhelmed by weeds. Birds devour native weed seeds by the tens of thousands and survive winters eating the seedy richness. If we

Backyard birds like the busy Carolina Chickadee, robust even in winter's grip, give me joy and soothe my soul.

didn't have vultures, we'd be knee deep in roadkill and other rotting, decaying, bacteria-laden carrion. If we didn't have hawks and owls, we'd be overrun by mice, rats, voles, snakes, even squirrels and rabbits. And if we didn't have birds, especially hummingbirds, we'd have a serious shortage of pollinators.

Mother Nature created an astonishing world of balance; each critter—including every bird—serves a purpose. Isn't it remarkable how the little guys are woven irrevocably into our lives? Gotta love 'em!

As naturalist John Burroughs wrote, "I go to nature to be soothed and healed, and to have my senses put in order." Watching, following birds' daily patterns—their interactions, their postures, their flights, their manners of behavior—creates a calming effect for me, distancing the stress and perils of the daily grind. Birds' seeming ongoing buoyancy and resiliency serve as a magical healing touch. They're beautiful. They're tough. They're amazing. They're incredible creatures whose lives intertwine with ours in more ways than most people suspect.

Watching birds also helps me learn, not just about them but about their connections with habitat—theirs and mine. And studying their habits and habitat teaches how biodiversity serves them—and us. Wild birds parallel the canary in the coal mine. Their struggle for survival foretells our own. And they're good teachers, if we watch. So let's watch. And learn.

Cool, Cold, Then Bitter

During January's cold, wind—or its absence—defines bird activity in my backyard. Birds tuck in, seeking shelter, when northwesterly gales zap warmth from their tiny bodies. On days that send me to hot chocolate and insulated underwear, the birds survive outdoors, sans hot drink, warm underwear, or wool socks. Awed, I spy on them. How do they survive?

Many birds, of course, simply leave, migrating south. Not a bad plan, if you don't mind the travel. Gone, for instance, are Gray Catbird, House Wren, Ruby-throated Hummingbird, Scarlet and Summer Tanagers, Indigo Bunting, Rose-breasted Grosbeak, Yellow-billed Cuckoo, all the flycatchers and gnatcatchers, all but one of the warblers, all the swifts, swallows, and martins, all the nighthawks and whip-poor-wills. They're gone, now snapping up bugs in places as far south as Brazil. Sounds tropically delightful—until I think about a single tiny creature, weighing perhaps less than an ounce, flapping its way more than 9,000 miles to Brazil and back. Oh, my. Can winter really be that bad?

In fact, many do stay. And those tough little winter-bird dynamos earn my respect. Big time. In Indiana, where I live, and to the north, winter hits stay-at-home birds with a four-way whammy. First, severe cold demands birds eat more calories in order to survive. Logically, finding more calories takes more time. But short winter days slash foraging time. There's a double whammy already. Next, add snow, maybe a foot deep or more, depending on where you live, and birds need their own snowplows to find sufficient food. Finally, as winter wears on, food grows more and more scarce: gobbled up, crushed, or spoiled, dwindling more quickly in years when summer's drought starves seed and berry crops. It's a tough go for overwintering birds.

So, bird-friendly backyard wintertime habitat—filled with food, water, and vital shelter—eases birds' wintertime woes.

FEEDER FOCUS
Feeder Folks Join the Crowd

According to a 2006 U.S. Fish and Wildlife Service report, about 50 million Americans feed wild birds, more than are members of AARP. Collectively they spend a stupefying $36 billion annually for optics and travel as well as for backyard supplies.

Feather Facts

Birds differ from all other animals is one respect: They wear feathers. Feather color and pattern denote species and sometimes gender and age. Think male and female Northern Cardinal. A bird's first set of feathers, however, tends to look a bit frumpy, disheveled, ragged. Think baby American Robin, speckled breast and overall ill-kempt look. But poor baby has an excuse. After all, it's growing feathers, muscle, organs, and bone, from egg to flight, all in a mere few weeks. Amazing, isn't it?

By summer's end, a month or three after fledging, youngsters need a better coat, warm enough to protect them against winter's meanness. So, about the same time as mom and dad molt, junior sheds his baby feathers and grows another set—a serious energy-drain on this youngster's overall well-being. Not yet astute at finding food, junior now lives on the edge. It's no wonder 80 percent of first-year birds don't survive. But the 20 percent that do are mighty tough critters, an asset to the gene pool.

I needn't explain that feathers make flight possible, but feathers also insulate and protect. Over the course of a year's four seasons, however, feathers take a beating. They fade and turn tattered from sun, rain, wind, snow, and ice; become worn from breeding activities, slipping in and out of cavities, through brambles, and among snagging twigs; go broken, missing, maybe soiled beyond a bath or preening repairs.

By the end of breeding season, when adults have finished building nests and raising kids, enjoying a literal "empty nest" celebration, they face no other energy obligations. Then they too get new winter coats. A few birds, like American Goldfinches, molt a second time,

During their autumn molt, American Gold-finches take on drab non-breeding plumage, the better to camouflage among winter's bare trees.

In spring, American Goldfinches molt a second time, gaining their lustrous name-sake golden plumage, handsomely trimmed in black.

in spring, growing spectacularly attractive breeding plumage. Hormones, triggered by length of day, kick in to produce the molt.

How do birds grow colorful feathers that set one species apart from another? Think crimson red or glossy black, startling blue or classy gray, neon yellow or rusty brown, fiery orange or iridescent green. Think, for instance, Black-throated Green Warbler or Northern Cardinal.

When we look at a bird, three factors combine to create color as we humans see it (as opposed to the ultraviolet colors birds see). It's all a little complicated, but here goes:

First, as a result of chemical processes and interactions in its system, the bird's body creates color pigments during feather growth. Those processes and interactions differ by species and so produce different colors. Second, feather structure creates color because of how light reflects from, or how light is absorbed by, the feathers. Ruby-throated Hummingbirds, for instance, don't have ruby-colored feathers at their throats. Instead, the color comes from light reflection. In many cases, though, color results from both pigment and light.

Third, environment can affect color. Diet, especially the absence of certain nutrients, can adversely affect color, so House Finches might turn out orange or cardinals pink. Usually in these cases, however, when the bird next molts and food supplies improve, plumage returns to normal. Makes me thrill to a bird's color all the more!

A combination of chemical processes and interactions in a bird's system cause it to produce species-distinguishing plumages, some in startlingly striking colors, like those in this Black-throated Green Warbler, one of our most common migrants.

BOTANY FOR BIRDS **Plants for Shelter**

Evergreen trees and shrubs, thorny bushes and tangles, and other dense vegetation like vines offer birds shelter and protection against winter winds and marauding predators. Few bird hosts have room for everything, so check the neighborhood and plant what's missing. Consider the following trees, shrubs, and vines for your backyard habitat, noting benefits beyond shelter that may help you choose. Check for your area's hardiness zones at http://www.usna.usda.gov/Hardzone/index.html.

Trees:	Common Name	Scientific Name	Additional Benefits
	Holly, especially native American holly	*Ilex* spp.	winter berries
	Pine	*Pinus* spp.	nest sites
	Eastern hemlock	*Tsuga canadensis*	nest sites; cone seeds
	Balsam fir	*Abies balsamea*	nest sites; cone seeds
	Hawthorn, for thorny protection	*Crataegus* spp.	winter berries; nest sites; bugs (attracted to blossoms); nectar
	Eastern red cedar	*Juniperus virginiana*	fall, winter berries (actually tiny cones)
	Spruce	*Picea* spp.	nest sites
Shrubs:	**Common Name**	**Scientific Name**	**Additional Benefits**
	Winterberry	*Ilex verticillata*	winter berries
	Northern bayberry, partly coniferous	*Myrica pennsylvanica*	fall, winter berries; nesting
	Wax myrtle, partly coniferous	*Myrica cerifera*	summer, fall, winter berries
	Wild rose, for thorny protection (avoid invasive multiflora rose)	*Rosa* spp.	fall, winter fruits (rose hips); nest sites
	Blackberry, raspberry, for thorny tangle	*Rubus* spp.	summer fruits; nest sites
Vines:	**Common Name**	**Scientific Name**	**Additional Benefits**
	Wild grape	*Vitis vinifera*	summer fruits; nest material; nest sites
	American bittersweet (avoid invasive oriental bittersweet)	*Celastrus scandens*	fall fruit; nest sites; bugs (attracted to blossoms)
	Trumpet creeper	*Campsis radicans*	nectar; nest sites
	Virginia creeper	*Parthenocissus quinquefolia*	nectar; nest sites; fall berries
	Greenbrier	*Smilax rotundifolia*	fall, winter berries; nest sites; bugs (attracted to blossoms)

Plants for Shelter (continued)

A yard bare of shelter offers little safety or protection for wintering birds. Brush piles and tangles, both quick backyard fixes, offer great winter shelter. White-throated and White-crowned Sparrows, Dark-eyed Juncos, and Northern Cardinals, among others, love the tangle of gone-to-seed zinnia, beebalm, and sneezeweed stalks left in the garden last fall. Now, their seed heads drooping dead, the mass of stalks remains upright, gathering wind-tossed leaves at the base, offering shelter from wind and snow to ground-loving birds and bunnies alike.

A brush pile, enhanced by a discarded Christmas tree or two, offers even greater protection, especially against a hungry Cooper's Hawk. The hawk keeps other birds' gene pools strong, picking off sick, slow, or slow-witted birds for lunch. But shelter provides a hideaway for the healthy, fast, and clever.

While many birds actually increase their number of feathers in fall, the addition doesn't fully insulate tiny bodies. And certainly added feathers would ultimately reach diminishing returns: A bird's body has only so much skin room to sprout more feathers. And too many more feathers would create too much additional weight—especially since most birds' feathers already weigh more than their bones.

At night, though, when wintering birds face their greatest survival challenges, some, like chickadees, go through an almost magical transition. They lower their nighttime body temperatures. Lowered body temps in turn lower metabolism and, therefore, conserve energy. So calories last a few hours longer, just long enough to get them through the night. What a biologically amazing built-in protection against winter's biting cold!

Nevertheless, like all birds, chickadees need a secure nighttime roost, out of the wind, safe from predators. So, they secret themselves away, tuck in behind evergreen foliage, buildings, or whatever other windbreak they find. Indeed, winter shelter may be one of the most important elements in any backyard wintertime habitat.

HABITAT—YOURS AND THEIRS
Give Birds a Break with Windbreaks

As you plan bird-friendly habitat, skip the landscape syndrome of a single feature tree surrounded by cropped grass. Instead, plant tree clusters, lots of them. Choose evergreen trees, preferably native to your area; and if you have room, add one or more clusters of deciduous trees, complementing all with shrubs and bushes, especially thorny ones, as understory. Evergreen and dense-shrub clusters form windbreaks, offering birds protection against icy blasts and storms.

As you plant, however, watch for utility wires, roof overhangs, septic tanks, and underground cables and pipes, anticipating your trees' growth patterns both above and below ground.

Even out of the wind, though, January, at least in our area, offers no tropical paradise. Still, I'm always amazed that some birds, in spite of the paradise lost, continue to sing. Carolina Wrens scold, American Goldfinches give flight calls, Tufted Titmice sputter *peter-peter-peter*, crows caw in flight, Red-shoulder Hawks screech *keer, keer, keer*. How do they have the energy—or even the willpower—to sing on these brittle days? All the more reason to call them awesome.

Putting on the Fat

What ultimately gets birds through the winter battle? One word: fat. If they've had enough fat calories during the day to last them through the night, if they can find enough fat calories at dawn to replenish their depleted reserves, and if they can find enough fat calories to gain enough reserves to last through the next night, birds will survive another day.

Below: *Carolina Chickadees stuff themselves with 250 to 300 seeds per day—60 percent of their body weight—in order to survive winter's most severe cold nights.* Left: *Eastern red cedar berries—actually tiny cones—serve up a tasty meal for most berry-loving winter birds, such as robins, mockingbirds, and bluebirds.*

And where do they find all this fat? In seeds, dormant bugs, insect eggs, and larvae—and lots of them. In summer, chickadees, for instance, need the equivalent of 150 seeds a day to stay alive. In winter, however, those same birds need the equivalent of 250 to 300 seeds a day—60 percent of their body weight—to survive severely cold nights. Unlike humans, birds need not limit fat consumption for fear of rising cholesterol or clogged arteries. Rather, they need fat. Lots of fat. Daily. No, make that hourly.

Will birds find fat in your backyard habitat? If you left some leaves last fall, the leaf litter harbors dormant bugs, insect eggs, and larvae. If your habitat boasts numerous trees and shrubs, bark harbors similar goodies. If you've left a rotting log along the back fence, perhaps among an array of perennials, it, too, will serve as a bird buffet.

For birds, winter survival is a frantic dawn-to-dusk search-and-feed operation—every minute, every daylight hour, every day. Their search includes, but is not limited to, your bird feeders. So assuming you're supplementing your natural backyard habitat with feeders, you'll help most if you're offering high-fat foods, the highest being black-oil sunflower seed (especially the hull-less and mess-free hearts), peanut kernels and peanut butter, and pure suet.

For instance, wintering birds consume huge amounts of energy flipping leaves and checking crevices, all while searching out seeds, insect eggs, and larvae. Since, in general, backyard birds must eat their weight in oil-rich seeds or other fat sources every day to survive a night's cold, black-oil sunflower seeds and hearts fill their bills with appetizer, entrée, and dessert. My weed patch and spent garden also still bear an abundance of seed, months after the first frost, and the birds busy themselves among the now-dead stalks and tangles.

HABITAT—YOURS AND THEIRS
Bed-and-Breakfast Trees

In our backyard, a little grove of native red cedar trees (*Juniperus virginiana*) serves as a bed-and-breakfast. The dense evergreen boughs offer shelter, a welcoming lodge for wintering birds. Highly drought-hardy, cedars never need pruning. Best in groups, they're slow growing and long lived. And they produce masses of tiny cones (sometimes called berries) that feed a whole host of winter birds, including, among others, bluebirds, mockingbirds, robins, and Cedar Waxwings.

HOW DOES YOUR GARDEN GROW?
Invasive Invasions—Check 'Em Out, Choke 'Em Out

As you add seed and berry producers to your backyard habitat for birds' winter fare, aim for natives. Some nurseries continue to carry exotic invasive plants that escape the garden, competing with natives, often to the point of destruction. Four of the most common and noxious invasives that choke natural habitats include purple loosestrife (*Lythrum salicaria*), phragmites (*Phragmites australis*), tree of heaven (*Ailanthus altissima*), and Russian olive or autumn olive (*Elaeagnus umbellate* and *E. angustifolia*). Check the United States National Arboretum's invasive plants website: www.usna.usda.gov/Gardens/Invasives.html. Then rid your property of intruders.

Caching In

If you watch birds' winter behavior, you'll likely catch several bird species "eating" far more seeds than seems possible. Look again! They may be, miserlike, stashing those fat-rich seeds against possible future winter shortfalls. Blue Jays, for instance, routinely fill their gullets until they bulge with six to eight shelled corn kernels. Then off they fly to bury kernels who-knows-where, guarding against the day when feeders may go empty. Next spring I'll discover a few forgotten caches when seeds emerge as errant cornstalks among the flowers. Meanwhile, Blue Jays are ever prepared.

BIOLOGY BITS   **Bill Color**

Sometimes a bird's bill color reveals secrets bird-watchers may otherwise miss. For instance, among Northern Cardinals, orangey-red bills denote mature birds. Juveniles wear dark bills. Sometimes bill color also denotes season. Wintertime American Goldfinches have gray bills that turn yellowish orange from the base to the tip when breeding time nears. Among European Starlings, bright yellow bills mark breeding birds. Wintertime starlings wear dark bills. House Sparrows' bills change from breeding black to winter tan.

Some bill color aids camouflage. Flycatchers, for instance, which often sport two-toned bills, have darker upper mandibles and lighter lower mandibles. Seen from above, the dark bill against dark undergrowth blends in, and seen from below, the light bill against light sky does likewise. And birds that forage in bright sun tend to have dark bills, perhaps to cut reflection, while birds that forage in shade typically have light-colored bills. Some authorities believe that, in this situation, bill color helps birds see.

Nuthatches hoard seeds, too, wedging them into tree bark. No way can the little Red-breasted Nuthatch eat an entire handful of sunflower hearts in a few days; but like its cousin the White-breasted Nuthatch, it snatches each one singly, carries it off, returns for another, and makes the round trip faster than it can crack and down a kernel. What the Red-breasted Nuthatch hides and forgets during its short winter stay with us, some bark-hitching wood-pecker will likely find next spring.

And what about woodpeckers in winter's frigid weather? Unable to find as many bugs in the bark as easily as they can find my feeders, they're gobbling down suet by the pound, Downy, Hairy, and Red-bellied Woodpeckers, and Northern Flicker alike, all waiting their turn.

A Hairy Woodpecker enjoys suet at a feeder.

Winter Water

Birds need water year round. True, they can eat snow, but warming snow to body temperature takes twelve times more energy than warming water to body temperature—a heavy toll in already severe conditions. So, provide open water no more than an inch deep. Our bubbling rock flows year-round, thanks to a thermostatically controlled submersible heater, available where pet or livestock supplies are sold.

Choose a de-icer according to wattage. Higher wattage puts out more heat. Consider your water feature's size and choose accordingly. As for power consumption, a 150-watt de-icer uses the same amount of electricity as a 150-watt light bulb. For your safety, plug the de-icer into a receptacle with a ground-fault circuit interrupter (GFCI). Finally, never ever add antifreeze or salt to your water feature; you'll likely kill the birds.

Water, Water Everywhere—Frozen

While shelter and food are two of the Big Four for habitat, birds also need a winter supply of water—thawed. Yes, it's 18 degrees outside tonight, but by morning, everyone wants a drink. When the first sun's rays sparkle on the bubbling rock, birds circle in, drop down for a drink, and maybe even flutter in a bit of a bath. Every bird needs water, both for bathing and drinking, and birds that never visit feeders will nevertheless belly up to the bar, perhaps because the bubbling rock looks natural, offers moving water, and, at ground level, offers water where Mother Nature would put it. But here's the rest of that story: Over half of the birds on my 160-species yard list have never put beak to feeder, but a good many of them have flown in solely for water.

Still, given the current deep freeze, even a heated water source can't help all birds. The Belted Kingfisher that undulated through last week's morning skies on its way to fish the now-frozen farm pond has flown on, seeking open waters, perhaps along the still-open river. While dabbling ducks and safety-seeking geese usually manage to keep favorite water patches open, ice robs kingfishers of any opportunity to fish. They're forced south.

Memorable Moments: Ice Storm Ices Birds

January's memories grip my mind like ice grips the land. They're hard memories. In January 2009, a widespread ice storm hit with brutal force in our three-state area. We humans huddled in power-outage cold but nevertheless had fireplaces and wood burners. Birds, however, faced the elements with nothing more that their feathers and instincts—and whatever our backyard habitat offered for food, water, and shelter. At first dawn, after the tree-crushing night, birds struggled to feed. Berries hung ice-coated, seeds drooped ice-coated, feeders stood ice-coated. Some birds flew in awkwardly, ice stuck to their heads and tails, skidding where they couldn't grip. Who knows how many never flew at all that morning.

Wildlife biologists agreed that the widespread damage would affect birds and other animals for years to come. Den trees downed by heavy ice left thousands of creatures homeless. Creation of new cavities will take years. Shrubby growth at forest

WHY DO BIRDS DO THAT?
Why Do Birds Bathe in the Cold?

Everything needs drinking water to live, but birds also need winter baths. Clean feathers are warm feathers. So, offering thawed water in winter allows birds to stay clean and warm.

During an overnight ice storm, roosting birds may accumulate ice on heads, backs, and tails, as seen on this Northern Cardinal—a situation that makes agile flight difficult and predation more likely.

edges, flattened, crushed by ice, no longer protects roosting or nesting birds. Old-growth forest canopy, devastated by ice and wind, no longer offers potential homes to treetop-loving birds migrating here to nest. What long-term effects will occur? No one knows for sure.

The ice storm dramatically altered food supplies. Berry eaters probably starved when ice-covered fruits remained encased for days. Foods cached in tree bark, cavities, and other niches were lost or exposed to rot. As the harsh weather continued, starvation worsened. We all suffered that January, but wildlife surely suffered the worst. At least short term. Other severe storms—hurricanes and tornadoes—create equal havoc for wildlife.

HOW DOES YOUR GARDEN GROW?
Set Your Sights on Improved Bird Sites

Garden catalogs jam January mailboxes. But avoid being tempted by the newest and brightest. Instead, look for bird-friendly plants offering food (berries, seed, or nectar), shelter, or nest sites. Beware of "bird friendly" labels, perhaps geared more toward marketing than birding and may reflect only modest suitability. Instead, look to add or replace with natives in your yard. To choose, check your area's native plants and hardiness zones on the Web, visiting reputable, non-sales sites that post without commercial biases. Or enter "native plants" and your state's name in your favorite search engine.

BIOLOGY BITS   **Who Lives Where—and Why?**

A bird's shape and size determine where it lives and, therefore, how natural events like storms affect it. For instance, wing shape dictates who soars and who flaps and where birds hunt. Long, broad wings, like a Red-tailed Hawk's, give soaring power, while narrow wings, like an Osprey's, power long-distance flight. So red-tails mostly stay year round or migrate only short distances while Ospreys depart for the winter, navigating to and from South America. Narrow, more maneuverable wings, like a Red-shouldered Hawk's, let it dart through dense woodlands. Birds at home in dense woodlands obviously face the consequences of storm destruction.

Tails also dictate lifestyle. Long tails assure maneuverability—quick, agile turns. Think Cooper's Hawk chasing a small songbird. Ground birds, typically poor fliers, wear short tails. Think Northern Bobwhite. Ground-loving birds likely benefit from storm destruction because undergrowth, opened to light, grows denser.

Legs likewise determine feeding behavior. Birds with thick, strong legs, maybe also strong feet and talons, come equipped to snatch heavy loads and fly off, with their prey in claws, typical of eagles and owls. Songbirds, on the other hand, have weak legs and feet, best used for scratching in leaves for insects or clinging to berry-laden branches. Storm damage alters their respective hunting grounds, perhaps eliminating suitable habitat, maybe forcing them out.

Relatively short, broad wings give this Red-tailed Hawk tremendous soaring power.

Why Neatniks Don't Have Birds

Wild birds like a little "wild," and most prefer quite a lot of "wild." For birds, a vast lawn equals a desert wasteland, and a lawn chemically treated for weeds and bugs equals a toxic dump. Birds favor habitat with abundant shelter—tall grasses and perennials, thick thorny shrubs, dense trees. Think protection. Even humans who love the beach don't want to spend stormy nights there, unprotected. So if a yard looks like a green beach, few birds venture through. None stay.

But wildlife—including birds—is generally resilient. Although habitat was altered by that January ice storm, some good came of much bad. The loss of shrubby vegetation, crushed and left to rot, attracted insects the following spring and summer, supplying hordes of tasty morsels for birds and their babies. Fallen limbs that collapsed into natural piles flooded the market with house-and-home sites for ground-dwelling birds. So, in the short term, birds that prefer large trees, continuous cover, and upper tree canopy lost their homes and moved out. But species that prefer early successional forest or tree gaps found a buyer's market of choice home sites. In forests ripped bare of limbs and with canopy shade gone, new vegetation replaced the old oak and other hardwoods. The entire forest community took on a new composition with new inhabitants and new visitors. Sort of like massive urban renewal. Out with the old, in with the new.

The ice storm, devastating as it was, taught us about natural habitat change. And it taught us about our own backyard habitats.

Ice Age Renewal

In our yard, the Great Ice Storm led to the Great Thaw followed by a months-long Great Clean-up. Like other area residents, we struggled to put our lives and yards back in order. Some folks, however, found positive use for the widespread debris. Three of our forty-year-old trees were nearly destroyed, seriously disfigured, jagged stubs jutting from trunks shortened by now-absent tops which were themselves the size of respectable trees.

Tree guys would need days, they said, to down the trees, haul out logs, and shred brush. Or not. What if we left the trees, allowing stubs to rot back, creating nesting and roosting cavities for woodpeckers, owls, bluebirds, flycatchers, creepers, nuthatches, swallows, chickadees, titmice, wrens, even Wood Ducks in the right location? All desperately need cavities. In fact, populations are limited by cavity availability: few cavities, few cavity nesters. By leaving disfigured trees, we had nothing to lose and everything to gain. Maybe, after all, "disfigured" is in the eye of the beholder. Maybe ragged trees that enhance bird habitat alter the eye of the beholder. Or so it is with this beholder.

Built-in Grocery Store

If ice or wind damage a tree in your yard and if your tree must come down, consider leaving the largest log to rot, maybe somewhere out of the way, perhaps along the back property line. Rotting logs, Mother Nature's grocery store, supplying fresh food for dozens of bird species, dressed up with hostas, shrubs, or perennials, dramatically enrich backyard habitat. As logs disintegrate, they enrich the soil for future growth. As for surplus debris, consider shredding the small stuff for next year's mulch. Natural mulch, another of Mother Nature's grocery stores, harbors a feathered friend's feast.

Feeders When Natural Habitat Goes Lacking

Except perhaps in the most severe weather, birds can do quite well without us, thank you. For many thousands of years, after all, long before sunflower seed and suet supplements, they survived. It's true, though, that we've made survival more difficult for them because we've destroyed overwhelming portions of their habitat. Historically, where my house stands, there was nothing but vast forest. Now, besides the footprint of my house, lands have been cleared for neighboring farms and agricultural fields. Original habitat hangs on as a mere remnant.

Over the years, we've tried to enhance the habitat, adding trees, shrubs, bushes, vines, perennials, tangles, brambles, wind breaks, weed patches, berry producers, nectar producers, dense evergreens—all the while reducing lawn, maintaining only paths and borders, creating bird-friendly habitat.

Given that, I nevertheless still feel compelled to supplement the wintertime habitat and feed birds the best foodstuffs I can. In some small way, I hope to ease their daily struggle to survive winter's rigors. Ages-old habitat changes altered original bird populations here, but for the ones that remain, I like to think—and really do believe—that my supplemental feeder buffet makes a difference, to them as well as to me. I take the effort seriously. They reward me with their presence. And soothe my soul.

Thus it is, then, that a late spring freeze, summer drought, early fall frost, and severe winter weather always play on my sympathies, nudging me to add more feeders for hungry wintering birds. More feeders mean more birds served, especially if the additional buffet line offers more variety in vittles and alternate serving sites, expanding the restaurant with a larger seating capacity.

Backyard habitat can be improved by eliminating most mowed lawn and adding coniferous and deciduous trees, thick and thorny shrubs, native vines, fruit-bearing tangles, and native grasses.

BIOLOGY BITS   **Who Eats What—and Why?**

For birds, who eats what is hardly a matter of being picky eaters. Rather, bill shape and size dictate who eats what. Northern Cardinals' strong nutcrackerlike conical bills let them crack open hefty seeds while Tufted Titmice's small bills restrict them to seeds they can hammer open. Hooked-billed raptors rip apart sizeable animal prey, but tiny-billed warblers eat only insects or berries. Long-billed snipe probe mud and sand for food while chisel-billed woodpeckers hammer holes in trees, extracting bugs. Bill shape and size thus ultimately determine who stays for the winter and who flees south. Birds that can eat only bugs necessarily disappear when and where bugs disappear.

But with feeder prices what they are and penny-pincher that I am, I set my sights on economical alternatives—and found them. So our yard birds are wallowing this January in the luxury of five new feeders offering a few new menu items.

A quick check at local shops revealed more than fifty kinds of feeders, standing rank and file, labels illustrating an amazing array of birds that they could attract. True, not all birds eat the same foods nor eat in the same ways. Bird-feeder manufacturers take all that into play and inundate us with choices. Tube feeders serve small to mid-sized perching birds, hopper feeders work for all but ground lovers, suet feeders attract clinging birds, and platform feeders, either ground level or elevated, accommodate almost everyone, shoulder to shoulder.

Commercial feeders also come in a variety of materials from cheap and chintzy to sturdy and expensive. Just remember: Birds can't read the price tag. Birds don't have degrees in feeder design. Birds don't know the difference between solid copper and the cheapest plastic. They just want to eat.

FEEDER FOCUS   **Quality Check**

What makes the best bird feeder? First, function. Does the feeder regulate seed dispersal but still keep seed dry and healthful? Can birds feed? Do perches fit birds' feeding postures? Does the roofline hinder birds' flight paths? For your sake, is it easily filled? Does it empty quicker than your schedule allows you to refill it? Is it easily cleaned? Wood is harder to clean than metal or plastic; grooves are harder than smooth surfaces.

Second, drainage. Are drain holes of adequate number and size to minimize mold and rot? In hopper and tube feeders, is there a bottom seed deflector? If not, bottom seeds will rot, spoiling seeds above.

Third, durability. Given squirrels and raccoons, metal or wood beats plastic. Check construction. Will anything rot, rust, crack, or break? Are joints tight, well-fitting? Moisture and sun deteriorate anything over time; look for components that are the most weather resistant.

Finally, attractiveness. A functional, durable feeder that's also decorative proves a real winner. You'll pay added dollars for fancy; birds won't care. Still, it's your yard, your view out the window.

Every winter finds me adding platform feeders under our hemlocks and junipers for visiting juncos and White-throated Sparrows. Made of aluminum screen wire, reinforced with half-inch hardware cloth, attached to a homemade footed frame, the economical feeders attract these birds and others, inviting them to dine together, assuring them safety beneath the overhanging boughs.

Some birds, however, don't like a crowd. Chickadees, titmice, and nuthatches dash to feeders, grab a seed, and scurry off to pound out the kernel. Each time, they lose their place at the table and must await another seat to grab the next quick bite. Little feeders for the little guys, though, will let them dine in comfort, away from the pushy big guys. My little feeders came free—in the form of last year's crop of assorted gourds, grown in the garden, gathered in the fall, stored to dry over winter, and now rattling dry, cut open for fly-through ease. They hold a mere cupful of seed, serving well, almost always one little guy at a time.

Nutritional Value of Common Bird Seeds

Seed	Percent Fat Content	Percent Protein Content
Sunflower chips	72	12
Peanuts	73	16
Thistle (Niger)	71	18
Black-oil sunflower	68	14
Corn	11	7
White millet	9	11

FEEDER FOCUS **High-Nutrition Feeder Foods**

Following yesteryear's habit of tossing out stale bread and cookies, popcorn and cereal, and other human foodstuffs probably hurts birds more than it helps them. They gobble up the offerings, of course, and fill their tummies. But food value—digestible fat and protein—totals near zero; their digestive systems can't process these human foods.

Since different birds prefer different seeds, offer several high-fat, high-protein foods. Some commercial blends meet the standard; others fail miserably. The Wild Bird-Feeding Industry posts these values, based on volume, with fat content important for winter warmth and protein content for breeding season. Compare labels. You'll get what you pay for.

A larger gourd, similarly cut for fly-through use, holds a chopped apple and a cup of crumbled suet for the mockingbird. He guards it with relish and gulps down the contents in two days. Yet another gourd offers a combination of peanut pieces and sunflower hearts, private treats for goldfinches, titmice, Pine Siskins, and nuthatches.

Growing woodpecker numbers begged for more suet feeders. Commercially prepared suet, made of rendered beef fat, often blended with seeds or fruit, comes shaped in squares, balls, and pegs to accommodate (or promote?) manufacturers' various feeders. The real stuff, a hard, crumbly fat from around beef kidneys, comes from the butcher shop. In my yard, the real stuff and pure suet squares (no seeds or fruits included), served in wire mesh feeders hanging from poles and tree trunks, vanish like smoke. Supply wasn't meeting demand.

Economical new suet feeders came from the woodpile. A limb 4 or 5 inches in diameter, cut about 2 feet long, drilled with 1½-inch diameter holes and stuffed with pure suet, an eye screw in the top for hanging, made the perfect natural feeder. Total cost: 30 cents (for the screw).

FEEDER FOCUS
Why Feed Birds?

All kinds of esoteric explanations surface about why we feed—or should feed—birds, but the bottom line, experts tell us, is simple and straightforward. Mostly we feed birds for selfish reasons. We feed them to lure them into our yards, near our windows, striving to enjoy their mere presence. We feed them to feed ourselves, to soothe our souls. And we trust that in some small way, we also make their lives better, as they do ours.

A male Northern Cardinal enjoys sunflower seeds, a favorite food among these handsome birds.

PROBLEM SOLVER   **Nuisance Birds at Your Feeders**

As a backyard bird host, depending on where you live, you may wring your hands in frustration at flocks of big noisy, pushy starlings, grackles, and Red-winged Blackbirds gobbling up pricey bird seed and crowding out songbirds. What's a conscientious host to do? Seeds that nuisance birds prefer tend to be cracked corn and millet. Avoid those seeds, and mixes including them, and you'll at least decrease the nuisance populations. Avoid ground-level feeding, keep the spills cleaned up, and you'll further decrease the so-called "blackbird" flocks.

Finally, another homemade platform feeder newly mounted on our wooden fence serves corn, now a magnet for Blue Jays, cardinals, and Red-bellied Woodpeckers. Since Red-headed Woodpeckers prefer shelled corn to any other seed, I'm hopeful the feeder may eventually lure them as well. I'm reminded, though, that their numbers have dwindled.

So my wintertime menu now offers black-oil sunflower seeds and hearts, thistle and safflower seeds, peanuts and peanut butter, apple pieces, shelled (but not cracked) corn and suet, each variety in its own feeder, some large and some small, sited down low and up high, under evergreens and awnings, out in the open and next to dense shrubs—a full-service buffet with something, and someplace, for everyone—all offered economically.

Conservation Corner: State of the Birds Report

In 2009, under the auspices of the North American Bird Conservation Initiative, nine bird conservation organizations cooperated to compile "The State of Our Nation's Birds." In part, that document reads, "The United States is home to a tremendous diversity of native birds, with more than 800 species inhabiting terrestrial, coastal, and ocean habitats, including Hawaii. Among these species, 67 are federally listed as endangered or threatened. An additional 184 are species of conservation concern because of their small distribution, high threats, or declining populations."

The report concludes with this formidable statement: "The birds we see in our backyards, fields, forests, deserts, and oceans have much to tell us about the health of the environment. Each year, thousands of citizen-science participants contribute data from across the United States, making it possible to identify birds in trouble. By understanding the message from birds and taking action, we can help them thrive and safeguard our own future."

Things to Do in January

- Watch birds to learn about their roosting and feeding behaviors.

A simple, inexpensive homemade suet feeder attracts many birds, including a female Downy Woodpecker.

[...]ls in your yard and [...]ly the availability of [...]anting accordingly.

[...]es for fat content, [...]est ratings.

[...]d bathing

[...]e it for function,

[...]in planning for [...]ing especially on [...] nest sites.

Sharon Sorenson
Website: www.birdsintheyard.com
sharonsorensonbirdlady
Email: sharon@birdsintheyard.com

[...] in January

Cold, [...] ld with 0 degrees wind chill, followed by seven i[...] ies gone.

Greater [...]		Eastern Towhee
Goose		Fox Sparrow
Canada [...]		Song Sparrow
Turkey Vulture	American Crow	White-throated Sparrow
Cooper's Hawk	Carolina Chickadee	Dark-eyed Junco
Red-shouldered Hawk	Tufted Titmouse	Northern Cardinal
Red-tailed Hawk	White-breasted Nuthatch	Red-winged Blackbird
Mourning Dove	Carolina Wren	Common Grackle
Great Horned Owl	Eastern Bluebird	Brown-headed Cowbird
Red-bellied Woodpecker	American Robin	House Finch
Downy Woodpecker	Northern Mockingbird	American Goldfinch
Hairy Woodpecker	European Starling	House Sparrow
	Yellow-rumped Warbler	

SPECIES PROFILE

NORTHERN CARDINAL

Above: *Northern Cardinal, male;* below: *Northern Cardinal, female*

VITAL STATS
Length: 8–9 in.
Wingspan: 10–12 in.
Weight: 1.6 oz.

Nearly everyone knows Northern Cardinals as common yard birds. Everyone east of the Rocky Mountains, that is. Seven states call it their state bird. Two major-league sports franchises and an untold number of colleges and high schools use it as their mascot.

The male birds' exquisite crimson plumage, however, causes them problems. While the International Migratory Bird Act protects them in the United States, the law doesn't apply in Mexico. And folks there crave having these gorgeous birds decorating their living rooms. I've seen Northern Cardinals for sale in Mexico, cooped up in small cages barely large enough to contain them—droopy, ill-groomed, sad-looking birds. They don't sing.

Still, during the Great Backyard Bird Count, Northern Cardinals ranked as the most frequently reported bird for five of the last six years. Refreshingly good numbers for refreshingly gorgeous birds.

But if these vibrantly plumaged, cheerful songsters were rare, serious birders would climb steep mountains, cross scorching deserts, hack through wild jungles—travel anywhere—to see one. And then, thrilled at sighting this stunning, brilliantly colored bird, they would have bragging rights over envious friends who wish they, too, could have seen it.

As common as they are in eastern backyards, however, they're anything but ordinary.

As a kid, I called these creatures "redbirds." Everyone I knew called them that. Then, when I learned they were more properly named Northern Cardinals, I puzzled over the "northern" part. Later, I learned that different species of cardinals also live in South America, so "northern" simply pegged the bird's habitat in North America. While their range has expanded northward, populations nevertheless remain greater in southern portions of the United States than north of the Mason-Dixon line.

NAME THAT BIRD

Cardinalis cardinalis (Northern Cardinal): The bird gets its name from the male's bright red color that matches the robes worn by cardinals in the Roman Catholic Church. Its common name reflects the scientific name, and "northern" denotes the bird's North American range. A common colloquial name is "redbird."

BIRD TALK: WHO'S CALLING?

Northern Cardinals claim an excess of twenty-five songs, mostly clear, down-slurred two-part whistles, repeated. The most recognized phrases include *whoit-cheer, whoit-cheer, cheer, cheer, cheer; bir-dy, bir-dy, bir-dy;* and *cheer, cheer, cheer.* The call is a sharp metallic *pik* or *tik.* During breeding season, females join males in duets, her song usually slightly softer than his.

SPOTTING THE SPECTACULAR **Northward Ho!**

Northern Cardinals are on the move—northward. Their expanding range, attributed primarily to human intervention, has created ample excitement. First, logging turned northern forests into shrubby edge habitat, perfect for cardinals. Then railroad construction built more perfect habitats, encouraging the birds to follow the shrubby channels north. When they reached Chicago 150 years ago, newspaper headlines touted their debut.

In 1958, nesting cardinals fledged their dark-billed babies in Concord, Massachusetts. Think about it. That means Henry David Thoreau, who died a century earlier, would never have seen them. Wouldn't he have thrilled to their flashes of red around Walden Pond?

Now, in the more recent past, backyard hosts from across southern Canada have begun to enjoy cardinals at their feeders, too. In 2008, cardinals were first reported in Fort Frances and Morson, Ontario.

Of course, winter backyard bird feeding offered cardinals an additional boon, and climate change has warmed northerly sites, enticing venturesome birds. But they do not live, and have never lived, in the Northwest United States.

ID CHECK

Readily recognized, male Northern Cardinals are distinguished by the following:

- Brilliant all-red plumage
- Bright red-orange bill
- Black face mask
- Crisp crest that can be raised or lowered

Females are distinguished by the following:

- Overall tan plumage with red tinges
- Bright red-orange bill
- Crisp crest that can be raised or lowered

FOOD FARE

Northern Cardinals prefer grain, including shelled corn, sunflower seeds and hearts, safflower (a favorite in my yard) and other birdseed. In the garden, they glean spent flower seed heads, grasses, and sedges and will forage among tulip poplar, dogwood, and mulberry trees for seed and berries. They feed their babies insects, including crickets, katydids, grasshoppers, leafhoppers, cicadas, and beetles.

While most bird-watchers know cardinals for their brilliant red, when males complete fall molt, new wing feathers show an overcast of gray, wrapping birds in a dusky winter cape. By springtime, the "cape" wears off, and the male exhibits the breeding all-red of a well-dressed gent. The female birds, gorgeously subtle, wear tan with red highlights in their hair and bright orangey-red lipstick on their bills. Juveniles, both males and females, look like females, minus the lipstick.

NEST NOTES

Nest Site: selected by male and female, 1–15 ft. up, wedged in forked branches of shrub, tangles, or other brushy plant, hidden in dense foliage

Nest Construction: by female alone, about 4 in. deep and 4 in. across, cup-shaped nest with four distinct layers: a foundation of a few coarse twigs, a leafy layer, a grapevine or cypress bark layer, and then fine grasses, stems, rootlets, and pine needles, as available, to form a cup

Eggs: 2–5 eggs, 1–2 broods, incubated only by female 10–13 days, male brings her food

Fledge: 7–13 days after hatch

Cardinal courtship leaves me waxing anthropomorphic. The birds flit about the yard together, perching side by side. Then, he pops the question, feeding her, their bills touching in a "kiss." Excuse me, but the endearing behavior seems quite touching. How sweet! Beyond the "kiss," mates then sing to each other, dueting phrase for phrase. They seem the perfect sweethearts.

Essentially homebodies, rarely wandering more than ten miles from their ancestral homes and usually no more than a mile, male cardinals maintain two- to ten-acre breeding territories year after year, courting the same mate, breeding earlier than their younger less-experienced counterparts. And doting lovers that males are, they feed their mates during incubation. Together, they feed their babies.

The two of them defend their territory. Sometimes, though, cardinals go overboard, notoriously defending the territory against an intruder that doesn't exist. If either bird sees its own reflection—in a window, automobile mirror, or shiny bumper, the fight is on. And on and on, repeatedly, tirelessly, ad infinitum. I fear for their well-being. As long as breeding season lasts, though, the battle continues. Only covering or breaking up the reflection stop the attacks.

Cardinals let me know when the day is done, joining compatriots at feeders in winter flocks. One snowy January evening, I counted fifty-two decorating backyard feeders and snow-covered hemlocks before darkness sent them to roost. Although they're last to feed at night, I know they'll also be first to feed in morning.

To attract more cardinals to your habitat, provide nest sites amid dense evergreens and tangles of unkempt thickets, all free from pesticides. Fill feeders with black-oil sunflower or safflower seed (although cardinals prefer seed spills on the ground). And keep water ice-free and fresh.

SPECIES PROFILE

CAROLINA CHICKADEE and BLACK-CAPPED CHICKADEE

VITAL STATS
Carolina Chickadee
Length: 3.9–4.7 in.
Wingspan: 5.9–7.9 in.
Weight: 0.3–0.4 oz.
Black-capped Chickadee
Length: 4.7–5.9 in.
Wingspan: 6.3–8.3 in.
Weight: 0.3–0.5 oz.

Carolina Chickadee, nearly indistinguishable from Black-capped Chickadee except by song.

Chickadees rank as the bird world's littlest piggy. Or biggest hoarder. Okay, we should refer to avian hoards as "caches," but that's only semantics. These cute, perky little birds pick favorite feeders, a couple of spots they check out multiple times a day, skipping other nearby feeders offering the same seeds, making choices we mere humans cannot understand. Maybe they're creatures of habit. Maybe one set of feeders feels safer. Maybe one feeder hangs closer to their secret caches.

At any rate, they've been recorded snatching up to two hundred or more wintertime feeder seeds a day. And all those one-seed-at-a-time trips back and forth from your feeder to some secret spot means a chickadee is beating a path to its private grocery store, stocking the shelves from your outlet, guarding against tough times. Clever shopper it is, taking in the sales, sometimes "buying" one and getting one free, stuffing a second seed in its tiny gullet before dashing off.

So now all this begs the question: Is the bird that's gathering groceries at your outlet a Carolina Chickadee or a Black-capped Chickadee? For all practical purposes, the two birds look nearly identical, and they're closely enough related that they hybridize where their ranges meet. The safest way, then, to determine who's who at your feeders is to consult a map. In the north, they're Black-capped Chickadees; in the south, they're Carolinas. In the Appalachians, Black-

NAME THAT BIRD

Poecile carolinensis (Carolina Chickadee): *Poecile,* from the Greek, means "two-colored" or "pied," for the bird's black and white color combination. *Carolinensis* refers to the state in which the bird was first found. Its common name recalls the bird's *chicka-dee-dee-dee* song and its habitat region.

Poecile atricapilla (Black-capped Chickadee): *Atricapilla* translates roughly as "black hair of the head."

capped inhabit the higher elevations (a range map will pinpoint the species in your area). Where the two species overlap, they're best told apart by their song.

Unlike many birds, neither chickadee shows interest in migrating. In fact, they don't wander far from home at any time in their lives, restricting themselves to about twenty-five-acre territories.

When I think chickadee, I think busy. They're busy foragers, hunting bugs, larvae, and seed. They're busy feeder guests, plucking single seeds and dashing off. Friendly, scolding, curious—and busy.

But busy as they are at feeders, I have to wonder just how these little guys, wearing only fluff, survive cold so severe that it sends us humans shivering into multilayered high-tech insulation.

Chickadees, seemingly ever cheerful, face a tougher time keeping warm than we do. First, they maintain a higher body temperature, about 108 degrees, even during winter's worst. Second, their tiny bodies produce proportionately less heat than ours do. Finally, relative to heat production, they have a much larger exposed surface than we do. Even with increased feather numbers in winter—about 30 percent more, totaling roughly two thousand—chickadees must really work to stay warm

You've watched; you know how busy they are. Zip in, grab a seed, zip off, eat it, zip back, repeat. Their busyness, however, increases heart rate, up to two thousand beats per minute. But even perched, chickadees continuously flex chest muscles, an avian version of shivering, to generate more heat. In short, they're half-ounce metabolic fireballs.

To maintain metabolism, however, the little fidgets must find 150 sunflower seeds—or the energy equivalent from insects, insect eggs, and spiders—every day. Sunny days, stormy days, icy days, snowy days, every day. On seriously cold days, that number doubles or even triples. Coupled with wintertime's shortened daylight hours, chickadees, like other birds, must meet increased food demands in about one-third less time. It's no wonder, then, that given a chickadees' proclivity to spend an entire season in no more than twenty-five acres, they know well every square inch of their habitat.

NEST NOTES   **Carolina and Black-capped Chickadees**

Nest Site: chosen by both adults, in nest box or tree cavity 2–25 ft. high, facing a clearing
Nest Construction: both adults excavate, although female spends more time inside cavity; female builds nest accompanied by male, but he rarely or never contributes nest materials; nest base is moss with thick lining of hair and/or plant fibers
Eggs: 3–10 eggs, 1 brood, incubated only by female 12–15 days; male occasionally brings her food
Fledge: 13–17 days after hatch

Given time restriction and food demands, put pencil to paper and check the figures. A chickadee must zip in, grab seed, zip off, and eat it, and repeat the process about every two and a half minutes all day long, just to stay alive. Never again will "eats like a bird" imply a skimpy diet.

To ensure constant wintertime food supplies, chickadees also cache seeds for snowy, ice-bound, or blizzard-blasted days. My peanut feeder gets blockbuster sale–type traffic when the weather turns, and I'm certain—although I've not seen—that part of the disappearing act gets stashed in holes or crevices or buried behind bark.

But do chickadees actually find all these caches later? High metabolism generates high brain temperature and correlates with better memory. Partner that with the extraordinary—and utterly amazing—ability of pea-sized brains to grow new memory cells; chickadees grow these new cells each autumn. So, yes, they find their caches, as much as a month later. Come spring, the now-useless cells die off, wiping the memory slate clean. (If researchers ever learn how chickadees annually produce new neurons, imagine the ramifications. Could a cure for Alzheimer's spring from understanding chickadee brains?)

SPOTTING THE SPECTACULAR
Friendly Fluff Balls

Chickadees likely hold the record for entertaining more backyard birders than any other species. They're widespread, reasonably abundant, and acrobatic, often dangling upside-down, foraging among branch tips. Their images decorate more sweatshirts, greeting cards, and coffee mugs than any other species—with the possible exception of cardinals. But unlike cardinals, they're also friendly little guys—really friendly. Folks with patience have had chickadees feed from their hands. The rest of us find the little black, white, and gray fluff balls waiting for us to fill their feeders, scolding if we're slow. Amazing, isn't it, that they feel comfortable near monsters like us, many times bigger than they are. Above all, though, you gotta love 'em for their cheery dispositions.

At night, chickadees tuck into a cavity, each to its own, perhaps in an abandoned woodpecker hole, changing locations every few nights but roosting as a flock within close proximity to one another. However, because daytime metabolism would cause them to starve by morning, the snuggled-in chickadees go into torpor, something like overnight hibernation, when heart rate slows to five hundred beats per minute and body temperature drops by 20 degrees. To conserve heat, they may also tuck their heads under their shoulder feathers.

In that condition, the birds fluff up, an act that changes temperatures between the surface feathers and the skin ½ inch away by as much as a mind-boggling 115 degrees. Still, overnight, the

BIRD TALK: WHO'S CALLING?

Among the Carolina Chickadee's thirty-five or so identified songs, the two most common are *chick-a-dee-dee-dee* and *fee-bee-fee-bay*, with the first and third notes higher in pitch. Both are sung about an octave higher, more rapidly, and sound less husky than the similar song by the Black-capped Chickadee. Black-caps also sing a shorter, simpler song than the four- to six-note Carolina song, *fee-bee-ee*.

FOOD FARE

Chickadees will take sunflower seeds and hearts, peanuts and peanut butter, and, especially in winter, suet. In the garden, they take seeds, berries, and insects. In spring, summer, and fall, 80 to 90 percent of their diet is insects, and they feed their babies exclusively insects. In winter, they form foraging flocks that include other species like titmice and Downy Woodpeckers.

ID CHECK

Whether Carolina or Black-capped Chickadee wanders your yard, it's easily identified by the following:

- Crisp black cap
- Bold black bib
- Soft gray back
- White breast and belly
- And its busy, busy behavior

birds lose about 10 percent of their weight just staying alive. Come morning, they'll be at your feeder, stuffing seeds and suet, regaining weight to survive another winter night.

SPECIES PROFILE

TUFTED TITMOUSE

VITAL STATS
Length: 6 in.
Wingspan: 10 in.
Weight: 0.8 oz.

Tufted Titmouse

The January caller had a simple question: "Do Blue Jays have babies now?" "Uh, no, not in January, not in the dead of winter," I answered, recalling the family of five Blue Jays that visited my yard on an irregular foraging route, the youngsters now indistinguishable from mom and dad. "Why do you ask?"

"Because I have this little Blue Jay in my yard. He's eating sunflower seeds from my feeder. Cute little guy. Do you think he'll grow up by spring?" the caller asked.

Indeed, "baby Blue Jay" may, in some sense, serve as a fair description of Tufted Titmouse. Both birds have perky topknots, both call frequently, and both . . . well, that's about it. Blue Jays dwarf titmice, and the two birds' outfits differ so much that it's as if one bought muted formal while the other bought Hollywood gaudy. Titmice wear the classic business lines, a soft lovely gray coat, tasteful, trim, freshly pressed—nothing as bold as a jay's brilliant blue and white. The titmouse's orangey-pink blush along its sides adds the delicately perfect touch of color, understated, classy, sweetly elegant.

To me, they look as if they wear sexy sunglasses. Big sunglasses. A bit bug-eyed, they seem like wide-eyed see-it-alls, eyes too big for their trim little heads. And when they flatten their crests—as they frequently do—their eyes look even bigger.

Juvenile titmice lack the spiffy black forehead of adults, and youngsters' crests show somewhat shorter than those of mature birds. By winter, however, most individuals look alike, and, unlike other members of the Paridae family, seasonal flocks formed by parents and their offspring commonly forage together, now a team rather than adults and dependents.

NEST NOTES

Nest Site: found cavities (cannot excavate their own), including former woodpecker cavities. Will accept nest boxes.

Nest Construction: nest cup of leaves, bark strips, grasses, and moss lined with soft materials like fur, wool, and hair, including that from raccoons, horses, cows, cats, opossums, squirrels, and humans; known to yank hair from sleeping dogs.

Eggs: 3–9 eggs, 1 brood, incubated only by female 12–14 days while male feeds her

Fledge: 15–16 days after hatch

Tufted Titmice carry on quite a conversation with their foraging buddies. Busily noisy, they chatter and squeak, whisper and yell, whistle and scold. Not that they say anything memorable—they'd just rather talk than listen.

In winter, Tufted Titmice typically join other birds, like Carolina Chickadees (or Black-capped Chickadees, depending on where you live), Downy Woodpeckers, and White-breasted Nuthatches, the flock foraging together not only to have more eyes alert to food but also more eyes alert to predators. Watch, and you'll find the flock of friends, with titmice, like their chickadee cousins, often dangling upside-down from branches and twigs. Listen, too, for the chatter. Research suggests many other birds tune in to titmice scold calls, racing to discover the problem or scurrying to avoid the danger.

Titmice lack wanderlust. Homebodies through and through, they nevertheless traipse about as much as a half mile in the course of a day's hunt for food. But it's likely the same half-mile route they wandered yesterday and the day before. Migration seems out of the question for most Tufted Titmice; but if northernmost birds face serious food shortages, they'll ease southward rather than starve.

When titmice visit my feeder, I smile at their antic routine. Grab seed, fly to favored branch, wedge seed between feet, and hammer. Hammer, hammer, hammer, until the seed cracks open. Gulp kernel, drop hull, dart back to feeder. Repeat. The calculated routine leaves little to anticipate, but their cocky alert attitude and brazen behavior pairs with a comic sense.

They're welcome little creatures, especially soul-soothing during January's dreary days.

NAME THAT BIRD

Baeolophus bicolor (Tufted Titmouse): *Baeolophus* translates roughly as "having a small crest." *Bicolor* refers to the two colors on the bird's face. Its common name is more interesting. "Mouse" does not refer to the familiar little four-legged furry creature but comes from *mase*, the Anglo-Saxon word for a little bird. The "tit" part comes from an Icelandic word, *tittr*, that means "little," and gives a nod to a Paridae family cousin, the Tit, an Old World species.

BIRD TALK: WHO'S CALLING?

Tufted Titmice give a clear, bright whistle, *peter, peter, peter,* up to eleven times in succession, as many as thirty-five a minute. They do, however, have many variations. Titmice also have a chickadee-like call, but more nasal, more complaining.

FOOD FARE

Titmice readily come to feeders stocked with sunflower seeds and hearts, peanuts and peanut butter, and suet. In summer, they eat insects almost exclusively, including beetles, spiders, ants, wasps, and snails. In the garden, they forage for berries, seeds, and bugs, feeding babies a diet solely of bugs, and will take nuts, acorns, and beechnuts.

ID CHECK

Easily recognized by small size and crest, Tufted Titmice also display the following characteristics:

- Wear soft gray on crest, wings, back, and tail
- Show black forehead when mature
- Wear white on breast and belly
- May flatten perky crests, then appearing round headed
- Often forage hanging upside down

SPOTTING THE SPECTACULAR

Hair-raising Cause

Some of the most amusing photos of Tufted Titmice portray their love of hair—dog hair, goat hair, cat hair—and, yes, human hair. The humor stems from the birds' fearless pursuit of said hair, so fearless, in fact, that they yank it out of living, sleeping animals, much to the dismay of the sleeper. The poor dog that starts from a sound sleep, confused by the tiny sting of yanked-free hair, invariably jerks to the alert, searching for the cause. Dozing resumed, he finally accepts the yank as some fluke and ultimately sleeps through the remaining nest-gathering activities. One woman reported retrieving her hat to prevent further hair loss. Who can help smiling at such antics, the risk, the daring, all in the name of building the perfect nest!

SPECIES PROFILE

CAROLINA WREN

VITAL STATS
Length: 5 in.
Wingspan: 7.5 in.
Weight: 0.7 oz.

This Carolina Wren, its feathers fluffed to hold warmth, looks fat in winter.

Bird-watchers rarely admit to having a favorite bird. In fact, if I sort "favorite" by category, I have many—my favorite songster (Wood Thrush), favorite migrant (Yellow-throated Warbler), favorite bushwhacker (Eastern Towhee), favorite forest bird (Great-horned Owl), favorite best-dressed (Red-headed Woodpecker), favorite waterfowl (Wood Duck).

But my overall favorite seems more a buddy, awakening me most mornings, keeping in touch with its mate all day, singing a cheerfully robust song, nesting in surprising sites, remaining loyal to its mate 'til death do them part, ushering its kids safely through the yard, staying with me year round, and, in general, creating a gigantic presence for such a tiny bird: Carolina Wren.

In short, Carolina Wrens have it all. I think no other songster their size can belt out a song with such gusto. And they burst forth with song sometimes on even the coldest winter days, even in January. What better cheer could I want? And they're certainly in the running for best-dressed, wearing corduroylike, pencil-fine barring on wings and tail, contrasting with a velvety smooth blush of warm buffy-orange underneath and rusty fine-leather brown above. I could never consent to describe them as just plain brown.

They're gorgeous—at least right now, sporting fresh, warm plumage after their fall molt. But, oh, what a sad sight they were in early September, worn feathers, missing feathers, ratty, rough, ill-kempt, rumpled. They looked like a homeless pair, down on their luck. Now, three months later, they're once again gorgeous.

Often shy, Carolina Wrens seem to get to know us and become friends. Brazen, then, they'll busy themselves among us, making themselves at home—in the garage, under the carport, in storage sheds, sometimes scolding us for entering our own buildings. Even so, around my yard, they prefer poking around the two rotten logs behind the shed, foraging there for bugs and larvae, or flipping leaves among the blackberry briars, or ducking in and out among tangles along the fencerow, or checking for delectable tidbits in the brush pile.

SPOTTING THE SPECTACULAR
Sighting Nest Sites

Carolina Wrens nest in strange places: in glove compartments of abandoned cars, in old shoes and tin cans, under household propane tank covers. They seem to love garages, especially if they find there an unused flower vase or pot, a hanging apron pocket, stacked baskets, or cardboard boxes in snuggly sizes. They use our nest boxes, especially if we tuck them under the eaves, and they like hollowed gourds if we hang them under the porch or awnings. But they're as likely to choose some odd spot that seems unlikely or inconvenient to us but obviously perfect for them—like our newspaper box.

NAME THAT BIRD

Thryothorus ludovicianus (Carolina Wren): Descriptive of the bird's behavior, *Thryothorus* refers to rushing through underbrush, or reeds. *Ludovicianus* actually refers to Louis XIV, King of France. But the bird was named not for the king but for the Louisiana Territory, where the bird was first found. Its common name comes first from its habitat range and second from the Anglo-Saxon word for this particular kind of bird.

BIRD TALK: WHO'S CALLING?

Loudly and clearly, Carolina Wrens are said to commonly sing *teakettle teakettle, teakettle* or *cheery, cherry, cheery.* I think he sings *hickory, dickory, dickory, dock.* But a male may have twenty-five to forty more songs, all highly varied. Unlike many other wren species, only the male Carolina Wren sings. Females only call and scold.

FOOD FARE

Insects and spiders make up most of a Carolina Wren's diet, but in winter, it will visit suet and peanut butter feeders. Generally, it does not eat seed, so when it visits seed feeders, it's most likely looking for spiders or other insects in feeder cracks.

NEST NOTES

Nest Site: males build multiple nests but females likely choose final site, open cavities 3–6 ft. up in trees, overhangs, stumps, mailboxes, empty flower pots, apron pockets, boots

Nest Construction: both adults build nest, males providing more materials than females; cup-shaped, usually domed or partially so, with side entrance, made of variety of materials, including bark strips, dead leaves, dried grasses, pine needles, hair, straw, snakeskin, lined with finer materials

Eggs: 3–7 eggs, 1–3 broods, incubated only by female 12–16 days during which time male delivers food to her

Fledge: 10–16 days after hatch

Since a pair of Carolina Wrens stays together and maintains a year-round territory, we also get to know them. They love the peanut butter feeder just outside my office window; and in early evening, I see the two of them, together, stuffing themselves against the upcoming cold night. They'll be back, chirring and calling, keeping in touch, first thing in the morning.

Yes, Carolina Wrens are my overall favorite birds, my friends, my companions. They make me smile. They cheer me. Sometimes I wonder if they hear me speak to them, greeting them hello. Oh, silly me, how anthropomorphic. But, then, why else would they cock their sweet little heads and look at me, quizzically. They know me. What a joy to know them.

ID CHECK

A Carolina Wren might be confused with a House Wren. But House Wrens are here only in summer, and Carolina Wrens stay with us year round. In winter, the wren is Carolina. In summer, to set it apart from House Wren, watch for the following Carolina Wren characteristics:

- Bold, distinct white eye line (opposed to House Wren's plain face)
- Reddish rusty-brown plumage on back, wings, and tail (opposed to House Wren's dull brown)
- Rich buffy-orange underparts (opposed to House Wren's drab gray-brown)
- Perky upright tail position
- Big-voice song of *teakettle, teakettle, teakettle* (opposed to House Wren's warbling rattles and trills)

February

When Nature made the bluebird she wished
to propitiate both the sky and the earth,
so she gave him the color of one on his back
and the hue of the other on his breast.

JOHN BURROUGHS

Filling feeders during last week's light snow, I was stopped dead-still in my tracks. Bird-song! From the woods, from the hay field, from the conifers, from the backyard tangles. Dozens of melodies! Just days after the groundhog promised six more weeks of winter, the birds promise spring. So, who's right?

The A Team was in place: Titmice shouted *peter, peter, peter.* Doves sighed their *coo-ahh-coo, coo, coo.* Jays name-called *jay, jay, jay, bubble-link.* Cardinals boasted *purdy purdy purdy.* Goldfinches whistled their trademark slurry *swee, swee.* Year-round residents, all of them, but are they tuning up for spring?

Then I heard the B Team, four tell-tale songs: *konk-la-reeeee* of Red-winged Blackbirds, *cherrily cheer-up cherrio* of American Robins, *kadee, kadee, kadee* of Killdeer in flight, and a lovely whistled appropriate *spring-of-the-a-year* of a single distant Eastern Meadowlark. Their songs drifted across the neighborhood, suggesting, at least, the advent of spring. The groundhog surely was wrong.

The joyous serenade came just three days after we'd spotted the Eastern Bluebirds. The pair was scouting out one of the eleven nest boxes on our little bluebird trail. Popping in and out, they checked singly and together for the perfect real estate.

HOW DOES YOUR GARDEN GROW?

Four-Category Garden

For many of us, February brings seed catalogs and gardening dreams, the time to plan. In order to keep your A Team well fed, aim to cultivate four kinds of plants: plants that produce seed, some that provide nectar, others that produce fruit, and among them, plants whose buds, flowers, and leaves attract bugs. Then aim to provide those four food groups during as many seasons as your climate allows. Next, consider layers of vegetation, from ground cover to towering trees. Think vines, short and tall shrubs, grasses, flowers—all among and surrounding trees, trees, and more trees, coniferous and deciduous.

HABITAT—YOURS AND THEIRS
Winter Lows

Last year, after embarking on my own Big Year in the Yard, I verified a pattern I suspected but had never confirmed. Logging bird species week after week helped me substantiate that my February backyard hosts the least number of bird species of the year. Oh, we had plenty of birds—numerous individuals—but from week to week, only twenty-one to twenty-eight species reported in to fill the A Team roster.

Male Northern Cardinals brighten February backyard habitats.

The activity comes not really without warning—or even without precedent—groundhog prediction or no. Our resident Red-tailed Hawk has been crying her descending *keeeeer* for almost a month. Two Barred Owls have been pillow-talking at unreasonable hours in our backyard pine trees, whooping it up occasionally to a full crescendo. Unnamed woodpeckers have begun tapping out love songs in our woods.

BIOLOGY BITS   **Why Don't Birds' Feet Freeze?**

Birds have several options for protecting their bare feet from freezing. Some stand on one leg and tuck the other under their feathers, wrapping it in the equivalent of a down comforter. Other birds squat down, covering both feet with feathers. Still other birds have entwined blood vessels in their legs, one carrying warm blood from the body and one returning cold blood. As the two flow together, cooler blood is warmed, and birds benefit from the happy medium.

Still, some birds, most notably Mourning Doves, actually do suffer frostbite, occasionally losing a toe or two. Newer to cold climates than northerly birds like titmice and chickadees, doves have not yet evolved the efficient solutions for circulation in cold weather we see in other species.

This early February bird activity promises that spring can't be far away. But do the poor creatures really understand that snow and subfreezing temperatures mean winter still lingers? Well, yes. As ornithologists tell us, though, it's not the weather. It's the length of day— that's what triggers avian hormones. And hormones tell birds when to sing, when to migrate, when to molt, when to nest. Have you noticed the longer days? Where I live, daylight lasts an hour and a half longer now in mid-February than at the Winter Solstice in late December.

Even so, in spite of birdsong and its seeming promise of spring, months will pass before insects return to the skies and plants blossom and their seeds mature. Birds forage longer and harder now to find the foods they need to survive.

A Northern Mockingbird guards a winterberry bush, his means of cold-weather survival.

WATER WAYS   ## Wade or Swim?

Hungry birds also need water—year round—and most prefer water served at ground level. Unfortunately, those lovely (and often expensive) pedestal birdbaths are more decorative than useful. After all, have you ever seen water three feet above ground in the wild?

Birds need shallow water. Very shallow. Think about how small most songbirds really are. Their legs, for instance, measure no more than an inch long, so water three inches deep equates to a neck-deep bathtub—useless to little birds. Choose a shallow birdbath with sloping sides, a rough surface, and water an inch deep or less. The combination lets birds step down securely to water's edge, check the level, and then drink or bathe in comfort.

Whichever Weather

Backyard bird numbers fluctuate with weather. If weather had personality, we'd surely call last week's stuff wicked. With seeds and berries heavily snow coated, birds suffered; so they came, an ice-snow mixture stuck to their tails—or with no tails at all—crowding feeders, desperate. Thus, what may have been fatal for some birds produced jaw-dropping backyard shows for bird-watchers.

Sparrows made the biggest show, droves of them, but not just annoying non-native House Sparrows. Winter regulars like White-throated and White-crowned Sparrows joined company with gorgeous Fox Sparrows, two-toned rusty red and gray; American Tree Sparrows, rusty caped and central-breast spotted; winter-plumaged Chipping Sparrows, Tree Sparrow–like minus the spot; perky Song Sparrows, mindless in winter of their name—all hungry.

Rare winter-visiting Purple Finches came searching, too, including seven females and one handsome raspberry-colored male—a yard record number. Their fellow winter visitors, Pine Siskins and Red-breasted Nuthatches, also came, also hungry.

NOTABLE BEHAVIOR   ### Jekyll and Hyde

Fooling us, birds can change their appearance. For instance, they change shape depending on the weather—but not because they ate too many cookies over the December holidays. During hot weather, birds look trim and sleek because, to keep cool, they flatten their feathers against their bodies. Alternately, when birds get cold, they fluff up, insulating themselves against the cold.

Birds prefer water no more than an inch deep, as this bathing White-throated Sparrow proves.

Even easier to see, however, is the bird with an attitude, showing aggression. Body language, we humans call it. Birds change their posture, leaning forward, standing taller, flaring their wings, standing head feathers on end, puffing up to look as big and mean as their little bodies will allow. Or, showing submission, they reverse all those stances, meek and mild in the presences of older, wiser birds—those higher up in the proverbial pecking order. Watch for their Jekyll-and-Hyde changes.

Other hungry species upped the count: an Eastern Towhee pair, vivid against the snow, picking at seeds; a shy Brown Thrasher flipping snow-free leaves under the junipers, seeking bugs; a Northern Mockingbird guarding its feeder of apple chunks, suet crumbles, and raisins; Carolina Wrens cracking the mocker's defenses, stealing its tidbits. And in late afternoon, a pair of Barred Owls asked each other, *Who cooks for you?*

Daily, however, a special time comes just before dark, after the raucous hordes of blackbirds and grackles depart, after hawk-mimic calls of jays go silent, and after squabbling starlings leave suet feeders quiet. Then cardinals gather, arriving in singles and pairs, feeding peacefully, red against snow and hemlock green, a quiet, celebratory alone-at-last atmosphere that even wicked weather couldn't erase.

FEEDER FOCUS **In Praise of Shelled Corn**

A daily scoop of shelled (not cracked) corn in a ground-level platform feeder keeps cardinals and doves well stuffed. Not much else feathered will tackle whole corn kernels, but cardinals patiently peel open the bounty and down the hearts. Doves, though, gulp kernels whole and love the fare. One day I watched a single female dove swallow thirty-eight kernels, popping down one after another, before a larger male made threatening moves and sent the female scurrying. Still not satisfied, she waddled over to forage under the thistle feeder, downing a few grains of safflower seed along the way. Shelled corn, though, always gets first dibs from doves.

Memorable Moments: Following Falling Feathers

Winter raises our hawk species tally from three to four. This new guy, however, is not a backyard regular. In fact, in forty-some years, only twice have I spotted it in my wintertime yard. Perhaps our resident pairs of Red-shouldered, Red-tailed, and Cooper's Hawks crowd it out of the neighborhood. But this year, it has moved in, made itself comfortably at home, and is terrorizing the yard.

This Sharp-shinned Hawk, little but mighty, sneaked in and proceeded to bombard me with memorable moments, sights now seared in my mind's eye, sights I'd rather not remember but do, because of their power, their speed, their impact, sights mixed with joy and sorrow—but not necessarily in equal parts.

While sharpies breed in some parts of the Northeast and through the Appalachians—maybe where you live—we typically don't see them here in southern Indiana until fall and winter. Residents of dense closed-canopy forests during breeding season, wintering Sharp-shinned Hawks willingly trade characteristic elusiveness for good hunting. And yards that support a nice population of feeder birds literally defines good hunting for them. Plucked songbird is their favorite meal—much to my consternation.

BIOLOGY BITS   **Dinosaurs to Birds**

Feathered creatures first appear in fossil records during the Jurassic Period, 150 million years ago. Called *Archaeopteryx*, it is ancestor to, or close relative of, modern birds. Meat-eating hawks followed fairly soon after on the evolutionary scale. But during the Tertiary Period, beginning 65 million years ago, rapid evolution of birds, especially of passerines— songbirds like finches, sparrows, thrushes—kicked in. The change came about with good cause: bugs. The rapid proliferation of new and varied plant foods, specifically the angiosperms, triggered the rapid proliferation of bugs. Even today, most insects depend entirely or in part on flowering plants. In turn, most little birds depend on bugs. Not hawks, though, that evolved earlier, eating chunkier kinds of meat.

So mixed feelings welled up inside when it first ripped through the yard. I admire its kind—their speed, their agility, their prowess, their flair—but I know why it's here. Sharpies are little guys—Blue Jay–sized—and I first mistook it for a dove, long tailed, perched in the dense pine boughs of our little backyard grove, surroundings familiar to a mini-hawk that grew up in northern conifers. It didn't look like a dove for very long, though, as it dropped, twisting, to several branches lower; popped up again several limbs to the right; flapped twice to make a long hop to a farther branch; then, eyeing me, slid effortlessly away, almost magically maneuvering through dense branches, its long tail a rudder, its flight speedy. In an instant, it was out of sight. I hoped it moved on. It didn't.

Within an hour, I heard feathers brush hard against the kitchen window, not a "thunk," but a controlled close encounter. A long tube feeder hangs less than a foot from the glass, within reach for easy filling from inside. Lately, it's been overflowing with goldfinches, feeding with abandon on sunflower hearts, keeping me entertained with their multitudes, dashing off each time I pass close to the window but returning posthaste. Thus, the commotion raised my worst fears. I dashed to see. The feeder hung shuddering, empty of birds, and I caught only an instant's glimpse of the sharpie, rushing into the pines.

FEEDER FOCUS
Single-seed Tubes

Tube feeders imitate nature— a sturdy plant with twigs for perching next to portals of food. Thus, by offering a single kind of seed per tube, you'll tap into natural and economic feeding. Birds won't flick unwanted seeds to the ground in order to find the seeds they prefer. Single-seed feeders save a mess, too.

Did it grab a goldfinch in its talons—right from the finch's perch? Sharpies hit with surprise and force, their long skinny toes, tipped with catlike claws, flexing as killing machines, piercing, constricting. Victims never know what hits. Other birds flee, screaming in terror.

I dashed out the back door, ignoring usual caution, and caught it in the act—standing on one foot, amid the pine tree's shroud, clutching a goldfinch in its talon. At my disturbance, it lifted off, flew west; I crashed through undergrowth, following. Into the cedar grove, it disappeared. I searched. No luck. Then, a feather drifted down. And another. Tiny pale yellow ones. And I knew.

NOTABLE BEHAVIOR   **Meat-eating Raptors**

Most raptors eat meat. Depending on the species, they prefer anything from grasshoppers to mice to rabbits to fish to carrion to, yes, even other birds. Sharp-shinned Hawks, like other accipiters, prefer fresh-killed meat. And while some raptors, like owls, gulp prey down whole, sharpies first pluck the prey bird's feathers, and then, using more delicate table manners, dine on their quarry one bite at a time. The sharpie's look-alike cousin, a Cooper's Hawk, once devoured a cardinal right outside my window. When the hawk finished, rested, and departed, I checked the dining room. It was neat and clean. Only three wing feathers remained. The Cooper's had eaten everything else—head, feet, wings, feathers, everything.

For more than a week, backyard feeders—all of them—hung idle, the yard barren of birds. Finally, cardinals drifted in, cautious, usually less threatened by sharpies than are the smaller birds. Another day passed. A Downy Woodpecker slipped to the suet. Then, over the next week, an occasional titmouse zipped in, grabbed a seed, and zipped out. Chickadees frequented only a feeder tucked in the corner of the trellis, protected from a sharpie's direct flight path.

Still, two weeks later, nothing ventured onto the long tube feeder, the scene of the crime. Do they know? Will they forget? Will they overcome their terror? Was the sharpie still nearby, secreted from my view but not theirs?

In the two-week respite from the backyard, goldfinches fed, sparsely, only at front-yard feeders, enjoying thistle and sunflower hearts, feeling safer, I suppose, because of close-by bushes and tree branches, not only obstacles for a speeding hawk but also protection in flight. Although the Cooper's Hawk regularly stands sentry in the front-yard oak, causing birds to disappear, it's a short-lived act, their "freezing" in position or melting into the landscape. Unlike a Cooper's, though, sharpies terrorize with speed, jetting in and out, snaring prey in fractional seconds, scattering feathers on the fly. Some memorable moments offer more pleasure than others.

BIOLOGY BITS
Gene Pool Party Pooper

Of course, birds aren't stupid. Threats to their safety send them fleeing in terror—at least those that survive to pass on their genes. To cope with the loss of a few goldfinches, I have to console myself by focusing on the Sharp-shinned Hawk's role in nature. Not only is everything lunch for something else (except for humans, at the top of the food chain), the speeding hawk hunting my backyard keeps the little birds' gene pools strong. It snares the sick, weak, old, and slow—or slow witted. Doesn't mean I like the situation, but that's the way it is.

WHY DO BIRDS DO THAT?
Why Do Woodpeckers Peck Wood?

Depending on the season, woodpeckers hammer for different reasons. Year round, they hammer seeking food, excavating rotten parts, sending bugs scurrying, then listening for movement. In spring, they're likely excavating nest sites. In fall, they hammer in caches of acorns and other nuts, storing a safety net of food against winter's hard times. In fall, they're also hollowing roost sites—since they rarely use nest sites as roost sites or vice versa.

Now, in February, they're hammering out Valentine's love messages. Loud. Staccato. Rhythmic. Tom-tom messages, tympani messages, bass-drum messages—each from a different woodpecker, each sending a hearts-and-flowers love note. And underlying every message is an equally clear call-to-war message, warning other males to stay off the drummer's territory.

A female Red-bellied Woodpecker prepares to cache a still-in-the-hull pecan, tucking it into the split of a rotting pine branch.

Staccato Beat

For those of us old enough to remember, the 1960s Sonny and Cher hit song claims, "The beat goes on. Drums keep pounding a rhythm to the brain." As seasons change, as winter begins losing its grip, as birds negate the groundhog's prediction, as days gain sunshine hours, the beat, indeed, goes on. This morning, the beat came from the woods. Woodpeckers seemed to drum the woods alive.

For folks with a keen musical sense, each woodpecker species hammers with an identifiable rhythm. The better the resonance, the farther the messages carry, whether the birds are hammering out territory or posting love messages. Resonance, however, comes from whatever they hammer on—hollow limb, decaying tree, utility post, or your gutter, chimney flashing, downspout, or vent pipe.

PROBLEM SOLVER

When "Hammer-Heads" Hammer Your House

Beware if woodpeckers hammer your house. They're not eating wood. Hammer-heads hammer for three reasons: to eat, carve out nest or roost sites, or attract mates within the breeding territory. If woodpeckers discover ants, carpenter bees, or other insects in your home's wood structures, they'll dine regularly, hammering small holes, often in a line. To verify that your home is free of pests, check with an exterminator. But houses sided with wood, especially in dark colors, also attract woodpeckers—bugs or not.

Of multiple deterrents tested, reflective streamers worked best to deter persistent woodpeckers from hammering on houses. Shiny coating and movement in wind kept birds at bay and eliminated damage at half of test sites.

While early morning downspout hammering probably falls short of a welcoming wake-up call, the hammer-heads surely earn a standing ovation for the complexity of the process. Woodpeckers can pound twenty beats a second—a fast pace for even a jazz master. And they can repeat that rhythm several thousand times a day. Physically, the pecking necessitates some dramatic muscular control, each peck requiring the bird to pull its head back as far as it will go and then blasting straight forward, a thrust measured at about 225 inches per second. Awesome stuff, don't you think?

Woodpeckers have evolved into odd little creatures. They nest in tree holes, eat bugs gleaned from tree bark, and sport stiff tails to lean against as they hitch up trees. While most birds have three toes forward and one back, woodpeckers have zygodactyl feet—two toes forward and two back—to better hang onto trees.

In the balance, woodpeckers play a major role in the lives of other birds, many of which commandeer old woodpecker dens for their own. Wood Ducks, wrens, nuthatches, bluebirds, most chickadees, titmice, Tree Swallows—all ill-equipped for hammering out cavities on their own—depend on woodpeckers for survival. So do a number of small mammals and reptiles.

BIOLOGY BITS
Why Woodpeckers Don't Get Headaches

Pounding wood seems a sure way to suffer brain damage—or at least cause a serious headache. But a woodpecker's reinforced frontal bones, extra-large brain case, and a set of muscle and bone structures at the base of its bill all work together to cushion the blows. In addition, unlike human brains, woodpecker brains are tightly packed into their skulls. Woodpeckers have no fluid surrounding their brains as do humans. Thus, when they hammer, there's no shock wave—the activity that causes human-brain concussions. As far as we know, they're headache free.

Heads or Tails

Okay, so woodpeckers don't get headaches. Beyond an incredible brain-protecting cranial cavity, however, they have some other remarkable adaptations that allow them to be peckers of wood, living not on the edge but on the vertical.

Let's start with the mouth. Compared to other birds, woodpeckers sport a powerful bill designed for serious wood work. Brawny, tough bones form woodpecker bills that, in turn, are tipped with a cutting edge any woodcrafter would treasure—chisel-like, sharp, thickset.

The most specialized part of a woodpecker's mouth, however, is not its bill but its tongue, a really long tongue, typically three times as long as its bill—so long that in order to store it, woodpecker anatomy allows it to loop up the back of the bird's head and, in some species, over its right eye, attaching near its right nostril. The extraordinary length—and strength—lets woodpeckers pry insects, insect eggs, and larvae from tree-bark crevices. Somehow "prying" seems the wrong word to describe

BIOLOGY BITS
Guiding Lights

In order to crack its tough eggshell and break out into the world, a bird embryo comes equipped with an "egg tooth," a little hook-like appendage on the bill tip. Knowing that the appendage drops off shortly after hatching, scientists thought the tooth's purpose ended at hatching. Recently, however, new research shows that the egg tooth has almost 100 percent reflective capability. Imagine being a minuscule just-out-of-the-shell woodpecker, nestled deep inside a dark, dark cavity. How does mom find you to drop food in your mouth? Mom and dad woodpecker, and likely many seabirds, apparently use the reflective egg tooth to direct feeding. What a trick!

NOTABLE BEHAVIOR
Signature Flight

Even without seeing a bird's color or field marks, bird-watchers can often ID a bird by its flight pattern. For instance, Red-headed Woodpeckers exhibit a beeline flight powered by slow, steady, shallow beats. Others in the woodpecker family, however, including red-belly, sapsucker, flicker, downy and hairy, fly in a flap-flap-flap-glide pattern that results in an undulating flight path.

A Carolina Wren enjoys a peanut-butter feeder.

the function of a tongue, but not for woodpeckers. In fact, its tongue is so strong and equipped with such a sharply barbed tip that it can spear—yes, spear—large insects. Mostly, though, the tongue works rather like flypaper, made sticky by special saliva glands that emit glue-like fluids. In short, woodpecker tongues seem more like weapons than tongues. Well, in fact, they are!

FEEDER FOCUS Peanut Butter on the Menu

To keep warm, wintering birds, including woodpeckers, need fat, and lots of it. Like suet, peanut butter offers high levels of fat. Personally, I feed crunchy style in a homemade feeder. Natural, salt-free works best for birds. Depending on where I hang the feeder, it attracts chickadees, titmice, cardinals, Carolina Wrens, Downy and Hairy Woodpeckers, and flickers.

A woodpecker's face sports one other customized feature. To protect chisel-billed woodpecker noses from flying woodchips and other debris, their little nostril slits are set farther apart than those of other birds. And they're also feather-covered. In fact, Downy and Hairy Woodpeckers get their names from the downy and hairy feathers that protect their respective nostrils.

A close look at a Downy Woodpecker's face shows the "downy" feathers for which the bird is named.

Beyond their specialized head and facial features, another specialized body part makes woodpeckers different from all other birds—and allows them to hitch up tree trunks in a way that no other bird can. It's their tails. Woodpeckers' customized tails give them traction to zip up and down trees. Supersized tail bones support super-strong tail muscles, and the tail sprouts super-stiff, super-tough feathers. As woodpeckers hitch up a tree, tails work with toes, forming a triangle, to scoot them along, two-foot hopping, suspended in midair for a fractional second as their toes stretch for the next highest grip on the bark—an astonishing means of locomotion. But don't try this at home.

Welcome Home

To welcome woodpeckers into your backyard habitat, first, most critically, offer nest sites. Every pair of woodpeckers requires nest and roost cavities to survive. Unfortunately, however, few woodpeckers readily accept human-made nest cavities. Thus, it's critical, when safely possible, to avoid cutting down dead trees or removing dead tree limbs—essential for woodpecker existence.

HABITAT—YOURS AND THEIRS   Snagging Birds

Dead trees, often called "snags," are Mother Nature's grocery store and nursery. Woodpeckers, wrens, creepers, nuthatches, and others pick larvae from under peeling bark or in rotting wood. Cavities offer nest sites for bluebirds, chickadees, titmice, owls, and of course, woodpeckers. If a yard tree is dying, of course you must protect your dwelling and those of your neighbors, so remove weak limbs. But allow the trunk to remain. Watch what comes to this magnet for shelter and food.

Second, offer food. Suet, raw unsalted shelled peanuts, natural unsalted peanut butter, sunflower seed, and sunflower hearts attract most woodpeckers. For Red-headed and Red-bellied Woodpeckers, you may choose to add shelled corn. Yellow-bellied Sapsuckers, Northern Flickers, and Pileated Woodpeckers rarely visit feeders, although flickers may take suet in winter; pileateds, in breeding season.

Although cracked corn will attract certain undesirable birds, both cracked and shelled corn are favorites with Red-headed Woodpeckers.

Suet by Any Name

Dozens of birds love suet. But given the glut of packaged suet combos available, how's a responsible bird host to know which to choose? Is it okay to pick the least expensive?

Suet is a specific kind of fat; it surrounds beef kidneys, as much as 20 pounds per creature. The real stuff, shiny and waxy, feels hard and crumbly. Soap- and candle-makers call it tallow. In the wild, without our help, birds glean suet from carcasses.

Suet offers much-needed nutrition for birds. Without concern for clogged arteries, birds require huge amounts of fat to maintain their astonishingly high metabolisms. Suet's concentrated form of fat ensures energy for nesting, migration, and winter survival.

What's the best suet cake? The answer is unequivocally simple: that with the highest fat content. Whether you buy it fresh from the butcher shop (100 percent fat) or packaged in rendered pressed cakes at the store (fat content can vary dramatically), understand what you're offering. Here are four key points:

First, suet cakes should not include seed, like cracked corn, millet, milo, or oats—for three reasons. Reason one: Birds that eat suet in winter are primarily birds that eat insects in summer; they're not seed eaters. Reason two: Seed-filled cakes crumble, so chunks fall to the ground and attract rodents, including rats. Reason three: Seed-filled cakes encourage non-suet-eating birds—like starlings—to rip into your offerings.

Second, suet cakes should include a high percentage of fat and little or no fiber. In this case, "fiber" translates as "trash" or "filler." Read the label. Some cakes contain 98 percent fat. That's good. Some have as little as 15 percent. That's pitifully poor—for birds and your pocketbook.

Third, fruit in suet works okay since birds that eat insects in summer typically eat berries in winter. Still, high fat content is key to nutritional value, so fruit should make up no more than 5 percent of the cake.

White-breasted Nuthatches will visit suet feeders.

Fourth, don't let packaging mislead you. A zippy name frequently reflects sales appeal rather than nutritional appeal. A careful read of some fancy-package labels reveals some real rip-offs. Watch out.

So do birds care? Yes. Run your own tests. Place several kinds of suet in feeders around your yard. My personal observation is that woodpeckers—and most other birds—prefer pure suet. And given a choice, they'll choose the real stuff from the butcher shop over the pure processed cakes. But processed cakes are easier to use, and they don't turn rancid nearly so quickly in above-freezing weather—a real drawback of the fresh-from-the-cow product.

Finally, how should hosts offer suet? Most suet lovers love to cling; feeders should accommodate that behavior. Tuck suet in mesh onion bags or in commercial or homemade suet cages (chicken wire works). Smear it on pine cones or bark, or mash it into a drilled log.

But above all, read those labels. Do it for the birds.

Housing Crisis

Woodpeckers carve out the wood cavities they require for raising babies, and abandoned woodpecker cavities serve as nest/rest sites for other species, including birds, reptiles, and mammals. But the crisis facing cavity-nesting birds goes well beyond woodpeckers and a dead tree limb here or a rotting tree snag there.

BOTANY FOR BIRDS
Cavity Nesters—Who Are They?

Nationwide, according to a U.S. Forest Service report, some eighty-five bird species use cavities for their nests—either cavities they hammer out themselves, cavities excavated by another species, or natural cavities created by decay. And because most cavity-nesting birds eat primarily insects—and feed their babies insects—these birds play a major role in controlling forest insect pests.

Consider the species list to the right and ways you might encourage them to be part of your backyard habitat with natural or constructed nest cavities.

Of the thirty-plus Eastern U.S. cavity-nesting species, all but maybe a half dozen can, depending on where you live, show up as yard birds. Imagine the competition. Those thirty-plus native species struggle to overcome dual problems. First, they must square off with hundreds of rival non-native European Starlings and House Sparrows. Squabbles over nest sites sometimes lead to dramatic battles, sometimes to the death. It's not a pretty sight. Second, birds find few dead or decaying trees or other natural cavity sites, because most folks cut down dead trees.

The seriousness of the situation is plain and simple: If cavity-nesters can't find cavities, they can't breed.

In short, that means for your backyard to meet the Big Four requirements for good habitat (food, water, shelter, and places to raise young), you'll want to provide nest cavities. Aside from waiting for a mature tree to die or a storm to rip a healthy tree apart, mounting commercial or homemade nest boxes will enhance your backyard habitat.

Now, in February, at least where I live, in spite of icy rims on birdbaths, cavity nesters begin staking out nest sites. They'll seek hollow trees, hollow wooden fence posts, gourds—or nest boxes. So, now's the time. Nest boxes, commonly called birdhouses, should be part of your landscape by the middle of this month.

CAVITY-NESTING BIRDS OF EASTERN UNITED STATES

Wood Duck
Hooded Merganser
Common Merganser
American Kestrel
Barn Owl
Eastern Screech-owl
Barred Owl
Northern Saw-whet Owl
Chimney Swift
Northern Flicker
Pileated Woodpecker
Red-bellied Woodpecker
Red-headed Woodpecker
Yellow-bellied Sapsucker
Hairy Woodpecker
Downy Woodpecker
Red-cockaded Woodpecker
Great Crested Flycatcher
Tree Swallow
Purple Martin
Black-capped Chickadee
Carolina Chickadee
Tufted Titmouse
White-breasted Nuthatch
Red-breasted Nuthatch
Brown Creeper
House Wren
Winter Wren
Carolina Wren
Eastern Bluebird
European Starling
Prothonotary Warbler
House Sparrow
European Tree Sparrow

Providing Nest-box Cavities

Different birds need different sized cavities with different sized entrances. Use the dimensions on the following page to choose for purchase—or to make—nest boxes appropriate for birds in your habitat.

Tree Swallows accept man-made nest boxes.

If you purchase nest boxes, watch for two kinds: those for people and those for birds. Birds don't want cute, decorative, or painted. Skip the fancy-schmancy. Instead, look for the following:

- Sturdy construction (¾-inch walls for durability)
- Untreated, unpainted wood, preferably cedar (for safety and durability)
- Extended sloped roof (for wind-blown rain protection)
- Recessed floor (for better waterproofing, preventing capillary action)
- Rough or grooved interior walls (so fledglings can climb out)
- Adequate drainage (to assure egg and nestling safety)
- Adequate ventilation holes (to prevent overheating in mid-summer)
- Smooth-to-the-touch openings (to avoid excessive feather wear)
- Easy access for monitoring and cleaning (to assure safety and to oust invasive species)
- No outside perches (to help prevent predation)

Openings range in size. For example, choose 1⅛-inch openings for chickadees, 1¼-inch for titmice and House Wrens, and 1½-inch for bluebirds, Carolina Wrens, Tree Swallows, and nuthatches. Opening size and nest-box location determine who finds your real estate attractive. Keep in mind, however, that nest boxes need maintenance, including preventative care that promotes good health among your tenants. Blowflies, parasitic mobsters that attack birds and babies in the nest, weaken and sometimes kill babies. To deter blowflies from laying eggs, crumble bay leaves and slide them gently under the nest. Help keep wasps from building nests inside by rubbing a bar of soap on the inside of the nest roof. And always monitor nest boxes to keep out House Sparrows and starlings.

Mounting Birdhouses

In order to provide safe, suitable housing for cavity nesters, follow these guidelines for mounting birdhouses:

- Choose nest box sites suitable for the intended species (open grasslands near trees for bluebirds, chickadees, and titmice; near or under eaves of buildings for House and Carolina Wrens; forest for woodpeckers; forest edge for kestrels; near water for Tree Swallows; at water's edge for Wood Ducks).

- Choose locations without large House Sparrow populations.
- Mount boxes on poles, not on trees or fence posts (which serve as ladders for predators), with openings facing generally southeastward.
- Mow the area near boxes. Bluebirds, for instance, abandon boxes in high weeds.
- For bluebird use, mount boxes at least 75 yards apart.
- Use predator guards to avoid creating snake or raccoon lunch boxes.
- Monitor boxes weekly, eliminating House Sparrow and European Starling nests, ants, wasps, and vacated nests.
- Leave boxes up year round. Wintering birds use nest boxes as winter roosts.

Recommended Dimensions for Birdhouses

Bird	Hole Diameter	Height Above Floor	Interior Floor Size	Total Box Height
Bluebird, Eastern	1½"	6"–7"	4" x 4"	11"–12"
Chickadee, Carolina and Black-capped	1⅛"–1½"	6"–7"	4" x 4" to 5" x 5"	9"–12"
Duck, Hooded Merganser	3" x 4"	16"–18"	10" x 10" to 12" x 12"	24"–25"
Duck, Wood	3" x 4"	16"–18"	10" x 10" to 12" x 12"	24"–25"
Flicker, Northern	2"–3"	10"–20"	6" x 6" to 8" x 8"	14"–24"
Kestrel, American	3"	10"–12"	8" x 8" to 9" x 9"	14"–16"
Martin, Purple	2"–2½"	1"	6" x 6"	6"
Nuthatch, White-breasted	1⅛"–1½"	6"–7"	4" x 4" to 5" x 5"	9"–12"
Owl, Barn	6"–9"	4"	16" wide, 22" deep	16"
Owl, Barred	6"–8"	14"–18"	13" x 13" to 14" x 14"	22"–28"
Owl, E. Screech-	2½"–4"	10"–12"	6" x 6" to 8" x 8"	15"–18"
Swallow, Tree	1¼"–1½"	6"–7"	4" x 4" to 5" x 5"	9"–12"
Titmouse, Tufted	1⅜"–1½"	6"–7"	4" x 4" to 5" x 5"	9"–12"
Woodpecker, Downy	1¼"–1½"	8"–12"	3" x 3" to 4" x 4"	10"–14"
Woodpecker, Hairy	1¾"–2¾"	10"–14"	5" x 5" to 6" x 6"	14"–16"
Woodpecker, Red-bellied	1¾"–2¾"	10"–14"	5" x 5" to 6" x 6"	14"–16"
Woodpecker, Red-headed	1¾"–2¾"	10"–14"	5" x 5" to 6" x 6"	14"–16"
Wren, Carolina	1½"	6"–7"	4" x 4" to 5" x 5"	9"–12"
Wren, House	1"–1½"	6"–7"	4" x 4" to 5" x 5"	9"–12"

The best way to mount small nest boxes is on free-standing metal poles or PVC pipes. In addition, be sure to add predator guards to deter snakes and raccoons; otherwise, you're inviting nest predation.

Artificial nest cavities make a huge difference in the scheme of avian life. Properly mounted, monitored, and maintained, they can also make a huge difference in your backyard habitat.

Great Backyard Bird Count

Mid-February marks the annual international Great Backyard Bird Count, led by the Cornell Lab of Ornithology and the National Audubon Society. The purpose of the four-day event is to "create a real-time snapshot of where the birds are across the continent." Because scientists can't be everywhere, each of us can serve as a citizen-scientist by reporting what's in our respective yards and neighborhoods. These data help ornithologists keep a finger on the pulse of bird populations. Find out how to participate and post your tally at www.birdsource.org. Then do it—for the birds.

Predator guards, like this one made of stove pipe, protect nest boxes from predation by raccoons and snakes; for safety's sake, never mount a nest box without a guard.

NOTABLE BEHAVIOR

Nest Box Roost Box

Bluebirds, among other birds, choose cavities for winter-night roosts, huddling together to better withstand bitter cold and driving wind. Consider the following comparisons in order to turn your own nest boxes into winter-sheltering roost boxes.

Differences between a Nest Box and Roost Box

A nest box . . .	A roost box . . .
serves birds for nesting in summer	serves birds for winter warmth and roosting safety
has varied sized entrance holes to meet needs of specific species (see page 49 for details)	has a 2½" entrance hole on front to serve most birds that accept winter roosts
has entrance hole near top for heat escape, ventilation, and protection against predators	has entrance hole near bottom to prevent heat loss
has adequate ventilation holes to cool incubating birds and nestlings during hot summer days	has no ventilation holes and is as airtight as possible
has no perches, inside or out	has inside perches: ¼" dowels, 4" apart, alternating so birds don't defecate on one another

Conservation Corner: Common Birds in Decline

According to the National Audubon Society (NAS), forty years of Christmas Bird Count data and Breeding Bird Survey tallies reveal "alarming declines for many of our most common and beloved birds."

The reports says, "Since 1967 the average population of the common birds in steepest decline has fallen by 68 percent; some individual species nose-dived as much as 80 percent. All twenty birds on the national Common Birds in Decline list lost at least half their populations in just four decades." Of those twenty birds, thirteen live in the Eastern United States.

According to NAS, "The findings point to growing impact from the many environmental challenges our birds face, from habitat loss from development, deforestation, and conversion of land to agriculture, to climate change. . . . The wide variety of birds affected is reason for concern. Populations of meadowlarks and other grassland birds [for instance] are diving because of suburban sprawl, industrial development, and the intensification of farming over the past 50 years."

Can we help? Yes, according to NAS. The organization recommends that each of us becomes "a citizen-scientist by participating in bird counts, volunteering at Important Bird Areas (IBAs), and bringing conservation home. At home, that means maintaining a healthy bird friendly yard"—which you can do by implementing the ideas in this book.

Northern Bobwhite, female

Once-common Eastern U.S. birds, some of which regularly visited backyards, are now in serious decline, no doubt soon-to-be candidates for the U.S. Department of the Interior's Red List (highest concern or endangered) or Yellow List (declining or rare), both addressed in this book's final chapter. Eastern U.S. birds in serious decline include the following:

American Bittern (wetlands)
Common Grackle (open areas)
Eastern Meadowlark (grasslands)
Evening Grosbeak (forest for breeding; suburban
    areas in winter)
Field Sparrow (grasslands)
Grasshopper Sparrow (grasslands)
Horned Lark (grasslands)
Little Blue Heron (wetlands)
Loggerhead Shrike (open woodlands)
Northern Bobwhite (grasslands)
Northern Pintail (water)
Snow Bunting (tundra for breeding; grassy fields,
    shores in winter)
Whip-poor-will (open forests)

Eastern Meadowlark

Things to Do in February

With winter in its depths, use February to complete the following to-do list:

- Serve nutritious foods (i.e., those with highest fat content) to help birds keep warm.
- Choose suet wisely, checking labels to choose cakes with at least 95 percent fat content.
- As daylight hours lengthen, listen for the first birdsongs of spring.
- Be alert to woodpecker activity as the birds begin hammering to advertise for mates.
- Check nursery catalogs and online to plan habitat improvements, choosing native plants of all sizes that produce seed, nectar, berries, and fruit, and attract bugs.
- Do your part as a citizen-scientist and participate in the Great Backyard Bird Count.
- Encourage a relative or friend to join you in protecting the birds.

---

35 Yard Birds in February

Two inches of snow early in month; then colder and more snow; much singing in spite of bitter weather.

Canada Goose	Pileated Woodpecker	Fox Sparrow
Turkey Vulture	Blue Jay	Song Sparrow
Sharp-shinned Hawk	American Crow	White-throated Sparrow
Cooper's Hawk	Carolina Chickadee	Dark-eyed Junco
Red-shouldered Hawk	Tufted Titmouse	Northern Cardinal
Red-tailed Hawk	White-breasted Nuthatch	Red-winged Blackbird
Mourning Dove	Carolina Wren	Common Grackle
Barred Owl	Eastern Bluebird	Brown-headed Cowbird
Red-bellied Woodpecker	American Robin	House Finch
Downy Woodpecker	Northern Mockingbird	American Goldfinch
Hairy Woodpecker	European Starling	House Sparrow
Northern Flicker	Eastern Towhee	

SPECIES PROFILE

DOWNY WOODPECKER and HAIRY WOODPECKER

VITAL STATS
Downy Woodpecker
Length: 7 in.
Wingspan: 11–12 in.
Weight: 1 oz.

Above, left: *Downy Woodpecker, female;* above right: *Downy Woodpecker, male*

VITAL STATS
Hairy Woodpecker
Length: 8.5–10.5 in.
Wingspan: 15–17.5 in.
Weight: 2.5 oz.

Above, left: *Hairy Woodpecker, female;* above right: *Hairy Woodpecker, male*

Downy Woodpecker, the smallest and most common of the woodpecker family, gets its name from short, soft bristles that seem to sprout from the base of its bill, covering its nostrils. From a distance, the little guy seems to have a tiny muff of fur rather than bristles. Hairy Woodpecker, the Downy Woodpecker's slightly larger look-alike cousin, gets its name from the same bristles. On the hairy, however, bristles look longer, stiffer, less furry than the downy's.

Given the right habitat, both woodpeckers can be regulars in the yard. Fortunately, both hang out all year in and around my yard and nest in the adjoining woodland. As a matter of routine, Downy Woodpeckers, frequently two at a time, dine at the suet feeder just 2 feet from my office window. They make me chuckle as one peers around the side to see if the other is still there. "Just checking," he seems to say, content that she's doing okay on her side.

Never, though, have I seen a Hairy Woodpecker at that same feeder. Instead, hairies prefer the feeder farther from the house, 15 feet or so from the kitchen window, between the old tulip poplar and dense hemlock.

NAME THAT BIRD

Picoides pubescens (Downy Woodpecker): The Latin word *picus* refers to a big black-backed woodpecker, thus *Picoides*. *Pubescens* refers to the short hairs at the base of the bird's bill and comes from the same root word as "pubescence" and "puberty," both connected to the onset of pubic hair.

Picoides villosus (Hairy Woodpecker): *Villosus* refers to the hairs at the base of the bill, longer and more bristly than those of the Downy Woodpecker.

As one might expect, downies, being overall more common than hairies, outnumber hairies in my yard by at least five to one—maybe more. I picked "five" because I regularly see five downies simultaneously, but seldom do I see more than one hairy—usually only on that rare occasion when mom brings junior to midsummer feeders.

Maybe their small size dictates nonaggression, but Downy Woodpeckers seem genuinely peaceful. Indeed, a family spat may decide who gets first dibs at the suet feeder, but they rarely pick a fight with other

ID CHECK
Use the chart below to make a positive idenification.

Identifying Downy and Hairy Woodpeckers

Downy	Hairy
Short bill	Long bill, equal to distance from base of bill to back of head
Outer tail feathers show black spots on sides	Outer tail feathers all white
Call is a sharp *pic*, whinny call descends in pitch at end	Call is a sharp *peeck*, higher pitched than a Downy's, whinny call does not descend
Feeds on small branches, weed stalks, cattails, moving acrobatically	Feeds on tree trunks, never on stalks, moving more heavily
In winter, flocks with chickadees, nuthatches	Generally forages alone

birds. Of course, starlings, always in a snit with other birds, will chase off downies and hairies from feeder stations. Somehow, though, to my mind at least, Downy Woodpeckers cast the image of gentle, quick-witted guardians of the flocks—perhaps not because they try to but because other birds take their cues from the loveable little guys. While downies rarely call out an alarm unless their mates can hear it, other birds take heed of the alarm as well. What's more, in winter, Downy Woodpeckers typically become members of mixed foraging flocks, ducking through woodlands along with chickadees, titmice, and nuthatches. Together, they have more eyes for protection and for finding hidden morsels in the dead—and deadly—time of winter.

Being the larger of the two woodpeckers, Hairy Woodpeckers prefer to feed on stockier, heavier tree parts than do downies. While acrobatic downies may dangle from branch tips, feeding on leaves and buds, and forage along slender twigs, weeds, and harvested corn stalks, hairies tend to feed on tree trunks or the largest limbs, or they drop down to rotting logs. In part because hairies tend to prefer more mature forest habitat than most yards offer, a good number of yards will be absent of Hairy Woodpeckers even though Downy Woodpeckers may be regular diners. If downies come to your yard, watch who eats where. Males and females don't feed on the same vegetation. Females scour the larger parts of branches while males forage among the more productive twigs.

FOOD FARE

Both species of woodpeckers will come to feeders for suet, peanuts, peanut butter, and sunflower seeds. Downy Woodpeckers will occasionally drink from hummingbird feeders. Both birds are primarily insect eaters, including larva, gleaning primarily from tree bark. In the garden, they consume pest insects: corn earworm, tent caterpillars, bark beetles, and apple borers. They also eat berries, such as dogwood and holly, as well as acorns and grain.

BIRD TALK: WHO'S CALLING?

Both Downy and Hairy Woodpeckers have a *whinny* call, down-slurred, beginning slow and ending faster. The downy's call is softer and lower pitched than the hairy's.

NEST NOTES

Downy Woodpecker

Nest Site: adults choose site together; tree cavity, especially broken stub, in fungus-softened wood, making excavation easier

Nest Construction: both adults excavate; entrance 1–1.5 in. wide and high, cavity 6–12 in. deep, wider at bottom, lined only with wood chips

Eggs: 3–8 eggs, 1 brood, incubated 12 days; males incubate at night; both adults incubate during day

Fledge: 18–21 days after hatch

Hairy Woodpecker

Nest Site: probably chosen by female; cavity in dead stub of living tree, especially one with heart rot, or in a dead tree.

Nest Construction: female may begin excavating alone; entrance 1.5 in. wide and 2 in. high, cavity 8–12 in. deep, wider at bottom, only wood chips for nesting

Eggs: 3–6 eggs, 1 brood, incubated by both parents, 11–12 days

Fledge: 28–30 days after hatch

Just-out-of-the-nest male woodpeckers—both hairy and downy—wear an odd little field mark that leaves me puzzled. A male Hairy or Downy Woodpecker sports a bright red patch on the back of his head, allowing us to readily separate males from females. Young males, though, wear little red caps, red on the tops of their heads. Then, when they molt from their juvenal plumage into adult plumage, the red spot emerges at the back of the head. Amazing, isn't it, that the red patch can "move" from the top to the back of the head!

SPOTTING THE SPECTACULAR   **Fending for the Flock**

You've watched. You've seen a Downy Woodpecker freeze along a branch or tree trunk, remaining motionless, sometimes for as long as twenty minutes—at least according to my clock. The behavior says "hawk" to one and all. But while the downy freezes for its own protection, to become invisible—or so it hopes—to the hawk's sharp eyes, news of its behavior spreads through the avian neighborhood at the speed of light. Within a split second, all other birds also melt into the landscape, also freeze, or at least tuck into dense foliage, well hidden. Downies serve the avian neighborhood well, rather like homeland security with feathers.

Given that Downy and Hairy Woodpeckers look mostly alike except for size, hairies being the larger, if they're clinging not side by side on the same tree, how can a person judge relative size—and, therefore, decide who's who? Skip size, and look at the bill. Their bills are of different proportions. The Downy Woodpecker's bill is about a third the length of its head. The Hairy Woodpecker's bill, designed for more serious hammering, is almost the same length as its head. Then, check page 54 for further comparisons.

SPECIES PROFILE

RED-HEADED WOODPECKER and RED-BELLIED WOODPECKER

VITAL STATS
Red-headed Woodpecker
Length: 8.5–9.5 in.
Wingspan: 17 in.
Weight: 2.5 oz.

Red-headed Woodpecker,
sexes indistinguishable

VITAL STATS
Red-bellied Woodpecker
Length: 9.4–10.5 in.
Wingspan: 13–16.5 in.
Weight: 2.4 oz.

Left: *Red-bellied Woodpecker, male;* right: *Red-bellied Woodpecker, female*

What handsome birds, these two woodpeckers! Red-headed Woodpecker dresses in formal attire—tuxedo black and starched white shirt—with a festive all-red head, front to back, neck to crown. The most omnivorous of our eastern woodpeckers, it nevertheless has experienced serious decline due to loss of nesting habitat.

Sometimes mistaken for red-heads, Red-bellied Woodpeckers do, indeed, wear a red crown. So, surely it's misnamed, right? Wrong. A red crown does not make a red head. Or so John James Audubon decided when, bird in hand, he named it Red-bellied Woodpecker. Although you may not have seen it, this woodpecker does have—yes—a red belly. But don't feel the need for a vision check if you've missed it, for it's really more a rumor than serious coloration. Call it a blush. Or a reddish wash. Either way, Red-bellied Woodpeckers wear red bellies only during breeding season, most clearly seen when they're hanging from a feeder or suet block that is way too small for them. And the red is minimal even then.

NAME THAT BIRD

Melanerpes carolinus (Red-bellied Woodpecker): *Melanerpes* translates roughly as "black on the side of the face" while *carolinus* describes the bird's natural range. The common name "red-bellied" seems all wrong—unless the bird is observed during breeding season when it has a distinct red wash across its belly.

Melanerpes erythrocephalus (Red-headed Woodpecker): *Erythrocephalus* comes from the Greek that means "red headed," so the common name describes the bird's appearance.

BIRD TALK: WHO'S CALLING?
Red-bellied Woodpeckers of
both sexes gives a loud rolling
churrrrrrrr and a hoarse *cha-
cha-cha-cha* as well as four
other less-common calls and
songs. Red-headed Wood-
peckers are fairly noisy, giving
a loud *queer, queer, queer.*

Regular visitors to our yard, Red-bellied Woodpeckers brighten my day. In addition to suet and peanut butter, red-bellies enjoy a regular supply of sunflower seeds, billing up one seed at a time, checking its heft, perhaps discarding it for a meatier one, flying no farther than necessary, and hammering the single serving open. For whatever reason, red-heads, on the other hand, rarely visit my yard, even though open woodlands and forest edge adjoin our property. While red-heads enjoy suet, they'd really rather have shelled, whole-kernel corn, but they will pluck it from the cob if it isn't already shelled.

Both woodpeckers suffer from habitat loss, especially the loss of nest cavities. A double whammy faces these beautiful birds. First, homeowners and landowners tend to take down dead or dying trees, eliminating potential sites for birds to hammer out suitable nests. Second, because nest cavities rank as hot commodities, competition soars. The most aggressive bird with the longest bill wins the choicest sites. Think European Starling. In a three-way battle over property rights, red-belly wins over red-head, and starling wins over all.

FOOD FARE

Red-bellied Woodpeckers eat mainly insects, especially gleaned from tree bark, but also nuts, acorns, and pine nuts. In the garden, they glean seed from annuals and perennials and forage for berries, like dogwood and holly, and fruit, like apples, cherries, peaches, and pears. At feeders, they enjoy sunflower seeds, peanut butter, and suet.

Red-headed Woodpeckers are the most omnivorous of woodpeckers and exhibit fly-catching behavior about 40 percent of the time. Commonly, they feed on the ground. Summer diet is about one-third insects and two-thirds grain and fruit; in winter, primarily hard mast like acorns and other nuts. At feeders, they take grain, especially shelled corn, and sunflower seed, suet, raisins, and nuts. In the garden, they glean insects from the ground and sometimes from tree bark and enjoy acorns and beechnuts.

When red-bellies or red-heads bring their babies out to show, my sympathies get tangled. I know they'll grow up beautiful—eventually—but the plain gray, scruffy-looking red-belly youngsters surely prove the adage "only a mother could love." By late fall, though, red-belly youngsters look thin, maybe a bit malnourished, but colorful. Red crowns, black and white zebra backs. Crisp. Polished. Red-heads, though, need almost until spring to take on their fully red heads. Until then, let's just say they lack luster.

A Red-bellied Woodpecker shows its namesake reddish belly only during breeding season.

NEST NOTES

Red-bellied Woodpecker

Nest Site: chosen by male who attracts female to the site; cavity in dead deciduous or pine tree or dead limb of live tree, sometimes using the same tree in consecutive years; newly excavated cavity usually lower than previous year's hole

Nest Construction: both sexes excavate a cavity nest about 3.5 in. by 5 in. and about 8 in. to 12 in. deep

Eggs: 2–6 eggs, 1–3 broods, incubated 12 days by both sexes

Fledge: 24–27 days after hatch

Red-headed Woodpecker

Nest Site: chosen by male who attracts female for her approval; cavity in dead tree, preferably one in which most bark is missing, typically near top of stub

Nest Construction: both construct nest but male does most of the work, excavating a cavity about 15 in. deep, the nest bowl about 3–4 in. by 5.5 in. with nest-entrance diameter of about 2 in.

Eggs: 4–7 eggs, 1–2 broods, incubated 12–14 days by both sexes, but male incubates at night and likely incubates more hours than does female

Fledge: 27–31 days after hatch

SPOTTING THE SPECTACULAR   Socially Challenged?

Red-bellied Woodpeckers, except during breeding season, take on the behavior of loners, foraging alone, hammering out a wintering cavity alone, roosting alone. Red-heads, too, tend toward antisocial behavior; but pairs sometimes winter together. The two species will tolerate one another in the same territory, assuming food supplies permit. Interestingly, red-bellies remain shy, fleeing people unless they've become familiarized with humans through feeding-station experiences. Red-heads, on the other hand, accept people rather readily, sometimes allowing close approach.

ID CHECK

Red-bellied Woodpeckers and Red-headed Woodpeckers are about the same size, larger than a Downy Woodpecker but smaller than a Northern Flicker. Distinguishing between the two requires only a quick look at their heads:

- Red-headed Woodpecker wears an all-red head, front and back, neck to crown.
- Red-bellied Woodpecker wears a red crown but not a red head—no red face or throat.
- Red crowns on female red-bellies stop well short of the bill while on males the crown is fully red to the base of the bill.

SPECIES PROFILE

PILEATED WOODPECKER

VITAL STATS
Length: 16.5–19.5 in.
Wingspan: 27–30 in.
Weight: 10–12.3 oz.

Left: *Pileated Woodpecker, male;*
right: *Pileated Woodpecker, female*

Think Woody Woodpecker. A crow-sized guy. The mighty bird that can render a mighty tree stump into a mighty pile of sawdust. Pileated Woodpecker, our largest, is named for its pileus, or large red crest. These robust handsome birds of the forest declined with the clearing of eastern timberland, then rebounded in the twentieth century, and now increase slowly.

Males and females look much alike except for the moustache. His is red, hers is black. A closer look shows that his forehead is red; hers is grayish-brown. Both have fiery red crests. Even youngsters just out of the nest wear red crests, rather like a Mohawk haircut, although junior's Mohawk stands a bit shorter than mom's or dad's. All in all, they're fine-looking creatures.

NAME THAT BIRD

Dryocopus pileatus (Pileated Woodpecker): *Dryocopus* means "woodpecker," originally a combination of two words that meant "oak tree" and "beating." *Pileus* originally referred to a bright red felt cap, a symbol of servitude among ancient Roman slaves. The bird's common name comes from the same word.

Growing up, I don't recall ever seeing or hearing—or even hearing about—Pileated Woodpeckers, even though we lived amid sixty acres of forest. In fact, marginal notes penciled in my ancient field guide record my first sighting in 1979. Listed then as "uncommon and local, a wary bird of extensive deciduous or mixed forests," pileateds have, in the thirty-five years since, outgrown their shyness and increased their numbers. Many folks tell me pileateds visit their backyard suet feeders, although, in general, those folks live in, or their property adjoins, woodlands.

Even in flight, pileateds put on a majestic show. White underwings flash during their dignified rowing flight, sometimes accompanied by their trademark *cuck cuck cuck cuck* calls. No matter what I'm doing, I'm compelled to stop and watch, following them until they slip out of sight.

Referred to as a "keystone" species, Pileated Woodpeckers help make the world go around—or at least the forest. Their large excavations, once the pileateds abandon them, serve as homes for numerous other species, including owls, Wood Ducks, and not a few furry creatures. Their preferred diet helps control pest infestations of forest beetles, and their chiseling through rotten trees, including fallen logs, speeds decomposition and thus nutrient recycling.

BIRD TALK: WHO'S CALLING?

Pileated Woodpeckers call to their mates with a *cuck cuck cuck cuck* that is both loud and deliberate. Males and females call *yucka, yucka, yucka,* similar to a flicker's call but slower, deeper, and louder and, unlike the flicker's, it changes in cadence and pitch.

FOOD FARE

Eats primarily insects, especially carpenter ants and wood-boring beetle larva but also fruit and nuts. Forages on logs, dead trees, stumps, and sometimes live trees. Rarely visits feeders unless located in or adjoining forested areas and will then take suet, especially if rendered and mixed with pecan or walnut pieces.

Not a migratory creature, Pileated Woodpeckers tend to be more numerous year-round in the Southeast than here in Indiana where I live. They like big old-growth forest for a simple reason: bigger trees, bigger dead snags, and bigger deadfall mean places to find bigger supplies of food. Once again, habitat is everything for birds. Change the habitat, as early settlers did by decimating eastern forests, and we change the birds in that habitat. Now that many small farms in the East have been abandoned, trees regenerate, and birds return. Watch your neighborhood for returning pileateds.

NEST NOTES

Nest Site: likely selected by male; cavity usually excavated in dead tree

Nest Construction: excavations by both sexes although male does more work; average 19 in. deep; diameter of cavity bowl about 6 in.; entrance hole diameter about 4 in. by 5 in.

Eggs: 1–6 eggs, commonly 4, 1 brood, incubated 18 days by both sexes; male always incubates at night; both during day

Fledge: 26–28 days after hatch

SPOTTING THE SPECTACULAR   **Chiseler on the Go**

Skip the hammer. Stow the drill. It's chisel time. We think of woodpeckers, "hammer heads" that they are, as drilling holes in tree trunks, hammering out cavities. Indeed, most woodpeckers do drill holes. But not Pileated Woodpeckers. They chisel out chunks. Power chisel. Big chunks. Look on the ground for a broad area showered with debris, shards of wood sometimes six or more inches long. Then look up. Look for an oval hole, a deep hole, sometimes so deep light shines through from the tree's opposite side. And sometimes the tree topples from the chiseled excavation. While oval holes distinguish pileated's feeding holes, nest cavities tend toward round. Big around.

ID CHECK

Our largest woodpecker (assuming the demise of Ivory-billed Woodpeckers), Pileated Woodpeckers are hard to misidentify. Look for a bird that has these three traits:

- Stands about a foot and a half long
- Wears a fiery red crest
- Shows white underwings in flight

SPECIES PROFILE

NORTHERN FLICKER

VITAL STATS
Length: 11–12 in.
Wingspan: 17–21 in.
Weight: 4.6–5.6 oz.

Left: *Northern Flicker, male;* right: *Northern Flicker, female*

They don't act like woodpeckers. They rarely hitch up tree trunks, although they'll perch upright on tree limbs. And they're ground feeders. Typically foraging among leaf litter, they're seen hammering not a tree limb but in the ground. And for good reason: They love ants. Indeed, it's an odd woodpecker, the plump, loveable Northern Flicker.

NAME THAT BIRD

Colaptes auratus (Northern Flicker): From the Latin, *Colaptes* means "to chisel like a bird." *Auratus* means "overlaid with gold"—a lovely description originally intended to describe only the yellow-shafted flicker. Its common name refers to its range and its fluttering, perhaps specifically its flash of white on the rump when it flies.

Last summer, during the first week of June, Northern Flickers abruptly ceased routine visits to our suet-smeared log feeder. Our yard, minus their *wick-a-wick-a-wick-a* chatter, remained quiet all summer. Twice, I thought I heard them off in the distance. But I never saw them. Then, in the fall, they returned, youngsters in tow.

FOOD FARE

Flickers eat primarily ants that they glean from the ground. In winter, they add fruits, seeds, and berries to their diet, including dogwood and holly berries. They do not commonly visit feeders, but in my own yard, they occasionally visit suet feeders, especially those placed 10 to 15 feet high, strung on a pulley for easy filling.

Northern flickers exude a soft and gentle, plump and loveable aura. Overall creamy-brown, flickers wear a cape of black-scalloped plumage accessorized in style. A broad black bib edges a buff-colored breast, heavily black spotted. Males and females both wear a back-of-the-head red chevron. Only a black moustache separates males from females: He has one, and she doesn't. In flight, they flash a surprise—yellow shafts on wing and tail feathers, as well as that bright white rump spot.

BIRD TALK: WHO'S CALLING?

Year-round call of an ascending *quew, quew, quew* is replaced during breeding season with *wicka-wicka-wicka* from adult pairs.

If you wander west, beyond the Rocky Mountains rain shadow—or if the mostly western birds wander east—you might question your vision. Instead of a flash of yellow, western birds flash red—signature of the Northern Flicker red-shafted subspecies. The red-shafted birds lack the pretty red chevron on the backs of their heads, but males wear a red moustache, not black.

Northern Flickers above 37 degrees latitude migrate, but southern birds stay put year round. So where were these gentle creatures all last summer? Nesting. Flickers need dead or dying trees or whopper-sized limbs for excavating 15-inch-deep cavities. Apparently our dead trees were already taken by a wide range of cavity-loving competitors: Downy, Hairy, Red-bellied, and Pileated Woodpeckers, bluebirds, Carolina Chickadees, titmice, House and Carolina Wrens, and Tree Swallows—plus imported European Starlings, the toughest, most numerous, and most aggressive competitors. So fighting for cavity sites rates as sometimes deadly work, depending on who's vying for housing rights.

NEST NOTES

Nest Site: both sexes thought to choose site; excavate holes in dead trees or dead limbs, especially trees diseased by heart rot

Nest Construction: both sexes excavate; male assumes major role; cavity excavated 13–16 in. deep, diameter of about 8 in. at bottom, with 3 in. diameter entrance hole; will reuse own or others' cavities

Eggs: 5–8 eggs, 1 brood, incubated 11–13 days by both sexes; male incubates at night

Fledge: 24–27 days after hatch

Sadly, over the last forty years, flickers have lost two-thirds of their population. Most authorities attribute losses to seven causes: suburban sprawl that reduces numbers of trees; prevalence of lawn and agricultural pesticides that kills ants and beetle larvae; removal of dead snags that eliminates nesting cavities; expansion of European Starlings that increases cavity competition; expansion of large-scale agriculture that further reduces forest edge; fire suppression that reduces numbers of dead and dying trees; and, somewhat ironically, regrowth of eastern deciduous forest that reduces the woodland openings flickers like.

The lessons for us as backyard bird lovers are obvious: First, never apply pesticides to lawns; such applications kill flickers' primary foods, ants and beetle larvae. Second, whenever safely possible, leave dead trees standing; they serve as nest sites for dozens of native birds, including flickers as well as other woodpeckers.

SPOTTING THE SPECTACULAR   **Tools to Suit the Job**

Flickers must surely boast the original ergonomic design. As prodders for ants and beetle larvae, they're equipped with slightly curved bills, the better to dig with. They're also equipped with long, barbed, sticky tongues, to better pluck out tasty morsels. When ants disappear for the winter, however, flickers switch to berries, especially flowering dogwood, wild black cherry, elderberry, and Virginia creeper.

When our 80-foot-tall pin oak died, we had it cut to 35 feet so if it uproots or falls, it won't hit the house. Now it's a busy buffet. Eventually, as the wood softens, we hope it will also serve as housing for cavity nesters. Fortunately, however, flickers will accept man-made nest boxes if mounted appropriately in open woodlands or along forest edges. (See nest box dimensions on page 49.)

Flickers can live up to nine years, so I'm already anticipating their loud drumming next spring. Meanwhile, maybe the old folks will teach the kids to enjoy our log feeder.

ID CHECK

Nothing else in the East resembles Northern Flicker, a chunky bird equipped with a serious bill. Make positive identification by noting the following markings:

- Overall creamy brown
- Pronounced black bib
- Red chevron on back of head
- Male's black moustache; female's plain face
- In flight, a flash of yellow on underwings and tail, flash of white on rump

March

Birds are indicators of the environment.
If they are in trouble,
we know we'll soon be in trouble.

ROGER TORY PETERSON

More birds die in March than in any other month. Yes, March heralds the vernal equinox, the month that finds Snow Geese receding to Arctic breeding grounds, Red-winged Blackbirds singing territorial mandates, Carolina Wrens stuffing last fall's leaves into secret nest sites, Canada Geese pairing and defending chosen territories, and spring peepers emerging in anyplace wet.

But March, fickle through and through, jerks us from winter to spring and back again, with freezing temps and snow boots one day and summertime shirt-sleeved weather the next, frosts and late freezes always in the wings, threatening the peach crop, nipping flower buds, and crusting the birdbath.

But why, with winter's worst behind us and the rush of spring upon us—why would birds die now? They've survived winter's trials and tribulations, these birds weighing mere ounces, covered with only a fluff of feathers, requiring increased fat calories to keep warm. Short winter days gave fewer hours to meet their greater need. Now, though, days grow longer. Shouldn't birds be thriving, with March offering a welcome respite?

HABITAT—YOURS AND THEIRS
Think Like a Bird for Birdy Habitat

Depending on where you live, this month, early or late, brings more birds looking for food, water, shelter, and now primarily, places to raise young. Indeed, March begins the mighty spring migration. Millions of birds will pour through the United States, some hanging out with us, others winging their way to Canada's boreal forest. Migrants have only one reason to come north: to reproduce.

So, what does a bird see when it flies over your yard? What does your habitat offer prospective nesters? Well-protected nest sites? Ample nesting materials like grasses, rootlets,

A Dark-eyed Junco plucks seed from weed stalks that now, in March, stand mostly depleted.

last autumn's leaves, soft mosses, and small twigs? A good source of bugs for babies? Water for drinking and bathing? Safe shelter against late spring and summer storms? Dense vegetation high to low, in large clusters, with little lawn and lots of tangle? Or mostly manicured lawn, evenly spaced feature trees, with all bugs under attack via pesticide application? If you were a bird mother- or father-to-be, would you choose your yard? Ah, yes, there's more to attracting birds to your yard than feeders and feed.

Warmer, sunnier days make us humans somehow feel the worst is over, that we can switch wardrobes, turtlenecks for T-shirts, winter woolens for cotton twills, long pants for shorts. For birds, though, the worst is still ahead. Here's why.

Winter Marches On

Many of our overwintering birds—both year-round residents and winter visitors—chow down mostly on seeds and berries. So let's start with seeds. Look around now at your habitat, and think about it from a bird's point of view. Grasses, forbs, and brushy plants that formed seed heads last fall have probably long since lost their seed to wind dispersal, pelting rains, weighty snows, and foraging birds like sparrows, cardinals, goldfinches, chickadees, and titmice. What few seed-bearing stalks remain now lie broken, likely "planted" by rain and snow, mudded in, no longer viable food for birds.

Tree seeds last a bit longer. If tulip poplar and sweet gum trees produced sizeable seed crops last fall, seed eaters sort through what remains. Still, in March, seed supplies have all but disappeared, and our tiniest birds seeking the tiniest seeds often come up short.

New seed, however, is on the way, right? Well, soon. But we must think in terms of months, not days or weeks, before new seeds appear. Plants have to green, grow, bloom, and produce seed heads. Then seed must mature before most birds find anything edible or nourishing. Among native grasses, maturity peaks more quickly than among some other plants. Still, edible seed production is a month or more away. As soon as spring buds form, however, some birds, such as Cedar Waxwings, Northern Mockingbirds, and Tufted Titmice, will gorge on petals and flowers, desperate for anything nutritious in the absence of seed.

FEEDER FOCUS   **Fruit Fixins**

Given some birds' love of fruit, consider offering some. Anything overripe—grapefruit, orange, or apple halves, pineapple, banana chunks—better feeds birds than fills garbage cans. Cut fruits open, place the pieces on a pie pan or jam them on a spike. For a perfect fruit server, drive a nail into something wooden—a fence post, fallen log, or tree branch—and cut off the nail head to make a spike. Or use "cups" of orange and grapefruit rinds and fill them with overripe citrus, apple, or peach chunks, halved grapes or cherries, and berries. If you don't mind the expense, offer dried figs, dates, prunes, raisins, currents, cranberries—chopped and rehydrated in hot water. Depending on where you live, you may attract woodpeckers, robins, bluebirds, thrushes, wrens, cardinals, grosbeaks, buntings, orioles, and waxwings.

Take the fruit fixins a step further and make your own fruit-suet blend. Melt pure lard (no substitutes here, please) and add chopped fruit (rehydrated if dried). Pour the mixture into tuna or cat food cans until it cools. Freeze unused portions.

By March, many birds, including Northern Mockingbirds, face a dearth of bugs and berries and turn to early blossoms for sustenance.

HOW DOES YOUR GARDEN GROW?

First Buds, First Blooms, First Bugs

Depending on your location, March gardens probably offer slim pickings for birds—except, of course, the lush buffet of insect eggs and larva in the leaf mulch. But what else? Maybe some crocuses, a few daffodils, or dandelions—nothing for a bird. Oh, wait. Dandelions? If they're blooming, chances are bugs are out, too, sipping on dandelion nectar. Early buds and blooms attract early bugs, so the nectar and protein together make tasty treats for desperate birds. So, never underestimate dandelions, not just for their bugs and nectar but especially for their seed-head fluff, a favored material for hummingbird nests.

What about berry-loving birds? Year-round residents in northerly climes that prefer summertime bugs switch in winter, by necessity, to an alternate diet, mostly berries. Like seeds, however, berries have mostly disappeared by March, gobbled up by hungry robins, waxwings, mockingbirds, bluebirds, and starlings. Other berries, probably those that birds find distasteful, simply rotted and dropped. The few berries remaining contain minimal fat calories, so birds must eat multiple times the usual amount in order to gain equal fat—assuming they can find those multiple amounts.

HABITAT—YOURS AND THEIRS

Sumac: Last of the Berries

By March, when berries have mostly disappeared, some birds turn to wild staghorn sumac (*Rhus typhina*), those teardrop-shaped clusters of fuzzy red berries squatting atop short rangy shrubs, usually growing along railroad rights-of-way, unmowed roadsides, or abandoned fields. According to one study, sumac makes up 85 to 95 percent of bluebirds' late-winter diet. Compared with other fruits, however, sumac berries have a low caloric content. Still, the berries may be the only means by which some birds, including robins and mockingbirds, avoid starvation. Consider cultivating some in a back corner. You may prefer hybrids: fragrant sumac (*R. aromatica*), smooth sumac (*R. glabra*), or my personal favorite, cutleaf sumac (*R. typhina*).

Very Berry

Backyard habitat improvements, however, can reduce March famine, maybe even turn it into a feast.

Curiously, about 70 percent of red berries that birds love ripen just in time for fall migration, helping them fatten up for the trip. While those berries bring a bonanza to hungry birds in autumn, the berry-ripening schedule doesn't do much to supplement the late-winter dearth in March. By providing a series of ripening berries over critical months, we can ease birds through dire times.

BIOLOGY BITS   **Fruit Eaters**

Birds called "seed predators," like cardinals and native sparrows, crush both fruit and seed and gulp it down. Chomped up seeds, of course, won't germinate. On the other hand, "seed dispersers" eat the whole fruit and then eliminate the smaller seeds or spit up the larger ones. So birds that act as seed dispersers aid in spreading and regenerating their own favorite plants—a sort of self-gardening for the future.

For instance, winterberry (*Ilex verticillata*), considered the hardiest and showiest of the hollies, is native to a large part of the eastern United States and may be a prized plant in your yard. Great berries, good nest materials, and terrific winter cover all mesh together for an urban-yard upgrade. Planted properly, depending on your space, winterberry or other shrubby berry producers can also provide a year-round corridor for birds, protecting them as they forage over widespread habitat, moving from roost sites to feeders to nest sites.

BOTANY FOR BIRDS
Plants for Berries

Depending on your region, a variety of berry-producing plants will provide a bird buffet to an otherwise lackluster property. See pages 72–73 for a list.

In short, by March, without adequate berries, the natural avian food supply falls seriously short. Foraging for food takes longer and produces fewer results. By scratching under leaf litter for overwintering bugs, larvae, eggs, or even the occasional still-edible seed, towhees, sparrows, and cardinals eke out a living. By searching tree-bark crevices for beetles and other insects, woodpeckers and nuthatches manage to survive. Many birds, however, perhaps weakened after a severe winter, suffer, sometimes seriously.

By March, sumac berries have shriveled and lost some nutritional value but may be the only remaining food source for berry-loving birds like robins and bluebirds.

A Partial List of Berry-Producing Trees, Shrubs and Vines
(Check hardiness zone for your area.)

Common Name	Scientific Name	Fruiting Season	Comments
Chokecherry (shrub)	*Prunus virginiana*	late spring/summer	weedy, rose family, works as hedge
Serviceberry (tree)	*Amelauchier* spp.	late spring/summer	very early bloomer
Blueberries (bush)	*Vaccinium* spp.	late spring/summer	attracts 35 birds
Black cherry (tree)	*Prunus serotina*	summer	attracts 50 birds
Red mulberry (tree)	*Morus rubra*	summer	attracts 40 birds
Alternative-leaf dogwood (shrub)	*Cornus alternifolia*	late summer/fall	attracts 35 birds
Grape vines	*Vitis* spp.	late summer/fall	attracts 100 birds; provides nest material
Sassafras (shrub)	*Sassafras albidum*	late summer/fall	good nest cavities
Red-osier dogwood (shrub)	*Cornus stolonifera*	late summer/fall	forms thickets
Silky dogwood (shrub)	*Cornus amomum*	late summer/fall	moist soil; part shade; good in masses
Elderberry (bush)	*Sambucus canadensis*	late summer/fall	voluntary
Pokeberry (herb)	*Phytolocca americana*	fall	dies back in winter
Inkberry (bush)	*Ilex glabra*	fall	male, female req.; forms thickets
Rusty blackhaw (bush)	*Viburnum rufidulum*	fall/winter	upland; fence- and hedgerows
N. bayberry (shrub)	*Myrica pensylvanica*	fall/winter	sandy soil
American beautyberry	*Callicarpa americana*	fall/winter	partial shade; best with two or more
Flowering dogwood (tree)	*Cornus florida*	fall/winter	attracts 40 birds
Gray dogwood (shrub)	*Cornus racemosa*	fall/winter	forms thickets; good border
Com. hackberry (tree)	*Celtis occidentalis*	fall/winter	Tolerates poor conditions
American holly (tree)	*Ilex opaca*	fall/winter	male, female req.
Deciduous holly (shrub)	*Ilex decidua*	fall/winter	male, female req.
Cotoneaster (bush)	*Cotoneaster* spp.	fall/winter	slow growing
Nannyberry (shrub)	*Viburnum lentago*	fall/winter	shade tolerant; fast growing; forms thickets; naturalize
Spicebush (shrub)	*Lindera benzoin*	fall/winter	widespread native
Pasture rose (bush)	*Rosa carolina*	fall/winter	also provides cover

Common Name	Scientific Name	Fruiting Season	Comments
Wild rose (bush)	*Rosa virginiana*	fall/winter	also provides cover
Virginia creeper (vine)	*Parthenocissus quinquefolia*	fall/winter	often confused with poison oak
Poison ivy (vine)	*Rhus radicans*	fall/winter	poisonous to humans
Mistletoe (parasitic)	*Phoradendron serotinum*	fall/winter	needs host tree
Black chokeberry (shrub)	*Aronia melanocarpa*	winter	moist soil
American bittersweet (vine)	*Celastrus scandens*	winter	invasive
Snowberry (bush)	*Symphoricarpos albus*	winter	tolerates many soils; sun to shade; spreads
Coralberry (bush)	*Symphoricarpos orbiculatu*	winter	spreading, arching shrub
American cranberry (bush)	*Viburnum trilobum*	winter	shade tolerant; ornamental
Smooth sumac (shrub)	*Rhus glabra*	winter	weedy; holds berries
Staghorn sumac (shrub)	*Rhus typhina*	winter	high tolerance for heat, drought
Common winterberry (shrub)	*Ilex verticillata*	winter	male, female req.; acidic moist soil
Crabapple (tree)	*Malus* spp.	winter	many biennial bearers
Eastern red cedar (tree)	*Juniperus virginiana*	winter	year-round cover; windbreak

Late spring/summer berries are high in carbohydrates (sugars) and coincide with the end of nesting season when fledglings are seeking food on their own for the first time.

Late summer/fall berries contain a large amount of fat/oil and, as a result, rot quickly. Thus, they must be consumed quickly as they ripen.

Winter berries have small amounts of lipids (a source of energy), but as a result, they don't spoil so readily. Some last even into very early spring and benefit from the freeze-thaw cycle that softens and sweetens them. Early migrants also seek these foods.

Flowering dogwood berries

NOTABLE BEHAVIOR   **Table Manners**

While many bird species eat fruit—both our resident birds and seasonal migrants—their table manners vary. Robins, mockingbirds, cardinals, and Rose-breasted Grosbeaks seat themselves politely, pluck one berry at a time, but gulp it down whole. By contrast, others, like House Finch and Downy Woodpecker, seat themselves and then nibble daintily. Some birds, perhaps feeding nestlings, elbow their way to the table, grab a berry, and flee. Some notables flutter around the table, too rude to be seated, snatching berries on the fly, particularly birds like Great Crested Flycatchers, which snatch bugs the same way. Finally, like household pets, some patiently patrol under the table, scouting for dropped berries, probably those that the pluckers and snatchers lost. Look for grackles, starlings, Blue Jays, and robins with these under-the-table manners.

But feeders can help. During most seasons, backyard feeders offer only a fast-food stop for birds that enjoy a wide feeding range. Now, however, feeders may actually make a difference. They may mean survival to some wild birds.

So if, during this transitional month, you've slacked off keeping your feeders filled, thinking warm days mean less-needy birds, please rethink. Or if you usually put your feeders away for the summer, please wait. When spring flowers have seeded and bug populations have grown, then birds can once again forage for an abundance of wild food. Meanwhile, they might like your help.

Memorable Moments: One for the Record Books

Where I live, mid-March marks a series of "firsts." The first Wood Ducks come whistling in, splashing down on the neighbor's farm pond, checking our nest boxes, discussing pros and cons, making choices. The first bluebird pair stakes out territory, popping in and out of a chosen nest box, checking the view, I suppose, then picking and defending the prime site. The first gold brightens American Goldfinches, slowly switching from winter drab to summer sunny. The first robin pair bustles through the yard, measuring potential construction sites. The first eager-to-nest pair of Carolina Wrens typically stuff our paper box full of leaves and grasses, only to discover that every morning's paper delivery crushes their efforts. Then the first Eastern Phoebe sings, rasping out his name from woods' edge, sounding just plain cross about the pronouncement. It's almost always the first migrant's song I hear in my springtime yard. The first American Woodcocks, also early migrants, perform their aerial mating displays in shrubby grasslands, calling their nasal *peent*. The first shorebirds zip through, always in a rush to rip northward to gain prime breeding spots. The first Wilson's Snipes poke long bills in muddy, puddle-filled fields. The first Tree Swallows swoop across the hayfields, and the first Purple Martins return to our neighbor's nesting-gourd condos.

Indeed, in this month of firsts, March brings our earliest wave of migrants. They stream northward following leaf buds. Leaf bud opening means bugs, and bugs mean food. But no bird outflies its food supply. So when snow and cold spells slow greening buds, that, in turn, slows birds' rush, thwarting their instinctive urge to be first on the breeding grounds.

Several years ago, however, March blew in a surprise "first," this time a dandy first for the yard. On March 23, outside my kitchen window, a Blue Grosbeak plucked sunflower seeds from my feeder. Whoa! Blue Grosbeaks rarely visit feeders, and at least where I live, they're mighty rare yard birds. So, excited that I'd added a new bird to my yard list, I posted my delight on our state's listserv.

Within minutes, a reply from our state's keeper of bird records brought more "first" news. Not only did I have my first yard Blue Grosbeak, a stunningly handsome male, but I also had a record early bird for the state. Oh my! He was a state record!

March brings Wilson's Snipe, among the first shorebirds to return, poking about in muddy fields.

My yard's first Blue Grosbeak briefly held the state record for earliest return. The following years brought even earlier arrivals in neighboring communities, likely an indication of climate change and birds' changing migratory patterns.

But, ah, the fleeting fifteen minutes of fame. The record was short lived. The next spring, another Indiana resident spotted a Blue Grosbeak several days earlier. And the following year, someone spotted the handsome little guy a week earlier. As climate changes, birds change their behavior, too, flying north with earlier leaf bud opening. For one whole year, though, my yard held the record early Blue Grosbeak. I'm sure no one else remembers, but I do. And the memory makes me smile.

NOTABLE BEHAVIOR   ## Birds Layer by Layer

Everyone lives somewhere—even birds. But we don't all live in the same kinds of places.

Just as some people prefer the seashore or plains while others prefer the forest or mountains, birds, too, have specific preferences—even within the same locale. For instance, some birds, such as tanagers, vireos, orioles, and many warblers, forage in lofty treetops. Other birds—catbirds, thrashers, jays, and cardinals—hang out midlevel. Still others, like towhees and native sparrows, seek the lowest levels of vegetation. Now consider what that says about suitable bird habitat: To welcome a variety of birds, the habitat needs ample vegetation from the ground up, the understory blending into the midstory blending into the upper story.

American Redstarts can be found in mid-level trees and shrubs.

Crane your neck way back to find Blackburnian Warblers in the upper canopy.

Look for Ovenbirds on or near the ground.

Clean-up, Fix-up Time

March means clean-up, fix-up time. Most fixes are simple, but all are important to birds' health and well-being. Here's the to-do list:

First, clean feeders. Moldy bits of uneaten seed and hulls, as well as yucky accumulated bird droppings on feeder trays, trigger disease and sickness in birds. To help keep birds healthy, take feeders down, empty the seed, and scrub all feeder parts with soapy water. To sanitize, wash again with a 9:1 water-bleach solution. Rinse thoroughly, dry, and refill. Then continue the clean-up plan on a monthly basis. Yes, snow is gone and spring is popping, but few insects are stirring; and certainly nothing has bloomed long enough to produce seed. Between now and early summer, birds fact a tough time as they turn their full efforts toward breeding and nesting. So don't neglect your feeders. Keep 'em clean, and keep 'em filled.

Mulching the garden with shredded leaves and "paving" paths with wood chips serves the plants well and avoids environmentally unfriendly use of cypress mulch.

HOW DOES YOUR GARDEN GROW?
Mulching Etiquette

As spring approaches and you're ready to tidy the garden, you'll likely plan to add mulch. Conservation-minded gardeners avoid cypress mulch. Here's why: Thousands of acres of cypress trees are chopped down to be ground to mulch, destroying much of Florida's wetlands and the wildlife—including thousands of birds—that depend on the old-growth trees. If there's no demand, the raping of these hundred-years-old trees will stop. But because so many of the huge trees have already been cut, currently available cypress mulch no longer serves as one of the best mulches. What was touted as rot- and termite-resistant is no more, since younger trees don't have those same attributes.

So consider more environmentally friendly mulch. Use recycled yard waste, hardwood mulch (from milling), pine bark and needles, and fallen leaves, perhaps shredded, from your own yard or neighborhood. Why kill a tree to save a flower?

With feeders clean, next clean the yard. Best estimates at our house are that in the past three months we poured out about four hundred pounds of birdseed. Residue hulls have piled up inches thick. They must go. While no one claims bird feeding is mess free, end-of-winter clean-up can be daunting. But clean up we must, for the accumulated waste harbors mold and spoiled seed, neither of which is good for birds. So rake it up, scoop it up, or vac it up.

But don't use black-oil sunflower seed hulls for garden mulch. They contain a substance harmful to most ornamental plants and tend to poison the soil where they decompose. They will inhibit the growth of annuals, and sometimes kill plants outright, although they aren't toxic enough to kill trees and shrubs. So do be thoughtful about where you dump the waste.

While you're cleaning, be sure to clean birdbaths. A wire brush makes quick cleaning of concrete baths. Avoid soap, chemicals, or pesticides. Then vow to keep the water clean and fresh—change it daily.

Next, clean house—birdhouse, that is. Birds can't. So if chickadees used your nest box last year, as a good landlord, you must clean out that amazing amount of moss and fine grasses so

---

WATER WAYS **Mighty Magnet**

Numerous birds on our yard list have never perched at a feeder, cracked a sunflower kernel, hulled a thistle seed, sneaked a peanut, or picked at suet. They've come for water. Only water.

A surprising number of birds, in fact, never visit feeders. Warblers, tanagers, orioles—truly handsome, colorful migrants—munch on bugs or lap up nectar, so they're checking the undersides of leaves, crevices in bark, and blossoms at peak. And water. Birdbath, yard pond, bubbling rock, or any other water feature, especially moving water, draws these nonfeeder birds.

Of course, all birds need water, our year-round residents, summer and winter visitors, and just-passing-through travelers. They need it to drink; they need it to bathe. When they're molting, as goldfinches do in spring, a bath surely feels sublime. Try to imagine having a body full of old, worn feathers working their way out. Sounds itchy, don't you think? And then try to imagine having a body full of prickly little pin feathers growing in, shedding the outer layer and bursting into full feather. Sounds really itchy. Ah, wouldn't a bath feel good?

Water attracts all birds, even those, like Cedar Waxwings, that never visit feeders.

A well maintained nestbox offers bluebirds a safe place to raise babies.

they can nest again this year. Time is of the essence. Our Carolina Wrens have already built this year's first nest in a favorite gourd.

Now for the fix-up part. Repair—or replace—nest boxes. No one wants a leaky house. If side or roof panels have separated, split, or begun to rot, make repairs or go for a new abode. If you're replacing a nest box, choose one designed not for people but for birds, one that is sturdy, utilitarian, unpainted, weatherproof, adequately ventilated, perch-free, and easily opened for cleaning and monitoring.

FEEDER FOCUS

Location, Location, Location

Different birds like different foods. And for every food, there's a feeder. Even if you buy the best feeder and best feeds, birds may snub your offerings. Ultimately, they also demand the right feeding location.

What's right? A site where they feel safe from predators while feeding, where a clear flight path opens to and from, and where little guys can feed in peace, away from big boisterous birds.

Case in point: In my yard, two identical peanut-butter feeders cater to crowds. One hangs on a T-pole in the backyard, 20 feet from the kitchen window, equidistant between two trees 50 feet apart, standing mostly in the open. The other hangs under a front-window awning, three feet from my office window, protected from elements, hidden from hawks.

Both draw a crowd—but different crowds. Downy Woodpeckers visit both, but Hairy Woodpeckers visit only the one in the open. Carolina Wrens pick occasionally at the backyard feeder but pig out regularly under the awning. Carolina Chickadees check out both sites but visit the front more often. To use a tired cliché, it really is all about location, location, location.

PROBLEM SOLVER

Squaring off with Squirrels

Cute as they may be, squirrels can empty a feeder of expensive birdseed in less than an hour and then destroy the feeder, their sharp rodent teeth ripping apart everything but metal. What to do?

Greasing feeder poles is an absolute no-no. According to the Cornell Lab of Ornithology, "If birds get into the grease, it can seriously impair their feathers' waterproofing and insulation," posing a serious survival risk. No one wants birds to die in order to keep squirrels at bay.

Many feeders and baffles boast "squirrel proof" labels, but the little varmints spend 24/7 figuring out how to outmaneuver any obstacles we present. Eventually they win. Sometimes in hours; sometimes in days or weeks. Squirrel resistant, maybe, but squirrel proof? Naaaah.

I've also offered an easy-access feeder just for squirrels while offering bird feeds elsewhere. Didn't work. Squirrels want it all—not just "their" feeders.

I've hung feeders under awnings, but squirrels climbed a brick wall, jumped from roof to awning, slid down the side, and tight-wire walked struts to feeders. Then they hung upside down by their hind feet, munching contentedly.

Expert George Harrison suggests the 5-7-9 rule. He writes, "Place the feeder at least 5 feet off the ground, 7 feet from the nearest tree or structure, and 9 feet below any overhanging branches. This has proven to be more effective than baffles, hot pepper, greased poles, and many other contraptions."

Next, fix predator guards. Without them, neat little birdhouses mounted on posts make perfect snake targets—unless, of course, the raccoons raid the boxes first. You'll find several styles of predator guards on store shelves. Or make your own. But be sure to use them. (See page 50 for an illustration.)

Finally, clear your shelves of pesticides and dispose of them properly. But don't use them in your yard. The more bugs you kill, the more birds you kill. Birds need bugs to survive. And while the pesticide industry would have you believe that lawn applications and other chemicals make your yard a better place, the facts prove otherwise. Chemicals kill. Indiscriminately. In worst-case scenarios, they also harm your pets, children, and grandchildren—not to mention the birds. These easy clean-up, fix-up efforts will reward you with healthier, happier, and probably more numerous birds.

CONSERVATION CORNER   **Pesticide Labeling**

The National Audubon Society says, "If you must use a pesticide, use the least toxic." NAS notes, "Pesticides labeled 'Caution' are considered the least hazardous to human health. 'Warning' signals more poisonous pesticides. 'Danger' (with skull and crossbones) identifies extremely poisonous pesticides."

Unfortunately, semantics play a role in pesticide labeling. The EPA registers pesticides, but it does not test, nor is it required to test, for impact on birds. So "registered" is not the same as "approved." As a result, sometimes pesticides deadly to birds sit ready for sale on store shelves across the country. In fact, according to the U.S. Fish and Wildlife Service, about 7 million birds die every year from "common household lawn pesticides," which can cause "neurological damage and cancers in both birds and people." We've not used pesticides in our yard for almost twenty years. With the resulting return of the balance of nature, we no longer even see a need to do so.

Things to Do in March

- Complete the clean-up, fix-up list of suggestions in your yard.
- Plan to add berry-producers to your habitat, as many as your space allows, knowing that if you're still cutting grass, there's room for more plants.
- Offer fruit fixins for your birds.
- Keep feeders in place during this most difficult month of the year, offering high-fat foods for birds hard-pressed to find seeds, berries, and bugs.

32 Yard Birds in March

Weather much warmer; almost summerlike by month's end.

Canada Goose	Tufted Titmouse	Fox Sparrow
Cooper's Hawk	White-breasted Nuthatch	Song Sparrow
Mourning Dove	Carolina Wren	White-throated Sparrow
Barred Owl	Eastern Bluebird	Dark-eyed Junco
Red-bellied Woodpecker	American Robin	Northern Cardinal
Downy Woodpecker	Northern Mockingbird	Red-winged Blackbird
Hairy Woodpecker	Brown Thrasher	Common Grackle
Northern Flicker	European Starling	Brown-headed Cowbird
Eastern Phoebe	Swamp Sparrow	House Finch
Blue Jay	Eastern Towhee	American Goldfinch
American Crow	Chipping Sparrow	House Sparrow
Carolina Chickadee		

AMERICAN ROBIN

Above: *American Robin, male;* below: *American Robin, female*

VITAL STATS
Length: 8–11 in.
Wingspan: 13–17 in.
Weight: 2.8 oz.

American Robins hop across all forty-nine continental states and roam from mountainous treeline to desert coast. Depending on where you live, robins may or may not be migratory. Robins in the northernmost tier of states form huge migrating flocks, with posted records of 60,000 birds passing a single checkpoint in five hours. Daily counts in November can reach 300,000 in places like Cape May, New Jersey.

NAME THAT BIRD

Turdus migratorius (American Robin): *Turdus* is Latin for "thrush-like bird" and *migratorius* means "wandering." Its common name describes its range, as opposed to robins in other parts of the world. The word "robin" is an English pet name for a bird, actually a shortened form of the proper name Robert.

FOOD FARE

Robins eat vast quantities of earthworms as well as insects and fruits, including hawthorn and sumac fruits. Generally not attracted to feeders. In the garden, forages for fruits, including cherries, chokecherries, and holly and dogwood berries.

In spite of those huge migratory numbers, however, in my area, wintering robins simply switch from pairs to flocks, sometimes three hundred or more in a single mass of foragers. Because frozen earth forces them to, robins switch from worms to fruit for wintertime fat supplies. They'll also bask in the abundance of crabapple, mountain ash, chokecherry, sumac, highbush cranberry, or other backyard winter-fruiting trees and bushes.

In berry-rich yards, robins swoop in by the dozens (even hundreds), make themselves at home, and, starting in the uppermost berried branches, pluck and gulp the fruits until their crops bulge full. As the first group retreats to digest, they're replaced by second and third groups, equally voracious. The to-and-fro flights generate more yard activity than virtually any other feeding frenzy backyard feeder hosts will likely witness. Depending on tree size and robin numbers, trees can go bare of berries in hours. Our two 35-foot, heavily laden holly trees last through only two days of frenetic feeding. So whether or not robins roam your wintertime yard depends on your abundance of berries. No berries, no robins.

In severe winters, though, especially during deep snows, robins move on, migrating only as far as necessary to find food. Their migration-on-demand habit became dramatically evident in 2007, when snow and ice in the Northeast and across Texas sent hordes of robins to Florida. During that year's February Great Backyard Bird Count, when more than 2 million robins were reported nationwide, folks in St. Petersburg tallied most of them—1.7 million in a single massive roost site. As one witness recounted, "Beginning in late afternoon, the robins flew overhead steadily for more than two-and-a-half hours."

Most of us think of robins as a lawn-loving, worm-pulling backyard favorite. In fact, they do love earthworms, but they're happiest among native mass plantings harboring their beloved feast. All too often, vast lawns have been contaminated with vast pesticide applications—known to kill robins outright. But barring pesticide applications, robins love us almost as much as we love them. They adapt well to our presence, enjoy our yards, and often find our structures suitable nest sites.

In fact, for four years running, a robin nested on the crook of our downspout. While I was tempted to think of her year after year as the same devoted mom, I would have been wrong. In reality, one robin's many-years' repeated use of a site is quite unlikely. With a robin's average lifespan of just over a year and a half, the repeated site use proves only that the site is ideal. Whichever robin finds it first each spring gains the advantage.

NEST NOTES

Nest Site: female selects site, typically in lower half of brushy tree on horizontal branches concealed by dense leaves. May also build on human-made structures: gutters, outdoor light fixtures, or eaves under porch roofs.

Nest Construction: only by female, working from inside; male may bring nest materials;
   use fine grasses and twigs, perhaps also rootlets and moss, pressed into cup shape to
   fit female's body using "wrist" of wing; then solidified with mud, and lined with soft
   grasses, 6–8 in. across, 3–6 in. high.
Eggs: 3–5 eggs, 1–3 broods, incubated only by female 12–14 days
Fledge: 13 days after hatch

Historically—and inaccurately—robins are labeled harbingers of spring. So, when folks spot a robin in mid-February, they email friends and family that spring has sprung. And maybe so. When length of day stirs hormones and temperatures stir earthworms, robins return to the lawn. Those are the birds that most folks proclaim as the first bird of spring. Likewise, it's one of the earliest birds to nest; in Georgia, robins may start nesting in mid-March.

Other myths about robins abound. The red, red robin does not go bob, bob, bobbing along. It runs, stops; runs, stops. At each stop, standing elegantly erect, black-tipped yellow bill pointing upward, appearing perhaps a bit arrogant, it cocks its head as if listening. But scientists say it's actually watching for movement, for any telltale sign of a worm working its way through the ground.

SPOTTING THE SPECTACULAR **Eying the Worm?**

Why do robins cock their heads to look? Because most songbirds' eyes are on the sides of their heads, they have 340-degree peripheral vision—enough to make humans envious but also enough to spot predators on the approach. The trade-off, however, is the loss of binocular vision, typically less than ten degrees in most birds. And unlike humans, birds can't move their eyes in their sockets. Given these two limitations, they have to turn their heads sideways in order to look down—while the other eye looks up. While we humans would go silly looking two directions at once, birds' brains let them sort out the directions.

While robins, with their potbellied silhouettes, look generally alike, the sexes differ subtly. Richer dark brown backs and heads and more vivid reddish-orange breasts and sides distinguish males from females. Juveniles, generally paler than adults, also wear heavy spots on their breasts. At 8 to 11 inches long, robins are the largest among thrushes, almost half again the size of their cousin the Eastern Bluebird.

Given their mortality rate, their vast numbers seem improbable. Nests carry only about a 40 percent success rate. Of those, only 25 percent survive until November. Only about half of the remaining robins survive the rest of the year. But robins typically raise three successful broods a year, accounting for their steady if not growing population.

Robins welcome mornings in song, and one could awaken to worse than robins whistling up the sun. But perhaps I should say "robin," singular, for only male robins sing, and only then during breeding season, singing about love and war, warbling to its monogamous mate and defending its territory. Unless your backyard habitat encompasses acreage, you'll likely have only a single pair during breeding season, and thus a single male. Researchers found, depending on habitat quality, robins need anywhere from a tenth of an acre to two acres for a family's territory.

BIRD TALK: WHO'S CALLING?
The familiar whistled liquid phrases *cheerily, cheer up, cheer up, cheerily* rise and fall in tone but keep a constant rhythm. The bird's call is a quiet *puck, puck, puck.*

ID CHECK

American Robins are unlikely to be confused with anything else. So common that we refer to "robin-sized" or "smaller than a robin" when we're describing other birds, it's a mainstay in many backyards. Look for the following colorations:

- A rusty breast
- A glossy dark brown head, back and wings
- A bright yellow bill
- The same colors but faded or muted among females

SPECIES PROFILE

EASTERN BLUEBIRD

VITAL STATS
Length: 6.5–8 in.
Wingspan: 10–12.5 in.
Weight: 1 oz.

Above: *Eastern Bluebird, male;* below: *Eastern Bluebird, female*

Everyone loves the "bluebird of happiness," the bird that's said to "carry the sky on its back." The Eastern Bluebird, pretty little member of the thrush family, merits both affectionate labels. But most telling of its many monikers is "comeback kid."

Bluebird populations declined by 90 percent after the introduction of House Sparrows and European Starlings in the late 1800s. Both of these exotic species rob bluebirds of their nest cavities, even killing incubating females and destroying their eggs. By the 1960s, bluebirds hit the point of near extinction. But they have since rebounded, thanks to the formation of the North American Bluebird Society and the establishment of bluebird trails, with groups of man-made nestboxes that bluebirds readily accept.

Bluebirds are much loved. They're gorgeous, they're sweet-singing, they have no bad habits, and they epitomize the perfect family. In fact, Julie Zickefoose, in her book *Enjoying Bluebirds More*, writes, "If you put all the familiar bird species in high school, the bluebird would be the kid who's elected to everything."

Well, let's see now. Surely the bluebird wins first seat in the orchestra's clarinet section for its sweet contralto warble. The choir would choose as soloist the enthusiastic leader of the dawn chorus. No speech team could be without birds that start "talking" twelve days after hatching, communicating with their siblings, mates, family groups, and flocks, making sure everyone knows everyone else's location and safety.

The male's performance for its mate, fluttering atop a proposed nest box, ducking in and back out to cheer the female's way, would ensure its election to the cheerleading squad.

NAME THAT BIRD

Sialis sialis (Eastern Bluebird): A rather nondescriptive, dull-sounding name; *sialis* means "a kind of bird." Fortunately, the common name describes both its range and its lovely color.

BIRD TALK: WHO'S CALLING?

The bluebird's song is a rich, quiet one- to three-note burble, like *tury, churwee, cheye-ley,* rapidly sung by both sexes, although the female sings more quietly than the male. When a male is off territory, however, a female will sing loudly when a predator nears. When the female is on the nest, the male sings more quietly. Both sexes call with a questioning *tuw-a-wee?*

SPOTTING THE SPECTACULAR
Prince Charming and His Princess

When a male bluebird meets a female and catches her eye, he takes her, as if hand in hand, to potential nest sites. There, each ducks in, checking the real estate, measuring its location, evaluating the area's food supply, eyeing possible guard perches, getting a feel for the surrounding area. The routine repeats, as each pops back out to let the other check again, all the while each assuring the other that this site is the real deal. Once a pair establishes preference for a home site, they tend to guard the site year round, not necessarily using it as a winter roost box but protecting it against any invaders who might want to take over come spring.

Bluebirds, which need a two- to five-acre territory for adequate food supplies, adopt and defend prime territory to outcompete migrant House Wrens and Tree Swallows, both of which arrive about a month after bluebirds first nest. Competitive battles with House Sparrows and European Starlings, however, rage year round.

FOOD FARE
Primary bluebird diet is insects caught on the ground: cater- pillars, crickets, grasshoppers, spiders. In fall and winter, the diet changes to fruits and berries: mistletoe, holly, sumac, currants, pokeweed, juniper berries, and honey- suckle. At the feeder, blue- birds occasionally take suet and regularly accept live mealworms. In the garden, bluebirds will hawk insects, including moths and butter- flies as well as caterpillars.

Who else for class president? The bluebird is admired by other bird species and seems to hold special attraction to House Finches. Finches sit on the nest box with a bluebird, follow it as it flies, both species singing. Finches share no competitive urges with bluebirds, desiring neither the bluebird's nest box nor its food, apparently only enjoying its company.

NEST NOTES
Nest Site: in well-documented "nest demonstration display" behaviors, male leads prospective female to possible nest site; choice accepted when both adults enter natural cavities, such as old woodpecker holes, or nest boxes
Nest Construction: entirely by female, loosely woven grasses and pine needles, lined with fine grasses and sometimes hair
Eggs: 2–7 eggs, 1–3 broods, incubated by female 11–19 days
Fledge: 17–21 days after hatch

Election to the honor society is assured, recognition of bluebirds' concentrated stu- diousness. For them, life is all about persistent perching on a lookout, studying a mowed meadow for grasshoppers, crickets, spiders, and beetles, then drop-hunting to snatch prey from the grass.

Come winter, with insects gone, bluebirds are great team players as they form nomadic flocks, helping one another seek berries for sustenance from dogwood, holly, wild grape, bit- tersweet, pokeweed, Virginia creeper, red cedar, and poison ivy.

If your habitat attracts bluebirds, consider offering nest boxes, using guidelines found in the February chapter, pages 48–50. Check the North American Bluebird Society website, www.nabluebirdsociety.org, for much more about these wonderful birds and how to help them.

ID CHECK
Male Eastern Bluebirds wear distinctive garb, but females wear a pale camouflaged version of the same outfit. Male Eastern Bluebirds are distinguished by the following markings:
• Bright blue head, back, wings, and tail
• Rust-colored breast
• White belly

SPECIES PROFILE

RED-WINGED BLACKBIRD
and COMMON GRACKLE

VITAL STATS
Red-winged Blackbird
Length: 7–9 in.
Wingspan: 12.5–15.5 in.
Weight: 1.1–2.7 oz.
Common Grackle
Length: 11–13 in.
Wingspan: 15–18 in.
Weight: 3–5 oz.

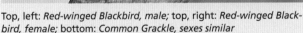

Top, left: *Red-winged Blackbird, male;* top, right: *Red-winged Black-bird, female;* bottom: *Common Grackle, sexes similar*

Consider three details about this bird: First, hands down, she wins honors for her intricate weaving. Surely no other bird can weave a solid, stable platform around vertical wiggly stalks rooted in water. Second, she's unlikely to win similar honors for her appearance, because she's dark and streaky, plain and unremarkable, and looks very much like a sparrow. But she isn't a sparrow at all. Third, according to experts, she's the most misidentified bird in North America.

Do you know her? These three clues point to none other than the female Red-winged Blackbird.

During late winter months, much maligned and unwelcome flocks of black-colored birds might well have burst into your yard, ravaging your snow-covered backyard feeders, startling your favored juncos, cardinals, and trim winter sparrows into flight. And maybe—just maybe—the flocks included this mystery bird. Oddly, the boisterous so-called blackbird flocks usually include far more European Starlings, Brown-headed Cowbirds, and Common Grackles than they do Red-winged Blackbirds. Even if flocks included a handful of red-wings, likely only two or three shy females fed among the dozens, often unnoticed in the crowd.

That's the way these girls like it—especially if unnoticed in a crowd translates to unnoticed, and therefore safe, on the nest. While the male red-wing brags about his showy red shoulder patches, strutting his stuff by spreading wings and tail, head thrown back, calling a repetitive *konk-la-reeee* atop the highest marshy roost, the female, on the other hand, skulks through the undergrowth, perfectly camouflaged in a dark, streaky dress.

Belittled plain Jane or not, the female red-wing is an unsung talent. It's here in the undergrowth, usually amid a cluster of vertical cattail stalks, that the female weaves her masterpiece. One naturalist, dismantling a red-wing's nest at the end of a season, found 32 strips of willow bark and 142 cattail leaves, some 2 feet long, intricately woven into a platform, around and over which were added wet leaves and mud. All of this fit neatly together into a snug nest about 5 inches wide and 6 inches deep.

Common Grackle

Nest Site: female chooses site; varies, but typically high in a coniferous tree, often near water

Nest Construction: built by female; bulky cup made of found materials such as paper scraps and string, along with twigs, leaves, and grass, reinforced with mud, and lined with fine grasses, 6–9 in. across, 3–9 in. deep

Eggs: 1–7 eggs, 1–2 broods, incubated only by female 11–15 days

Fledge: 10–17 days after hatch

The tightly woven basketlike abode makes us wonder how the female red-wing can produce such a work using only her sharp, slender bill. But equally full of wonder is that the bird looks as if it too has been woven of the same grass and stalks, streaky white on brown, the streaks as sharply defined as the stalks themselves.

Still, every girl likes a touch of makeup, and the female wears a clear white eyebrow stripe, and sometimes a blush of pale salmon pink across its throat and face—nice touches on an otherwise cryptic bird.

SPOTTING THE SPECTACULAR
Multimillion-Dollar Birds

Common Grackles love corn. All kinds of corn. Corn sprouts. Corn on the cob. Shelled corn. Cracked corn. In fact, they love corn so much that, because they forage in flocks of thousands, they cause multimillions of dollars in damage to agricultural cornfields, yanking corn sprouts from the ground and ripping ripened corn from the ears.

While Red-winged Blackbirds are our most abundant native bird and mass together in winter flocks of millions, these flocks are now, in March, dispersing, and males are beginning to stake out territory, singing to mark boundaries. One male may attract as many as fifteen females, each with its own nest, all crowded into a single cozy watery habitat.

Together, males and females defend their territories, females using their subdued camouflage to secret their nests, slip through dense vegetation to forage for food for their babies, and remain unnoticed in the crowd. How odd that such a common, much-maligned but secretively talented bird is the most misidentified bird in the country.

The male, all black except for those lustrous red epaulettes, rarely flunks the ID test—unless it's confused with Common Grackles. Grackles lack any red. In fact, while from a distance they mostly look all-over black, closer up, in bright sunlight, grackles show a lovely iridescent glossy blue and purple. While red-wings lack the grackle's iridescence, males sometimes hide their red epaulettes. They have the uncanny ability to perform a wing-patch disappearing act, especially when they choose to avoid aggression. See no red; see no fight. Ah, that all life should be so simple.

Grackles, however, sport hefty sharp beaks, much more stout than the delicate pointy bills of red-wings. In fact, grackles

FOOD FARE

Grackles and blackbirds are not particularly welcome at most backyard feeders but are attracted to small grains like millet, wheat, and cracked corn. Grackles and blackbirds eat insects in summer with grackles taking slightly larger bugs. In winter, when insects are gone, both species switch to grass and weedy seeds like ragweed, cocklebur, native sunflower, and waste grains.

outmuscle red-wings on every front: they're longer, taller, larger, broader, with longer tails and longer legs. Meaner. Bigger. Oh, and don't forget their bright gold eyes. Startling. Intense. Riveting.

In the backyard, however, grackles' heft hinders their feeding at tube feeders. Short perches can't accommodate their muscle. Platform feeders, however, invite grackles in hordes.

In their defense, though, grackles also deal with hordes on their own—hordes of insects, that is. About 30 percent of their diet is bugs. The result? Diminished bug populations. Not a bad trade-off for us.

So set apart red-wings from grackles by size and heft. And know that along southern coastal areas of the Eastern United States, Boat-tailed Grackles typically outnumber Common Grackles, distinguished by a still-larger size, even longer tail, louder voices, and equally larger presence at feeders.

ID CHECK

Separate black-colored birds by checking for the following:

- Overall black body with red shoulder patches on male Red-winged Blackbirds
- Overall streaky body with buffy eye stripe on female Red-winged Blackbirds
- Sharp, pointy bill on red-wings
- Overall black-looking body that shows glossy iridescence close up on Common Grackles
- Longer tail, longer legs, larger body on grackles
- Larger, heavier bill on grackles
- Gold eyes on grackles

Compare these two black-colored birds with European Starling (in September's chapter) and Brown-headed Cowbird (following), all of which flock together in winter foraging hordes.

BROWN-HEADED COWBIRD

Above: *Brown-headed Cowbird, male;* below: *Brown-headed Cowbird, female*

VITAL STATS
Length: 7.5–8.5 in.
Wingspan: 12–14 in.
Weight: 1.5 oz.

Up until the late 1920s, folks in western states routinely referred to Brown-headed Cowbirds as Buffalo Birds or Cow Buntings.

Brown-headed Cowbirds, native birds with a changed lifestyle, originally followed bison herds, eating insects stirred up by thousands of hooves. As on-the-go birds tagging along hundreds of miles with the bison, being tied down by building a nest and incubating eggs just didn't work. So, they parasitized other birds' nests. In other words, they laid eggs in whatever ready-made nests they found, relying on a surrogate mom to raise their babies.

But then the bison herds disappeared. Cowbirds had to adapt. And we humans presented an alternative on a grand scale: we cut down the forests and developed agricultural areas. Since cowbirds love open grasslands, especially areas abutting forest edge, they found luxuriously comfortable digs in our newly formed fields and pastures. Cattle substituted perfectly for buffalo. And cowbird numbers exploded.

Even though cowbirds no longer need to roam hundreds of miles in an effort to follow buffalo herds, and even though they can stay in a relatively small area following cattle, they continue to parasitize. In fact, over a single season, a single cowbird will lay thirty to eighty eggs in other birds' nests. Scientists have documented cowbirds parasitizing about 220 different kinds of host birds.

It's quite a system the female cowbird has worked out. Since her eggs typically hatch a few days earlier than hosts' eggs, and since her babies are typically larger than host nestlings, cowbird babies have the advantage. In fact, nestling cowbirds typically crowd "siblings" from the nest. And if other nestlings do remain, cowbirds are still big enough to hog the food that "mom" brings, causing almost certain demise of all or most of the foster mom's own babies.

Seeing a beautiful cardinal—or even worse, a sweet little Chipping Sparrow—working itself to exhaustion to feed a ravenously hungry baby cowbird makes my stomach churn.

Fortunately, some host birds, instincts having evolved, will pitch out foreign eggs. Blue-gray Gnatcatchers typically abandon a parasitized nest, deserting their own eggs. Yellow Warblers often build a new nest floor directly on top of a parasitized nest, perhaps fooling the cowbird into thinking it's been successful at that spot.

But birds have no doubt also learned that cowbirds also seek revenge. The female cowbird routinely checks the nests where she has left eggs, and if she finds her own missing, she will sabotage those remaining—the "punishment" side of the cowbird Mafia. So apparently some birds figure out that they have a better chance to raise at least one of their own if they tolerate the cowbird baby. Can birds think through such scenarios? How did they learn? Hmmmm. I think it's called evolution.

NEST NOTES
Nest Site: never build nests, parasitizing nests of other birds, especially those birds whose eggs are somewhat smaller than their own, including about 220 species
Eggs: 1–7 eggs, incubated 10–12 days
Fledge: 8–13 days after hatch

Unfortunately, as a result of all the ramifications of their parasitic behavior, and as a result of their being one of our most abundant birds, cowbirds breed to the detriment of others, especially our lovely little warblers who fly thousands of miles to breed here.

So feeding cowbirds disgusts me.

I also cringe when I watch summertime cowbirds. Females sit in strategic spots around the yard, watching, noting who goes where, following, and then slyly slipping in when the adult at a host potential nest dashes out for lunch. She can dart in, lay an egg, and slip out within less than a minute. Often she tosses out one host egg so that, in case the owner can count, the addition isn't obvious. Talk about tricks of the trade!

Sometimes instead of taking the sly and quiet route, female cowbirds will disturb the nesting host, flapping wings, calling, generally creating a scene. When the host is startled off the nest, the cowbird's opportunity opens up.

FOOD FARE
Not particularly welcome at backyard feeders, cowbirds will come for small birdseed like millet or grains like wheat and cracked corn. About a fourth of its diet in summer is insects, especially as stirred up by cattle and horses with which these birds congregate. Otherwise, their diet is grass and weed seeds and waste grain.

SPOTTING THE SPECTACULAR   **Who Am I?**

One of the most amazing aspects of the cowbird's parasitic nesting behavior is what happens when the cowbird babies grow up. Most infant animals imprint on the creature that cares for them. We've all heard stories about critters that mistake their own identities, like wild creatures that imprint on humans who have rescued them. Young cowbirds, however, instead of imprinting on whichever host raised them, somehow know who they are, that they are, in fact, cowbirds, and they join their own kind in autumn flocks. The question: How do they know? We don't know.

As native birds, however, cowbirds are a protected species. Unlike nonnative European Starlings and House Sparrows, which also cause the demise of many or our native birds, cowbirds legally "take over." Only in certain areas, like in Michigan pinelands where critically endangered Kirtland's Warblers are protected, can cowbirds be legally trapped.

What's a good backyard bird host to do? Watch what they eat and avoid offering that feed. Cowbirds generally won't touch striped sunflower seed or safflower seed. So, given an invasion of the critters, consider switching.

ID CHECK
Several all-black birds may show up at backyard feeders. Closer observation, however, especially in good light, reveals that Brown-headed Cowbirds do, indeed, have brown heads and females look mostly grayish brown. To confirm identification, look for the following clues:

- Stocky black-colored bird with shorter tail and shorter neck than other black-colored birds
- A heavy finch-like bill much shorter and stockier than that of other black-colored birds
- Males with overall glossy black bodies and dark brown heads
- Males that look black overall in poor light or at a distance
- Females with overall gray-brown bodies, darker on back and tail, finely streaked bellies

April

*The dandelion tells me when to look for the swallow,
the dog-toothed violet when to expect the wood thrush,
and when I have found the wake-robin in bloom
I know the season is fairly begun.*

JOHN BURROUGHS

Early April bursts with bloom here in southern Indiana, maybe a few weeks earlier or later where you live. Drab browns turn a dozen shades of golden green—plus white and yellow next, followed by pink, red, orange, purple, blue, and lavender. Sugar maples, forsythia, redbuds, flowering dogwoods, and lilacs, followed by azaleas and rhododendrons, sprinkled beneath with tulips and hyacinths, followed by locust and wild black cherry trees. Ah, indeed, color has washed away winter and painted a welcome spring.

Transformations Galore

So it is in April; the backyard undergoes total transformation. The dramatic makeover, though, leaps well beyond budding and blooming vegetation. Our backyard bird population transforms itself, too, with April's burst of birds. By month's end, I'm absolutely giddy over the magic of migration.

April's very earliest avian transformations, however, aren't the result of new arrivals at all. Instead, they come about because birds change clothes—and colors. They molt. Or at least some do.

Only a few birds expend the significant energy to molt twice a year, spring and fall. Of those that do, over several weeks, they alternately lose some feathers, produce replacements, and then lose a few more until they're decked out in fresh, bright—and usually different—colors, often taking on the appearance of an altogether new species. Spring molt, however, typically lacks the full-body molt of autumn, with only the bodily contour feathers gaining a new look.

In my yard, the Most Elegant Wardrobe Change award goes to American Goldfinches. Of course, a bright gold bird in a bare winter tree would shine like a beacon, like a restaurant's neon sign flashing "Eat Here," a tasty attraction for hawks, cats, and other predators. So in winter, goldfinches might better be named olive finches and could be confused with assorted sparrows and other finches at winter feeders. Only their *swee* call and their distinctive whitish wing markings set goldfinches apart from other LBJs (little brown jobs)—well, that and the fact that they're hanging on thistle feeders. Few other birds find thistle seed a gourmet delight.

In recent weeks, however, gold has fully returned on goldfinches, the bird colloquially named "wild canary." During the early part of their molt, they're splotchy little ragamuffins who look as if they've had the worst end of a feather-pickin' fight. Now, transformation complete, males wear bright hurt-your-eyes yellow and sport perky solid-black skullcaps, black wings with yellowish-white wing bars, and black tails.

The female goldfinch, poor dear, even after spring molt, retains drab olive plumage, remaining nearly void of her namesake claim-to-fame color. Only the softest yellow wash around her face and neck marks her species, a camouflage protection for nesting.

Male Yellow-rumped Warblers molt now, too, debuting in gorgeous breeding plumage. When that happens, though, I know they're about to leave, heading for their breeding grounds up north—maybe where you live.

FEEDER FOCUS
Upside-down Feeders

In late summer, watch how goldfinches feed in the garden, foraging on coneflower, zinnia, or sunflower seed heads. Have you noticed how they'll habitually hang upside down to reach the tastiest morsels? Thus, thistle (niger) seed feeders designed for birds to feed upside down tap into goldfinches' natural habits—and help keep other bird species from gobbling down your pricey offerings.

PROBLEM SOLVER
What a Mess! How Do I Clean Feeder Areas?

Part of the yard's April transformation should come in the form of spring clean-up. If you didn't get the job done during the March clean-up/fix-up, do it now—or maybe again—to reduce the risk of disease. Remove accumulated seed hulls from a winter's worth of feeding. Rake up hulls, or use a shop vac to suck 'em up. Discard hulls safely, perhaps bagged for trash pickup, since sunflower hulls are toxic to delicate plants, both perennials and annuals.

A male Northern Cardinal in fresh winter plumage shows a gray wash over its wings.

After a winter's wear, the male Northern Cardinal's plumage turns all-over brilliant red.

A few other birds change color, too, but less dramatically. During early winter, after last fall's molt, male Northern Cardinals wore a grayish "wash" across backs and wings. Now, by early April, the "wash" has worn off, and males wear vivid, vibrant red. European Starlings, too, have worn off the rice-like spots from their fall plumage so that now they're overall black, even iridescent in the right light. I know it sounds all wrong to say that wear makes feathers brighter, but with these two species, that's exactly the case.

April's Bird Bonanza

April in southern Indiana, however, marks yet another dramatic form of backyard transformation. Your backyard transformation may occur a few weeks earlier or later, depending on where you live, but the progress runs the same cycle. I'm talking about migrants, some going, some coming.

BIOLOGY BITS   **Migration: Tools for Tracking**

A double handful of tools helps scientists understand migration:
- **Radar** detects and tracks migrating birds, sometimes even identifying large masses by species.
- **Acoustic monitoring** of migratory flight calls, especially at night, identifies migrating species.
- **Spotting scopes and binoculars** aimed at the full moon allow birders to count birds.
- **Citizen science** online reporting sites such as eBird (www.ebird.org) compile citizen-reported sightings into time-series migration maps.
- **Bird counts,** completed by local bird-watchers on the second Saturday of May and again in late December, have generated more than one hundred years of data.
- **Bird banding stations** provide abundant data of how and when birds move through areas.
- **Cooperative international studies** help document birds' winter and summer habitats.
- **Existing large datasets** archive long-term information on annual, seasonal, monthly, and daily migrations.
- **Stable isotopes** measured in feather samples identify by longitude, latitude, and altitude the geographic location in which those feathers grew.
- **Radio-telemetry,** including devices like geolocators, trace bird movements.

The "going" part refers to our winter visitors who leave this month. No more Dark-eyed Juncos confusing me with songs that sound quite like those of Chipping Sparrows or Pine Warblers—at least to my ears—causing me to wonder if I'm hearing the last of the winter visitors or the first of spring's arrivals. By month's end, no more White-throated Sparrows will call their soft *chink* to one another at dusk. This month, they'll navigate by some unseen beacon on their way to the home of their song—or at least one mnemonic version of it: *Oh, sweet Canada, Canada, Canada.* The males in our yard have practiced that song for two months, a bit off-key, notes missing, not quite right. Until recently. Now, hormones raging full blast, they have it just right. Females will surely flip beak over tail at the perfection.

So our winter visitors drift north this month, until one day, without knowing exactly when it happened, I realize they're all gone. If you live way north, maybe they're coming to your backyard. But here, I'll miss them. In fact, I already do. Watching their bouncing, friendly behavior, foraging beneath my thistle feeders, popping in and out of the hemlock, flipping last fall's leaves in search of bugs—it's all become a part of my winter long-afternoon-with-a-hot-cup-of-tea routine.

A Least Flycatcher snags bugs in mid-air, darting out from an advantageous perch, snaring a bug, and returning to its perch to devour the bounty.

BOTANY FOR BIRDS
Bug-eating Manners

Birds arriving from the tropics come for our bugs, often the only item on their picky little menus. Of course, many of our year-round residents, having foraged all winter on now-depleted seeds and berries, become bug connoisseurs, too. Now, in April, budding vegetation supports the bugs they all seek. But they don't all eat the same bugs, as big birds tend to eat big bugs. And they don't all forage for them in the same way. Depending on the vegetation on which they forage, look for the following:

- **Leaf gleaners,** including chickadees, titmice, and certain warblers, pluck bugs from leaves, often hanging, maybe even upside down, from limb tips in the search.
- **Bark gleaners** like nuthatches and creepers, search crevices of bark.
- **Wood and bark probers,** most notably woodpeckers, hammer into trees, dead or alive.
- **Air salliers,** including flycatchers, dart out, snag a bug, and return to perch to eat.
- **Gleaners** of tiny aerial bugs, like swallows and swifts, fly, mouths open, taking in food on the wing.

Birds entirely dependent on bugs for survival have evolved physically to better catch them, even on the wing—wide mouths (swifts, swallows, and nightjars), tweezers-bills (warblers), and dart-and-snare behavior (flycatchers, gnatcatchers, and others).

By month's end, replacing our departing winter visitors, tropical birds arrive for summer nesting. They, too, transform the backyard population in wild and wonderful ways, splashing the habitat with their rainforest colors—scarlet red, orange, brilliant blue, rosy pink, and a myriad combination of yellows, golds, and greens.

The Low-down on High-flying Migrants

Birds come and go freely across our borders, without passports, driver's licenses, or other ID. No one builds barriers to stop their traffic; no one funnels them through checkpoints to verify their purpose. Instead, birds move from South America through Central America and Mexico into the United States and Canada and back every year, going about their instinctive business of breeding and nesting, intent on propagating the species.

BIOLOGY BITS   **Who's Flying?**

Some birds migrate; others don't. Some migrate only a few hundred miles; some, as much as 24,000 miles—literally the distance around the world every year. Some only drop to a lower elevation. Some fly 8,000 miles nonstop; others hop, skip, and jump, stopping every day to refuel. And some species complete only partial migrations, with some individuals staying put while others move out. Why the variation?

In a short-sighted sense, migration is a response to food supplies. Birds with bills designed to snap bugs from the air, from leaves, or from bark don't have bill strength to crack seeds. When cold kills bugs, the bug eaters move to better food supplies farther south, maybe as far south as South America. Some bug eaters switch to berries when bug

Hundreds of tropical birds, including Black-throated Green Warblers, migrate thousands of miles to nest and raise their babies here.

How do these tropical beauties, many tipping the scales at a fractional ounce, find their way from South America to Indiana or Pennsylvania or Maine? And why seek out such far-flung destinations? Scientists understand enough to answer a few of these questions, but they're a long way from knowing the definitive answers to all.

Let's start with what we know. In general, we in the eastern United States have five groups of birds. One loyal group stays with us year round, including troopers like Northern Cardinals, Blue Jays, Carolina Wrens, American Robins, and Carolina Chickadees (or Black-capped Chickadees if you live in the northern tier of states).

A second group, including American Goldfinches and House Finches, seems to be nonmigratory but actually isn't. These birds roam. Bird-banding studies show that while

supplies diminish, but when berry banquets close, these birds, too, leave town, although maybe only to the southern tier of the United States.

For birds on the long-distance migratory circuit, however, migration is more about breeding success, albeit food supplies obviously weigh in on that success. North American breeders face less competition for bugs to feed their babies than they do in South America. So, tropical birds, seeking better bug supplies, migrate here to breed. For them, it's a business proposition: Benefits outweigh risks.

How migration came about, however, reflects a bird's evolutionary history. One possible scenario, at least for our neotropical migrants, plays out like this: During the Pliocene epoch, some 3.5 million years ago, in the course of vast ice formations, oceanic water levels dropped, forming a land bridge between North and South America. The land bridge, what we now call the Isthmus of Panama, gave many creatures, including birds, the freedom to move between continents, traveling a land route. When northern birds moved far south, however, they created havoc in an already avian-crowded South America.

Over the next several million years, as glaciations advanced and retreated, birds evolved migratory patterns to correspond. Their northward movement gained them the advantages of northerly breeding cycles, but their feeding limitations created by bill structure chased them back south each winter. As thousands of generations repeated the pattern, migratory patterns changed. Only the fittest individuals, breeding the most successfully, survived.

Who, then, doesn't fly but stays with us year round? The birds whose bill structures allow them to eat whatever resources winter wonderlands offer. Crossbills eat pine-cone seeds. Cardinals crack grain and heavy seeds. Native sparrows and finches munch smaller weed seeds. Woodpeckers and nuthatches find bugs and larva in tree-bark crevices. So, migration isn't really about escaping cold, snowy, blustery weather. No, it's about food. If birds can find suitable food, they can stay warm.

Seems that no matter where we begin thinking about who migrates and who doesn't, we end thinking about food. For birds, it's always about habitat, including the food that habitat offers.

---

one little flock drifts out of your yard, another little flock moves in. We never know the difference—unless the populations overlap. Then, we're off to the bird seed store for more supplies.

The other three groups migrate. One group migrates here to nest, like Ruby-throated Hummingbirds, Scarlet and Summer Tanagers, House Wrens, all the swallows, including Purple Martins, and orioles, flycatchers, and some warblers.

Another group, migrating to and from their northerly breeding grounds, flies through in spring and fall, giving us gawking rights for only days or weeks, including (at least where I live) Rose-breasted Grosbeaks, several thrushes, and a more than two dozen warblers. If you live far enough north, some of these spend the summer with you.

The final group shows up only in winter, again depending on your location; but where I live, that group includes Purple Finches, Pine Siskins, Yellow-bellied Sapsuckers, Dark-eyed Juncos, Short-eared Owls. Individual waterfowl number in the tens of thousands and represent about three dozen species.

PROBLEM SOLVER **Feeding Hungry Migrants**

Hungry migrants, having flown all night, drop down as dawn breaks to rest and refuel, feeding primarily on bugs. Obviously, then, seed-filled feeders mean nothing to these travelers. Instead, suitable stopover sites, necessarily pesticide-free, must include blossoming trees and shrubs, early berry producers, and other plants that attract bugs. In short, to feed these birds, we must first feed the bugs. Rest sites must also include dense, sheltering vegetation and fresh, preferably moving, water.

Migration Distances of Select Birds

Migrant Bird	Extreme Migration, from Where to Where?	Migration Round Trip, Maximum Straight-line Miles
Arctic Tern	Polar ice cap of Antarctica to high Arctic	22,000
Red Knot	Southern South America to Arctic	20,000
Barn Swallow	Southern tip of South America to Arctic	16,600
Purple Martin	Central South America to Midwestern U.S.	15,000
Common Nighthawk	Argentina to most of U.S. and Canada	15,000
Blackpoll Warbler	Northern coast of South America to Alaska	12,000
Chimney Swift	Central South America to southern Canada	10,200
Scarlet Tanager	Bolivia to Nova Scotia	10,200
Black-and-white Warbler	Northern Peru to upper Canada	10,000
Baltimore Oriole	Northern South America to central Canada	8,800
Summer Tanager	Bolivia to northern Illinois, Indiana, Ohio and east	8,000
Ruby-throated Hummingbird	Costa Rica to eastern U.S. and Canada	8,000
Yellow-rumped Warbler	Central America to upper Canada	8,000
Black-throated Green Warbler	Northern tip of South America to central Canada	7,800
Gray Catbird	Central America to southern Canada	7,400
White-throated Sparrow	Northern fringe of Mexico to northern Canada	5,400
Wood Thrush	Panama to eastern U.S. and Canada	5,400
Snow Goose	Middle U.S. to Arctic	5,000

Some migrants move only from northern to southern states. Many, like House Wrens, may venture no farther than Mexico. By contrast, the Blackpoll Warbler migrates to Argentina, completing a 6,200 mile trip each way each year. The long-distance record holder, however, may be the Arctic Tern, which flies annually from the Arctic to the Antarctic and back.

How Do They Know the Way?

How do birds find their way? Most scientists believe different migrants use different guidance systems or even a combination of systems. Some species seem hardwired to fly a given route, thus explaining how hatch-year birds, flying alone, find their way to specific Central or South American wintering grounds and then, amazingly, recognize their destination when they arrive.

Others migrants, however, appear to follow landmarks, like coastlines, mountain ranges, or rivers. For instance, the Mississippi River serves as an aerial-highway guide for hundreds of thousands of birds, especially hawks and waterfowl.

Perhaps more fascinating, however, is the scientific exploration of how birds migrate by the sun and stars and, most likely, by magnetic fields—still very much a mystery to scientists who once thought iron-rich cells in birds' bills helped them navigate, a theory now debunked.

Whatever the means, these absolutely amazing creatures, their migratory urge triggered by length of day, can fly thousands of miles and return to the same tree from which they departed the previous year.

BIOLOGY BITS   **Myths of Migration**

Biology has nixed a number of migration myths. For instance, our ancestors watched geese fly across the face of a full moon and surmised that birds flew there for the winter. Early historical documents recount the belief that swallows survived the winter by burying themselves in a lake's bottom mud. Some European cultures presumed that Barnacle Geese turned into barnacles for the winter, thus as a unique type of seafood, making the goose an acceptable Lenten meatless meal. How about that for convoluted logic? A more persistent myth, however, claims that hummingbirds migrate on the backs of geese. All these make for great stories, even if all are myths.

Miracle of Migration

Migration is big. Billions of birds pour through our skies, mostly unnoticed and unannounced, the general human population oblivious to the phenomenal activity above them. In fact, about 75 percent of the birds that nest in North America migrate at least to some degree, and about half of our nesting birds migrate beyond the southern borders of the United States. Given the distances of some migrations, the twice-a-year travel can take up more than half of some birds' lives.

Of course you notice the feathered frequent fliers' comings and goings in your backyard. But take a closer look at these mind-boggling details, a sampling of migration facts and figures that amaze me and transform our April yards.

Among the prettiest of migrating warblers, Yellow Warblers such as this male spend their winters in Central and South America.

HOW DOES YOUR GARDEN GROW
Wild about Willows

Ever since I played as a child under the long drooping limbs of a weeping willow, I've loved willow trees. All kinds of willow trees (*Salix* spp.)! And so do birds. A watchful eye this spring led me to where migrants were feeding, and I understood the true benefits of willows: Dozens of species of birds foraged among their branches, fattening up on bugs for the remainder of their journey. If you do plant willows, be mindful of placing them near sidewalks, underground utility lines, or water and sewer pipes. They have insidious root systems.

First, think about how high birds fly. Contrary to first guess, it's way above tree-top level. True, 95 percent of migrating birds fly at less than ten thousand feet. In fact, most fly below three thousand feet—as detected by radar—with long-distance migrants flying higher than short-distance fliers.

But time of day or night that birds migrate affects their preferred altitude. Most song-birds—but not all—migrate at night. For whatever reason, they tend to fly higher earlier in the night and then, by about midnight, begin dropping slowly. So there's a big variation in even a single bird's highest flight. Radar studies suggest, however, that most small birds find an altitude between five hundred and one thousand feet most comfortable.

But what about that 5 percent that flies above ten thousand feet? Shorebirds have been recorded flying transoceanic at fifteen thousand to twenty thousand feet. That's high—right alongside some airplanes, an altitude at which we mere humans would begin suffering from lack of oxygen. On the other hand, small shorebirds and certain sea ducks often migrate so

Comparisons of Migration Altitudes

Comparison	Altitude in Feet
Ruppell's Griffon Vulture, record verified flight altitude	37,000
Mallard, record verified flight altitude, struck by airplane	21,000
Mt. McKinley, highest mountain in North America	20,032
3 miles high, in feet	15,840
Shorebird transoceanic migration range	15,000–20,000
95 percent of bird migration occurs below this altitude	10,000
1 mile high, in feet	5,280
10 percent of bird migration occurs above this altitude	5,000
Songbird migration range	500–6,000
Most flight occurs below this altitude	3,000
65 percent of bird-aircraft collisions occur below this altitude	2,000
Raptor migration range	700–4,000
Waterfowl migration range	200–4,000
Height of Empire State Building, including roof	1,250
Most small-bird migration range	500–1,000
Approximate height of 35-story office building	500
Daytime hummingbird migration	500

low over water that they're visible only between waves, rarely lifting up more than two hundred feet above water.

Why so high for some birds? High altitude gives better perspective on location, lets birds fly above clouds and high obstacles, perhaps lets them take advantage of tailwinds, and allows them to fly in cooler temperatures. It's hot work, after all, flapping hours on end, much like running on a treadmill—except I can't fathom doing that all night. But birds fly higher with tailwinds and lower with headwinds, since at lower altitudes, winds tend to be less strong. Still, isn't it astonishing that some birds fly so high?

WHY DO BIRDS DO THAT?
Why Do Birds Follow Weather Maps?

While some folks mark their calendars by the arrival of the swallows of Capistrano, sometimes calendars lie. Well, it's not really the calendar, of course. It's the weather—especially wind direction and speed. Everyone who watches weather forecasts on television knows about warm and cold fronts and highs and lows. Winds move clockwise around highs and counterclockwise around lows. So check the weather map and think like a bird.

If, like most warblers, you weigh less than an ounce and you're flying north, where do you want the winds? Bingo! You'll fly north on the backside of a high or in front of a low,where the winds push you north. In autumn, of course, you'll reverse that track to fly south. Spring storms can pin birds down for weeks at a time. Then, when weather breaks and winds shift, vast migration waves wash through, air currents pushing the birds along. Keep an eye on the sky to know when weather will bring wings.

I'm also in awe of migration speeds. Generally, we're told, birds fly between 20 and 50 miles per hour, depending on circumstances. Logically, headwinds make for slow going; tailwinds speed birds along. But day-to-day crises result in speed change, too. A songbird with a Cooper's Hawk on its tail can, in panic, sometimes double its speed. Birds that use flight displays during courtship typically fly then at their speediest—and, thus, sexiest! A bird alone in the open, surely vulnerable, flies faster than when in safe habitat. Flocks fly faster than loners. Big birds generally fly faster than little guys. Spring migrants, driven by raging hormones, fly faster than do the same birds during fall's return. Sustained flight by any bird at any time, however, typically slows.

Selected Migration Flight Speeds

Bird Species	Migratory Flight Speed
Peregrine Falcon	100+ mph in a stoop
Ducks and geese	30–50 mph
Shorebirds	45 mph, sustained over water
Mourning Dove	up to 35 mph
Songbirds	30 mph, sustained
Herons, hawks, ravens	22–28 mph
Flycatchers	10–17 mph

Still, I have a tough time getting my mind wrapped around those kinds of speeds given the necessary *flap, flap, flap* and the corresponding muscular—and metabolic—demands. What's more, during migration, birds maintain those speeds for hours at a time. I'm exhausted just thinking about it. *Flap, flap, flap, flap.* Astonishing, this miracle of migration.

NOTABLE BEHAVIOR
Close Encounter with the Avian Kind

An avian behavior that will remain a personal cherished memory for a long time happened in less than 60 seconds and left me awestruck.

Sitting on the ground, in the open, hunkered low, trying to remain motionless, I was watching the antics of newly arrived Barn Swallows. Then the gnats arrived. They didn't bite, but they annoyed me, landing near my eyes, sitting on my forehead, buzzing my nose. The urge to swat nearly overwhelmed my effort to sit still.

Barn Swallows eat vast amounts of bugs—all caught on the wing.

Then the swallows swooped toward me, six of them, dashing past, soaring up and around, and back again. Mesmerized, I stayed still, moving only my eyes, watching their acrobatics. They swooped nearer, then nearer still, until finally, on each pass, they were only inches from my head. I could hear their wing beats, feel the rush of air past my face. At one point, two zoomed directly toward me, side by side, separating as they reached me, one going left, the other going right. It was exhilarating to see them so close, speeding past. And then they were gone. Just like that. All of them.

Suddenly, after a moment's pause, I understood. The gnats were gone, too. The swallows had snapped up every one.

Memorable Moments: Catching Up on Gossip

No matter how great the early spring vacation, I love returning home to catch up on backyard gossip. Bird gossip, that is—in their songs and actions.

Having been gone the last two weeks of April, I'm up early on this first day back home, the last day of the month. At dawn, gossip choruses through open windows, cardinals, robins, chickadees, titmice, and a tireless mockingbird, talking all at once. But the first feathered friends to hold my bleary-eyed focus speak only by action: Three Wood Ducks—one hen on the nest box, two drakes in the water—show me their battle with starlings is ongoing, with the woodies winning.

Then brilliant blue-green iridescence registers "Tree Swallow" in my foggy brain. Sentinel-like, the male is perched on a tree branch nearest a nest box, his posture proclaiming intent to lease for the season. The female swallow's face in the nest hole tells the rest of the story: In the real-estate battle between House Sparrows and Tree Swallows, the swallows have won. So here the male sits, preening, filling me in on the news.

Tree Swallows nest in cavities and will accept manmade boxes. The males will perch nearby preening, watching, and protecting.

NOTABLE BEHAVIOR   **Migrants Learn from Locals**

Migrating birds face a variety of predators, different not just from one hemisphere to another but also in each area through which they travel. How do they know who's who, like the difference between a benign bunny and a hungry fox or between a snake and a lizard? In fact, they apparently learn from the locals, watching our year-round resident birds and how they react with others in their habitat. Migrants tune in to mobbing behavior, listen for alarm calls. So our locals help these frequent fliers along the way—knowingly or not.

Meanwhile, activity in the maple tree sends me for binoculars. A Blue-headed Vireo, sporting its white-rimmed "spectacles," has dropped in for food and respite after its all-night migratory flight. Tanking up, readying for tonight's push farther north, its bug-eating visit signals that our pesticide-free backyard habitat meets its needs.

NOTABLE BEHAVIOR   **Mobs on the Move**

"Mobbing" refers to the act of small birds, sometimes a mixed flock, ganging up to drive an unwanted critter from the territory—like an owl, hawk, squirrel, fox, cat, or snake. But mobbing is risky business. The mob's target could attack, even kill. Mobbing also costs the gang precious time and energy, away from their territory, nests, and nestlings. But the mob clearly serves notice to the predator that it's been discovered and serves notice to family and friends to beware—all of which seriously impedes the predator's chance of success and frequently serves to drive the predator away.

Dickcissels are in decline, likely because of disappearing grassland habitat and because hayfields, convenient substitutes grasslands, are usually mowed before babies fledge from their ground-level nests.

Then I realize I'm missing one persistent song; without looking, I know that in our absence the neighbor has mowed the hayfield. Red-winged Blackbirds, whose nests are thus destroyed, sing no more. Sure, we've an abundance of red-wings, but I'm saddened by the loss for Bobolinks, Dickcissels, Eastern Meadowlarks, and Northern Bobwhites that also nest in grassy meadows—and hayfields.

As I pad to the kitchen to start coffee, a backyard survey adds to the gossip. The raccoons have partied hardy. One feeder lies on the ground, another missing entirely, the remaining feeders empty, including suet feeders I'd stuffed full to ensure they'd last my absence. Bird baths need water. Birds chatter that I attend to these matters sooner rather than later.

WATER WAYS   **Pedestal or Plain?**

The vast array of bird baths available at shops and online boggles the mind. So how to choose? It's not about the prettiest, most decorative, or most elegant. Instead, think about where you see birds bathe naturally—in street puddles or along pond or stream edges. Choose the bath that most closely imitates nature. Have you noticed? No natural water puddle sits three feet above ground.

Of course, it's likely that a slightly raised birdbath protects bathers from certain ground-level predators, like cats. So it's a bit of a dilemma. I use both.

Pedestal or not, next look for shallow. Water should not exceed 1 inch deep. Aim for gently—very gently—sloped sides, allowing birds to creep down to water's edge. Look for a rough surface for birds' good footing but also something easy to clean. A stiff wire brush works well; I scrub once a week but every day or every other day in summer when mosquitoes breed. Place the bath near vegetation, allowing bathing birds to flee danger and dash to a safe place to preen. But prune away dense ground-level vegetation that might protect marauding predators.

Coffee mug filled, I ease open the front door, letting in more morning song-gossip. By its burble, I spot the male bluebird perched on the tip of a broken limb, head cocked toward its nest box. Activity soon confirms that the pair are feeding babies now. Our stove-pipe predator guards have protected mom and babes from snakes and raccoons.

The Brown Thrasher's quiet murmur draws my attention. Sitting above the nest, the pair is tucked into the juniper at the corner of the driveway. The male may be whispering that their babies are okay, too, nearly ready to fledge.

A male Eastern Bluebird perches near his nest cavity.

WHY DO BIRDS DO THAT?
Why Do Birds Sing?

"Oh, the birds are so happy! Listen to them sing!" Scientists would shudder at such statements and label them as anthropomorphic, noting that we're assigning human emotions to nonhuman beings. Sometimes I convince myself that I do see love, happiness, anger, frustration—the whole gamut of human emotions—among birds. In turn, though, logic convinces me that I'm probably transferring my own emotions onto them.

Birds do, however, have two nonanthropomorphic reasons to sing—love and war. Well, okay, "love" is another anthropomorphic term, but I use it here to describe the very significant effort of choosing a mate, breeding, and reproducing. In short, they sing to attract and keep mates. The "war" part is more easily understood. They sing to define and defend nest territories and chatter to scold predators. While the love and war labels oversimplify song, they are handy tools to sort through what we hear in our backyard habitats.

Feeding activity renders more news. The earliest arriving hummingbirds, still few in numbers, busy at coral bells and columbine, whisk by nectar feeders for quick sips. Surely nesting now, females spare only seconds to feed. Indigo Buntings pick at thistle-seed feeders, their blue a brilliant contrast to goldfinches. A female among them says they're nesting here, too. Twittering Cedar Waxwings gossip about the ripening mulberries. A Belted Kingfisher's chatter reports it's back fishing alongside the Great Blue Heron on the neighbor's farm pond.

HOW DOES YOUR GARDEN GROW?
Early Bloomers

Early arriving Ruby-throated Hummingbirds seek nectar-producing flowers, not just feeders. Personal favorites in my April garden include trumpet honeysuckle (*Lonicera sempervirens*), coral bells, sometimes called American alumroot (*Huechera americana*), and native, salmon-blossomed columbine (*Aquilegia canadensis*). All early bloomers, hummingbirds know these natives and recognize them as great nectar sources.

A female Ruby-throated Hummingbird makes a quick trip to a nectar feeder, fending off competition with a threat display. Note the slight indentation on her breast feathers, called a "nest band," where a snug-fitting nest has pressed against her feathers like too-tight socks around your ankles.

And so it goes. Song and action tell all. Caught up on backyard gossip, ready now for other news, I settle into my morning paper, glad to be home again.

For the Love of Trees

Spring's unsettled weather often wracks us with violent storms. Recently, vicious thunderstorms wrenched thousands of trees from area backyards, losses ironically underscoring their inherent but virtually immeasurable value.

Their absence leaves holes in the skyline and gaps in the landscape. We miss them for their shade, reducing utility bills, and their natural air purification. We miss them as old friends, for we sipped morning coffee under their spreading branches, afternoon lemonade in their shade, and evening sweet tea with their limbs framing the sunset. But we'll miss them, too, for the birds they sheltered in their arms.

Recent destruction gave me pause to think about trees that seem—at least in my yard—most attractive to birds. Native species all, the list admittedly reflects highly personal biases.

HABITAT—YOURS AND THEIRS
Pesticides: What Do They Kill?

Pesticides and lawn. It's a deadly combination. And many homeowners, dedicated to lush lawns, embrace the combination that kills an estimated seven million birds every year in the United States. Yes, that's a "7" with six zeroes.

If birds breathe, touch, or ingest only a droplet of pesticide, or if they eat bugs or drink nectar from flowers or other plant matter contaminated by pesticides, even indirectly through the food chain, they can die quickly. Worse, the effects accumulate in birds' bodies, perhaps affecting reproduction, vigilance, navigational skills, or general health. Much is unknown, but risks are real.

We would do well to move past our addiction to lush lawns. We spend millions of dollars fertilizing, mowing, treating, and cutting grass—only to bag it and haul it to the landfill. It's a well-tended crop that we cannot eat, sell, or use. For birds, a lawn is a wasteland. Add pesticides, and lawn turns into a toxic dump. Wildlife and humans would both benefit from eliminating lawn and replacing it with native trees, shrubs, vines, and perennials that provide food, shelter, and nest sites. In short, if you're still mowing grass, you have room to plant more for the birds—improving habitat for you, your birds, and your neighborhood.

For me, wild black cherry takes top pick. An odd choice, perhaps, but that was the tree that introduced me to warblers. Because wild cherries drape with blossoms in early May, their sweetness attracting bugs, migrant warblers feed frenetically among the branches. On a single morning, I remember identifying eight warbler species gracing a single black cherry tree.

By June, when pea-sized fruit ripens, Cedar Waxwings, Northern Cardinals, Blue Jays, woodpeckers, robins, mockingbirds, and grackles keep the limbs a-flutter as they yank berries from slender twigs. Bluebirds feed the fruits to their babies, keeping them hydrated in summer's excessive heat. You'll find upchucked pits in the nest when babies fledge. Phoebes and kingbirds snatch bugs attracted to the fruit. Doves sun on the branches. Wild cherries are truly "birdie" trees.

NOTABLE BEHAVIOR   **Brutal Battles**

Competition for nest sites can turn brutal, and this year's tree loss ratchets up the battle. House Wrens arrive well after year-round residents have begun nesting. So, with preferred nest cavities already holding families-to-be, House Wrens go on a serious search for vacancies. Finding none—or finding none to their satisfaction—the wrens resolve the problem by eviction, piercing and tossing out other birds' eggs and, given the opportunity, killing the female on the nest. We've lost more than one Eastern Bluebird family to House Wrens. But even year-round residents vie for nest sites. House Sparrows, too, practice eviction—to the death.

One solution? Offer more nest cavities. Situate them in appropriate but varied sites to meet the varied preferences of the species in your backyard habitat. With enough cavities to go around, battles become less brutal.

My next favorite tree: native pecan. Even our most mature ones produce nuts too small for bragging rights, but in late fall, Blue Jays keep branches bouncing as they gather winter stores. In summer, bluebirds perch on lowest branches, hunting grass-dwelling bugs for their broods. All woodpeckers check out our pecans—Red-headed, Red-bellied, Pileated, Downy, and Hairy Woodpeckers. Upper reaches serve a vigilant Red-tailed Hawk.

HOW DOES YOUR GARDEN GROW?
                    Wind-up Plants

Vines that wind up tree trunks, trellises, fences, or other support structures enhance habitat variety with vertical growth, a significant asset to a backyard environment. In addition, however, vines provide birds with shelter, nest sites, protection, roost spots, and—yes—food, especially in the form of berries and nectar. Consider two of my favorites: Virginia creeper (*Parthenocissus quinquefolia*) and trumpet creeper, sometimes called trumpet vine (*Campsis radicans*). While adding a splash of autumn red foliage, Virginia creeper produces lovely deep-purple berries, a favorite among thrashers, cardinals, robins, bluebirds, and other thrushes. My other personal favorite, trumpet creeper attracts not only hummingbirds but also orioles, which poke holes in the flower base to get at the nectar.

Gotta love sassafras trees, too. Sentinels along untended fence rows provide abundant lipid-rich fall berries for jays, cardinals, and mockingbirds; nesting branches for doves; cavities in abundance for nesting and roosting; and in one wild corner of our yard, a perch for Belted Kingfishers and Green Herons fishing the adjacent pond. In winter, White-throated Sparrows, juncos, Carolina Wrens, and Yellow-rumped Warblers roost there, and occasionally a Cooper's Hawk makes it a hunting blind.

Red and sugar maples, both superior to silver maples, rank high with birds. True, the tiny spring blooms bring millions of whirling seeds that seem to sprout in all the wrong places. But blossoms also bring bugs, and birds love bugs. Think phoebes, pewees, bluebirds, Song Sparrows, kingbirds, and warblers. Lots of warblers.

In spring, native oaks—any of many—harbor migrant warblers that find bugs among the branches. Friends have verified that if they're looking for spring migrants, they hunt for native oaks, take a seat, and watch. Later, hummingbirds perch on lower shade-killed twigs

Native trumpet vine, sometimes called trumpet creeper, attracts a variety of birds to its rich nectar.

from which they hawk tiny bugs, guard nectar feeders, or perform courtship flights. In winter when acorns litter the ground, Blue Jays throng to clean up ahead of the squirrels. Flickers, Brown Thrashers, Eastern Towhees, and Fox and Song Sparrows come for the ants and bugs that the decaying acorns draw. By spring, the acorns are gone.

PROBLEM SOLVER

Seed-filled Feeders Empty of Birds

Given spring's transformation, seed-filled feeders empty of birds demand inspection. First, check for mold. Spring rains followed by hot days readily promote rot and mold. Dump damp feed, scrub feeders to remove yucky remnants, dry them thoroughly, and add fresh seed.

If birds still turn up their beaks at your offerings, purchase a new batch of seed. If birds find the new seed acceptable, you know that your earlier offerings have gone buggy or otherwise become unacceptable to birds.

Also in spring, tulip poplar trees host Orchard and Baltimore Orioles, poking their heads into nectar-filled blossoms; by winter, seed eaters descend. Year around, nuthatches skitter down poplar trunks, hunting bugs.

And I can't omit sycamores. From their tops, Baltimore Orioles, Yellow-throated Warblers, and Summer Tanagers feed and sing; Northern Parulas keep house just below. Our tallest sycamore cradled a Red-shouldered Hawk's nest; its hollow limb housed a flicker family. Nor can I skip over sweetgum trees that last winter attracted a little flock of Pine Siskins, feeding on the mast.

Tree Planting Plan

Before you lovingly plant that pretty little tree you hauled home in your car, consider its size at maturity. Trees in a three-gallon pot look deceptively small but over time grow into giants. In general, then, avoid planting trees under power lines, above buried cables and septic systems, too close to your home's foundation or other structure, and too near a sidewalk, driveway, or street. Consider the window view from inside your house, your roofline, and your neighbor's property rights. After checking information about the tree's diameter and height at maturity, roll out the tape measure for a reality check and put imagination to rest.

Evergreens, especially red cedars and hollies, offer berries and buffers against bitter blasts for multitudes of wintering birds. This year our pines hosted a Barred Owl; in previous years, Eastern Screech Owls whinnied from them nightly.

So while I grieve for the area's precious tree losses, I grieve, too, for the birds' losses.

And so it goes with April. Transformation abounds. Winter visitors stream north. Summer nesters stake out territory. Long-distance migrants navigate unmarked skies, at dramatic altitudes and dramatic speeds. Spring storms tear apart habitat—theirs and ours. The backyard undergoes dramatic changes as the annual cycle rolls on.

Conservation Corner: Eight Ways to Make a Difference for Migrating Birds

The National Audubon Society (http://athome.audubon.org) offers these suggestions by which backyard hosts can aid migrating birds:

- Reduce or eliminate pesticide and herbicide use. Using fewer chemicals in your yard and home helps keep wildlife, pets, and people healthy.
- Plant native plants. Natives provide birds with food in the form of fruit and seeds and house tasty invertebrates like bugs and spiders.
- Keep cats inside. Keeping cats indoors ensures that birds outdoors stay safe, and indoor cats live much longer than cats that go outside.
- Prevent window collisions. Make sure birds can see and thereby avoid your windows by putting up screens, closing drapes and blinds when you leave the house, or sticking multiple decals on the glass, spaced no more than two to four inches apart.
- Provide cover in your backyard. Leave snags for nesting places and stack downed tree limbs to create a brush pile, a great source of cover for birds during bad weather.
- Help birds stay on course. Close your blinds at night and turn off lights you aren't using. Some birds use constellations to guide them on their annual migrations, and bright lights can disrupt them.
- Create or protect water sources in your yard. Birds need water for drink and bath. Change the water every day or two when mosquitoes are breeding.
- Landscape for birds. Use layers, including understory, ground cover, shrubs, vines, and trees. Multiple plant levels give birds different layers for different purposes, such as nesting, feeding, and singing.

Things to Do in April

- Empty your shelves of pesticides and pledge to discontinue their use.
- Reduce or eliminate lawn, instead planting ground covers, bushes, native low-grow grasses, trees, perennials, and vines.
- Add nest cavities, situated in a variety of locations attractive to the bird species in your backyard habitat.
- Follow suggestions to eliminate window collisions.
- Urge your neighbors and friends to join you in habitat improvement.

83 Yard Birds in April

Spring has transformed the yard!

Canada Goose	Blue Jay	Yellow-throated Warbler
Wood Duck	American Crow	Pine Warbler
Mallard	Purple Martin	Palm Warbler
Northern Bobwhite	Tree Swallow	American Redstart
Double-crested Cormorant	Northern Rough-winged	Common Yellowthroat
Great Blue Heron	Swallow	Yellow-breasted Chat
Turkey Vulture	Barn Swallow	Eastern Towhee
Cooper's Hawk	Carolina Chickadee	Chipping Sparrow
Red-shouldered Hawk	Tufted Titmouse	Field Sparrow
Red-tailed Hawk	White-breasted Nuthatch	Song Sparrow
Killdeer	Carolina Wren	Lincoln's Sparrow
Mourning Dove	House Wren	White-throated Sparrow
Barred Owl	Golden-crowned Kinglet	Dark-eyed Junco
Common Nighthawk	Ruby-crowned Kinglet	Summer Tanager
Chimney Swift	Blue-gray Gnatcatcher	Scarlet Tanager
Ruby-throated	Eastern Bluebird	Northern Cardinal
Hummingbird	American Robin	Rose-breasted Grosbeak
Belted Kingfisher	Gray Catbird	Blue Grosbeak
Red-bellied Woodpecker	Northern Mockingbird	Indigo Bunting
Yellow-bellied Sapsucker	Brown Thrasher	Red-winged Blackbird
Downy Woodpecker	European Starling	Eastern Meadowlark
Hairy Woodpecker	Cedar Waxwing	Common Grackle
Northern Flicker	Tennessee Warbler	Brown-headed Cowbird
Pileated Woodpecker	Nashville Warbler	Orchard Oriole
Eastern Wood-pewee	Northern Parula	Baltimore Oriole
Eastern Phoebe	Yellow Warbler	House Finch
Eastern Kingbird	Magnolia Warbler	American Goldfinch
Philadelphia Vireo	Yellow-rumped Warbler	House Sparrow
Red-eyed Vireo		

SPECIES PROFILE

HOUSE WREN

VITAL STATS
Length: 4.5–5.1 in.
Wingspan: 6–6.5 in.
Weight: 0.4 oz.

House Wren (sexes alike)

BIRD TALK: WHO'S CALLING?

The long, jumbled, flute-like musical song of House Wrens, delivered as a gurgling out-burst, can be repeated 9–11 times a minute and includes 12–16 identifiable syllables. During breeding season, they sometimes sing nonstop for long periods. The females answer their mates in a high squeal.

M y love-hate relationship with House Wrens began when they chose our wren box attached to the side of the shed, hatched five babies, and sang their way into my heart. Then something happened to the female—probably a cat—and the male sang two days and left—for two years.

NAME THAT BIRD

Troglodytes aedon (House Wren): *Troglodytes* comes from the Greek meaning "one who creeps into holes." In English, the word refers to people who live in caves. So, the term refers to the bird's habit of foraging among crevices. *Aedon* means "nightingale," alluding to the bird's robust song.

Three springs later, I was thrilled to hear that song again: The house wren (or one of its kind) was back. In typical male House Wren fashion, he stuffed two nest boxes and a nest gourd with twigs, touted his vocal prowess, and showed off his house-building expertise to a coy little female.

The female House Wren chose the gourd. After topping the pile of sticks with grasses, she settled in to lay and incubate eggs; and the male pampered his mate, checking on her regularly, singing arias from dawn to dusk.

During heavy post-hurricane rains, we commented how clever the female was, to choose a gourd tucked under the awning, snug and dry during the downpours.

Babies hatched, papa sang, and both parents racked up frequent flier miles carrying bugs for breakfast, lunch, and dinner. Dedicated parents, busy and successful bug zappers, they tended the babies with the equivalent of religious fervor.

Since the gourd hung only two feet from my office window, I rarely missed a departure or landing and smiled at their perky dedication, reflecting that humans could learn much from them about family care.

Watching their activities also gave us a twinge of satisfaction, that we managed by trial and error to offer a cavity nest that the song-masters found attractive. The side opening fit their tiny little bodies; the drain holes guaranteed a dry house; and the under-the-awning mount protected all from the elements.

It made for a perfect home. Or so we thought.

NEST NOTES

Nest Site: male guards available old woodpecker holes or similar natural cavities, nest boxes, or "found" man-made cavities like boots, mailboxes, or discarded cans immediately upon claiming territory; avoids heavily wooded nest sites but rarely nests more than 100 ft. from trees or shrubs; will evict other, larger birds from preferred cavities

Nest Construction: male fills multiple cavities with twigs; female chooses her favorite and makes a skimpy soft-lined cup within the twig pile

Eggs: 3–10 eggs, 1–2 broods, incubated by female only 9–16 days; male stands guard

Fledge: 14–17 days after hatch

Sunday afternoon, the wrens set up a chatter that alerted us to something out of order. We studied their behavior, trying to interpret the cause. They scampered from awning's edge to bush to awning's strut to roof then back to awning's edge, scolding, scolding, forever scolding.

Investigating, we found nothing. We poked in the bushes, spread apart the flower stalks, checked under rocks, examined crevasses in the awning, but found nothing. Back inside, we watched the wren's behavior return to normal. They resumed on-time arrivals, feeding, singing.

SPOTTING THE SPECTACULAR   **Tell-tale Behavior**

When House Wrens demonstrate strange behavior, it's time to monitor the nest cavity. Unusual chatter or unusual silence both point to trouble. In this instance, the pair flew from awning's edge to strut to roof, but between landings, they fluttered in front of their nest gourd, peered in, and shot away. Occasionally one sat quivering, almost as if in fear— or horror. From the awning strut, they stretched upward, straining to gape in the gourd's opening. Then they'd streak away, only to return in minutes to repeat the behavior. Something was seriously wrong.

But strange behavior resumed the next morning. Perhaps they were ready for the babies to fly? But no, they weren't calling, only searching. Silent. Surely, something was wrong.

Positioning a ladder, I climbed up, flashlight in hand, and with some trepidation, peered in. There, digesting its feast, curled a snake.

Logic tells me this is nature's way; snakes have to eat, too. But logic aside, my heart cried out for these hard-working, devoted little birds. Oh, I know, really they're just following instincts. But when we removed the gourd and relocated the snake, I couldn't help counting the five little bulges in its belly.

For the next two days, the wrens repeatedly checked the cleaned gourd, peered in, leaned back, looked again, and flew.

FOOD FARE

House Wrens maintain a 100-percent animal diet, including a wide variety of insects and spiders. They do not visit feeders except, perhaps, to forage for spiders in feeder crevices.

Next morning, I heard the male sing twice, from across the neighbor's hay field. Then, silence. I hoped, with a catch in my throat, that it wouldn't be two more years before my visitor returned.

But the next spring when he did return—or one of his kind—he arrived as an aggressive, commandeering male who evicted the bluebirds from their nest box, killed their babies, and stuffed the box with sticks, full to the roof. Now his song leaves me empty, sick for the bluebirds and their equal dedication to family affairs. Bluebirds live with us year round and hold a special place in my heart, so when House Wrens arrive from the southern coast or even Mexico, I see them as seasonal intruders. True, they come here only to raise babies, feed them our abundance of bugs, and family responsibilities complete, return to the parts south.

But I want visitors to play nice. Unfortunately, Mother Nature's ways don't follow the Golden Rule.

ID CHECK

Distinguish House Wren from Carolina Wren by looking for the following characteristics:
- Distinct, white eye line on Carolina Wren's face
- Relatively plain face of House Wren
- Loud *teacher, teacher, teacher* song of Carolina Wren
- Long warbling song of House Wren

EASTERN PHOEBE and
EASTERN WOOD-PEWEE

VITAL STATS
Eastern Phoebe
Length: 5.5–6.5 in.
Wingspan: 10.2–11.0 in.
Weight: 0.65 oz.

Above: Eastern Phoebe (sexes alike); below: Eastern Wood-pewee (sexes alike)

VITAL STATS
Eastern Wood-pewee
Length: 5.9–6.5 in.
Wingspan: 9.1–10.5 in.
Weight: 0.4–0.5 oz.

Last month, March 20 to be exact, marked the vernal equinox. Whether your calendar hangs its bulk on the kitchen wall, spreads its pages on a desk, folds compactly into purse or wallet, or displays its chronology on some electronic gadget, it labels March 20 as the first day of spring.

But I beg to differ. This year, for me, the first day of spring arrived March 8.

Nature has its own calendar, totally oblivious to anything in print or on screen. And spring reaches different places on different dates in different years, entirely dependent on global weather patterns.

For me, spring's certainty arrives on wings—on the wings of the first migrant, one of those amazing birds that last fall sailed somewhere south, probably somewhere among the southern tier of states, bugging there over winter, and now returns to nest this summer. In fact, it's back so early that perhaps I should more accurately say it returns not in early spring but in late winter—indeed, before the vernal equinox. Either way, it's the harbinger of spring, joining the daffodil blossoms, making me smile.

NAME THAT BIRD

Sayornis phoebe (Eastern Phoebe): *Sayornis* is derived from "Say's bird," that is, Thomas Say, an American Naturalist and prolific scientific writer. The word *phoebe,* which means "bright and shining," may refer to one of the mythological Greek Titans, or it may simply be descriptive of the bird's song. So, its common name describes its range and, most likely, its song.

Contopus virens (Eastern Wood-pewee): *Contopus* means "short footed" as this bird family has particularly short tarsi. *Virens* means "greenish" and refers to the pale green underparts. The bird's common name describes its range and its song.

BIRD TALK: WHO'S CALLING?

Both birds say their names. Eastern Phoebes sputter *fee-b-b-bee,* accented on the first syllable; Eastern Wood-pewees sing *pee-uh-wee,* the tone dropping on the second syllable and rising on the third.

FOOD FARE

Both birds eat small flying insects, captured by watching from a perch, flying out to snap up the insect, and returning to the same or nearby perch.

That happened March 8. An Eastern Phoebe, one of our earliest migrants, announced with raspy exclamation his arrival, proclaiming his name first from the pecan tree, then from locust, then from maple, *FEE-bee! FEE-bee!* a summertime song that brought me bolt upright from my gardening, turning an ear toward the sound, listening to be sure. *FEE-bee! FEE-bee!* Yes!

Plain little birds, phoebes wear dark gray-brown on back and head, an all-black bill, white underparts, but no distinct wing bars or other decorative accessories. Oddly, they're loners; even during breeding season, mated pairs rarely stay together. The male sings atop his low-level fly-catching perch, bobbing his tail, pausing to dart out, snag a passing bug, and return, repeating the process as fly-by bugs allow.

In spite of its loner tendencies, the phoebe ranks as our most common flycatcher. But while shunning others of its own kind, it typically nests near humans, its neat little cuplike abode, shaped of a mud-moss-grass mix, plastered under eaves of buildings and under bridges and culverts. In remote areas, it tucks its nest among the fissures of cliffs.

NEST NOTES

Eastern Phoebe

Nest Site: chosen by female, under cliff, bridge, or eave of building

Nest Construction: entirely by female but with male's presence; open cup, 4.5 in. outside diameter, 2.5 in. inside diameter, just under 2 in. deep; made of moss and leaves mudded together, lined with fine grasses and hair, and cemented with mud to side of structure near ceiling or other overhang

Eggs: 2–6 eggs, 1 brood, incubated only by female, 16 days

Fledge: 16–18 days after hatch

Eastern Wood-pewee

Nest Site: on horizontal tree limb or sapling, details unknown

Nest Construction: shallow cup less than 1 in. deep, of woven grass, pasted over on outside by lichens, lined with fine grasses, moss, hair, plant fibers, 3 in. diameter; few details known about manner of construction

Eggs: 2–4 eggs, 1 brood, incubated by female 12–13 days; male remains nearby

Fledge: 14–18 days after hatch

Eastern Wood-pewees, on the other hand, nest in the open, on a horizontal limb, the abode neatly camouflaged with lichen. Nearly the same size as Eastern Phoebes, pewees can be distinguished from look-alike phoebes by their bold wing bars and two-toned bills—and by their persistent name-calling song, *pee-ah-wee, pee-ah-wee*. Both flycatchers, phoebes and pewees forage at somewhat different canopy levels, pewees typically feeding higher than phoebes. But as their name suggests, Eastern Wood-pewees tend to move farther into woodland while phoebes range in the open.

While phoebes serve as harbingers of spring where I live, pewees are among the last migrants to arrive from their South American wintering grounds. Their repetitive *pee-ah-wee* translates, from my human perspective, into "we're all here now."

ID CHECK

To separate Eastern Phoebe from Eastern Wood-pewee, check these comparisons:

Comparison of Eastern Phoebe and Eastern Wood-pewee

Eastern Phoebe	Eastern Wood-pewee
No wing bars	Double wing bars
All-black bill	Two-toned bill; lower mandible pale yellow
Short wings, extend just beyond base of tail	Wings extend about halfway down tail
Rounded head	Back of head peaked
Bobs tail while perched	Does not bob tail
Says its name, a raspy "FEE-bee," accented on first syllable.	Says its name, adding a syllable, as in "pee-ah-wee"
Prefers streamsides, bridges, farms, field edges, towns, roadsides.	Prefers woodlands and groves
Nest under eaves, cliffs, and bridges, in culverts.	Nests on horizontal limb in forest.

SPOTTING THE SPECTACULAR
Homebodies Homing In

Phoebes bear the distinction of being the first birds scientifically tracked. In 1804, John James Audubon tied silver threads on baby phoebes' legs to see if they returned in successive years. And they did. Unless you live in a forest, it's unlikely you'll have Eastern Wood-pewees nest in your yard; but if you've had Eastern Phoebes nest under your eaves once, chances are they've been there before and will return again. By late March, in our area, the early arriving phoebe migrants have nests built, ready, awaiting the insect "bloom." Nest-site fidelity is a big deal with clever little phoebes. Renting the same condo year after year offers time-saving efficiency. They know where everything is, how to find the shopping center, and what threats lurk nearby. Watch for these homebodies in your yard!

SPECIES PROFILE

BLUE-GRAY GNATCATCHER

VITAL STATS
Length: 4–4.5 in.
Wingspan: 6 in.
Weight: 0.2 oz.

Above: *Blue-gray Gnatcatcher, male;* below: *Blue-gray Gnatcatcher, female*

When the late-April warbler wave washes through southern Indiana, I know that among the migrants will be a warbler-like nonwarbler: Blue-gray Gnatcatcher. In my yard, the gnatcatcher arrives along with Yellow-throated Warblers and Northern Parulas—almost to the day. And usually I hear them—each of them—before I see them, the Blue-gray Gnatcatchers calling their high-pitched burry *speee*.

When I do see the male, all dressed up in breeding plumage sporting a dainty little black bridle-like band just above its beak and eyes, he's usually scooting about in our cluster of apple trees, picking along the branches, supping on tiny edibles hidden in the bark. The female shows up a few days later, perhaps in response to the male's song. She's missing the dainty black trim. Together, though, their white-edged tails flit much like the Dark-eyed Junco's tail. Since, at least in my yard, juncos depart for their northerly breeding grounds often on the same weather front that brings in the smaller gnatcatchers, those little flicks of white tail feathers now ID this new guy in town. Look for a bluish-gray bird with a tail nearly equal to the length of its body.

At my house, Blue-gray Gnatcatchers are yard birds, and I hear and see them regularly during their five-month visit with us, from mid-April until mid-September. But I've never found their tiny little nest. I've watched them gather nesting material from a pile of long grasses, cut and raked from the winter garden. I know why I've not spotted the little nest. Photos I've seen show a nest so cleverly concealed by bits of lichen and bark that it's more a lump on a limb than a well-defined nest. Clever construction!

NAME THAT BIRD

Polioptila caerulea (Blue-gray Gnatcatcher): *Polioptila* translates roughly as "gray feathered." *Caerulea* also refers to the bird's color, a bluish gray. Its common name not only describes the bird's color but its behavior, catching small gnat-like insects in the air.

NEST NOTES

Nest Site: male leads site search with female "testing" sites until both agree; on tree limb about halfway between trunk and tip

Nest Construction: by both sexes; open cup with 3 in. high elastic walls, made of various plant matter held together with spider webbing or caterpillar silk and lined with plant down or other fine fibers; 2 in. outside diameter, 1.5 in. inside diameter, 1.5 in. deep; males often build alone for second nesting

Eggs: 3–6 eggs, 1–2 broods, incubated about equally by both sexes, 13 days

Fledge: 10–12 days after hatch

Any time these birds catch my eye, it's either their chitty-chatty with one another or their consummate busyness that has attracted my attention. They flit from branch tip to branch tip, dangling, nibbling, picking, zipping to the next, all the while exchanging *speee* calls. Who can ignore their enthusiastic, energetic, bubbling busyness? Always, I stop to watch, judging that their winter along the Gulf Coast or perhaps farther south, in Mexico, Costa Rica, or the Caribbean, must have served them well. And my heart swells as I think about how many millions of times their tiny wings beat to fly the hundreds of miles to return to my yard. Such awesome little creatures!

SPOTTING THE SPECTACULAR **Tailing Bugs**

As Blue-gray Gnatcatchers zip busily about, they constantly flick and fan their tails, allowing those white outer tail feathers to flash, even deep within the darkest foliage. Some observers speculate that the tail motion stirs up bugs, flushing them out for a ready meal.

While the birds in my yard tend to sneak along the branch tips gleaning bugs, they will dash out, snare a treat midair, and return to their on-limb foraging. Occasionally, they hover, moth-like, as if making sure no bug goes unseen.

Rarely do gnatcatchers hop about on the ground. And they seem repulsed by pine trees. Instead, they hang out on broad-leafed deciduous trees, defending somewhere between 2 and 4.5 acres for their territory. So I never see more than one pair in the yard. Whatever fights have ensued in territorial defense, I've missed—probably just as well. Sometimes these tiny creatures battle to the ground, revealing a tenacious mean streak when it comes to calling a home their own.

All in all, though, the male is a good guy. He helps the female build the nest, and stays with her while she's laying her eggs. He shows up during incubation only to change shifts, and during nestling period only to help feed. Well, at least it seems the male is a good guy—attentive, helpful, responsible. Or, on the other hand, maybe he's just guarding his female against other males, making sure the typically monogamous relationship stays that way.

FOOD FARE

As its name suggests, the Blue-gray Gnatcatcher eats small insects and spiders.

BIRD TALK: WHO'S CALLING?

This little bird sings softly, warbling a jumble of complex wheezy notes in a steady rhythm. Its call is a thin, high-pitched *speeee*.

ID CHECK

Blue-gray Gnatcatcher, trim, neat, tiny bird that it is, separates itself from other little guys by sporting the following traits:

- Blue-gray head, back, tail, and wings, minus any wing bars
- White underparts
- Breeding male's black bridled face pattern and bluish head and nape
- Distinct white eye ring
- White outer feathers on long tail
- Small, thin, bug-catching bill

SPECIES PROFILE

BALTIMORE ORIOLE

Above: *Baltimore Oriole, male;* below: *Baltimore Oriole, female*

VITAL STATS
Length: 6.7–7.5 in.
Wingspan: 9.1–11.8 in.
Weight: 1.1–1.4 oz.

For most of a week, the female oriole sailed in regularly to the arbor outside our backdoor, paying homage, it seemed, to the wisteria vine there, tugging on slender stems, stripping off threads of bark, leaning so far back that she seemed certain to tip over. Of course, she never did. She would let go, move closer to where the thread remained attached and ease back again. Over and over she manipulated the stems, obviously striving for the longest threads possible—for good reason. This Baltimore Oriole was nest building.

NAME THAT BIRD

Icterus galbula (Baltimore Oriole): *Icterus* means "jaundice," a yellowish color of the skin, and *galbula* reinforces the idea: It means "yellow bird." The bird's common name honors George Calvert, Lord Baltimore, wealthy investor in colonial Maryland whose colorful orange and black coat-of-arms colors matched those of this bird. The term "oriole" comes from Latin, meaning "golden." European immigrants named the American bird after similar-looking but unrelated birds at home. Orioles were once thought to cure jaundice.

SPOTTING THE SPECTACULAR
Swing 'n Sway Masters

The Baltimore Oriole weaves an incredibly intricate nest that hangs by mere threads—long tough strands of grass or bark—a swinging pouch dangling and bobbing near branch's end, safe from snakes, raccoons, and most other predators. The female, however, typically builds the nest alone, the male occasionally visiting the site, as if in some supervisory capacity. The female stitches, using her beak as a needle, threading strands one at a time, knotting them loosely, apparently understanding instinctively that the stitches and knots tighten as the nest grows. Masterful, indeed!

Nest building among Baltimore Orioles surely requires the greatest talent among all avian contractors. But the female Baltimore Oriole comes well equipped. Her pointy bill, the perfect aid for stitching nests, reminds me of the oriole's cousin, the Red-winged Blackbird. Red-wings, too, have the ability to weave, winding cattail leaves around cattail stalks, suspending their tightly woven nests above water level. Some gene in the blackbird family must want their girls to be weavers and stitchers, for the exceptional skill is their mark of superiority.

Aside from the female's nest-building expertise, Baltimore Orioles come highly recommended for their stylish appearance. These lovelies wear carefully tailored orange and black outfits, the female's somewhat more subtle but unmistakable. Confusing costumes, however, can leave us mere humans scratching our heads. The tricky part, from the human perspective, lies in the fact that yearling males resemble mature females and do not molt into their more recognizable fiery-orange and black plumage until the fall of their second year. While some yearling males breed successfully, most don't breed the first year. So when a yearling male does breed, he and his mate seem a strange pair to bird-watchers trying to figure out who's who. Mostly, however, females look brown, not black, and lack any evidence of dark coloration at the throat. But then there's the age issue: the older the female, the brighter her plumage. If she lives long enough, it will be orange enough to closely resemble adult males. Is it any wonder that sometimes even the experts have been fooled!

NEST NOTES

Nest Site: selected by female, within male's territory; hangs from near ends of branches especially in elm, maple, cottonwood, and sycamore trees

Nest Construction: usually by female alone; sock-like hanging nest is woven of long, slender fibers, usually 4 in. deep, 3.5 in. nest cup diameter, and 3 in. opening, usually nearly invisible because of surrounding leaves; male occasionally brings nest materials, watches construction

Eggs: 3–7 eggs, 1 brood, incubated by female alone, 11–14 days; male remains nearby

Fledge: 11–14 days after hatch

Orioles tend to be hardy souls. If weather permits, some over-winter along the Gulf Coast. Most, however, arrive mid-April along the coast, having wintered farther south—in Mexico, Central America, and the very northern rim of South America. Thus, most of us in central and northern states don't see these summer nesters until about Mother's Day. Then, with breeding over, most orioles, young and old alike, disappear by mid-September, earlier the farther north you live. In general, many of us have the pleasure of these birds' company no more than three months or so, but what pleasure they bring us during their short stay.

BIRD TALK: WHO'S CALLING?
Flute-like paired notes, repeated two to seven times, are somewhat robin-like, full and rich, and last 1–2 seconds. The female also sings but her songs are shorter, quieter. Occasionally mated orioles duet.

Not only do we find pleasure in seeing their lovely plumage and marveling over their remarkable nests, but we enjoy the pleasure of the clear, whistled song. In fact, because Baltimore Orioles tend to feed in the high canopy, foraging for bugs, fruit, and nectar, we more often hear than see them. In my yard, during spring migration, when I do hear them, I crane my neck way back, searching for a glimpse of them high in the old tulip poplar tree where they'll be sipping nectar from the tulip-shaped flowers, sometimes dangling upside down, fluttering and stretching for nectar, and snagging bugs that the flowers attract.

Probably because I live a bit far from water, orioles have never nested in our yard. Mostly I find their nest sites near rivers and lakes, the nests sometimes dangling over roads or over the water itself. Preferring open areas to dense forest, orioles frequent parks, orchards, forest edge, and open areas, especially near large bodies of water.

FOOD FARE

Orioles eat insects, fruit, and nectar, occasionally visiting hummingbird feeders. In the garden, they eat pest insects, including tent caterpillars, fall webworms, and larvae within plant galls. They will also eat purple mulberries, garden fruits like raspberries, dark cherries, purple grapes, oranges, and bananas. At feeders, they accept nectar, orange halves, and grape jelly.

While some folks have great luck attracting Baltimore Orioles to nectar feeders, typically that happens only in spring during migration. Once breeding begins, orioles tend to abandon sweet stuff and go for protein, foraging entirely for insects in order to raise their babies. But early in the season, consider offering fruit, especially orange halves—tropical fruit for tropical birds—to draw hungry orioles to your yard.

Baltimore Orioles are attracted to orange halves and feed readily from them. Note that this male is banded.

ID CHECK

Because the eastern half of the United States hosts the small Orchard Oriole (so small it's often mistaken for a warbler) along with the larger and more common Baltimore Oriole, identify the Baltimore Oriole by looking for these specific markings:

- Male's bright fiery orange breast and belly
- Male's full black hood and bib
- Male's black wings with single bold white wing bar
- Female's yellow-orange breast and belly
- Female's brownish gray head and whitish throat
- Female's brownish gray wings with double, bold white wing bar

May

A bird does not sing
because it has an answer.
It sings because it has a song.

CHINESE PROVERB

April's transformation shaped the way for a gorgeous May. I marvel at the cycle, the renewal, the rebirth of both birds and bloom. In full leaf, trees that budded golden green in April's transformation now define "forest green" in deep, lush, verdant masses. Flowers that a month ago began wan and pale, in white and soft yellows, now burst bold. The rush is on. Life renews. And we celebrate.

The last week in April and the first two weeks in May rank, hands down, as my absolute favorite time of year. My giddiness over April's first migrant is replaced by my excitement over May's many migrants. While April holds title to "birdiest" month in the yard, the number reflects logistical overlaps: Winter visitors leave the first of the month, and spring and summer migrants flow in by month's end.

May, though, brings the hot-and-heavy wave of marvelous birds. Thrushes. Orioles. Tanagers. Grosbeaks. Vireos. And warblers. Ah, the warblers. Some pass through, perhaps nudging northward to where you live. Some sail in here to stay the summer.

In the avian world, since 1992, May marks International Migratory Bird Day, a day to celebrate the birds' migratory cycle, their annual return to our yards, forests, wetlands, and grasslands. The second Saturday in May boasts festivals and bird counts galore—maybe including a count in your own backyard habitat.

Marveling at Color

Among the May marvels: color. Oh, how I ogle the spring birds' rich colors. Breeding plumage literally defines "full color," like HDTV. Surely nothing lands at feeders prettier than male American Goldfinches, wearing brand-new bright gold suits, crisp black caps, and newly painted yellow-orange bills. They feed next to male Northern Cardinals, attired in brilliantly royal crimson, seasonally bright to impress the girls.

Together, in juxtaposition, the two residents form a hurt-your-eyes side-by-side gold-red that tops the "gorgeous" list. Nothing could be more striking.

HOW DOES YOUR GARDEN GROW?
Prime Planting Time

Here in southern Indiana, May means prime planting time. Oh, sure, the early cole crops went in last month, but May marks the time to add perennials, vines, bushes, trees, even annuals to the bird-friendly backyard. Maybe you made plans last winter, plotting better landscaping to add food, shelter, and nest sites for birds. If so, now's the time to cruise the nurseries in search of plants—preferably native—that offer nectar, berries, or seed; thorny shelters; and dense vegetation.

Didn't make plans last winter? It's not too late. Check suggestion lists throughout this book for a wide variety of ideas. The index will help you find lists quickly.

Oops! Wrong! Add a male Indigo Bunting, decked out in intense blue, broadening the color spectrum. Mother Nature doesn't paint many creatures blue; but when she does, it's an eyeful. So with the indigo's arrival, there you have it—gold, red, and blue, all vivid, all startlingly bright, all at the feeder together.

The combination makes me catch my breath. I know absolutely nothing could be more stunning.

Oops! Wrong again! A male Rose-breasted Grosbeak joins the rainbow, adding his crisp black and white suit and snappy rose-colored ascot to the colorful array.

Bright colors sprinkle the yard as migrants flow through, with some staying to nest while others move on. The Prothonotary Warbler (top, left) flashes brilliant yellow, the Indigo Bunting (top, right) splashes bright blue, the Rose-breasted Grosbeak (center, left) adds his bright-rosy throat patch, the Baltimore Oriole (center, right) is citrus orange, and the Chestnut-sided Warbler (left) combines rufous and dandelion yellow.

HABITAT—YOURS AND THEIRS
What Birds Teach Us about Habitat

Choosing plants for a bird-haven backyard habitat is complicated by the fact that different birds prefer different habitat. You already know that some birds like shrubby unmowed grasslands, others choose forest edges, some favor dense conifers, and so on. Watching birds we hope to attract, however, teaches us what they like.

So venture out and watch multiple habitats. Go early. Migrants have traveled all night. At dawn, they drop down to feed and rest for the day before taking to wing again at dusk. As a result, early morning yields best migratory bird watching. Listen for unusual songs, track down the source, and note the habitat. Then mimic that habitat in your backyard.

The migrant additions are all we need to prove that the color spectrum among springtime visitors brings the tropics to our doors.

And I've not yet mentioned the whole bevy of nonfeeder birds: Baltimore Orioles, their fire-bright orange and black combo. Or Scarlet Tanagers, their startlingly black wings against all-over deep red. Or Summer Tanagers, their robes of overall orangey red. Or Blue Grosbeaks that wear their name.

Other nonfeeder birds, the whole family of warblers, add dashes of lemon yellow, some solidly sunny, others flashing gold on heads, wings, backs, or breasts. Think Yellow, Yellow-throated, Canada, Wilson's, Black-throated Green, or Pine Warblers, just to tease your memory.

But it's no figure of speech to say these newly arrived rainbow birds bring us the tropics. They are, indeed, tropical birds. They spend the bulk of their lives in Central and South

The Blue Grosbeak, looking somewhat like a super-sized version of an Indigo Bunting, also boasts russet on wings and back.

America. But come spring, they fly thousands of miles to come here to nest, some spending more than half their lives in transit.

And every year their arrival reminds me that nothing can be prettier than a springtime backyard's rainbow, even beyond our beloved goldfinches and cardinals—a marvel of May, the ongoing cycle.

Dawn's Chorus

Another of May's marvels bursts forth in the form of what we affectionately call the dawn chorus, the blend of hundreds of bird voices: some high, some low, some raspy, some bell-like, some short and simple, some complicated and varied, some far off, some close by. Together, the jumble of notes sometimes makes who's singing what tough to sort out.

But what a delightfully marvelous way to start the day.

NOTABLE BEHAVIOR   **Stand Up and Sing!**

For birds, song is serious business. And just like an opera star, no bird sings sitting down. Many stretch to their tallest, as if somehow that makes the song more boisterous, more far reaching. Some throw their heads back, as if singing to the heavens. Some even sing on the wing. And here's an ID tip: Different birds take on different singing postures.

Watch! You'll see!

The clock reads 5:35 a.m. My wake-up call trills with robust enthusiasm two feet from the open bedroom window. A House Wren, only recently returned, has chosen one of our nest boxes as its own, and his early morning song, the first to awaken me, seals the deal.

Coming out of my sleepy fog, I recognize another dozen dawn choristers. Why do birds sing? Why more in spring than in other seasons? And why do they sing with greater gusto at dawn than at any other time?

BIOLOGY BITS   **How Birds Sing**

Humans have a larynx, or voice box, that gives us voice. Most birds have a syrinx instead. But it's all about location. The larynx is located at the top of the windpipe; the syrinx is located where the windpipe divides into the two tubes that go to the lungs. So birds are blessed with not one, but two voice boxes. They can sing duets with themselves!

For birds, song is communication, and as we noted in April, they expound on two topics: love and war. At dawn, most females lay their egg of the day; and at dawn, sound travels well in the quiet. So, yes, it's about love (meaning, in avian terms, reproduction) and war (stak-

A male Common Yellowthroat throws his head back to belt out his "witch-ety, witchety, witchety" song.

ing out and maintaining territory). And part of love and war is staying in touch. Somewhat amusingly, in fact, the Red-eyed Vireo seems to say, *Here I am,* and then ask, *Where are you?* Paired geese talk to each other as they fly, her honking higher pitched than his, assuring each of the other's well-being. Other birds talk to their mates quietly in chips and churrs, keeping in touch.

Bird songs, however, vary as much as birds themselves. Bluebirds burble soothing lullabies. Mourning Doves coo, yes, mournfully. Eastern Screech-Owls emit a quavering whistle that can strike fear among the brave. Scarlet Tanagers are said to sing like robins with a sore throat; Summer Tanagers, like robins that have had voice lessons. Yellow-breasted Chats jumble their song so much that they make me chuckle. Great-blue Herons squawk as annoyingly as fingernails on chalkboards. And eagles? Their cackle belies such a magnificent bird.

But birds have calls as well as songs—a chip, chirr, or chatter—also about love and war. Chips warn a nesting mate that trouble lurks or an intruder that it has trespassed. Calls lure fledglings from nests. Sometimes calls rally other species, urging their aid in ganging up on predators like snakes, cats, or roosting owls.

BIOLOGY BITS   **How Birds Learn Their Songs**

Some birds, like flycatchers, are born with their species song genetically ingrained. No learning, no practicing, no mistakes—and no variation. Most songbirds, however, learn their songs by listening during their infancy, a short frame of time in which they memorize what they hear, taking it for their own. Carolina Wrens, for instance, may sound somewhat different from one another, depending on where they grew up and what they heard as kids. Even so, these same birds don't usually get the song quite right until they've practiced, using their own ear to measure their song against the memorized melody. By the time breeding hormones kick in, they have it just right. And they have to get it right. How else can they impress the girls?

But variations occur. Song Sparrows, for instance, sing regionally different songs, reflective of their fathers, grandfathers, and great-grandfathers. Still other birds learn not from their fathers but from the other neighborhood guys, like Indigo Buntings, whose songs change over time to reflect the combined variations. And some birds break free from that narrow band of time in which they must memorize song and instead learn all their lives, compiling a vast array of melodies, as do mockingbirds, catbirds, and Brown Thrashers. One single Brown Thrasher was documented vocalizing 2,400 songs—a sure winner among the ladies.

For me, though, song and call serve another purpose. They catch my attention, sometimes because I know—or because I don't know—what I'll enjoy seeing when I locate the source. Last night, out for our evening walk, I heard a Common Nighthawk. I doubt I would have looked straight overhead without it alerting me of its presence.

Sometimes, however, finding the source drives me silly. At every opportunity, I listen and look for a Kentucky Warbler. When I hear him, I eye the undergrowth, straining for a glimpse of this stealthy, dense-woodland bird. Sometimes I actually track the sound to a bird, only to find not the warbler, but a Carolina Wren, whose song, at least to my ears, sounds similar.

The Kentucky Warbler can best be found by recognizing its song and then searching dense forested undergrowth for the bird.

Sometimes, though, the source of song or call eludes me, despite my best efforts. Even then, I'm pleased to know the bird is there, expounding on love and war. And when spring's dawn chorus seeps through my sleepy brain, I awake smiling, even at 5:35 a.m.

May Brides

Whether its song or its flight draws my attention, an unfamiliar bird in the yard guarantees an adrenaline rush, accompanied by a hushed "What's that?" But beyond the puzzle of identification—a puzzle usually solved with a quick flip through a field guide—the puzzle of a bird's behavior often remains unsolved. The intrigue is my favorite part of watching birds. Questioning who does what, when, and why, often leads me on lengthy chases through reference books and correspondence with those in the know.

Most decent early May mornings find me in the yard, huddled against early morning chill, watching treetops and tangles for migrants. But I'm easily distracted by who's doing what.

BIOLOGY BITS　　　　　　　**Changing Tunes**

Because of habitat degradation, many birds, especially those in the city, find themselves forced into less than desirable breeding habitat. The noise level—from traffic, industry, and construction—can dramatically interfere with their ability to communicate. They can't hear each other sing. Or call. And since song is about love and war, a bird whose song can't be heard faces life without love.

As a result, some birds are actually changing their tune. They may sing louder or at a higher pitch. Sadly, not all birds can make such changes. Populations of these species have fallen markedly in noisy zones.

Consider the love triangles that unfolded this week. A feisty foreign male Eastern Bluebird tried its best to break up a happy home. While the mated male fought his competitor to the ground, wings clashing like mini gladiators' swords, his loyal lady awaited the male's return atop their nest box. Surely all the wing fluttering and bobbing at battle's end was akin to welcome-home hugs and kisses.

NOTABLE BEHAVIOR

Territorial Terrorists Defending the Home Front

Have you seen them declare war? Breeding birds rise to battle against any intruder. Male goldfinches battle competing males, bill to toenail, right to the ground, sometimes with deadly results. Cardinals pursue interlopers in scolding hot-on-their-tails flight. Mockingbirds attack cats—even humans—pecking with vengeance any who venture into their territory. I've seen a Brown Thrasher pair take on a six-foot snake. The snake won, devouring the babies, but the battle was ferocious and brave, surely worthy of an avian Purple Heart. Little birds fearlessly take on big birds—like the diminutive Blue-gray Gnatcatcher I

watched bombarding a nesting Cooper's Hawk. The hawk ignored the persistent gnatcatcher, but what a dive-bomber that little gnatcatcher was! Even when accidental flight takes an innocent avian into the wrong part of town, attack brews. Only a hasty retreat saves the day.

When they were nest building, these two love-bird bluebirds, I watched the female tirelessly ferrying wads of pine straw into their chosen abode, stuffing beakful after beakful inside. Topside, the male waited, a pudgy green caterpillar in bill. When the female popped back out, he fed her the tasty treat, saving none for himself. How sweet. Surely the equivalent of roses and chocolates, don't you think?

I caught the Carolina Chickadees kissing, too, when they were plucking bugs along the dangling twigs of a little elm, hanging upside down, perhaps the better to see the underleaf sides where bugs hide. The site of their little tryst was none too secret, right there along the woods' edge. One flew to the other. The male fed the female a select morsel, and they touched beaks, twittering in the quiet way they have of talking privately to each other.

Cardinals kiss, too, did you know? It's rather like the groom kissing the bride at the conclusion of the wedding ceremony. The deal is sealed. The male offers the female a seed, and beak to beak, she gently plucks it from him. Can't you hear those wedding bells? A Red-shouldered Hawk, however, gave me a glimpse of coy and clever. Breaking off a foot-long willow branch, it carried the

A female Eastern Bluebird carries nest materials to the nestbox she and her mate have chosen.

branch in its beak to an adjoining tree, shifted the branch to its talons, and made three more lead-the-observer-astray flights before ducking through dense trees to where I'm sure its mate had hidden a nest. Then it repeated the process. Two days later, I watched it repeat the process yet again, this time with a cluster of last year's oak leaves. Maybe not chocolates and roses, but surely equal to tidying up for its beloved.

Marvels of the Air Arrive

Another set of his-and-her behaviors ranks all-out fascinating. Ruby-throated Hummingbirds, little marvels that they are, can fly in any direction, backward, forward, even upside down. Iridescent jewels of the air, they usually arrive at my feeders in mid-April, but only in numbers few, as they move through on their way, perhaps, as far north as Canada. But now, in mid-May, multiple males battle over feeders while females slip in, sip quickly, and zip off. If I didn't work where the feeder hangs 3 feet from my window, I'd miss their 5-second visits. The mating ritual, though, that daring, dizzying, jet-speed swooping flight up and down and back surely impresses the girls.

FEEDER FOCUS
Six Criteria for Choosing a Hummingbird Feeder

When hummingbirds show up in your yard, treat them well and they'll return. Consider the following criteria for a hummer-friendly feeder:

- Appearance. Choose a feeder designed for birds, not for people; functional, not fancy.
- Durability. Glass feeders last longer than plastic ones.
- Color. Red attracts hummingbirds. Use red *on* the feeder, *not in* the feeder.

Female Ruby-throated Hummingbirds make only quick stops at feeders during incubation season.

- Size. Larger is not always better. Choose feeders that hummers can empty in less than three days.
- Ant/bee Guards. Look for feeders with built-in guards to discourage ants and bees.
- Perches. They're optional but give hummers a chance to rest and you a chance to watch.

By mid-May in southern Indiana, female hummers have built nests, mated, laid eggs, and are incubating. Eggs hatch in two weeks. Late this month or early next, females will be feeding young. By the last two weeks of June, female hummers' lives grow even more hectic. Babies fledge, so they're feeding fledglings and, simultaneously, building new nests for another brood—at least where the season allows a second nesting.

We can't expect hordes of hummers at feeders now. The female leaves her nest for only two minutes or so. Without her 108-degree body incubating eggs, they cool quickly.

But one final factor changes May's hummingbird feeder landscape. When lush and profuse blossoms offer hummers bountiful nectar, they have little reason to seek feeders. And given hummers' habit of returning to ancestral flower patches, birds may, in fact, neglect feeders for some weeks. Sometimes an idle feeder means an abundantly productive native habitat—lots of bugs (60 percent of their diet) and nectar (40 percent). So, watch how your garden grows.

HOW DOES YOUR GARDEN GROW?
Feeding Hummers the Natural Way

I know folks who never hang hummingbird feeders but have a yard full of delightful little hummers. It's all about their gardens. Good hummingbird plants offer nectar, attract tiny

Sage with feeding hummingbird.

insects, and draw the birds. Since more than half of a hummer's diet is bugs, choose a good combination of bug-loving nectar-producing plants. Here are my top ten picks:

- Columbine, *Aguilegia canadensis* (native; cultivars not as attractive to hummers)
- Coral bells, *Heuchera americana* (native; cultivars not as attractive to hummers)
- Trumpet honeysuckle, *Lonicera sempervirens* (native)
- Scarlet runner bean, *Phaseolus coccineus* (annual vine; excellent fall nectar source)
- Zinnia, *Zinnia* spp. (annual)
- Hyacinth bean vine, *Dolichos lablab purpureus* (annual vine; excellent fall nectar source; beans edible)
- Rose of Sharon, *Hibiscus syriacus* (non-native; will naturalize)
- Butterfly bush, *Buddleia* spp. (can be invasive in southern zones; illegal in some states)
- Beebalm, *Monarda didyma* (native)
- Sage, *Artemisia* spp. (many colors; hummer favorite in my garden: blue)

Memorable Moments: Monster Memory

Hummingbirds possess the uncanny ability to remember—and return to—a given spot where in previous years they found nectar, either in flowers or feeders. Or so I've read. But one year, that uncanny ability hit home. The window at my kitchen sink frames two hummingbird feeders, so the little jewels entertain me while I work. What pleasures I enjoy, following their tactics for commandeering feeders and waging their ferocious battles. I've always heard that hummers may look cute, but if they were big enough, they'd eat you! Ferocious, indeed.

WATER WAYS **Frogs in the Water—A Threat to Birds**

Good habitat of course includes water, and water attracts frogs. In fact, a good variety of frogs and toads indicates healthy habitat. But, startling as it may be, frogs rank as the number two predator of hummingbirds. But, oh, please don't do anything to eliminate or harm the frogs. Rather, avoid planting hummer-attracting flowers overarching the edges of your water feature where the frogs bask. As hummers hover to feed, frogs flip out a long tongue and snag lunch. Beware.

In the midst of my kitchen-sink tasks one mid-April, I was brought up short, suddenly realizing that I was tardy hanging my feeders. And what reminded me? A hummingbird perched two feet from the window, on the rod that last year held its feeder. It seemed to be peering in the window at me, as if to say, "Hey, I'm here. Where's the food?" Okay, that's what my anthropomorphic mind read into the bird's perching. In reality, It had simply returned to the precise spot where it remembered feeding last year. Who knows exactly where it's been since then on its travels to and from Costa Rica. Yet it knew exactly where to return, the exact yard, the exact perch. And I have trouble getting across town on the orange-barrel express. Need I add that feeders were filled and out within minutes?

Why Do Hummingbirds Visit Last Year's Flowerbeds?

Even though they've traveled thousands of miles and have been absent from your yard for seven or eight months, returning hummingbirds remember exactly where they found flowers last year. Given their minuscule brains, they have remarkable memories. In fact, research shows that while feeding, they remember which specific flowers they've already visited and remember how often and when those same flowers will replenish nectar. Why go elsewhere when you know the neighborhood?

Dying to Try Dye?

Let's be up front and honest here: Red dye in hummingbird nectar has seriously negative effects on the birds. Well, true, you won't find the ground under your hummer feeders littered with tiny dead bodies. No, the danger is far more insidious than that, less visible, but of equally serious consequences.

Everyone knows red attracts hummers; so some years ago, folks began adding red dye to nectar. Until now, manufacturers, retailers, and even some hummer hosts claimed there was no evidence that red dye could be harmful. At the same time, however, we know that initially in Europe and finally here, we've banned certain red dyes for human consumption. "So what?" you ask. Hummers aren't human, right?

Responsible hummingbird hosts put red on the feeder, not in the feeder. In one day, swarms of hummingbirds can nearly empty feeders filled with clear nectar, made with one cup of granulated cane sugar and four cups of water. Red dye in feeder nectar has been proven to be harmful to hummers' health.

Now, however, the evidence is in. Sheri Williamson, author of the *Peterson Field Guide to the Hummingbirds of North America* and one of this nation's foremost experts on hummingbirds, writes: "Hummingbird experts have long discouraged the use of colored feeder solutions as unnatural and unnecessary, but there was little more than anecdotal evidence to suggest how synthetic dyes might affect the birds' health. Now studies on humans, lab animals and even cell cultures are providing that evidence without turning the hummingbirds into 'guinea pigs.'"

FEEDER FOCUS
A Dozen Do's and Don'ts for Hummer Feeding

- *Do* hang feeders April 1 until December 30.
- *Do* keep feeders clean, fresh. Change syrup (four parts water, one part white granulated cane sugar) every two or three days.
- *Do* wash feeders with each filling, using hot water and bottle brush. For heavy soil, use soapy water; rinse, rinse, rinse.
- *Do* use cotton swabs or pipe cleaners to clean crevices.
- *Do* use denture cleanser to effervesce tiny parts like bee guards.
- *Do* use moat-type ant guards. They contain only water, not pesticides, and last for years, saving you money.
- *Don't* use pesticides. Hummers' diet is 60 percent protein from tiny flying insects. Kill bugs in your yard and you kill hummers' food supply.
- *Don't* use ant guards that contain pesticides or say "Keep out of the reach of children." Choose water-filled moats instead.
- *Don't* use red dye or commercial nectars that include red dye. Dye may harm birds' kidneys and may affect their reproductive ability.
- *Don't* use commercially prepared nectars that include additives; they can be harmful to birds and waste your money.
- *Don't* use molasses, honey, or artificial sweeteners.
- *Don't* hang feeders in direct sun or within reach of frogs or cats.

While citing research and resulting bans of synthetic red dyes in places around the world—from Great Britain to Japan, including Austria, Belgium, Denmark, France, Germany, Sweden, and Switzerland—Williamson notes that American researchers found that in high doses, some red dyes "significantly reduced reproductive success, parental and offspring weight, brain weight, survival, (and) increased behavioral abnormalities."

Referring specifically to the red dyes used in manufactured hummingbird nectar, Williamson notes, "The most alarming aspect of these studies is that many of the harmful effects were dose-dependent: The larger the dosage of dye, the greater the effect."

Given that, think about this: A hummingbird weighs one-tenth of an ounce. Depending on the quality of the nectar, a hummer may drink two or more times its body weight in nectar daily. As Williamson concludes, "If that sugar-water is dyed . . . the bird would take in 10 times the daily dosage of dye that produced DNA damage in the Japanese study."

It gets worse: Given cold weather or weight gain necessary for migration, hummers may double their nectar intake, further exacerbating an already serious problem.

FEEDER FOCUS   **Responsible Hummingbird Feeding**

Given the serious ramifications of red dye in commercial hummingbird nectar, what's a good hummer host to do? Make your own syrup, mixing 1 cup water and ¼ cup white granulated cane sugar. Stir well and serve. By replacing syrup every other day, there's no need to boil and cool. Making your own saves dollars. But if it's too much trouble to stir and serve, then at least purchase only clear nectar. If that's not possible, hummers will be better off without your feeders.

In short, here's the mantra for hummer hosts: Put red *on* the feeder, not *in* the feeder. Please pass the word.

Learning from Birds about Habitat

Because birds are linked irrevocably to the vegetation around them, when you add vegetation, you add birds. Not only do you increase the number of birds, but you also increase the number of species. At the same time, you will improve the health of the environment as well as your own and that of your neighborhood. Who can argue with that?

So watch the birds in your yard—not those at your feeders but in your habitat's vegetation. Over the past weeks, I've watched Scarlet Tanagers and Rose-breasted Grosbeaks frequent tulip poplar trees, enjoying the blossoms' nectar and the bugs the nectar attracts. As nectar lovers, Baltimore Orioles also love tulip poplar blossoms, but they also readily feed in our oaks and black locusts, also now in bloom.

Baltimore Orioles fly in regularly to forage for bugs and feed on nectar-rich black locust blossoms.

PROBLEM SOLVER **Helping Avian Orphans**

Assuming your habitat merits nesting birds, sooner or later you'll likely find a baby bird, seemingly alone, perhaps on the ground, maybe low in a bush. What should you do? Generally, nothing. Unless cats roam your yard (a serious problem in itself), leave the baby alone. The parents are nearby; they know where their baby is; they will tend to it. Meanwhile, keep the cats at bay.

Magnolia Warblers, Yellow-breasted Chats, and Red-eyed Vireos seem drawn solely to the black locust trees. And among them, a trio of flycatchers—Least, Yellow-breasted, and Acadian—dart about, also in hot pursuit of bugs the locust nectar attracts. The Great Crested Flycatcher, however, prefers tall trees and darts after bugs from forest edge.

A Gray Catbird sings daily from the thicket down the backyard's hill, an area we quit mowing about fifteen years ago. Native grapevines now wrap through downed sugar maple branches and climb an old black cherry tree. Brambles reign supreme. Catbird paradise!

HABITAT—YOURS AND THEIRS
Vegetation Magnets

You can improve vegetation in the tiniest of yards. Even little patches of special habitat will attract additional birds and additional species. Consider an unmowed section filled with seedy weeds, a cluster of fruiting shrubs, some rambling vines grown over a trellis or draped across a fence. Leave a dead tree standing (if it's not dangerous, of course) for woodpeckers. Shrubby undergrowth draws birds like a magnet.

After having done these things myself, my yard list soared from about 100 species to 166—and still growing. As my habitat grows more lush, my bird list grows, too.

Common Yellowthroats pop up from the low tangles of our wild blackberry patch. But they also explore a monster brush pile formed with this year's apple-tree prunings. The brambles and brush pile share two characteristics that attract secretive birds: They offer low-to-the-ground dense cover, and they're largely impenetrable by hawks and some other predators.

What do these birds teach us? They like native plants—tulip poplar, oak, black locust, black cherry, native grapevines, wild blackberries. Native plants attract birds because they and their blossoms host native bugs. Result? Bird magnets.

Many migrants, however, prefer upper canopy cover, so nectar-producing trees draw more birds than shrubby

Skulking birds such as Common Yellowthroat like dense tangles offered by wild blackberries.

nectar plants. And secretive species demand dense cover. If dense cover also harbors bugs, birds hit the jackpot. And how many migrants do we see in well-manicured, chemically treated lawns? Mmmm? None.

A watchful eye will teach you more.

Pledge to Cut Your Grass—At Least in Half

Here's a conversation starter: Annually, we spend $25 billion on a crop that we douse with ten times more chemical pesticide per acre than we do farmland. The crop? Lawns.

According to the EPA, we pour 30 to 60 percent of our water consumption onto lawns so that 70 million tons of fertilizers work to make the grass grow. Then we cut it. To run lawn-mowers, we burn 580 million gallons of gasoline, which at $4 a gallon, amounts to $2.32 billion each year. That's billion, with a "b." Adjust the figures according to today's price of gas.

Let's make the situation worse: According to the National Vehicle and Fuel Emissions Lab in Ann Arbor, a lawnmower spews out in one hour as much hydrocarbon as an auto driven fifty miles. (String trimmers are twice as bad; leaf blowers, three times worse.) Then we bag the grass, put it at the curb and, nationally, fill up 20 to 40 percent of landfill space. According to the National Wildlife Federation, a 40- by 100-foot lawn produces 1,200 pounds of clippings annually.

Female Baltimore Orioles love the long, stringy bark from wild grape-vines to weave into their hanging-basket nests.

HOW DOES YOUR GARDEN GROW?
Heard It on the Grapevine

If you watch birds in the wild, migrants and nesters alike flock to wild grapevines. A whole array of warblers and vireos, for instance, dine on the bugs the vines attract. Many avian species cherish the little grapes as they ripen in June or July. And female orioles reach great lengths—literally—to strip grapevine bark for weaving their hanging-basket nests. If for no other reason, birds seek the vines to cradle their own nests and to find protection against winter winds.

So, in some of that space you gain by foregoing lawn, plant grapevines along an arbor or trellis or any other support—even a dead tree—and watch the birds love it. Or, if you're so fortunate, nurture a wild grapevine already in place in your habitat.

As a nation, we spend these billions of dollars, pollute the air, waste water, overrun landfills, and contaminate our water wells only to produce biological wastelands—or worse. Lawns have virtually no value to wildlife, offer no food, no cover, no nesting sites. But worse yet, the applied pesticides and chemical fertilizers turn wastelands into toxic dumps. Then we send our pets and children out to play.

Ninety-eight percent of all birds feed their babies bugs, including larval forms, like the cater-pillar this Eastern Bluebird carries to his nestlings.

A friendly backyard wildlife habitat can't exist in a toxic dump. For instance, typical pesticide applications eliminate up to 90 percent of earthworms, major contributors to soil health. Annually, pesticides poison 60 to 70 million birds. Less than 10 percent of insects are harmful to plants, yet pesticides kill them all. Since most birds eat insects, the handwriting is on the wall—or, rather, in the grass.

WHY DO BIRDS DO THAT?
Why Do Birds Attack Windows?

A common question goes like this: What should I do about this bird that keeps throwing itself against my window? It's making a terrible mess.

And the answer goes like this: Your bird sees its reflection in your window. It doesn't see the reflection as a companion, but as an intruder into its territory. So you're witnessing a soldier at war, not a lover in pursuit. The only solution: eliminate the "enemy." That is, eliminate the reflection. If you have screens for your windows, put them in place to break up reflection. Or tack mesh in place over the windows. Find rolls of very light-weight, screen-wire-like plastic mesh at hardware or big box stores. Stretched across the outside of the window, it's hardly noticeable from inside. Other folks have come up with similar inventive methods to break up the reflection. A hint to the efficient: The cleaner the window, the sharper the reflection. Good enough excuse for me to skip washing windows—especially during breeding season.

Mow borders and paths to reduce lawn and improve habitat—yours and theirs.

Think about this. In summer, bluebirds live entirely on insects and caterpillars and feed their babies the same. Hummingbirds sip nectar to have the energy to be the bug-eating machines that they are. Barn Swallows, Tree Swallows, and Purple Martins consume vast numbers of flying bugs—and only flying bugs. Flickers stick to a diet of ants. Song Sparrows and Eastern Towhees pick bugs from the leaf litter and low-growing plants. All the flycatchers, including pewees and phoebes, live entirely on bugs. A habitat without bugs is a habitat with few birds. Pesticides kill the bugs.

BOTANY FOR BIRDS **Instead of Grass**

Most conservation organizations recommend that we cut our lawns—in half. So how can we implement the recommendation?

Mow borders and paths instead of vast stretches. Let a back corner grow wild. Plant it with brambles and dense shrubs for wildlife cover. Plant a patch of native grasses and perennials. Blossoms and seeds serve up a fine menu for nectar- and pollen-loving birds, bees, and butterflies. And seed-loving birds get the dessert.

Use natural mulch (shredded leaves or hardwood chips) around shrubs and trees, among flowerbeds, and along walkways. Add ground covers. They offer protection and nursery sites for some critters, including ground-nesting birds.

And for what lawn remains, use a mulcher mower and put the nutrients back in the ground. Skip the chemicals. And enjoy the influx of birds.

Conservation Corner: Migratory Stopover Sites in Decline

According to the Smithsonian Migratory Bird Center (SMBC; http://nationalzoo.si.edu), the serious decline and/or degradation of stopover sites for migratory birds significantly reduces the probability of the birds' breeding success—and even of their very survival.

Think about it this way: Imagine you're driving a 1,200-mile route you've taken before. You know the way. As your low-fuel warning light blinks on and as you realize you're hungry, you look forward to the travel/gas station you know is just ahead. Unfortunately, however, when you arrive, the facility is closed. No gas. No food. But, unlike birds, you can summon help. It's just a cell-phone call or GPS calculation away. For birds finding familiar stopover sites bulldozed and developed, no such help exists. They perish.

So the push is on to conserve stopover sites. As the SMBC notes, "Inland stopover areas will continue to be affected by land use policies, especially with regards to development, ranching, agriculture, forestry, and oil exploration. A balance between economic needs and the needs of migrants will have to be sought in order for the grand phenomenon of avian migration to continue. Economic growth based on bird watching and ecotourism is proving to be a successful alternative in a number of key stopover areas across the globe."

In some small way, each of us can help by creating good habitat in our own backyards and encouraging our neighbors to do the same. All of us together can make a difference—in fact, a big difference. And then we can continue to enjoy a marvelous May.

Things to Do in May

Given the waves of migrants moving through the yard in May, give these to-do matters priority:

- Keep water fresh and, preferably, moving, since the sound of bubbling, dripping, rippling, or cascading water helps thirsty migrants find your water feature.
- Avoid any application of any kind of pesticides—now and forever more.
- Take the pledge to cut your lawn—at least in half.
- Use spring planting time to add more vegetation: bushes, shrubs, trees, perennials, vines.
- Hang hummingbird feeders filled with clear nectar, using red only *on* the feeder, not *in* the feeder.
- Set aside an unmowed corner of the yard this year, allowing native plants to flower and seed.

79 Yard Birds in May

The Second Birdiest Month of the Year!

Canada Goose
Wood Duck
Mallard
Northern Bobwhite
Green Heron
Turkey Vulture
Cooper's Hawk
Red-shouldered Hawk
Mourning Dove
Black-billed Cuckoo
Yellow-billed Cuckoo
Barred Owl
Common Nighthawk
Chimney Swift
Ruby-throated
   Hummingbird
Red-bellied Woodpecker
Downy Woodpecker
Hairy Woodpecker
Northern Flicker
Pileated Woodpecker
Eastern Wood-pewee
Yellow-bellied Flycatcher
Acadian Flycatcher
Least Flycatcher
Eastern Phoebe
Great Crested Flycatcher

Eastern Kingbird
White-eyed Vireo
Philadelphia Vireo
Red-eyed Vireo
Blue Jay
American Crow
Purple Martin
Northern Rough-winged
   Swallow
Barn Swallow
Carolina Chickadee
Tufted Titmouse
White-breasted Nuthatch
Carolina Wren
House Wren
Blue-gray Gnatcatcher
Eastern Bluebird
Gray-cheeked Thrush
American Robin
Gray Catbird
Northern Mockingbird
Brown Thrasher
European Starling
Cedar Waxwing
Tennessee Warbler
Nashville Warbler
Northern Parula

Chestnut-sided Warbler
Magnolia Warbler
Cape May Warbler
Blackburnian Warbler
Yellow-throated Warbler
American Redstart
Common Yellowthroat
Yellow-breasted Chat
Eastern Towhee
Chipping Sparrow
Field Sparrow
Song Sparrow
Lincoln's Sparrow
White-crowned Sparrow
Summer Tanager
Scarlet Tanager
Northern Cardinal
Rose-breasted Grosbeak
Indigo Bunting
Red-winged Blackbird
Eastern Meadowlark
Common Grackle
Brown-headed Cowbird
Baltimore Oriole
House Finch
American Goldfinch
House Sparrow

SPECIES PROFILE

RUBY-THROATED HUMMINGBIRD

VITAL STATS
Length: 2.8–3.5 in.
Wingspan: 3.1–4.3 in.
Weight: 0.1 oz.

Top, left: *Ruby-throated Hummingbird, male;* bottom: *Ruby-throated Hummingbird, female;* top, right: *Ruby-throated Hummingbird, hatch-year male*

In late February, after they reach the Gulf Coast from Central America, Ruby-throated Hummingbirds feed several weeks, replacing fat losses from their super-heroic, nonstop, roughly 800-mile flight across the Gulf. Then, it's northward, ho!

NAME THAT BIRD
Archilochus colubris (Ruby-throated Hummingbird): This bird's name honors Greek lyric poet Archilochus who created a number of poetic forms. *Colubris* (*colubri* or *colibri*) translates as "hummingbird" in French and Spanish. Its common name recognizes the male's throat color while the term "hummingbird" refers to the sound the bird makes in flight, especially while hovering.

The arrival of Ruby-throated Hummingbirds announces spring for more backyard birders than that of any other bird, maybe because these birds are tiny, ferocious, beautiful, fast, curious, nimble, smart—and well traveled. That a tiny bird can fly 2,000 miles, spend the winter, then fly 2,000 miles back, fighting storms, cold fronts, and sometimes freezing nighttime temperatures, and return to a specific ancestral nesting and feeding site—well, it leaves us lumbering, land-bound humans awestruck.

Consider the amazing details: Ten hummingbirds together weigh 1 ounce. During migration, hummers fly 18–20 hours nonstop across the Gulf of Mexico, losing half their body weight. High metabolism powers wing beats of 60 times a second in normal flight, 200 beats a second during courtship flights (songbirds beat their wings only about 5 times a second), body temperature of 108°F, respiration rate of 250 breaths a minute, heart rate of 1,000 beats a minute. By comparison, a 150-pound human with similar metabolism would have to eat 80 meals of 1,000 calories a day just to stay alive.

BIRD TALK: WHO'S CALLING?
The most common hummingbird sound is nonvocal—that of their wing whir. They also call a very rapid monotone chip or *tidt-tidt-tidt* to each other during a chase or sometimes during flight.

While hummers can fly in any direction, including upside down, they can neither walk nor hop. They can shuffle sideways, awkwardly, along a branch, but they're not anatomically designed to navigate other than by wing.

Called "jewels of the air" for their iridescent emerald-green backs and the male's glowing ruby-red throat, hummers are anything but gem-like. If you've been paying attention, hummers are neither gentle nor sweet. They're warriors. Fierce and mean. If they were big enough, they'd eat you. While maybe their battles look playful, the appearance is likely only the result of their tiny size. If hummers were the size of eagles, you wouldn't let your children watch. Think dirty wrestling, body slamming, foot fighting, bill poking, biting.

Why the ferocious territorial fights? Food. Because hummers have an especially high metabolism, they're only hours from starvation at any moment in their lives. Protecting their food sources—your feeder or your garden flowers—is tantamount to survival. Battles are, quite literally, a matter of life or death.

FOOD FARE
Contrary to popular belief, 60 percent of a hummingbird's diet is small insects. They also take nectar, especially from tubular flowers, and they come readily to nectar feeders. Sometimes they dine on tree sap, especially when nectar is scarce.

The aggression, however, goes beyond other hummers. In fact, hummingbirds will attack hawks to protect territory. Ironically, though, they're lunch for frogs and praying mantises. In fact, Asian praying mantises (as opposed to our native insects) carry the unlikely title of hummingbirds' number-one predator.

Of course, the earliest hummers to arrive in Indiana and parts south don't stay. They're in a hurry, on their way north, perhaps as far as Canada, racing for the best territories and the prettiest girls. The earliest birds have the farthest to go.

"Our" hummers, the ones that nest here in southern Indiana, arrive in late April, making quick feeder forays. They, too, seem in a rush, here to get an early start on double broods. In fact, early season feeder visits are typically so seconds-quick that, *zip*, and they're gone, back to building nests and incubating eggs. Unless we have nothing else to do and monitor our hummer feeders 100 percent of the time, most of those speedy visits we never see.

Nevertheless, feeders do draw hummers up close for backyard bird lovers. But feeders, while they satisfy our viewing pleasure, offer only convenience for birds. Tiny bugs and natural nectar, both found among annuals, perennials, vines, shrubs, bushes, and even trees, rank far more important to hummers than do feeders. But early, before flowers bloom profusely, hummers also visit sap wells. In our yard, Yellow-bellied Sapsuckers drill rows and rows of sap wells on sugar maples, enjoying—and unwittingly providing for hummers—their own version of maple syrup.

SPOTTING THE SPECTACULAR
Sipping Soda through a Straw—Not

Until recently, scientists thought hummers sipped nectar, almost as if through a straw, the straw-like function attributed to the bird's tongue and capillary action. But in 2011, a University of Connecticut graduate student, Alejandro Rico-Guevara, videographed a high-speed, high-definition recording that showed a bird with a fringed forked tongue.

When a hummer inserts its tongue into nectar, the tongue, less than 1 millimeter thick, which is about half the thickness of a dime, spreads out into forked tubes. The tubes are fringed with hair-like fleshy extensions, and the fringes fan out to gather nectar. As the hummer retracts its tongue, the tubes zip closed, trapping the nectar, carrying it into the bird's mouth. As Rico-Guevara says, "The hummingbird tongue is a fluid trap, not a capillary tube." And hummers can slurp syrup 20 times per second.

As birds go, a female hummingbird faces a daunting lifestyle. The perfect single mom, she builds her nest, incubates eggs, and while building a second nest, feeds her first young—all entirely alone. Once second nests are underway and the breeding cycle ends, the male, having fulfilled his only purpose, returns to Costa Rica. Where I live, that means he's gone by mid-August, and the only males at feeders after that are those moving through from parts farther north.

NEST NOTES

Nest Site: selected by female, located on top (not in a fork) of a slender branch 10–40 ft. up, often in coniferous trees but also in pine

Nest Construction: by female alone, made of dandelion or thistle fluff, pasted together with spider web, sometimes "painted" on the outside with pine sap for sturdiness, and covered with lichen or moss, 2 in. by 1 in., resembling a large thimble

Eggs: 1–3 eggs, 1–2 broods, incubated only by female, 12–14 days

Fledge: 18–20 days after hatch

As soon as the female fledges her second brood, she feeds heavily, fattening up, doubling her weight in only 7–10 days. Then she, too, heads south, leaving youngsters to fend for themselves. These two groups of juveniles join migrants to swarm feeders in late August through most of September, the busiest time for hummer hosts. From banding studies, we know that these creatures of habit visit the same feeding sites on almost the same day year after year.

While length of day tells hummers when to leave, it appears that their migration may be timed to coincide with the peak flowering of jewelweed, sometimes called touch-me-not (*Impatiens biflora*). Thus, adding the native plant to your garden may be a life-saver for late migrants.

How hummers know the route to Costa Rica and how they know the wintering site when they arrive—these remain mysteries. But by late September or early October, many ruby-throats have reached their destination, ready to molt and fight a new round of battles for food.

No wonder backyard birders treasure these fascinating jewels of the air.

ID CHECK

With some winter-time exceptions, Ruby-throated Hummingbirds hold a hummer monopoly in the eastern United States, so we mostly concern ourselves with differentiating among males, females, and juveniles.

- Mature males wear a throat patch, called a gorget, which shows ruby red in good light but black in poor light.
- Males and females have iridescent green backs, wings, and tails.
- Mature males have solid-colored forked tails; females have rounded tails with a white dot on the end of each tail feather.
- Immature males and females closely resemble mature females.
- In late fall, immature males may show a few red throat spots, the beginnings of a gorget.

INDIGO BUNTING

Above: *Indigo Bunting, male;* center: *Indigo Bunting, female;* bottom: *Indigo Bunting, first-spring male*

VITAL STATS
Length: 4.7–5.1 in.
Wingspan: 7.5–8.7 in.
Weight: 0.5 oz.

In late April, when the Indigo Buntings first return to my yard from Central America and the Caribbean, they arrive in multitudes. Typically ground feeders, a dozen or so may dot the yard under niger-seed (thistle-seed) feeders. Surely nothing in the spring yard is more eye-catching than indigo blue feeding shoulder-to-shoulder with red Northern Cardinals, gold American Goldfinches, and another new arrival, rose-bibbed black-and-white Rose-breasted Grosbeaks. What a foursome, this treat for the eyes!

NAME THAT BIRD

Passerina cyanea (Indigo Bunting): *Passerina* means "sparrow-like," a term used to refer to many small birds. *Cyanea,* a Greek derivative, means "dark blue," the bird's overall color. Its common name, "indigo," also names its color, while "bunting" is believed to come from an Old English word meaning "plump."

Some Indigo Buntings, however, arrive a bit ragged looking, as if they've somehow missed the assembly-line paint booth. Splotchy back and wings, they're poor excuses for an Indigo Bunting. But just give them time. These are first-spring males, not yet molted into their full adult plumage. Some weeks from now, molt complete, they, too, will be dazzlingly gorgeous and meet our highest expectations of blue.

The dirt-drab female, though, remains destined to be the true plain Jane of the avian world. Of course, if I had to sit quietly in a nest where she prefers to build, I'd want drab dress too, for she nests about 3 feet off the ground where predators seem likely. Concealment means protection—and survival.

Early in the season, before annual vegetation has reached sufficient height, the female will choose thorny brambles or shrubby understory for her nest. Later, however, she may nest a second or even third time, building a new nest for each brood, in now-lush annuals like goldenrod, stinging nettle, cow parsnip, or Joe-pye weed, weaving its masterful abode firmly to lateral or oblique branches. Sometimes in late winter, I'll find its nest, still tight, still snug, despite the ravages of wind and rain, on a stoic stalk in my weed patch: a marvel.

NEST NOTES

Nest Site: chosen by female, in shrubs and annual vegetation located in fields, woods edges, roadsides or railroad rights-of-way, usually within 3 ft. of ground

Nest Construction: built by female alone, open cup of dead leaves, grass stems, and bark strips; lined with fine grasses, thistle down, rootlets; outside diameter about 3 in., inside 2 in., inside depth 1.5 in.; early nests often larger than later nests

Eggs: 3–4 eggs, 1–2 broods, incubated by female alone, 12–13 days; males show no interest in nest or nestlings

Fledge: 10–12 days after hatch

All spring and summer, I hear the male indigo singing, usually from a high, open perch, proclaiming his presence to the world. For such a tiny bird, his paired-notes song seems overly loud. And way too persistent. Sun up to sun down. Sometimes he sings within the same minute he's feeding. Does he never pause for breath? Gotta love his persistence.

BIRD TALK: WHO'S CALLING?

Males warble a consistent pattern of paired notes. While the pattern remains essentially the same throughout the male's life, his pattern will be different from that of other male Indigo Buntings. Listen for a song more patterned than melodic.

Among birds, song is always about love and war, and a male indigo defines and defends his territory aggressively. On average, a single pair of Indigo Buntings will call 3.5 acres home. But make no mistake: This bird is no knight in shining armor. The female builds the nest alone, incubates alone, feeds babes alone, all without any overt support from the master of song. Occasionally, after babies fledge, males accept certain parenting duties, especially if this participation encourages the female to start another nest.

So these lovelies from the tropics tend to arrive in my yard in late April and busy themselves with nests and babies until late August. Song ceases. But I may see stragglers even in October—most likely northerly birds making their way south, using my habitat for a welcome stopover along their approximately 1,200-mile journey.

FOOD FARE

Indigo Buntings eat a variety of small insects and spiders, especially during breeding season, and add small seed and buds to their diets as available. At feeders, they will forage on the ground for spilled thistle seed.

SPOTTING THE SPECTACULAR
Learning the Musical Score

We might expect that an Indigo Bunting sounds like an Indigo Bunting in Ohio, Florida, or Maine. But maybe not. They'll likely be enough alike to recognize wherever you are; but indigos, like most oscine passerines, learn their songs from their fathers or their neighbors. It's possible, then, that the local dialect may vary slightly from one region to another, but Indigo Buntings in the same neighborhood sound remarkably alike—very much like a cultural dialect. Over 20 years or so, though, even the neighborhood song might change slightly, as individual males add their variations and the neighbor's kids pick up the dialect, in turn adding their own variations. I have to wonder: Who keeps track of the original score?

ID CHECK

The male Indigo Bunting is our only overall-blue bird. Note the following details.

- Male overall blue with black wing feathers
- Female overall mousey gray-brown with hint of blue on tail feathers and outer wing feathers
- Silvery conical bill
- First-year spring male splotchy blue, some more solidly blue than others
- Distinguished from Eastern Bluebird by bluebird's rusty breast and white belly
- Distinguished from Blue Grosbeak by grosbeak's chestnut-colored wing patches and larger size

SPECIES PROFILE

ROSE-BREASTED GROSBEAK

VITAL STATS
Length: 7.5–8 in.
Wingspan: 12–13 in.
Weight: 1.6 oz.

Above: *Rose-breasted Grosbeak, male;* below: *Rose-breasted Grosbeak, female*

The calls and emails early this month went something like this: "I have the most beautiful bird at my feeder. In 20 years I've never seen anything like it."

Or, "I've had these birds at my feeder before, but only one or two. This morning there were 30."

Another claimed, "This bird looks like something from the rainforest."

Well, you know what? It is from the rainforest! During winter, the stunning Rose-breasted Grosbeak feeds on fruit, seeds, and insects in the Costa Rican rain forests. Now, during migration, it's pausing here in southern Indiana, garnering energy to navigate only a few more hundred miles farther north to breed.

The male's rosy-red triangular bib, a startling contrast to his otherwise black-and-white plumage, makes him a spectacular favorite springtime yard bird—or maybe a summer nester where you live. His parrot-like bill works handily for plucking fruit, chomping insects, and now, hulling the backyard-feeder sunflower seeds he deems so tasty. He stands out in a crowd. The female, however, like most avian females whose nesting practices demand good camouflage, looks like an oversized sparrow, mostly brown, her only beauty spot a distinct white eye line, making her easy to miss. Really easy.

In spring and early summer, Rose-breasted Grosbeaks forage in the highest branches of the tallest trees, gobbling tree buds, flowers, and seeds, as well as insects that will become the prime food fare during breeding season. Even hidden among treetops, foraging, their songs tell us they're here, as they whistle rich arias that resemble a robin's songs after voice lessons. Often, their calls, though, rather than their songs, help me locate them.

In late summer and autumn, especially when rosies stop here along their way south, they've lowered their feeding altitude, then seeking fat-rich berries in the low- to midlevel vegetation. Dogwood trees, pokeberry, and other fall fruits draw them down and help them fill their tummies while I feast my eyes during their brief autumn visit.

For a bird weighing only 1.5 ounces, the Rose-breasted Grosbeak follows an astonishing twice-a-year routine, winging across thousands of migratory miles. Summer finds it aggressively defending territory. During winter, however, when territorial defense serves no purpose, rosies sometimes form small foraging flocks. Come migration time, the flocks may travel together, perhaps because multiple eyes reduce predation risks and improve feeding success along the way. Some of us, then, see little wavelets of rosies in the yard, here one day, maybe two, then scooting on, perhaps another handful following in their wake. And that's when I get those calls and emails about 30 or more tropical rainforest birds stuffing themselves at area backyard feeders. Then they're gone.

NAME THAT BIRD

Pheucticus ludovicianus (Rose-breasted Grosbeak): *Pheucticus* translates roughly as "shy," a reference to the bird's reclusive habits. *Ludovicianus* honors King Louis XIV, connecting the French king with the Louisiana Territory, where the bird was first found. Its common name notes the male's prominently colored bib as well as its hefty beak.

BIRD TALK: WHO'S CALLING?

Song is a rich, slow warble. Its call, sometimes more easily recognized, is a sharp *skeetch*, like the sound of a sneaker on a gym floor.

FOOD FARE

Rose-breasted Grosbeaks eat primarily insects, but if insects are few, in early spring they eat leaf and flower buds; in fall they enjoy seeds, small fruits, and berries like dogwood, pokeweed, and elderberry.

NEST NOTES

Nest Site: in trees, shrubs, or vines in widely varied habitat from woods to shrubby fields to roadsides; little known about process of selection

Nest Construction: both sexes construct; female usually selects materials; flimsy-looking loose open cup, 6 in. diameter, made of sticks, twigs, grass stems, dead leaves, lined with rootlets, fine twigs, inside cup about 5 in. by 2 in.

Eggs: 1–5 eggs (average 3), incubated at night by female, during day by both sexes, male incubating about one-third of time, 12–13 days

Fledge: 9–12 days after hatch

As with many migrants, rosies travel only at night, likely using the stars for navigation, and feed during the day to prepare for another all-night flight. When surging hormones leave them restless and push them speedily toward their breeding grounds, their migratory stopovers are of short duration. In autumn, however, they may dawdle over berries and bugs, taking time to fatten up for the remaining journey. Ironically, though, you may not notice them then, when males start losing their glory and begin molting into more female-like plumage.

SPOTTING THE SPECTACULAR

Rosies by the Numbers

One spring, the big buzz among backyard birders was all about Rose-breasted Grosbeaks—multitudes of them. After late freezes destroyed blossoms and fruits on which they normally feed, the tropical migrants swooped in on sunflower seed feeders. Desperately hungry, the eye-catching birds dominated backyard scenes, including ours. One afternoon forty-two fed in our yard, and other folks saw as many or more. What a sight!

Lately, however, growing human intervention makes the Rose-breasted Grosbeak's genetically imprinted migration flight less and less tenable. Not only do North American destinations now offer less reliable food sources, but increased obstacles along the way—such as forest reduction and fragmentation, increasingly numerous high-rise windows, and growing abundance of transmission towers and wind farms—also take their toll, reducing bird populations by up to 80 percent.

Further, some folks view rosies as more a pest than a pleasure in the backyard habitat. Because rosies eat fruits, flowers, plant buds, and garden and commercial crops of peas, they're often perceived as pests by farmers, gardeners, and orchard growers. But rosies also gobble up an abundance of harmful insects and insect larvae, including the pestiferous potato beetle larvae. They're part of the system of checks and balances, always welcome in my yard.

ID CHECK

Mature male Rose-breasted Grosbeaks, with the colorful colloquial name "cut-throat," are virtually unmistakable. Females, on the other hand, can be confused with sparrows or finches. So watch for the following keys to their identification:

- Mature male with rosy-red throat and bib, white belly and rump, black hood and upper parts
- White wing patches in flight; white wing bars at rest
- Reddish wing linings that show in flight
- Autumn males more brownish, throat mottled, bib duller
- Mature female painted in brown and white streaks
- Distinct white eye stripe over brown face mask and conical bill separating female rosie from sparrows
- White on belly and under tail; tail brown
- Wing bars similar to those on males

SPECIES PROFILE

AMERICAN GOLDFINCH

Above: *American Goldfinch, summer male;* center: *American Goldfinch, summer female;* bottom: *American Goldfinch, winter (sexes similar)*

VITAL STATS
Length: 4.5–5.0 in.
Wingspan: 7.5–8.7 in.
Weight: 0.4–0.7 oz.

Amerian Goldfinches nest late in the season. The more experienced females set up house-keeping first, beginning in mid-July. Youngsters making their premier appearance at backyard feeders in August come from those early nests and are recognized by their incessant monotonous *chip-eee, chip-eee,* still begging to be fed.

NAME THAT BIRD

Carduelis tristis (American Goldfinch): *Carduelis* stems from a word meaning "thistle" (the bird's favorite food) and in Latin means "goldfinch." *Tristis* means "sad" and supposedly refers to the bird's song. Its common name sets our bird apart from the European finch. "Goldfinch" suggest both the color of the bird and the sound of its call.

Nesting period peaks, however, when first-time moms start tending nests in late July or early August. At that time, backyard feeder hosts watch niger-seed feeders empty at record rates as goldfinches gorge to meet burst-of-energy needs for nest building and egg production. Then, suddenly, female goldfinches seem to disappear, becoming rare sights at the feeder. They're incubating, of course, and their mates are feeding them.

Late nesting, however, doesn't mean goldfinch girls are lazy. Two peculiarities cause them to part from the norm.

First, they are one of only a few birds that molt twice a year, and the only member of the finch family to do so. That means in early spring, they exert considerable energy to produce an entirely new set of feathers, males changing from drab winter camo to dashingly brilliant gold and females changing into fresh but still-drab olive-yellow. If a female also needed to produce eggs simultaneously, she would likely die. So late nesting makes sure sense for this species.

Second, they're particular. They prefer certain plant materials to build their tight, snug little nests, choosing fibrous thistle and milkweed seed fluff. Goldfinches weave a compact nest, built in three layers, so tight that it's firm to the touch. They lash a foundation to a triangle of forked branches using spider webbing, form a cup of rootlets and other plant fiber, and line the cup with thistle or other plant down. But opportunists that they are, goldfinches, like other birds, often substitute readily available materials for the more traditional.

NEST NOTES

Nest Site: pair explores sites, female likely makes final choice; in open area in shrub or sapling, usually where three stems come together

Nest Construction: by female alone, in three stages; foundation fastened to stems with spider webs, topped by open cup of grasses and rootlets woven so tightly it will hold water; lined with thistle fluff; thus, goldfinches are one of the latest nesters, awaiting the ripening of thistle seed

Eggs: 2–7 eggs, 1–2 broods, incubated by female 12–14 days while fed and attended to by male

Fledge: 11–17 days after hatch

SPOTTING THE SPECTACULAR
Webworm or Spider Web?

One mid-August afternoon, I sat idle, watching a female goldfinch gather nest materials—gathering at this late date perhaps because of an earlier failed nest or maybe because she was preparing for a second brood. Either way, she found a bonanza as the result of a moth. In early fall, fuzzy orange caterpillars called webworms build long-stranded silken masses that look like cotton candy hanging from the ends of tree branches. The caterpillars eventually turn into moths. While spider webs abound throughout the yard, stretched taut between bushes, across windows, and among flowers, this goldfinch chose, for whatever reason, to ignore the readily available spider webs for her nest and, instead, to repeatedly visit this webworm nest. She picked and tugged at the web, hopping up, hopping over, separating strands and yanking out whole clumps, rearing backward, stretching the web, taking another bite, fluttering, legs braced, head upright.

Then she would pause, her bill so filled with web that it looked as if she were sporting a bushy moustache, and off she would go, apparently not far, returning in less than two minutes for more.

What a delightful use for webworm web. I can think of little else to recommend webworms—well, except that they're the Yellow-billed Cuckoo's entree of choice. Kudos to both birds!

And being vegetarians, goldfinches prefer certain seeds to feed their babies; so they put off nesting until those seeds mature. Indeed, unlike most other birds, there are no bugs for goldfinch babies.

What's their gourmet babyfood choice? Think grasses and composites—as in the daisy, aster, goldenrod, zinnia, or sunflower families, all late bloomers. Goldfinches' food preferences also explain certain of their behaviors. Ever notice how they tend to feed together? Since most of their favorite seed plants tend to grow in patches, goldfinches are forced to forage together in those (sometimes small) patches, often clinging to stalks only inches apart as they harvest the seeds.

FOOD FARE
Goldfinches are strict vegetarians, consuming a wide variety of seeds. At feeders, they enjoy thistle and sunflower seeds.

When it comes to feeding the kids, goldfinches rely on an efficient team effort. Dad feeds seeds to mom on the nest. In turn, she feeds the partially digested regurgitated seeds to their babies.

So these year-round yard birds keep a calendar unlike their peers, creating some fascinating out-the-kitchen-window observations.

BIRD TALK: WHO'S CALLING?
Males sing a complex series of twitters and warbles lasting several seconds. Songs vary from one rendition to the next and from one male to the next, and males learn new variations throughout life. Their contact call, often in flight, sounds like a quiet, evenly pronounced *po-ta-to-chip*.

If your little goldfinch flock seems to mushroom in winter, you're likely watching birds who have joined you from farther north, roaming through your habitat to flee severe weather that may have buried their seed sources. So while goldfinches don't migrate in the sense of sailing off to the tropics, they do roam to find seasonal foods.

ID CHECK

While male American Goldfinches in breeding plumage are unmistakable, note these details about goldfinches in general and females in particular:

- Both sexes wear a distinct white pattern on black wing feathers year-round
- Both sexes show notched tails and whitish-edged tail feathers
- Males have tiny, drab brown, conical bills that turn orange-yellow in summer
- Females have tiny, drab brown, conical bills that turn pinkish in summer
- Breeding males have a striking black forehead
- Both sexes wear overall drab grayish olive in winter, the male with a bit more yellow wash on face and neck
- Females in summer still wear grayish olive but with yellowish wash on throat and sides of neck

---

June

There is nothing in which the birds differ more from man
than the way in which they can build
and yet leave a landscape as it was before.

ROBERT LYND

In June, backyard bird activity hits its peak. Cherry trees and native red mulberry trees droop heavily with ripe fruits; strawberries beg for salads, desserts, and cereal toppings. Birds take their share of the riches without asking, gobbling some for themselves and snagging more for their babes. The earliest out-of-the-nest youngsters, like bluebirds and robins, snatch a few fruits of their own.

Now, at peak production, birds work overtime, taking advantage of the year's longest days, their nesting and breeding behaviors in-your-face obvious, even from the kitchen window. Year-round residents have fledged first broods; their eggs tucked in camouflaged nests promise second broods. Migrants' nests, secreted within dense vegetation, likewise cradle eggs, maybe even naked little nestlings.

Watching the goings-on, I feel compelled to proclaim June as the Month of the Nest.

And what amazing activities and results we backyard bird-watchers see. Every bird nest, unique to its species, weaves a story. Wrens build differently and in different places than do cardinals; chickadees build differently and in different places than do doves. Each species maintains its own blueprint, genetically hardwired into its brain. In fact, a bird's unique nest can be so readily identified by its builder that specialized field guides illustrate and identify virtually every yard bird's abode.

Nest Building 101

To begin to appreciate the marvel of nests, here's a challenge: Gather sticks, twigs, grasses, pine needles, feathers, moss, and maybe a little mud. Choose the best components, and build a nest. It must hold a mamma bird and three to six eggs, withstand rain and wind, and endure a pile of babies romping, clawing, competing for food. Oh—and you can't use your hands to complete this abode. Birds don't have hands. Now complete a nest two or three times this

An American Robin enjoys a ripe cherry, one of June's best offerings for birds.

summer. Each time, though, you must start from scratch. No reusing a nest filled with feces and parasites. The only part you can reuse is the blueprint. Welcome to the avian version of home construction. Fairly amazing, don't you think?

BOTANY FOR BIRDS **Building Supplies**

Birds choose to nest in locations that offer preferred building materials, so providing those materials whenever possible in your backyard habitat may bring on the birds. Building supplies fall into three categories: vegetation, animal products, and inorganic materials. Vegetation covers the gamut, anything that grows. And, of course, some form of vegetation makes up the primary component of most nests. Birds, irrevocably connected to the plants around them, look to all manner of plant life for building material: rootlets, leaves, bark, twigs, sticks, flowers, seed pods, mosses, seaweed, lichens, grasses, reeds, sedges, fungi, and more.

Vegetation also accommodates most bird nests: They're situated in tree branches and cavities, deciduous and coniferous; shrubs and bushes, especially dense and thorny; tangles and grasses, from understory to meadow. The more botanical variety your habitat offers, the more bird species will find the kind of nest site they like, and the more of them will choose to join you.

Many birds, however, also incorporate animal products into their clever little nests, especially feathers, some from other bird species, some from the nesting female's own breast. Other animal products used include bits of fur, hair, skin, and spider silk. Inorganic materials include such oddities as mud, human trash, and—go figure—little stones.

Most of us likely "saw" our first bird nests in children's books. Remember them? Invariably made of small twigs, they straddled a branch about midway out from the trunk and hosted happy, singing bird families.

In reality, few nests straddle a branch. Even fewer sit midway out. And almost none are made entirely of small twigs.

For instance, Baltimore Orioles build miraculously woven, six-inch-long pouch-like nests suspended from the tip of a branch by a few long fibrous strands. Vireos likewise build pendulous nests, suspended between two twigs near their fork, situated low, amid dense vegetation.

Brown Thrashers, Eastern Towhees, and Song Sparrows situate their nests on or near the ground, protected only by stealth and dense undergrowth.

Woodpeckers carve out tree cavities in which to raise their young, but a nest? Forget it. They don't build nests inside. And since woodpeckers use a cavity for only a single year, the following year that ready-made nest site may host Wood Ducks, Great Crested Flycatchers, Prothonotary Warblers, titmice, or nuthatches—none of which can carve out their own cavities. Except for Wood Ducks, these second-time users bring something soft and insulating to the cavity, a sort of remodeling effort to suit themselves.

Kingfishers may take the prize, however, for oddest nest site. They excavate tunnels in mud banks, building their nests at the upper end. Runners-up for the award surely include swallow species that stick mud-dab nests under eaves of buildings or under bridges. Or Chimney Swifts that use their own saliva to spit-glue nest materials inside chimneys. Or maybe Killdeer that lay eggs in a mere scrape, often among driveway rocks. Ouch.

NOTABLE BEHAVIOR   **Flirtations**

During breeding season, watch birds flirt. For instance, to attract the girls, a male Red-winged Blackbird sings, hunches forward, and raises his "shoulders" to show off namesake brilliant-red epaulettes. In a different courtship routine, a male Mourning Dove coos, bowing repeatedly, head almost to the ground, eyeing a chosen female. A male White-breasted Nuthatch behaves out of character, giving up his upside-down travel to scoot horizontally along a branch, carrying a seed to his potential mate.

Male Red-winged Blackbirds display to females by singing, thrusting forward, and spreading their wings to show off brilliant red epaulettes.

A Mallard drake swims around his preferred female performing the likes of a ballet—neck, head, tail, and wings all part of the pirouette—ending in a surprising splash toward the female. You may spot a male Ruby-throated Hummingbird swooping in a U-shaped display, beginning 40 to 50 feet up. The lowest point of the dip occurs immediately in front of the female, wing whirs making an audible buzz. Eagles clutch talons and cartwheel through the sky.

HABITAT—YOURS AND THEIRS
Mr. Green Lawn and You

Some folks yearn for perfect lawns, weed free, lush, green. But the toxic materials in lawn-care products used to create the perfect lawns also create seriously imperfect habitat for birds or their babies. If you must use some kind of insect control, choose only organic products and read labels carefully. Otherwise, why not use the best insect control Mother Nature offers: birds. We do. And we have for years. It works.

Other birds use an equally wide array of nesting arrangements. Carolina Wrens shape closed nests with a side entrance. Most flycatchers build cup-shaped nests in tree forks. Incubating Mourning Doves sit, unblinking, on their flimsy collection of sticks, camouflaging their nests by motionlessness. Brown Creepers stuff their nests behind loose tree bark. American Goldfinches tuck their tiny cup nests in forks of shrubs, small trees, even sturdy weeds—cups so solidly compact that they feel and sound wood-hard when tapped. Osprey build stick-pile nests atop man-made platforms over or near good fishing waters. On the other hand, owls never build nests, instead commandeering old hawk nests or natural tree—or man-made—cavities. Once I chuckled at a Great-horned Owl nesting in a former Bald Eagle nest, nearly lost in the bulk of sticks.

WHY DO BIRDS DO THAT?
Why Do Birds Deck Their Nests with Greenery?

Some birds, like European Starlings, Red-tailed Hawks, and Bald Eagles, add bits of greenery to their nests during incubation and sometimes throughout the use of the nest. While scientists continue the debate over the purpose of this greenery, many believe herbal-like qualities act as a natural insect repellant, a theory supported by the fact that birds that reuse their own or others' nests often incorporate greenery. Other experts propose that the aroma of certain greenery masks the baby birds' odor and thus deters predators. Some suggest greenery merely camouflages the nest and its regular replacement maintains nest secrecy.

PROBLEM SOLVER
Unwanted Guests in Your Bird Houses

Birds that sign on to rent your nest boxes for the season sometimes find unwanted company—pests like ants, wasps, and parasites that can infest the nest to the detriment, perhaps even the death, of babes or adults.

So what to do? To help prevent pests in general, remove nests immediately after birds fledge. And remove any broken egg that might attract pests.

If ants infest an active nest, check your local pharmacy for a bottle of flowers of sulphur, a bright yellow powder also known as brimstone. Assuming your nest box opens for access, place a scant tablespoonful of flowers of sulphur on a wide-bladed putty knife, the size that will slip easily into the bottom of the box. With another similarly sized putty knife, gently lift the nest enough to slide the sulphur-laden knife underneath, gently jiggle off the powder, and lower the nest back in place.

To prevent wasps, smear the ceiling with bar soap. To control parasites, sprinkle the nest cavity floor with diatomaceous earth, available at garden stores. It scratches the surface of parasite's bodies, causing death from dehydration, but it's completely harmless to other life forms. For blowflies, place crushed bay leaves under the nest.

Nest materials differ almost as much as the nests. Canada Geese pull surrounding vegetation toward themselves, forming a loose nest on the ground, and then line it with their own downy breast feathers. Goose down—now there's a nice, soft, insulated bed! Male House Wrens stuff every available cavity with twigs; then, females choose their favorite and build a cup of soft grasses amid the twigs. Cousins Carolina Wrens prefer dried grasses and last fall's leaves.

For comparison, a pencil eraser shows the miniscule size of a Ruby-throated Hummingbird nest, here with two nestlings.

Female Ruby-throated Hummingbirds assemble lichen-covered nests from dandelion and other plant down, fastening their abodes with spider web to the limbs they straddle. Tree sap "glue" makes nests snug. Blue-gray Gnatcatchers employ a similar lichen-cover disguise and spider-web attachment technique. Quite a combination of building materials, don't you think? If you could ask them, I bet they'd tell you to skip killing off all your dandelions and spiders.

Cardinal and Brown Thrasher nests include shreds of bark from bald cypress or wild grapevine. Chickadees lay foundations of moss on which they construct neat cups of plant down, hair, and plant fibers.

NOTABLE BEHAVIOR   **Appreciating the Nesting Effort**

Birds exert significant effort gathering nest materials. Each twig, each leaf, each blade of grass requires the bird to find the material, fly it stealthily to the nest site, and weave it carefully in place so that the nest will hold eggs, babies, and mom. One Northern Cardinal nest, when analyzed, included more than three hundred pieces of twigs, bark, leaves, and grasses. So, think about it: This particular nest represented three hundred repetitions of that find-fly-weave scenario.

When finished, a nest construction holds its shape, tightly, firmly. Building it demands time, energy, and effort—all significant economic output in a bird's way of life.

But even more significant is the female's biological contribution—the energy and nutrients required to develop the eggs, the output of calcium for the shells, the overall physical drain of producing eggs that, together, nearly equal the bird's own weight. Simultaneously, she must remain strong and healthy enough to incubate, brood, feed, and defend her young.

While we glimpse something of birds' personalities by the nests they make, we also recognize their amazing—if innate—skill in weaving secure cradles for their young. They do with bill and feet what we can't begin to do with two hands and assorted tools—and an illustrated guide.

Your Home Depot

Okay, so we can't for the life of us duplicate the intricate nests our wild friends build instinctively. But we can help them along—and encourage them to build their abodes near our abodes—by being the one-stop big box store for nest supplies. Here's how.

Offer eggshells. Females of all bird species need added calcium for egg production. Natural sources being somewhat limited, eggshells suffice. Before offering them, however, kill bacteria by baking for half an hour at 200°F. Scatter the crumbled shells near feeders or serve on a solid surface.

Leave leaves and grass. Mockingbirds and Carolina Wrens use last fall's leaves to make this summer's nest, so don't be too fastidious about raking your yard. Likewise, raking or bagging grass leaves a clean yard, but cardinals, bluebirds, titmice, and others need grass for nests. Neat and well-manicured may look good to you, but wild and wonderful looks better to birds.

Pick up sticks—not. We're not talking branches here. It's those little twigs that House Wrens stuff into nest boxes or that Mourning Doves gather for their flimsy-looking nests. No twigs, no nests! So pick up the big stuff but don't rake up the little stuff. Keep aiming for wild and wonderful.

Protect spider webs. Several species of birds, including hummingbirds and gnatcatchers, use spider webs to line or bind nests.

Let moss gather. The north side of buildings provides a perfect place for moss, especially if soil is damp. You don't plant it; moss grows naturally given the right conditions. If you have no moss, you'll have no nesting chickadees. Other birds use moss, too.

Make mud. With a dry spring or midsummer, robins and Barn Swallows have to hunt for mud to build nests. One way to maintain a "mud hole" is to put a pin hole in the bottom of a plastic milk jug, fill the jug with water, and hang it above loose soil. The continuous drip will maintain a nice muddy patch. (Butterflies will love it, too.)

BIOLOGY BITS
Home Construction

Birds create nests one of two ways. They may excavate—remove grasses, twigs, leaves, rocks, or other objects—to create a shallow bowl or scrape to hold eggs and babies. Or they may assemble—weave or interlock, stick together (as with mud or saliva), or pile up. The outside may be camouflaged, especially with lichen or mosses, or it may be waterproofed, as with tree sap. Small birds tend to add sophisticated nest linings to conserve heat loss.

HOW DOES YOUR GARDEN GROW?
Zinnias: Non-native Magnets

How I love zinnias, the head-high brightly blossomed ones. But I love them only because the birds love them, especially the American Goldfinches. In late June, when the backdoor opens, a veritable cloud of golden birds lifts from the patch. And it's a big patch that I plant, about 80 feet of a foot-wide row that produces abundant blossoms until frost. Zinnias also attract more butterflies in my garden than any other plant, including the aptly named butterfly bush (*Buddleia* spp.). Give 'em a try!

Hang out a string mop. You'll never miss a few strings on an old mop, but you'll have a hoot watching eager nest builders pull and tug until a few strands pop loose.

Wait to prune. Several species strip grapevine fibers to build nests. And every spring I wait until the female Baltimore Oriole strips the stringy fibers off the native wisteria vine before I prune off the dead. The oriole yanks and rears backward until I'm sure she'll flip over, but the fibers finally break loose and off she flies, long streamers trailing behind. The female oriole will use those fibers to build that wonderful hanging nest that somehow stays put well into winter.

Skip dryer lint. We used to think soft dryer lint was a good means by which to keep eggs warm. Warm, maybe, but not dry or safe. When dryer lint gets wet, it packs. Unlike natural fibers, like milkweed silk, it doesn't fluff up again when dry. Thus, if a bird uses dryer lint to construct its nest, the first rain will cause the nest to sag or even collapse.

Maternity Ward Yard

So you've seen a new face in your yard? Okay, maybe it's not just another pretty face. In fact, maybe it's not very pretty at all, just the face of some strange, pale new bird, streaky and splotchy, no clear field marks, leaving you wondering to whom it belongs.

Best bet? A baby. Fledglings, those youngsters just out of the nest, often look much like mom and dad, maybe a bit more scraggly or not quite as plump. Young Tufted Titmice, Black-capped and Carolina Chickadees, and Blue Jays all closely resemble their parents. Those are easy. It's the one that doesn't look like its parents that gives us the sense of a strange new bird in the yard.

Woodpeckers likely lead the parade of strange new faces. Surely only a mother Red-bellied Woodpecker could love her fledglings, those sad-looking—dare I call them ugly?—little creatures with overall-gray heads offering no hint of their species except by silhouette and checkered backs. And fledgling Downy Woodpeckers, while cute, look like neither the adult male, with a red patch on the back of his head, nor adult female, without any red. No wonder folks assume they have a new species when they see a pale red cap on a wood-pecker's forecrown.

A fledgling Chipping Sparrow perches on a purple coneflower begging its parents for a snack.

Most folks recognize young robins by their black-spotted breasts, less dapper than the adult's brick-colored plumage that gives us the cliché, "robin red-breast." But bluebird fledglings, being in the same thrush family as robins, also wear the spotted breast feathers. To add to the spotted effect, juvenile bluebirds also wear an eye ring, a bold white circle around each dark eye.

BIOLOGY BITS   **Nest Failures**

Why did two baby bluebirds and our Tree Swallows die in their nests? Why did one robin egg not hatch? What poked holes in chickadee eggs but left them in the nest box? Why did House Wrens quit feeding their young?

Most nests aren't readily studied, so we frequently don't know breeding results. Unfortunately, nest failure

Oddly enough, an immature Downy Woodpecker wears red on top of its head. When it matures, a male will have red on the back of its head. The mature female will lack any red.

Just hours out of the nest, an Eastern Bluebird fledgling shows a spotted breast that best identifies it as a member of the thrush family.

rates are astonishingly high, for some species a startling 75 percent. Consider the following half-dozen common causes:

- Predation ranks as primary cause. Common predators include snakes, cats, raccoons, skunks, opossums, foxes, crows, jays, squirrels, House Sparrows, and others—any of which will eat eggs and nestlings. In addition, if a predator kills one of the parents, the remaining parent likely can't feed the brood alone and typically abandons the nest.
- Weather ranks second. Storms wrench nests from their anchors, bombard incubating birds with hailstones, and crash nest-cradling limbs to the ground. An unusual cold snap promotes infertility. Too much rain and/or cold drives insects to the ground, starving insect-catchers as well as their young. Intense heat can "cook" eggs.
- Nest contamination by ants, wasps, and parasites exerts a toll.
- Cowbirds parasitize nests of some 220 species. Baby cowbirds' early hatching crowds out the hosts' own babies and/or causes their starvation or their being pushed from the nest.
- Human intervention also causes failures. Pruning protective branches or clearing tangled areas that serve as nest sites invites predation. Mowing grasslands in early June destroys ground nests before babies fledge. Pesticides take a massive toll on nestlings and adults. Ninety-eight percent of all birds feed their young insects; so not only does pesticide destroy birds' food supply, it sickens remaining insects so that babies—and often adults—die from contaminated food.
- First-time nesters may build inadequate nests. Construction fails and the nest falls from its anchor, comes unraveled in rain, or drops contents through its bottom. And especially for first-time nesters but others as well, eggs may be infertile, for reasons we can only guess.

Cardinals, on the other hand, closely resemble their mothers. If you've noticed an increase in female cardinals in your backyard, look closely. If a "female" has a dark bill, it's a juvenile, its sex as yet unidentifiable. Adult cardinals, both males and females, have reddish-orange bills.

Sometimes, though, the clue is not the bill but the eye. Young Cooper's Hawks, for instance, keep pale eyes for a year or more. Adults sport red eyes.

BIOLOGY BITS   **Growing Babies**

Scientists use two words to differentiate between baby birds' condition at hatch: *precocial* and *altricial*.

A precocial baby breaks out of the shell alert, eyes open, covered in downy feathers, leg muscles ready to go. In short, it's fairly well developed and tuned in to the environment the moment it cracks the shell. Just think about how we use a similar word, "precocious," to refer to human children, and you'll get the idea. Killdeer, goslings, and ducklings are obvious examples.

An altricial baby, however, hatches naked with eyes closed, totally helpless, barely able to hold its wobbly head up to beg for food. Even while searching for food, parents must continue to brood these tiny, naked creatures. But these nestlings grow incredibly fast. Muscles, bones, organs, feathers, and brain all reach maturity in a matter of two or three weeks. Rather astonishing, when you stop to think about it. Songbirds, like cardinals, bluebirds, and goldfinches, are all altricial.

Young Northern Cardinals have black bills that gradually turn bright orange-red. Their dark bills mark the easiest way to distinguish immature cardinals (both males and females) from adult females.

One of the biggest teasers among new faces in the yard is that of the fledgling towhee. Only its silhouette and conical-shaped bill reveal its identity. For unlike its handsome tuxedoed father, who wears black with a rusty open vest, and its subtly plumaged mother, who wears brown and rust, the juvenile is nothing more than a mix of brown, tan, and white streaks and splotches, its sparrow-like appearance identifying its family but disguising its true identity.

Mostly, of course, we recognize a new face by the company it keeps. Juveniles stick to their parents like Velcro, twittering pathetic pleas of *Feed me; feed me; feed me.* Fluttering wings add a show of desperation. But there's one exception: baby Brown-headed Cowbirds. The world's worst avian moms, female cowbirds lay their eggs in other birds' nests, and the host birds raise the nestling cowbirds as their own. It's disgusting to see a tiny Chipping Sparrow, its own babies likely dead from starvation, now standing on tiptoe, stretching high, trying to feed a fluttering, incessantly calling young cowbird twice its size.

So watch for pale bills and legs; streaky, fluffy plumage; big mouths; and fluttering wings. And listen for nonstop calls of little beggars—all new faces but no new species.

Memorable Moments: Pruning Nightmare

Knowing where yard birds nest always presents a challenge; for when it comes to nest sites, well concealed equals well protected. Still, noting where a male sings to mark his territory, watching where the pair carries grasses, leaves, and twigs, and listening for quiet chips of an incubating female and, later, cries of hungry babies often reveal where birds have set up housekeeping. So last week I was really angry with myself for missing clues, and sick about nearly destroying a Brown Thrasher's nest.

One of our trumpet honeysuckle vines overarches a trellis adjoining the sidewalk to the garage. Anyone who enjoys this magnificent hummingbird-magnet plant knows, however, that its vigorous growth demands seasonal pruning. Ours overflowed the sidewalk, forcing us to walk around, tromping a path through the yard, rendering pruning essential.

WATER WAYS   **Keep It Moving**

No matter where you live, summertime assuredly means mosquitoes; and these pesky insects seek water in which to breed. So you see the problem: A backyard water feature that readily attracts birds, without proper maintenance, also readily attracts mosquitoes. Adding some sort of insecticidal mosquito control to your water feature is to offer toxic drink and baths to your birds. Your water feature turns deadly.

But here's the key: Mosquitoes don't breed in moving water. So, whatever water feature you choose, keep its waters moving. Electrical pumps, including solar powered, turn the trick. In winter, pumps also deter freeze-ups—depending on the size of your reservoir, the size of the pump, and the severity of the cold.

Without something to keep the water moving in summer, though, you'll need to empty the water and scour the reservoir on a daily basis. Otherwise, you may promote more than just mosquitoes; you and yours may face West Nile Virus.

Overwhelmed by rain-delayed spring yard chores and oblivious to everything but getting the job done, I whacked away. Suddenly, close by, a sound that I can only describe as growling, halted my work. A Brown Thrasher, arm's length away, exploded into aggression, bouncing here, jabbing the air there, flicking its wings, its deep angry chirring loud, insistent.

I stopped midwhack. A nest, maybe? Peering into dense tangle, gingerly pulling a branch aside here, nudging another up there, I saw it, right where I was about to whack off another mass of overgrowth.

Suddenly sick in the pit of my stomach, I backed off, certain the pair would now abandon the well-made nest, the result of days and days of avian work, gathering hundreds of twigs and hundreds of grasses, weaving them together into this avian mansion. But hours later, the female was back, barely visible yet certainly more poorly concealed than before.

Will my scent on the vine now attract predators, like snakes and raccoons, egg eaters that otherwise would be indifferent to the tangle? Will the diminished cover no longer adequately camouflage nest-side activity, the coming and going of parents feeding young? Will they lose their babies because of my invasion?

The really sickening part is that I know better. In spite of my attention, I'm fully aware that I don't know where every bird is nesting. I know that hidden nests make successful nests. I even know that honeysuckle tangle—like other dense tangles—makes some of the safest nest sites. And I even know that Brown Thrashers are nesting here because I've heard their quiet mockingbird-like song and watched their furtive flights in and out of nearby shrubs. I know they like thick tangles about chest high. Yet I whacked away, unthinking, failing to connect the proverbial dots.

So now we're willfully tromping a path through the yard, avoiding sidewalk and honeysuckle. I watch for but rarely see the thrashers. Secretive birds that they are, I hope they're still there, yet I'm not about to push back the tangle to look.

Having learned the bitter lesson, I hereby humbly share it: In spite of conscious effort, we're unlikely to know where all our yard birds nest. They're apt to like best the parts of the yard most overgrown, those we most likely want to prune. So, if we must prune, we must do so cautiously. But preferably we should skip efforts to tame wild parts of the yard—the parts most attractive to birds—until nesting ends. Where I live, that's most likely August.

FEEDER FOCUS **Safflower Seed for the Savvy**

No matter the season, June or January, cute little squirrels can turn into unruly pests, draining your feeders and your wallet. While they're only doing what comes naturally—taking advantage of easy, reliable meals—backyard hosts sometimes find the little piggies annoying, so much so that they peg them with the nickname "tree rats."

What to do? Savvy backyard bird hosts offer safflower seed. Most mammals don't like it, probably because of its somewhat bitter taste, but birds don't notice. In fact, when I've offered safflower and sunflower seeds side by side, some birds, especially Northern Cardinals and House Finches, shun the sunflower in favor of the safflower. It's worth a try!

Living the Long (?) Life

Breeding season makes me pause to contemplate an avian question: How long do birds live? Given that lifespan, how many babies can they raise? And given the fact that 80 percent of all songbirds perish in the first year of life (and therefore obviously do not breed), how do birds maintain their respective species populations?

The business of a bird's longevity has also piqued my personal interest lately because of a cardinal in my yard. She's not just any cardinal; she's a specific female, easily recognized by a genetic quirk—her partially white head. She's leucistic, meaning "partial-albino." I call her, not very creatively, Pretty Girl.

WATER WAYS   **Down and Dirty Baths**

Birds "bathe" in dust as well as water. For dust-bathers, keep a bare patch of dirt, perhaps under some shrubs or against the foundation of your house. To maintain the patch as "dust" rather than hard-packed dirt, loosen the soil, crush or sift it, perhaps add a bit of sand if your soil is really clayey. Birds prefer dust baths over water baths to control parasites. Give 'em the down and dirty!

My first photos of Pretty Girl date back two years, likely when she was about five months old. Of course, she could have been older; I only first saw her then. What fascinates me most, though, is that she's still here, still strikingly attractive, still visiting our feeders.

I try to imagine the hazards she's faced. Hawks snatch songbirds for high-protein meals. Neighbors' cats venture into our yard. Raccoons romp in numbers. Snakes make themselves at home. Skunks, coyotes, and foxes all take their toll. Bitter cold, snow, and ice increase her food demand, but summer's drought reduces the seed production that might keep her alive. Oh, how she must struggle.

Scientists tell us that birds that survive their first year are more likely savvy enough to avoid predation in the future. Still, it's only a matter of time. Rarely, in fact, do birds die of old age, eventually succumbing instead to predation, window crashes, disease, winter starvation, migration perils, and human interference.

Leucistic (partially albino) birds show up fairly often among many species. This oddly colored cardinal happens to have a white head, but other leucistic birds may have white wings, white tails, white bodies, or any combination of white patches.

BIOLOGY BITS **Avian Lifespan**

In general, large birds live longer than small birds, but exceptions to the generality abound. According to statistics compiled by Stanford University, large birds like geese, swans, eagles, Red-tailed Hawks, and Great Blue Herons hold long-life records in the wild of twenty years or more.

By comparison, cardinals, as well as doves, Blue Jays, Downy Woodpeckers, and Red-winged Blackbirds, hold records beyond fifteen years. Even chickadees, robins, Song Sparrows, Tree Swallows, and juncos have lived past ten years. One Ruby-throated Hummingbird survived a record nine years.

These numbers, however, are highly misleading. Record maximum lifetimes are far, far different from average lifetimes.

Consider this comparison. The current undisputed record maximum lifetime for humans is 122.5 years. But the average lifetime for humans is about seventy-seven years. The dramatic difference between maximum and average also applies to avian lives.

In fact, for birds, average life expectancy can be as short as ten months, mostly because so many babies die in the nest (70 to 80 percent of nests fail) or face predation right out of the nest before they can fly well or learn to recognize threats. After having reached adulthood, though, their chances of survival increase, even though a songbird in the wild has less than a 50 percent chance of surviving two years. What a joy, then, to have had Pretty Girl so long. I hope she stays strong, smart, careful—and pretty.

HOW DOES YOUR GARDEN GROW?
Ground Covers

Good ground cover offers not only foraging areas but also nest sites for certain birds. But before you grab the routine (and non-native) Boston ivy (*Parthenocissus tricuspidata*) or periwinkles (*Vinca* spp.), do some research. In the northern half of the United States, check out plants like bearberry (*Arctostaphylos uva-ursi* Massachusetts), bunchberry (*Cornus canadensis*), or creeping juniper (*Juniperus horizontalis*). In the south, consider creeping mint (*Meehania cordata*), green and gold (*Chrysogonum virginianum*), or one of many carex sedges (*Carex* spp.). Depending on your hardiness zone, one or more of these will add desirable wildlife habitat to your backyard. Check http://plants.usda.gov.

To be effective, plant in drifts—at least seven individuals of whatever species you select.

Cherry Tree Birds

The cherry tree next door hosted last week's birding hotspot. Much to the neighbor's chagrin, at least seventeen bird species winged in for a scarlet snack of ripening fruits.

Woodpeckers—downy, hairy, and red-bellied—carried cherry hunks off to nestlings. Chipping Sparrows joined House Finches in the fray. That little rascal of a mockingbird who zealously guarded my suet- and fruit-filled gourd feeder last winter only to trail after a female—well, he came back, lured by the abundant red fruits—and all alone.

Cardinals, robins, bluebirds, Blue Jays, House Sparrows, titmice—they were all regulars at the cherry buffet. Even hummingbirds stopped by, but only to check out the bug supply the

Cedar Waxwings often arrive in flocks to feed on ripening fruits, including cherries.

sweet fruits attract. The most numerous visitors, however, were those that, when I was a kid, we called—appropriately—cherry birds, a species whose little flocks seem to materialize out of nowhere just when cherries turn pink: Cedar Waxwings.

Baby birds, however, especially fledgling bluebirds and robins, made for humorous cherry picking. Babies like berries because, unlike bugs, the berries sit still. Easy to "catch," nutritious berries pop down with little effort, a calorie-saving meal for growing birds and their nutrient-demanding feather production. Sometimes, however, the cherry is beyond the bird's best stretch from any direction. After tipping, flipping, and fluttering, fledglings' expressions seem to say, "Okay, Mom, what do I do now?" Even success in grabbing a cherry doesn't necessarily mean the fruit breaks from its stem, so the added flutter and fluster make for a comic routine.

NOTABLE BEHAVIOR   **Flight Patterns**

As birds zip in and out of a cherry tree—or anywhere else—I'll bet you've noticed that not all species fly the same way. Consider this human comparison: Even from a distance, you can pick out your loved ones in a crowd, even from the back, only by the way they walk—how they swing their arms, how long their stride, how they carry themselves. So it is with birds. On the wing, birds display distinctive flight patterns that allow us to identify them, even in silhouette against the sky.

For instance, American Goldfinches fly in a deeply undulating path, a sort of *flap-flap-flap-freefall.* Thrushes, on the other hand, swoop along in a flight pattern similar to that of a robin. Some birds fly a steady, unvarying *flap-flap-flap,* bullet straight. Some *flap-flap-flap-glide,* as do Song Sparrows. So watch for wing beat pattern as well as directional pattern. You'll see.

Sometimes, when the fruit is just out of reach, a flying leap allows a fledgling bluebird to capture lunch.

Most fun, however, were the robins. Waxwings, cardinals, and other more mannerly birds nip hunks of cherry, eyeing the rosiest cheeks for the tastiest nip. Robins, on the other hand, like to down their berries whole. But when cherry is larger than gullet, what's a self-respecting robin red-breast to do? Squeeze and mash, drip and dribble, and the cherry turns to mush, soft enough to down with a few big, gullet-bulging gulps, causing tense moments when I wondered if the poor bird would choke. None did.

Alas, after one flight-filled week, the tree is bare. So, dear neighbor, I'm sorry about the lattice-top cherry pies you planned; but oh! what the birds and I enjoyed—they, the bits and pieces and mushy whole fruits, and I, the antics of their feeding.

So, marking the Month of the Nest, June offers backyard bird-watchers quite an array of activities to watch. Enjoy!

Conservation Corner: Backyard Conservation

The Cornell University Lab of Ornithology notes (www.birds.cornell.edu/AllAboutBirds/ conservation/habitat) that successful habitat maintenance follows several guiding principles, and "these can be used by anyone, on both public and private land, to conserve breeding habitat, wintering habitat, and migratory corridors of all sizes." Cornell offers the following suggestions for backyard conservation:

- Grow native plants that provide fruit or seeds.
- [Maintain a] woodlot with fallen limbs and leaves, dead plant material, and other woodland debris [that] harbor insects on which migratory birds thrive. Leave as much dead plant materials as possible on the land (without endangering your home, of course).
- Seek alternatives to chemical pesticides. Use biological controls for unwanted insects and vegetation.

- Reduce the risk of bird predation by keeping pet cats indoors. Refrain from putting out table scraps, which attract predators such as raccoons.
- Invite neighboring landowners to join your backyard effort. Plan cooperatively!
- Build (or buy) and maintain a bird feeder or bird house.

Things to Do in June

- Maintain breeding safe havens in your backyard habitat.
- Avoid pesticides so that birds have ample bugs to feed their babies.
- Delay pruning until the end of breeding season, no earlier than mid-August where I live.
- Keep moving water fresh and mosquito free.
- Monitor nest boxes and remove old nests as soon as babies fledge.
- Avoid dead-heading flowers in order to provide natural seeds for birds.

58 Yard Birds in June

Very hot entire month; black cherries ripened

Northern Bobwhite	Great Crested Flycatcher	Brown Thrasher
Great Blue Heron	Eastern Kingbird	European Starling
Green Heron	White-eyed Vireo	Cedar Waxwing
Cooper's Hawk	Philadelphia Vireo	Northern Parula
Red-shouldered Hawk	Red-eyed Vireo	Yellow-throated Warbler
Killdeer	Blue Jay	Common Yellowthroat
Mourning Dove	American Crow	Eastern Towhee
Yellow-billed Cuckoo	Purple Martin	Chipping Sparrow
Barred Owl	Northern Rough-winged	Field Sparrow
Chimney Swift	Swallow	Song Sparrow
Ruby-throated	Barn Swallow	Summer Tanager
Hummingbird	Carolina Chickadee	Northern Cardinal
Red-bellied Woodpecker	Tufted Titmouse	Indigo Bunting
Downy Woodpecker	White-breasted Nuthatch	Red-winged Blackbird
Hairy Woodpecker	Carolina Wren	Eastern Meadowlark
Northern Flicker	House Wren	Common Grackle
Pileated Woodpecker	Blue-gray Gnatcatcher	Brown-headed Cowbird
Eastern Wood-pewee	Eastern Bluebird	House Finch
Acadian Flycatcher	American Robin	American Goldfinch
Eastern Phoebe	Northern Mockingbird	House Sparrow

NORTHERN MOCKINGBIRD

VITAL STATS
Length: 9–10 in.
Wingspan: 12.5–13.8 in.
Weight: 1.8 oz.

Northern Mockingbird

A Northern Bobwhite called its bell-clear ascending *Bobwhite! Bobwhite!* It was so near that I caught my breath and froze, peering into the dense underbrush, looking for movement, hoping to catch a glimpse of the bird.

Over the past weeks, I'd heard the bobwhites across the hayfield, calling to one another along the brushy fencerows, happy in their habitat. But hearing them in the distance isn't nearly as exciting as hearing them from 20 feet away. Now, if I could just see him.

Stock still, I tried to spot him. Maybe in the honeysuckle tangle along the fence? Maybe skittering at the edge of the woods? Maybe in the corner, under the tangle of blackberry brambles?

He called again, closer, just above me. Wait. Above me? A bobwhite? The call seemed to come from the very top of the old sycamore tree at the yard's edge. Puzzled, I wondered if it had been startled from its usual ground-level habitat. Had it flown up to escape some predator? But why so high?

Shading my eyes to check out the very top of the tree where several dead branches splay from the green, I squinted at a long-tailed silhouette. Then the call changed to *FEE-bee,* the call of the Eastern Phoebe.

That's when I knew. I'd been fooled again. How many times now? That clever gray mimic, the Northern Mockingbird burst with song from his favorite territorial high point, his repertoire mocking every yard bird in the area. Within the next minutes, he shared the bluebird's burble, the cardinal's *purdy, purdy, purdy,* the Red-shouldered Hawk's screaming *keer, keer, keer,* and then moved on to a series of unidentifiable whistles, chirps, and chatters followed by the *beep-beep-beep* of the trash-pick-up truck's backup warning. Whatever he sang, however, he always repeated three or more times.

NAME THAT BIRD
Mimus Polyglottos (Northern Mockingbird): *Mimus* means "mimic." *Polyglottos* means "many tongued." Both words refer to the bird's unoriginal song that only mimics other birds. Its common name makes the same reference and differentiates the U.S. bird from that in Central and South America.

FOOD FARE
Mockingbirds eat mostly insects in summer and berries in winter. At winter feeders, they occasionally take suet and rehydrated, chopped dried fruits like raisins. They rarely visit summer feeders.

I have to love these virtuosos—not because of their original scores but because males mimic to perfection all the greatest arias from all the greatest operas. The female mockingbirds love the music, too. In fact, according to some research, the male with the best rendition of the most scores has the best chance of attracting a female. So being a virtuoso isn't just a credit on a resume or a blue ribbon at the county fair; it's success as a mate.

In the early 1900s, however, its song rendered the mockingbird a popular caged bird and nearly caused its demise. In fact, while president, Thomas Jefferson kept a pet mockingbird named Dick in the White House. But they can be pets no more. Recovered now after the passage of laws preventing the capture or killing of any migratory bird, the Northern Mockingbird's territory has expanded from its more southern climes into areas as far north as Canada.

SPOTTING THE SPECTACULAR   **Territorial Terrors**

During breeding season, mockingbirds vigorously, even viciously, defend nest territories, attacking any intruder, including dogs, cats, and sometimes humans. Come winter, however, when they must switch diets from insects to berries, they stake out berry-rich winter feeding territories. By singing, the mockers—male and female—claim, "This berry patch is mine, everybody, all mine." So the advent of winter really marks the advent of the female's most melodic arias. In summer, while nesting, the bird is quiet. In autumn, though, the female is on its own and most capable of blasting out its own aggressive "Buzz off, buster," to any other mocker—mate included—who might eye the female's cache of berries.

So, loners by design, mockers guard winter food sources for simple survival. And the rigors of guarding winter territory equal that of guarding summer territory.

How do mockingbirds learn to sing like mockingbirds? While some bird species are born hard-wired with the songs of their species, mockers are not. They learn by listening. They listen to good ol' dad; they listen to dad's competition; they listen to the guys next door. Then they listen to everything else around them: car alarms and horns, back-up warning beepers, train whistles, emergency vehicle sirens, and depending on where they live, whatever else they hear on a regular basis.

BIRD TALK: WHO'S CALLING?
Males and females both sing, mimicking birds around them, learning new songs all their lives, some males having more than 200 songs in their repertoire. They repeat each phrase usually three to six times before changing to a new phrase, a repetition count that separates them from fellow mimics, the Gray Catbird and Brown Thrasher.

Mockers keep learning new songs all their lives. Some virtuosos, in fact, become so artful that they know as many as two hundred or more song phrases. But to keep the girls coming, they never repeat all those songs in the same order. Variation apparently keeps the act fresh.

Sometimes, though, a male gets lonely, especially in spring. And he's lonely all day—and, unfortunately, all night. So he sings. The more lonely he is, the more he sings, from your rooftop, your satellite dish, your tallest tree, your yard light post, your backyard fence, moving from one spot to the next to show off the perimeter of his territory. If the repertoire keeps you awake at night, I'm sure he would apologize, but time is limited and the need urgent. Breeding season is brief.

NEST NOTES

Nest Site: probably selected by male, in low dense shrubs and trees, 3–10 ft. high, thorny vegetation favored

Nest Construction: built by male; dead twigs form an open cup, lined with grasses and leaves, sometimes including human trash, like foil, cigarette filters, shreds of plastic or paper, dental floss

Eggs: 2–6 eggs, 2–3 broods, incubated only by female, 12–13 days

Fledge: 12–13 days from hatch

The male's robust song, accompanied by upward loop flights in which it flashes its white wing bars and white tail edges, surely proves irresistible to a female. Having attracted her and knowing she is hunkered in a nearby nest, he sings more quietly, perhaps a soothing auditory signal to her of her—and her brood's—protection.

ID CHECK

Northern Mockingbird, both male and female, is identified by the following traits:

- Overall gray coloration with darker wings and whitish gray breast and belly
- Two white wing bars
- White wing patch obvious in flight
- White outer tail feathers obvious in flight
- Long tail, long legs
- Relatively long bill, slightly decurved
- Narrow dark eyeline

SPECIES PROFILE

GRAY CATBIRD

VITAL STATS
Length: 8.3–9.4 in.
Wingspan: 8.7–11.8 in.
Weight: 0.9 oz.

Gray Catbird

NAME THAT BIRD

Dumetella carolinensis (Gray Catbird): *Dumetella* refers to a thorny thicket, ideal habitat for this bird. *Carolinensis* refers to the Carolina colonies where the bird was first found. Its common name refers to its overall color and part of the bird's call that sounds much like a cat's meow.

BIRD TALK: WHO'S CALLING?

Gray Catbirds sing like Northern Mockingbirds, mimicking other birds around them as well as frogs and insects, and adding an assortment of squeaks and whistles. They sing each phrase only once before moving to the next. Their call, a raspy mewing, earns this bird its name. Females sing occasionally but much more quietly than males.

They look alike, the male and female Gray Catbirds. All gray. At least from a distance they look all gray. Get a closer look, though, and you'll see the fashionably dark gray cap and—surprise!—a bright chestnut-brown patch under the tail. Strange place for a strikingly contrasting color, but Gray Catbirds boast several quirky characteristics.

Part of the purpose of that mostly hidden chestnut-brown patch may be connected with breeding. When the two undergo courtship rituals, it's a fast-paced chase through the undergrowth, dashing out and back in, a rapid pursuit, a bit of flirtatious catch-me-if-you-can. Then, when the chase ends, he turns his back to her, bows, droops his wings, and raises his tail, displaying that single patch of color. Who knows what goes through her mind, for she, too, wears the chestnut-brown patch.

Catbirds lead secret lives. They like to hide in dense vegetation, especially brushy undergrowth, the closer to impenetrable the better. Situate this dense undergrowth near water and *voila,* you've found catbird heaven. So replicating catbird heaven in your yard may be a bit tricky. In my southern Indiana yard, it's come down to wild blackberry brambles—half a hillside of them. Only in recent years, after we quit mowing the hillside and clearing only a path along the bottom, have I had the joy of living with this songster.

Even though they've moved in with me, catbirds never visit my feeders. In fact, rarely do I see these secretive birds. But I hear the male sing. In differentiating his song from those of the Northern Mockingbird and the Brown Thrasher, I've come to think of the catbird as a bit more quiet, more tentative, singing each phrase only once, as if speaking only to one during a lovely dinner for two, rarely repeating phrases, burbling along in an uneven tempo with its own improvised material.

SPOTTING THE SPECTACULAR   **Posting Guard**

When the female catbird leaves the nest to feed, the male stays close by, keeping an eye peeled, guarding the nest, watching for any intrusion. As a result, when a Brown-headed Cowbird tries to slip in and deposit its parasitic egg, it is either chased off before the deed is done, or the catbirds puncture and toss out her egg. Thus, cowbird parasitism among catbirds is a rare event. Other birds should take lessons from the clever little catbirds.

In the catbird world, however, the guy with the most songs wins the girl. It behooves him, then, to imitate every bird—indeed, every sound—possible. I try to imagine a catbird listening to the Northern Mockingbird and the Brown Thrasher, striving to imitate everything they sing. A mimic mimicking the mimics!

Catbirds, however, distinguish themselves as caregivers, quick to the defense of their own. Let nests, nestlings, or fledglings come under threat, and the distress calls bring in the troops.

In fact, catbirds are so geared to come to the aid of each other that, unlike other species, they even care for orphaned baby catbirds. Ironically, bird banders, having caught catbirds in their mist nets, frequently capture additional catbirds that respond to netted birds' distress calls.

During winter, many catbirds migrate to the Atlantic Coast where the species lives year-round. Others migrate to Florida, the Gulf Coast, and into Central America. As a result, the destruction and reduction of coastal habitat is beginning to cause population declines among these amazing songsters.

FOOD FARE

In summer, Gray Catbirds eat mostly ants, beetles, grasshoppers, caterpillars, cankerworms, Japanese and June beetles, and gypsy moths but supplement their diet with berries and fruits. In the garden, they enjoy elderberries, grapes, blackberries, cherries and holly, poison ivy, and dogwood berries. They rarely feed in the open, and to the best of my knowledge, they never come to a feeder.

NEST NOTES

Nest Site: usually made about four feet off the ground but can be on the ground, well concealed in dense shrubs, vines, or tangles, on horizontal branch; site selection process unknown

Nest Construction: built by female but male sometimes brings nest materials; bulky open cup of grapevine bark, twigs, bark, straw, trash, lined with soft grasses, hair, pine needles, about 5.5 in. wide and 2 in. deep

Eggs: 1–6 eggs, 2–3 broods, incubated only by female, 12–15 days; some males may bring food

Fledge: 10–11 days after hatch

Given the bird's behavior and preference for dense vegetation, and given its catlike mewing call, the bird seems to be mocking cats, taunting them if you will, while remaining perfectly camouflaged—and safe! But don't overlook the bird's preference for singing from the highest spot in its territory. That brings me to the question: Have you heard that smug expression about someone, "sitting in the catbird seat"? Mirroring the catbird's manner, the phrase means that a person enjoys a position of favor, living the good life, protected from the cruel world, perhaps conveying a bit of snobbery.

Amazing, isn't it, how we cloak humans with labels reflecting bird behavior, sometimes as a compliment and sometimes not!

ID CHECK

Gray Catbirds of either sex display the following markings:
- Overall somber gray body, minus any streaking, spots, or wing bars
- Dark gray cap
- Chestnut-brown undertail patch
- Long, slender, round-tipped blackish tail
- Narrow straight bill
- Broad rounded wings in flight

SPECIES PROFILE

BROWN THRASHER

VITAL STATS
Length: 9.1–11.8 in.
Wingspan: 11.4–12.6 in.
Weight: 2.8 oz.

Brown Thrasher

They nested in a dense spreading juniper, the handsome Brown Thrasher pair. Deep inside, well protected from hawks and raccoons by closely spaced twigs and branches, the nest already harbored babies. I know only because I could hear their tiny peeps and could watch the adults on their routine feeding missions.

NAME THAT BIRD

Toxostoma rufum (Brown Thrasher): The bird's slightly down-curved bill somewhat resembles the curve of a strung bow, thus *Toxostoma*, meaning "bow mouth." *Rufum* refers to its reddish color. Its common name downplays the reddishness to "brown," and "thrasher" comes from an English word that means "like a thrush."

Puttering about in the garden near the protective juniper, I heard what I first thought was squirrel chatter. As I refocused, however, I understood that chatter was, instead, the Brown Thrasher's churring scold. Were they scolding me? I didn't think so, but I backed off, weeding in another part of the garden, farther from the nest site.

The scolding continued, grew more insistent, the birds more agitated, more physical, bouncing about inside the juniper, evidenced only by shuddering branches. Something was surely amiss.

As I approached the head-high shrub, the birds ignored me, focusing instead on their nest, scolding, darting, diving. Separating the branches, I peered in. There, along the branch that cradled the nest, lay a huge snake, partly curled inside the nest, oblivious to the agitation around him. The thrashers, emboldened by their preservation instincts, landed directly on the snake, pecking it vigorously, endangering themselves, risking the snake's lightning-fast strikes. But the snake, apparently somehow content in spite of the attacks, remained curled in the nest.

NEST NOTES

Nest Site: selected by both sexes; situated on or very low to ground, in or below dense tangle, especially thorny vegetation

Nest Construction: both sexes build, relatively flat bulky nest of 4–12 in. twigs, about 7 in. diameter, 2 in. deep, lined with leaves topped with rootlets

Eggs: 2–6 eggs (average 3), 1–2 broods, incubated by both sexes, 11–14 days, although females incubate about twice as long as males

Fledge: 11–12 days after hatch

Then I understood. The snake was digesting its dinner. The lumps along its body were four, the four precious babies of the Brown Thrashers. I understand that this is nature's way, that the snake has to eat, too. Still, I was sick to my stomach, knowing how hard the thrashers had worked, building the nest, one stick at a time, a flight out and back for each twig and stem, the female exerting the physical energy to lay eggs, the four of them, then committing to the time to incubate minute by minute for nearly two weeks, and most recently, finding bugs, ferrying them to the nest, and carefully feeding the babies. And now the babies are gone, lunch for a snake. That incident occurred many years ago. Never again did thrashers nest in the juniper.

But they've nested somewhere, secreted off in another part of the yard where I've not discovered their nest—and maybe the snakes didn't discover it, either. I know they're here, though, because the male sings from the top of the oak tree, from the top of the sweetgum tree, from the top of the holly tree, his quiet, repeat-everything-twice song, distinctly different from that of the mockingbird that likes to sing from similar tip-top spots.

BIRD TALK: WHO'S CALLING?
Brown Thrashers sing a series of songs reminiscent of a Northern Mockingbird or Gray Catbird, both relatives; but in addition to mimicking other birds, they add their own variable phrases, repeating each twice, and pausing before the next phrase.

SPOTTING THE SPECTACULAR **Believe It or Not**

Thanks to Donald Kroodsma's work, the Brown Thrasher holds an entry in *Ripley's Believe It or Not* for the number of songs rendered by a single bird. Are you ready for the number? Would you believe over 2,400? Thus, the thrasher's repertoire far exceeds that of both Northern Mockingbirds and Gray Catbirds. Now for the other question. Which is more amazing—that the bird has so many songs or that someone was able to count them?

The male and the female look alike, at least to us, a lovely bright rufous brown on head, back, wings, and tail with whitish breast cleanly streaked with black. Larger than mockingbirds and catbirds, long tailed, and conspicuous during courtship, thrashers turn secretive and seem to disappear once nesting begins. Because so many of those shrubby overgrown areas that attract them have disappeared, Brown Thrasher numbers slowly decline. So you can then add a star to your crown if your habitat helps thrashers reduce their population slide.

FOOD FARE
Brown Thrashers eat mostly insects, especially beetles, as well as other arthropods and fruits, berries, and nuts. I've never known a Brown Thrasher to come to my feeders, but they will forage in leaf litter.

Considered short-distance migrants, they disperse to warmer climes when severe winter weather makes foraging for bugs difficult or impossible, but they rarely leave the United States.

ID CHECK

To identify a Brown Thrasher, look for these characteristics:
- Long-tailed large bird with long, strong bill
- Bright rufous-brown on head, back, wings, and tail
- Whitish breast with clearly defined black streaks

SPECIES PROFILE

CHIPPING SPARROW

VITAL STATS
Length: 4.7–5.9 in.
Wingspan: 8.3 in.
Weight: 0.5 oz.

Chipping Sparrow

Friends tease me that my favorite bird is whichever one I'm watching at the moment. Mmmm, well, maybe. But my favorite sparrow, at least in spring and summer, hands down, is the Chipping Sparrow. It's trim, neat, well groomed, cute, and relatively tame. And that snazzy rufous-brown cap it wears above that black stripe through its eye makes it readily identifiable in any situation. So, if you'll allow me, given what I deem as a racing cap and slim eye goggles, might as well add "sporty" to the list, too!

Long tailed, Chipping Sparrows show off a silhouette readily identifiable. Add their smaller-than-usual bills, and you'll key in to the birds' identity. Look for them in tall grassy areas supporting a scattering of trees. In spring, they'll tee up on tall weeds, saplings, or sometimes in upper tree limbs, preferably evergreens if available. There, they'll sing, a loud, clear, long monotone trill, readily recognizable, even by folks not familiar with bird song.

BIRD TALK: WHO'S CALLING?
Males sing a long series of rapid, dry, mechanical-sounding chips (hence, the bird's name), similar to that of Dark-eyed Juncos. So if you live where both birds breed, listen for a somewhat more musical series of chips from juncos to separate the two.

While chippers breed across most of North America, they retreat to the more southerly climes when severe winters cover their favorite seeds with ice or deep snow. Considered "partial migrants," generally chippers fly no farther than necessary, and never any farther than southern Mexico. (An apparently nonmigratory subspecies lives year round in Central America.) Banding studies show that at least some chippers from Ontario winter in Florida.

Still, some years we'll see a few chippers during the winter in our southern Indiana yard. Then, though, picking among the fallen feeder seeds, they blend in with all the other LBJs (little brown jobs), harder to sort out minus their sporty colorful caps, turned streaky and dull for the winter.

Chippers distinguish themselves from other sparrows by their preference not for grasslands but for scattered open woodlands. So if your backyard habitat includes small shrubby trees amid short grasses and other slender vegetation, chippers may choose your yard for nesting. And if those small trees include evergreens, like juniper or cedar, your chances improve significantly. Add a gone-to-seed weed patch for foraging, and I can almost guarantee their presence. Then they'll thank you kindly with song and babies, visiting your feeders for seed.

While chippers feed primarily hopping along on the ground, I've seen them bobbing from grass stems, plucking seeds. It's rather amusing behavior, their extortions at reaching the seeds, causing the stems to shudder all the more violently. But they know the drill and manage quite well, downing every ripe seed before moving on.

NAME THAT BIRD
Spizella passerina (Chipping Sparrow): *Spizella* means "little finch," and *passerina* is Latin for "sparrow." The common name refers to the bird's song. "Sparrow" comes from a word meaning "flutterer" or "small bird."

FOOD FARE
Chipping Sparrows eat seeds, especially from a wide variety of grasses and weeds. During breeding season, however, they turn to insects for added protein and to feed their babies. They regularly take grit.

NEST NOTES
Nest Site: selection by both sexes; 3–10 ft. up, usually at tip of branch, hidden by vegetation, often in evergreens
Nest Construction: by female with male in close attendance; flimsy see-through nest, 4.5 inches by 2 inches, of dried grasses and rootlets, lined with fine plant fibers
Eggs: 2–7 eggs, 1–3 broods, incubated by female only, 10–15 days
Fledge: 9–12 days after hatch

From time to time, I've managed to spot a Chipping Sparrow nest, almost always in a low shrubby cedar tree, usually surrounded by moderately high grass but near mowed areas. One year, though, I spotted a baby, obviously just out of the nest. It sat neatly atop a purple coneflower blossom, barely taking up a third of the flower surface. While the babe sat seemingly helpless, chittering, mouth agape, mom and dad fed it regularly, keeping tabs, I'm sure, on others from their brood. Although I never saw the others, the adults moved routinely from spot to spot in the garden, almost certainly tending to them.

They are delightful little creatures in the garden and are common enough to probably be in yours as well.

SPOTTING THE SPECTACULAR   **Flocking Chippers**

At the end of breeding season, Chipping Sparrows form flocks of 20 to 40 birds and forage together for weed seeds along roadsides, among grasslands and parks, and at well-stocked feeders, especially near trees and preferably near evergreens. Happy with human-altered vegetation, including the scattered trees of suburbs and parks, they're doing well as a species across most of North America.

ID CHECK

Chipping Sparrows can be readily identified by spotting these field marks:
- Streaked back and wings
- White wing bars
- Whitish underparts in breeding plumage, darkly streaked in winter
- Bright rufous cap in breeding plumage, turned duller, streaky brown in winter
- Black stripe through eye
- Small black bill in breeding plumage, pinkish in winter
- Pink legs
- Long tail

July

The presence of birds at any time is magical in effect.
They are magicians that transform every scene,
make of every desert a garden of delights.

CHARLES C. ABBOT

Dog days, they call them, those hazy, lazy days of summer. In the heat of July, with June's summer solstice now weeks gone by, the earth's annual cycle begins its downhill slide, almost imperceptibly but nevertheless relentlessly, inching onward toward autumn and winter. July's partly-gone-to-seed garden blooms in spite of the heat, the plants biologically bound to produce seed, to reproduce themselves. In spite of our midsummer human mindset, most birds never quit living life in a hurry. Now, in July, the avian world marks a nesting season that ends for some birds, begins for others, and continues in full swing for multiple-brood families.

Detective Work in the Neighborhood

Even before nesting season ends, new kids have slipped into the neighborhood, once again changing the monthly landscape. Fledglings try to stay hidden, shy about their limitations, instinctively fearful of predators. But I know they're here. They call in their squeaky little baby voices, begging for food, testing the duration of mom and dad's willingness to serve it up.

So who are these new kids on the block? A quick survey of our immediate neighborhood tallied fifty-two species breeding here. Did I see fifty-two nests? Oh my, no. Did I see most of them? Not in my wildest dreams. So how do I know they nested?

The detective in me found a whole set of revealing clues. Here they are:

First, back in May, I had a sneak peak at courting behavior: male cardinals offering bill-to-bill gifts of sunflower seeds to flirting mates; bluebird pairs ducking in and out of nest boxes, comparing the merits of one location over another; a male Wood Duck swimming nervously around a female, awaiting her decision; and Red-shouldered Hawks copulating.

Sometimes I know they nested because I saw bird pairs, not courting, particularly, but their breeding-season togetherness pointing to their family ways: Eastern Towhees, the male in black and rust, the female in brown and rust; Brown Thrashers, both nearly indistinguishable but together; Indigo Buntings, the male in brilliant blue, the female in plain-Jane brown.

A pair of Wood Ducks, the handsome drake in the lead, paddle across the farm pond, approaching the nest box we've provided.

HOW DOES YOUR GARDEN GROW?
A Weed Patch in the Corner

By July, my weed patch wears a lovely garment of white. White panicle asters (*Aster lanceolatus*) sprinkle their tiny white flowers across the crown. Bees, butterflies, and of course, birds—especially hummingbirds, flycatchers, wrens, warblers, and native sparrows—frequent the flowers, some to eat nectar and some to eat the nectar eaters. More of these wildflowers—which some folks might mistakenly call weeds—will bloom next month and the next, attracting still more fauna, until frost turns the whole patch brown. Then seed heads draw migrant native sparrows to the treats.

To let a corner go wild, to let it grow up in "weeds" and form a wildflower garden, is to draw an amazing array of wildlife, especially birds. On the other hand, if a weed patch goes totally untended, you may have nothing but Asian exotics. So depending on where you live, welcome natives like wild asters (*Aster* or *Symphyotrichum* spp.), goldenrod (*Solidago* spp.), milkweed (*Asclepias* spp.), native thistle (*Cirsium* spp.), American bittersweet (*Celastrus scandens*), prairie grasses, and sedges. But try to keep the exotics at bay, like Japanese honeysuckle (*Lonicera japonica*), multiflora rose (*Rosa multiflora*), oriental bittersweet (*Celastrus orbiculatus*), and bull thistle (*Cirsium vulgare*). The birds will reward you for your lovely native garden.

Panicle asters bloom in profusion along my yard-path edges, attracting multiple avian species, both year-round residents and summer nesters.

The extended family of seven crows, the young from last year and the previous year helping mom and dad with this year's brood, busied themselves in their territory.

Birds carrying nest materials—sticks, grasses, pine straw, last year's leaves, bits of string, gobs of mud—clearly showed they were building a nursery. The female Baltimore Oriole yanked shreds from our native wisteria vine to weave into her hanging nest. Carolina Wrens scooped up bills full of shredded leaf mulch, filling their bills so full they surely couldn't see to fly. Carolina Chickadees tugged tufts of moss from the ground where it grows on the north side of the shed to line their cavity nest. House Wrens executed contortions to stuff 8-inch twigs into 1½-inch holes in a gourd.

HABITAT—YOURS AND THEIRS
The Fifth Component of Habitat

Besides food, water, shelter, and places to raise young, we must add a fifth ingredient to backyard bird habitat: safety. Avoid pesticides. Take strides toward preventing window kills. Keep cats out of your backyard habitat.

Bottom line: If we invite birds to our yards, we have an obligation to make habitat safe for them to accept our invitations.

In addition, territorial defense told nesting stories—and made for entertaining backyard bird watching. Mockingbirds chased and fussed. Great Crested Flycatchers called from a chosen tree cavity. Red-winged Blackbirds dive-bombed the Red-shouldered Hawk as it hunted too close to their territory. The Summer Tanager sang from treetops around his territory's perimeter, drawing an audio map.

Birds singing during breeding season are either defending territory or advertising for mates. If they're singing, you can bet they're nesting, or will be soon. Sometimes, of course,

Northern Parulas sing early and again now, in mid-summer, when they begin their second nesting.

songs are more easily heard than secretive birds are to see, like Northern Parula, Northern Bobwhite, Eastern Wood-pewee, Red-eyed Vireo, Common Yellowthroat, Yellow-throated Warbler, and Wood Thrush. Lately, Yellow-billed Cuckoos, awaiting caterpillar reproduction to begin nesting, registered their territorial boundaries with their resonating *klok-klok-klok*.

Occasionally, I'd get a peek at breeding pairs feeding their young. Tree Swallows fed young in the nest and fed fledglings on the wing (a spectacle to watch); woodpeckers—downy, hairy, and red-bellied—brought their youngsters to our suet feeders; a pair of nuthatches showed three babies how to snap up sunflower-seed snacks; Chipping Sparrows taught their family birdbath-splashing techniques.

FEEDER FOCUS **Thistle from Afar**

Thistle seed, the common name for niger seed and trademarked "Nyjer," really isn't thistle at all. Rather, it's a centuries-old African herb (*Guizotia abyssinica*) that flowers yellow and produces an oilseed. Crushed, it yields cooking oil, commonly used in Africa and Asia, similar to canola or safflower oil. Because niger doesn't grow in North America, however, every seed we offer birds comes from elsewhere. In fact, the bulk of an estimated 70 million pounds imported annually comes from India and Ethiopia. Thus, given the foreign origins, regulations require niger seed be heat-sterilized to destroy weed seeds without affecting the feeder seeds. Together, shipping and sterilization make niger pricey.

Pricey or not, the rich and nutritious seed offers about 40 percent fat and 18 percent protein; so birds like goldfinches, Indigo Buntings, and Pine Siskins love it. But fat promotes spoilage, so storing niger in conditions too hot or for periods too long turns it rancid. Watch feeders. If birds stop feeding, seed has likely grown rancid or turned moldy. Wash feeders; add fresh seed. Birds will return posthaste.

Eventually, I saw or heard fledglings. Two Barred Owl babies cried out a hair-raising combination *hiss-scream-bark* every night, a call that merits the Scariest Halloween Sound Effect award. Two Red-tailed Hawks practiced aerial acrobatics with their parents over the hayfield. Three kingfishers showed up to hunt at the farm pond—one more than usual. And the resident Green Heron pair became four. Now, in July, a multitude of young hummingbirds squabbles regularly at nectar feeders. Successful nestings!

Now, in mid-summer, goldfinches feed heavily in preparation for their late nesting season. Thistle (niger) seed is their preferred oil-rich feast.

BOTANY FOR BIRDS   **Top 15 Summer Garden Flowers**

In my garden, some flowers get more attention than others—and not just from me. Birds have their favorites, too. Whether birds like the nectar, seeds, or bugs that the nectar attracts, or whether they nibble the flowers themselves (as goldfinches love to do), the following fifteen perennials are tops in my southern Indiana garden. Many also attract butterflies. Check hardiness zones and native species for your area at http://plants.usda.gov.

A native prairie plant, purple coneflower rises sturdy and tall amid other garden flowers and draws birds to its seed and butterflies and bees to its nectar.

WHY DO BIRDS DO THAT?
Why Do Birds Carry Little White Sacs from Their Nests?

You may have seen birds carry little white sacs from their nests. Think of the little sacs as self-contained diapers. And some moms—but not all—keep a fastidiously clean house. So when an adult bluebird, for instance, feeds babies, it waits a few seconds until baby excretes the little sac; and then the adult carries it off, dropping it well away from the nest, preferably in water (yikes! maybe your pool!), to prevent predators from tracking the scent. But according to an unpublished report, some birds, including mockingbirds, actually eat the fecal sacs, especially those of really young birds whose digestive tracts are not yet fully developed and thus eliminate certain remaining good nutrients. Okay, maybe that was more than you wanted to know.

And well, yes, I actually spotted a few nests: the cardinal in the flame honeysuckle vine, the robin on the curve of the downspout, a dove under the trellis, and the Song Sparrow only a foot from the ground in the abelia bush. Of course, the nest boxes housed families of blue-

Common Name	Scientific Name	Attraction
Aster	*Aster* spp.	nectar, bugs
Beebalm/Oswego tea	*Monarda didyma*	nectar, bugs
Black-eyed or Brown-eyed Susan	*Rudbeckia* spp. (choose one native to your area)	seeds
Blanket flower	*Gaillardia pulchella*	seeds
Butterfly bush	*Buddleia davidii*	nectar, bugs, flowers, seeds
Coreopsis	*Coreopsis* spp.	seeds
Coneflower (Eastern purple)	*Echinacea purpurea*	seeds
Cosmos	*Cosmos* spp.	seeds
Hollyhock	*Althea* spp.	nectar, bugs, seeds
Jewelweed	*Impatiens* spp. (choose one native to your area)	nectar, seeds
Morning glory	*Ipomoea* spp.	nectar, bugs
Salvia, esp. red and blue varieties	*Salvia* spp.	nectar
Sunflower (avoid fancy hybrids)	*Helianthus annuus*	bugs, seeds
Verbena, esp. tall	*Verbena bonariensis*	nectar, bugs
Zinnia, esp. tall, large-flowered	*Zinnia elegans*	nectar, bugs, seeds

Depending on where you live, Mourning Doves may nest year round.

birds (including one unusual pair that has for three years laid white eggs) as well as chickadees, House Wrens, Tree Sparrows, titmice, and Wood Ducks.

Try the detective work in your backyard. You may be surprised!

HABITAT—YOURS AND THEIRS

Nice in the Neighborhood

Many communities enforce some form of weed ordinance. No one can have "weeds" more than, say, ten inches tall. The ordinances come with good intent—to make sure people maintain their yards and keep the neighborhood tidy.

But those of us who aim for a wildlife habitat may find ourselves at odds with the rule-makers, accused of being in violation of the ordinances, especially when neighbors don't understand what they're seeing. They may perceive wildflowers as weeds. So keep neighbors informed. Name the native wildflowers, and explain why they grow in your garden or along the back fence. Use borders or fences to demark the garden boundaries. We use short stretches of split rails to edge mowed paths. Maybe a picket fence or wrought-iron fence better suits your style.

Plant hedges, and let them grow high enough to block what neighbors may find objectionable. The more vegetation you plant, the more private your yard—and the happier the birds.

Keep a list of birds you see in your yard. Then, list in hand, invite the neighbors to your yard to enjoy the habitat and join you in your endeavor to attract more birds. Share information with them, perhaps in the form of this book. Make wildlife habitat a neighborhood project, perhaps suggesting as a goal a certified wildlife neighborhood. Most people like birds; they just don't know how to provide for them beyond feeders and feed. You can help!

Midsummer Madness

BIOLOGY BITS
Going the Distance

Species that fly farthest—like Purple Martins, Summer and Scarlet Tanagers, all the vireos and swallows—leave first, followed by those that travel to middle distances and then those that travel least. Bird-feeders don't lure birds out of migration but, depending on the species and what your feeders and habitat hold, you might help migrants refuel along the way.

All birds live in a hurry. They search for food in a hurry, forced by necessity to find daily nutrition. They breed in a hurry, biologically driven to reproduce at all costs. They feed their babies in a hurry, instinctively alert to predators watching. They prepare for winter in a hurry, innately knowing without understanding the annual cycle. Life is urgent, hurried, short—a bit mad, if you will.

In July, despite our own human midsummer doldrums, the avian madness persists. As the annual cycle spins on, birds sense the coming changes. In fact, believe it or not, now in July, some birds are already preparing to leave us, to fly south, perhaps way south. After all, their kids are growing fast and can now fly and eat on their own. Housekeeping is history. So, the well-deserving moms and dads will rest a bit, put on some fat, and boogie south. Among some species, the kids will follow later, when they're ready.

Our year-round residents, though, never face the problem of taking the kids on a long journey. And when the migrants leave, there's more food for everyone else. So, given extra time and extra bugs, our locals often raise an extra brood.

The resulting midsummer madness raises the curtain on some crazy and wild activity—much of it in juxtaposition.

Last weekend, for instance, at a wetlands mudflat a few miles from our backyard, sixty-two Killdeer fed ravenously, together, peacefully. Now, that's a behavior you'd never see during breeding season. Then, territorial pairs keep others of their kind at a distance. No cozy get-togethers allowed.

Among the sixty-two Killdeer, however, another example of midsummer madness wandered along. Three little shorebirds called Least Sandpipers poked about in the mud, feeding on worms, putting on fat, readying themselves to continue south. Among our earliest migrants, these little sandpipers, in mid-July, have already been on the wing for hundreds of miles. In fact, they left their Arctic breeding grounds as soon as their youngsters fledged, leaving the tykes to fend for themselves. Now, in midsummer, they've already flown from the Arctic to where I live in southern Indiana.

HABITAT—YOURS AND THEIRS

Happy Habitats

Obviously, shorebirds aren't typical yard birds—unless, of course, you live on the shore. While other birds' preferred habitats may not be quite as clear cut as that of shorebirds, all birds hang out in their respective preferred habitats.

Compare birds' preferred habitats with your own. For instance, Cerulean Warblers and Acadian Flycatchers choose only forest interiors. American Redstarts, Blue-winged Warblers, and Gray Catbirds enjoy tangled woods' edges or areas only somewhat cleared. But large clearings like mowed yards tend to attract Common Grackles, American Robins, and Brown-headed Cowbirds. Add livestock and human habitation to the large clearings, and what prefers that habitat? Starlings, House Sparrows, and pigeons.

Aim to replicate—as much as possible, of course—desirable natural habitats in your backyard. It will forever be a work in progress, but progress will prevail.

While I now read daily online reports of the season's first migrants, I'm also noting birdlife changes right in my own backyard, a sort of restlessness, a sense of pending drama, waiting for the perfect time. Tree Swallows have fledged but continue their aerial flycatching among the dozens of Barn Swallows sweeping the pasture. A pair of Eastern Kingbirds hawks bugs from tree-top vantage points, contentedly munching their catches, no longer bound by hungry, squawking nestlings to share the tasty catch. They seem to be biding time.

If your backyard habitat becomes "woodsy" enough, you may attract Acadian Flycatchers that will help rid the yard of bugs.

Eastern Kingbirds snatch bugs from vantage points along open limbs or fencerows.

In juxtaposition, though, after the early summer semi-silence when birds busied themselves nesting and feeding young, among some birds, midsummer brings a return of song. Now during early evenings, the Summer Tanager's melody brings joy to my soul. From the woods, the Wood Thrush song, a flute-like aria and my favorite of all bird songs, makes me smile. I like knowing he's here. Occasionally from the woodland edge, a not-so-melodious Yellow-billed Cuckoo sings a song that, when I was a kid, earned the bird its "rain crow" moniker. But its sporadic same-location calls suggest its late busyness, perhaps still—or again—feeding young.

Among some birds, however, only occasional melody marks midsummer madness. The Eastern Wood-pewee, one of those typically busy flycatchers, sits patiently on a leafless limb, darts after bugs, and returns to devour its catch, no longer busy toting bugs to babes. Like a contemplative long-distance flier relishing the day, it seems to sing

One of my favorite forest birds and huge consumer of caterpillars, the Yellow-billed Cuckoo is heard more often than seen.

By July, the Eastern Wood-pewee once again is calling his name—although often only half of it—and flycatching over my garden.

to itself, often singing only half its song, the downward slur, and then, as if rethinking, stops.

By contrast, year-round residents—chickadees, wrens, cardinals, bluebirds, doves, robins—dedicate their mid-summer madness to additional broods, producing second or even third nestings. Makes me tired just thinking about the urgency of the task.

WATER WAYS   **Yucky Green Stuff**

In July's typical oppressive heat, water draws a crowd. But nobody—not even birds—likes yucky algae in a back-yard water feature. Three factors contribute to algae growth: sunlight, nutrients, and low oxygen. So, it's a simple matter to naturally control algae growth.

First, plants in and around the water add shade, reducing algae's source of sunlight. Second, hardy water plants zap significant nutrients from the water, thus starving out algae. Finally, plants add oxygen—some more than others—that renders the water too oxygen-rich for algae. So add plants; you'll reduce algae and, at the same time, add a lovely natural graceful touch to a man-made water feature. Consider natives like sweetflag (*Acorus americanus*), yellow marsh marigold (*Caltha palustris*), water iris (*Iris virginica*), pickerelweed (*Pontedaria cordata*), and swamp rosemallow (*Hibiscus grandiflorus*).

Of course, small birdbaths can't accommodate plants. To keep these water features sparkling clean, change the water daily and give the basin a few good swishes with a wire brush. If you've been on vacation and the green stuff accumulated in your absence, use equal parts hot water and plain white vinegar and apply the wire brush for a vigorous rubdown. Rinse thoroughly.

Meanwhile, midsummer madness continues as juveniles arrive at the feeders: speckle-breasted robins, speckle-breasted bluebirds, dark-billed female-looking cardinals, and down-tufted brown thrashers. While all full sized, each carries the stigma of teenage plumage. Woodpeckers—downy, hairy, and red-bellied—coax their young to the suet. I hate to admit that I hurt for the Red-bellied Woodpecker, its babies almost painfully plain. But they'll grow up gorgeous, and I guess that's mom's consolation. At any rate, the assortment of babes at the feeders makes for amusing sightings—their odd plumage, their awkwardness, their vocal insistence, their Velcro-like stick-to-itiveness to mom and dad.

Who's "Immature"?

When babes leave the nest, they change from "nestlings" to "fledglings." As soon as they can feed themselves and fly well enough to fend for themselves, they change from "fledglings" to "immatures." But the immature stage varies dramatically among species before the bird becomes a bona-fide adult.

A Northern Cardinal reaches maturity in a matter of months—from the time it leaves the nest, perhaps in early July, until it molts into adult plumage, likely around November. At the other extreme, however, Bald Eagles take at least five years to reach maturity, not until then gaining the all-white head and tail. In any case, maturity in birds implies more than so-called adult plumage. Biologically, a mature bird is able to breed.

Immature Bald Eagles look splotchy, even dirty, before they gain mature plumage at about age five. When Bald Eagles reach maturity, they wear regal all-white heads and all-white tails, while the remainder of their contrasting plumage is rich brown.

A nectaring immature Ruby-throated Hummingbird, characterized by its streaked throat and tan-edged feathers on head and back, will molt on its wintering grounds and return next spring in mature plumage.

But midsummer madness guarantees expanding activity in three more places: in the flower garden and at the hummingbird feeder, as young hummers fledge and northern hummers move south over the next two months; and in the sky, as Chimney Swifts gather in growing flocks, creating thronging social groups prior to mass migration.

At long last, as part of midsummer madness, goldfinches begin nesting. They've been waiting for thistle to bloom and go to seed, for it's the soft seed fluff with which they line their nests and the seeds with which they feed their babes. Lately I've seen bursting thistle seed heads along the roadsides—another sure sign of midsummer change.

So it's a crazy time—some birds already following the relentless tug south, some packing it on in preparation to leave; some singing to retain territory; some, of all things, filling new nests. And the migrants' fledglings? They're still trying to get things straight—what to eat, how to find food, where to roost, when to hide, where to go. Soon, they, too, will feel the relentless restlessness, the instinctive urge to gorge, the push to leave, the understanding, somehow, that they must migrate. They're hardwired to know when to go, where to go, and when they arrive, a set of instincts beyond my comprehension. Mad, indeed.

PROBLEM SOLVER
Battle of the Bees at the Hummingbird Feeder

Depending on where you live, one or more kinds of bees looking for fast food may join your yard's midsummer madness—unfortunately, at your hummingbird feeders. If they find sweet stuff, they'll tell all their friends. Your feeders will be swamped with bees. At my house, small ground bees, sometimes called yellow jackets, most frequently make pests of themselves.

The solution, however, is simple: If bees can't get to the syrup, they won't hang around. So if they're clinging to your feeders, one of two conditions exists. First, the feeder may be leaking. If so, decide whether or not you can stop the leak. If not, replace the feeder.

Second, a poor feeder design may allow bees access. Generally, a deep reservoir prevents bees from poking their proboscises (tongues) far enough into the feeder to sip syrup. Since some larger bees have tongues nearly a half-inch long, you may need to replace your bee-loving feeders with those having deeper reservoirs or longer "throats" on the feeding ports.

All that having been said, however, hummingbirds are messy eaters. When they drag their bills in and out of the feeder ports, they leave a bit of nectar residue. Bees go after that, too.

Summer Storms

Seek shelter! Alerted by meteorologists' severe-storm predictions, we dive to our basements, cowering against fierce winds, driving rain, lightning pops, and ear-shattering thunder. But what do birds do? They've no basement, no roof over their heads, not even a meteorologist's warning.

But birds have reckoned with storms since before time as we know it, and they understand what do to. They, too, seek shelter. Depending on the species, birds tuck in on the lee side of a natural or artificial structure—a tree trunk, steep bank, building, or dense thicket. Or amid tall grasses, shrubs, brush piles, thick cedar groves, or other natural windbreaks. Some seek shelter in cavities, natural or man-made, like roost- and nestboxes.

Still, winds can rip birds from their roosts, or rip the roosts from their structure. Rains soak seed, cover it or cause it to rot. Bobwhites, towhees, Brown Thrashers, and Song Sparrows may find their ground nests flooded, eggs destroyed, or nestlings drowned. Extended cold rains ground flying insects, eliminating food for Purple Martins and other swallows, swifts, phoebes, and pewees, all birds that feed on the fly. And no bird can feed during a pounding deluge.

NOTABLE BEHAVIOR   **Feeding on the Wing**

Purple Martins, Tree Swallows, Barn Swallows, Rough-winged Swallows, Common Nighthawks, Chimney Swifts, and others feed only on the wing. Watch and you'll know. They dive, dart, dip, and stall, all on the chase of a sky-level buffet. They feed, however, at different altitudes. Barn Swallows, for instance, fly foraging low, maybe only a few feet off the ground. Chimney Swifts fly foraging high, sometimes quite high. Thus, you guessed it—the swallows and swifts prefer different bugs that live at different levels in the atmosphere. When extended rain or cold weather puts bugs on the ground, however, these birds face starvation.

Perhaps that accounts for the busyness at feeders immediately after storms. Hungry survivors come to the quickest, most reliable food source they know, ready for some free fast food—that is, free for the taking with no extra energy expended on the hunt.

The larger the bird—like a crow, for instance—the longer it can go without feeding, its reserves sustaining it for a day or so. But at the other extreme, hummingbirds need sustenance every twenty minutes. The hummer swarms at our feeders after a forty-minute storm surely demonstrate their need for quick energy and verify the lack of sustenance in rain-pounded flowers, nectar rinsed, maybe stalks smashed to the ground.

BIOLOGY BITS   ## Keeping Their Cool

Given July's often blistering heat, how do birds keep cool during midsummer madness? Their average body temperatures range between 104 and 109°F, some a bit higher; so perhaps they don't feel "hot" at temperatures we find uncomfortable. Still, birds, young and old alike, do suffer from the heat.

Birds don't sweat, however, so perspiration can't cool them. They have to do something else. In winter, most birds fluff up their feathers, trapping air that retains body heat, keeping them warm. In summer, then, for starters, birds flatten their feathers, taking on a slimmer look and a cooler body.

Beyond that, however, hawks, crows, and sparrows breathe open-mouthed, panting. Cormorants vibrate the upper parts of their throats, an act called gular fluttering. Herons and egrets droop their wings to allow cooling air against their bodies. Most birds take an afternoon siesta in the heat, restricting activities to early and late.

Birds that nest in the open turn to face the sun, thus minimizing the body surface exposed to direct rays. And vultures and storks, I'm reluctant to say, defecate on their legs and feet, enjoying the cooling effect of evaporation. I guess you gotta do what you gotta do.

Scientific avian reports say little about the effects of summer storms, even severe ones. Rather, research focuses on hurricanes, ice and snow storms, and migration calamities that typically affect thousands of birds. So I'm speculating when I say most birds survive violent thunder-lightning-deluge storms. After all, we don't find piles of dead birds afterward. In fact, as the thunder distances itself, even in continuing but lighter rains, goldfinches resume their twitters and trills, feeding as usual.

But obviously, some do suffer. Birds most susceptible to storm fatalities are likely nestlings or juveniles still unsteady on their wings. But reproduction suffers other ways, too. Storms strip cardinal nests from their moorings, wash away the robin-nest mud, scatter the dove's flimsy pile of sticks. Sometimes even the massively sturdy osprey or eagle nest succumbs to wind when the entire support tree comes crashing down.

NOTABLE BEHAVIOR   ## ID Birds by Behavior

Especially on cloudy, stormy bad-weather days or in otherwise poor light, identifying birds gets tricky. But watching a bird's behavior can help nail the ID. For instance, flycatchers perch, dart out to catch a bug, and return, yo-yo like, to their perches. Warblers, which also flycatch, bushwhack by flushing out bugs and grabbing them on the fly. They dart. On the other hand, vireos methodically drop through branches, bugging, looking like leaves gently tumbling down. They're deliberate. Some birds bob their tails, and signature tail-bobbers include the Palm Warbler and the Hermit Thrush. Check your field guide for other identifiable behaviors when you find a puzzler in your yard.

Make no mistake; storms kill. Calamitous devastation to healthy adult birds, however, occurs most frequently during migration when birds may be caught away from shelter. For instance, on April 16, 1960, migrants left the Indiana shore, boosted by strong south winds, to wing their way across Lake Michigan on their way to Canadian boreal-forest breeding grounds. But a sudden storm switched winds to the west, increased wind speeds to seventy-five miles per hour, and pummeled the migrants with hailstones. They had nowhere to go but down. The next morning, thousands of dead birds floated along the shore.

Nature, however, revitalizes itself in the cycle of storm and renewal. If some birds die, more food and nesting sites become available for the remaining birds that can then reproduce more successfully. For them, good backyard habitat offers protection when their instincts scream, "Seek shelter."

BIOLOGY BITS   **Sleepy Time—When and Where?**

Studying birds' sleep behavior is even more difficult than studying their storm protection behavior. Birds don't offer ready observation in either case. We do know, however, that birds sleep only when they can't forage. So shorebirds sleep when high tide submerges food. Owls sleep during the day when their preferred critter-foods hide. And songbirds sleep at night when darkness hides bugs and seeds.

Birds sleep in various places and positions, mostly where they otherwise live—perched on a branch, clinging to a tree trunk, sitting on the ground, tucked into a cavity, floating on or standing in water, or yes, flying the distance. Bobwhites sleep in a circle, facing outward. If disturbed, each flies the direction it faces, confusing predators. Whip-poor-wills sleep parallel to roost limbs, thus camouflaging themselves for the day. Snow buntings sleep in tiny snow caves.

A dozing Mourning Dove, shoulders hunched as a head rest, seems oblivious to its surroundings, seemingly sound asleep.

Recent encounters with a Mississippi Kite recall my first sighting twelve years ago this month, an experience I remember well.

In winter, many birds drop body temperatures by twenty degrees or more at night, and some, adapting to human habitation, have learned to roost near heat sources, like neon signs or street lights. A few birds, most notably hummingbirds, go into torpor, something like overnight hibernation, to conserve energy. Birds do not, however, sleep with head tucked under a wing. They may tuck their heads under shoulder feathers, or they may, like most Mourning Doves, hunch their shoulders as a head rest.

Memorable Moments: Kites Kiting

How well I remember the first time I saw a Mississippi Kite. It was in 2000, and we were celebrating my husband's late-July birthday, making a day-trip to the Lincoln Boyhood National Memorial two counties away. And there, across the lake, it soared. And soared and soared. What a beauty! We agreed that the spectacular sighting added a special omen to an already special day. Little did we imagine how, over the next twelve years, the memorable moment would grow.

BIOLOGY BITS   **Eyeball to Eyeball**

When birds sleep, you may see something that looks like closed eyelids. But birds' eyelids differ from ours. For instance, when birds like Mississippi Kites, eagles, Ospreys, and falcons rip through the skies, their eyes need protection. A raptor with an eye injury is soon a dead bird. Strangely enough, though, birds rarely blink—except for owls and parrots and a few others. When they do blink, and when they close their eyes to sleep, their eyelids move from bottom up, not top down like ours. To keep their eyes moist and washed clean of dirt, dust, and debris, however, birds have another eyelid-like structure called a nictitating membrane. This translucent "eyelid" moves horizontally across the eye, front to back. Sometimes a photo catches the nictitating membrane in place, an image that gives the bird a ghostly aura.

Sleek, handsome, falcon-like, pearly gray birds with black tails, 3-foot wingspans, 15-inch-long bodies, and red eyes, Mississippi kites typically live in the south, near the Gulf Coast and westward in Oklahoma and northern Texas. Having ranged northward up the Mississippi and Ohio River valleys, however, the kites typically arrive in southern Indiana in early May.

When caught on camera, a Bald Eagle's closed nictitating membrane gives the bird a ghostly aura.

They choose a tall treetop for nest building, incubate eggs for thirty to thirty-two days, fledge young another month later in early August, and leave by Labor Day on their way back to regions of Brazil and Bolivia for the winter. Surely that merits a long-distance flier designation.

<hr>

WHY DO BIRDS DO THAT?

Why Do Birds Sleep So Little?

If birds knew how much we humans sleep, they'd surely think us true sluggards. Given their odd sleep patterns, by comparison, they'd be right.

No matter where or how they sleep, let's call it dozing—minimal and light. Being asleep as we humans think of it would seriously risk a bird's life, a time when predators can snatch, kill, and devour. So, birds instantly awaken at the least sound or unusual movement. Or maybe just because it's time for a frequent, periodic check. Birds that hang out in flocks, like geese, can sleep more soundly, always knowing one or more in their midst acts as sentinel for the flock. Mallards sleep in big flocks so that those in the center sleep with both eyes closed while those on the outer edges sleep with only one eye closed. I presume they take turns.

Even at night, though, most birds sleep light, always alert to predators. In fact, many if not most birds engage in something called unihemispheric slow-wave sleep (USWS) in which half the brain sleeps and one eye is closed. Simultaneously, the other half of the brain and the other eye are alert and watchful. Quite a trick, isn't it?

Preferring woodlands and riparian zones for nesting, kites nevertheless like grasslands, woodland edges, and even human-altered areas—like farms and golf courses—for hunting. They frequently snatch and eat large insects in the air, so their aerial acrobatics can be breathtaking to behold.

Until 1992, only two Indiana state records existed for Mississippi Kites, one in 1937 and another in 1959. Rare birds here, indeed. But in 1992, news broke that two pairs were nesting four counties upriver. Every year since, kites in those territories have successfully produced young, the offspring expanding the kites' range nearer and nearer to our home.

NOTABLE BEHAVIOR   **Fly-through Showers**

Especially in times of midsummer drought, you may be able to create some memorable moments of your own. Birds enjoy a refreshing shower as much as we do. So, when rain fails to fall, offer a built-in shower that will entertain you with birds' notable behavior— and perhaps attract new birds for your viewing pleasure.

Place in your garden a sprinkler or mister. Hummingbirds will fly through, *zip, zip,* darting through the droplets, stopping beyond to flutter and preen, returning for another *zip, zip,* and repeating the routine. Other birds engage in the same notable behavior. Yesterday, I watched a mockingbird fly from one vantage point to another, repeatedly fluttering through the neighbor's sprinkler "rain."

Now this year, neighbors three miles to our south have had daily kite sightings throughout June and July, obviously a nesting pair. It can't be long, can it? Surely, it will be a yard bird soon, and our skies, too, will host these special birds. A memorable birthday moment thus returns as an annual reminder that the flight to Bolivia is a long, long way.

Conservation Corner: Birds Kill Bugs Dead

The Smithsonian Migratory Bird Center (SMBC; http://nationalzoo.si.edu) reminds us that birds play a dramatic role in keeping insects under control. Without birds, we'd be buried in bugs. Consider these fascinating details from SMBCs report:

- Birds are technologically advanced, highly motivated, extremely efficient, and cost-effective insect-pest controllers.

- Birds' breeding season occurs when insect populations peak. During insect outbreaks, some birds increase the number of offspring they raise in order to take advantage of the abundant food supply.

- Birds are highly mobile, so they will move to take advantage of insect outbreaks. Some of these invasions can increase the normal bird population in an area by eighty times.

- Birds can alter their diets to take advantage of an insect outbreak and adjust their foraging techniques in order to better capture the insects, even moving from a preferred foraging habitat to an entirely different habitat.

Things to Do in July

- Keep birdbath water fresh and clean.

- Keep feeders free from mold.

- Store birdfeed where summer's heat and humidity don't spoil the oil-rich seeds.

- Remain vigilant to keep your backyard habitat safe for birds—free of pesticides, cats, and other predators.

- Clean hummingbird feeders every other day, each time you fill with fresh nectar.

- Use red on hummingbird feeders but never in hummingbird feeders.

44 Yard Birds in July

Record-breaking heat with high humidity; reduced my diligence in watching.

Canada Goose	American Crow	Northern Parula
Northern Bobwhite	Purple Martin	Yellow-throated Warbler
Great Blue Heron	Barn Swallow	Eastern Towhee
Red-shouldered Hawk	Carolina Chickadee	Chipping Sparrow
Mourning Dove	Tufted Titmouse	Song Sparrow
Yellow-billed Cuckoo	White-breasted Nuthatch	Summer Tanager
Barred Owl	Carolina Wren	Northern Cardinal
Chimney Swift	House Wren	Indigo Bunting
Ruby-throated	Blue-gray Gnatcatcher	Red-winged Blackbird
Hummingbird	Eastern Bluebird	Eastern Meadowlark
Red-bellied Woodpecker	American Robin	Common Grackle
Downy Woodpecker	Northern Mockingbird	Brown-headed Cowbird
Hairy Woodpecker	Brown Thrasher	House Finch
Northern Flicker	European Starling	American Goldfinch
Pileated Woodpecker	Cedar Waxwing	House Sparrow

SPECIES PROFILE

PURPLE MARTIN

VITAL STATS
Length: 7.5–8 in.
Wingspan: 15.5–17.5 in.
Weight: 1.7–2 oz.

Left: *Purple Martin, male;* right: *Purple Martin, female*

As the only bird in the eastern United States totally dependent on humans for nest sites (western birds still nest in natural cavities), Purple Martins give landlords ample reasons to host them. Acclaimed as the most graceful and agile birds in the world, their long, pointed wings and forked tails grant them elegance even perched. In sunlight, the male glows with a drop-dead gorgeous, all-over deep purple. Their gurgling musical twitter literally sings of camaraderie. But above all, their single interest besides breeding is eating—bugs and only bugs and more bugs.

NAME THAT BIRD

Progne subis (Purple Martin): This bird's name comes from the Greek mythological character Progne (the spelling a form of Procne) who was turned into a swallow. *Subis,* however, refers to a bird that breaks eagle eggs—a behavior unknown among Purple Martins. So, it's a mystery how the bird got that part of its name. The common name, though, is more gentle—"purple" for its overall color and "martin," from the French pet name for this kind of bird.

Contrary to popular myth, however, Purple Martins do not eat mosquitoes. In a seven-year study of over five hundred purple martins, not a single mosquito was found in their diets. It makes sense. After all, martins feed on the wing, and they feed high. Mosquitoes hum low, near the ground. And for the most part, martins have gone to bed by the time mosquitoes come out. Instead, our largest swallows eat the largest bugs, like dragonflies.

FOOD FARE
Purple Martins eat only flying insects caught on the wing.

Another myth abounds about Purple Martins: that "scouts" come first to check out territories. The first martins to arrive at a colony site are just that—the first. First arrivals don't leave and guide others. Instead, they are mature birds who remember their ancestral nest site and make a beeline to the colony to claim first dibs on preferred cavities.

Purple Martins, famously finicky, scorn hundreds of nest boxes mounted by well-intentioned folks, leaving the fancy abodes to starlings and sparrows and setting up housekeeping elsewhere. Designer apartments rust, languish into eyesores, and attract not a single burbling, bug-eating feathered acrobat.

And therein lies a tale—a tale of woe. Purple Martin colonies demand high maintenance: daily checks, weekly care, winter take-down, spring opening, and annual clean-up fix-up efforts. Most wannabe Purple Martin hosts put up a house and forget it. They should save their money.

When it comes to successful Purple Martin abodes, placement dictates success. The colonial homes must be situated at least 40 feet from trees, with unobscured flight paths to nest cavities. Avoid wire running to nest boxes as it can provide predator access. Avoid apartments attached to fence posts. Predator pole guards and owl guards are essential.

Purple Martins in the eastern United States depend entirely on human-provided nest colonies.

The box size is just as important: it should measure 7 by 12 inches deep with entrance holes 2⅛ inches in diameter. Horizontal gourds are most successful and safest, with the highest rate of acceptance by the birds themselves. A telescoping or winch-equipped pole serves best. Avoid houses that require the removal of the roof and/or sections to access compartments for weekly monitoring and seasonal cleaning.

BIRD TALK: WHO'S CALLING?

Purple Martins sing a number of songs, including while in flight, that can be roughly described as low-pitched, liquid gurgling, sometimes like a descending *cheer,* a more complex chortle, and musical chirps and raspy twitters, charming and soothing to the human ear.

Colony nesters, adult Purple Martins can fly up to 350 miles a day on their return trip from South American wintering grounds, responding to the urgency of reaching their last-year's colonial nests early and thereby claiming the best sites. By comparison, while one martin took 43 days to reach Brazil during its fall migration, it returned in only 13 days.

So, depending on where you live, the first martins, those who lived with you last year, return mid- to late March. Typically, however, only subadults (last year's offspring) will populate new colonies. Since subadults arrive four to six weeks later than adults, hosts hoping to attract new colonies should keep compartments sealed until about April 15, again depending on where you live, thus thwarting House Sparrows and European Starlings.

According to the Purple Martin Conservation Association (PMCA), folks hoping to become martin hosts "should not buy or build a martin house before thoroughly researching the subject. They may find the yard is too tree enclosed, or that the martin house is difficult or impossible to manage."

NEST NOTES

Nest Site: in colonial bird houses
Nest Construction: mostly by female, somewhat skimpy nest of twigs, plant stems, mud, and grasses; male may carry greenery to nest
Eggs: 1–8 eggs, 1 brood, incubated mostly by female 15–18 days; male stays at nest or on eggs while female forages
Fledge: 28–29 days after hatch

Predation ranks first among reasons why hosts lose colonies. Raccoons climb seemingly impossible heights for nighttime raids on eggs and nestlings. Owls, also nocturnal hunters, snatch startled adults from their nests, leaving eggs to rot and babies to die. Daylight hours, however, can be equally deadly. Hawks and crows snatch birds and eggs, again causing survivors to abandon the colony, sometimes permanently. Once predated, a colony abandons the site and rarely returns.

SPOTTING THE SPECTACULAR
Marveling at Multitudes and Miles

When breeding season ends, just weeks after babies fledge, Purple Martins return to South America. But they don't return in pairs or even families. Instead, along the way, martins congregate to form huge migratory flocks, some flocks amassing 700,000 or more birds, roosting near large bodies of water, many roosts large enough to be detected by Doppler radar. In some areas along the Gulf Coast, these mass gatherings become the focal point of birding festivals.

Fall migration is somewhat leisurely, with some birds, tracked by geolocators, covering 300 miles a day for about 5 days and then resting 3 or 4 weeks before flying on, taking an average total of 44 days to travel 4,150 miles to Brazil. In spring, however, the rush is on, and one bird traveled 4,660 miles in 9 days, resting 4 days along the way. That's a whopping average of 518 miles per day on flying days.

Where I live, Purple Martins arrive in late March and depart by late July, a short four-month visit. After congregating along the Gulf Coast, martins take one of two routes to Brazil. Some island-hop from Cuba to Haiti, the Dominican Republic, Puerto Rico, through the Virgin Islands, down the Lesser Antilles chain, touching down perhaps in Antigua, Martinique, and Grenada, and then to Venezuela and Brazil.

Others take a shorter but more difficult flight directly across the Gulf of Mexico, reaching land along the Yucatan, then through Belize, Guatemala, Honduras, Nicaragua, Costa Rica, Panama, Columbia, Peru, and Brazil, nearly 5,000 miles each way.

ID CHECK

Unless you host a Purple Martin colony or live near someone who does, you're unlikely to see martins during the breeding season. If you do, most likely you'll see them on the wing, darting after bugs to feed their hungry families. Look for these tell-tale signs:
- Long, pointed wings
- Forked tail
- Large head, broad chest

To identify Purple Martins perched, note the following:
- Males are all-over deep blue-black, glossy
- Females are blue-black on back, head, and tail; lighter underneath
- Immatures look like drab, pale females with brown wing and tail feathers

SPECIES PROFILE

SONG SPARROW

Above: *Song Sparrows, with their highly variable plumage, may have an overall dark appearance.* Below: *Some Song Sparrows show a dark breast spot but may be predominantly pale.*

VITAL STATS
Length: 4.7–6.7 in.
Wingspan: 7.1–9.4 in.
Weight: 0.4–1.9 oz.

Ah, sparrows. LBJs—little brown jobs. Streaky, look-alike birds that drive new birders a little goofy. However, since Song Sparrows live across Canada from Newfoundland to Alaska and south to Mexico, and since they're one of the most numerous sparrows in North America, a little streaky brown job in your yard that looks like some kind of sparrow could well be a Song Sparrow.

NAME THAT BIRD
Melospiza melodia (Song Sparrow): The full name translates roughly as "finch with a pleasant song." Its common name also refers to its penchant for melody. "Sparrow" comes from the Anglo-Saxon meaning "a flutterer," a word originally referring to any small bird.

Song Sparrows differ quite a lot across the nation. Some bulk up to nearly double the size of others. Some show more—and more striking—streaks than others. Some dashingly dark birds sport dramatic plumage contrasts while certain of their fellows literally pale by comparison, their plumage muted, faded, washed out. Some take on a gray cast; others tend toward reddish (properly called rufous) streaks, from coarse to fine. So how's a bird-watcher to know?

SPOTTING THE SPECTACULAR   **Same but Different**

Song Sparrows show so much variation across North America that most scientists recognize at least thirty-eight subspecies. A few ornithologists have actually proposed fifty-two subspecies. That's a lot of variation! Even though some Song Sparrows are twice the size of others and have rather dramatic differences in plumage coloration, their behavior and habitat sort them out from other sparrow species. No other sparrow earns a similar reputation as songster. And no other native sparrow is as widespread and numerous as the Song Sparrow.

Here's the best ID plan: Tune in to Song Sparrows in your area. They'll look mostly alike, so become familiar with them in your habitat instead of sorting through all the variations in a field guide. For instance, in the eastern half of the continent, look for a rusty and gray bird, broad gray stripe above the eye, gray patches below the eye, striped crown, dark brown moustache, heavy dark-brown streaking on white chest, and a white belly. The breast streaking often includes a dark central spot that looks as if the poor bird flew into a splat of oil that stained one area then streaked down and out.

This bird's name, however, says more about identifying it than all those streaky details. This bird sings. Sings its little heart out. Even in winter. It tees up, perching on the tallest weed or shrubby twig, leans back, throws its head back, and belts out a cheery tune. Once you catch their song, you'll readily recognize Song Sparrows—any time of the year.

FOOD FARE

Seeds and berries make up the bulk of a Song Sparrow's diet, although they feed their babies bugs. In the garden, they enjoy most any spent-flower seed heads and will take small seeds, including thistle, from spilled feeder fare. They forage secretively, mostly on or very near the ground.

BIRD TALK: WHO'S CALLING?

Song Sparrows, like humans, have dialects: Birds from one region will have a slightly different song than birds from another. All, however, begin with a sharp three-note phrase and follow with a variety of trills and/or buzzes. Call includes a high thin *ssst*.

Two years ago, I heard what partly resembled a Song Sparrow's song, but it wasn't quite right. So who was that singing? Off on a search I went, following the song until I found the singer. And there he was, handsome Song Sparrow, teed up in the weed patch, claiming the area for his own, singing to attract some sweet thing to join him. But he was a stranger to the neighborhood. How do I know? His dialect.

Song Sparrows have accents. Birds that grow up in Kentucky have a slightly different lilt, rhythm, and melody than those that grow up in Pennsylvania, say, or Florida. Rather like us human residents. The three-note introduction, however, gives them away. That immigrant "stranger" stayed with us for a year. After that, he either moved on or met his demise. His off-spring, however, learned a vocal variation that combined its song and that of our "natives." What a delight to know we have a blended neighborhood.

NEST NOTES

Nest Site: likely chosen by female; usually hidden in grass, sometimes directly on ground, occasionally as high as 15 ft., often near water, sometimes in flower beds, at the base of grass clumps or rose bushes

Nest Construction: built by female; simple sturdy cup of loose grasses and weeds but lined with tightly woven materials, including grass, rootlets, hair

Eggs: 1–6 eggs, 1–6 broods, incubated only by female 12–15 days; male stays in area during incubation to guard site

Fledge: 9–12 days after hatch

ID CHECK

Song Sparrows, in spite of their variations, can be readily identified by their preferred habitat (thickets, brushy areas, weedy sites, marshes, roadsides, and feeder areas) as well as by the following characterics:

- Rusty-brown backs with muted streaks
- White chest and belly with central spot and heavy streaks
- Long rounded tail
- Broad grayish eyebrow
- Dark moustache on white bib

SPECIES PROFILE

BARN SWALLOW

Above: *Barn Swallow, male;* below: *Barn Swallow, female*

VITAL STATS
Length: 5.9–7.5 in.
Wingspan: 11.4–12.6 in.
Weight: 0.6–0.7 oz.

They show up in flocks when we cut what little grass we cut, swooping in front of and behind the mower, giving us cause to fear for their safety. But their erratic flight paths, their dodge-and-dart aerial acrobatics, guarantee they're swift enough to avoid any harm.

So, what are they doing, these Barn Swallows? Catching bugs! The mower startles the bugs up in swarms, and the swallows snap up the swarms. No doubt about it, Barn Swallows are bug-eating maniacs. They eat mostly on the wing and mostly bugs, snapping 'em from the skies, feasting on bugs, bugs, and more bugs. Gotta love 'em!

FOOD FARE

Barn Swallows eat primarily flying insects but will occasionally in autumn take berries. They do not visit traditional feeders, but they will pick up calcium-rich crushed egg or oyster shells from pavements, sidewalks, or rooftops.

These bug-eating maniacs also top the gorgeous list. Male Barn Swallows sport long forked streamer tails, gracefully long wings, and a handsome steel blue and tawny orange wardrobe that would make a fashion designer envious. Females, slightly less flashy, aren't too shabby, either.

Mighty spiffy, these swallows!

If you have Barn Swallows in your yard or neighborhood, you're in good company. In fact, Barn Swallows are the most abundant and widespread swallows in the world, breeding throughout North America, Europe, and Asia, and wintering in South America, Indonesia, Australia, and Africa. Ours mostly winter in Central and South America, some venturing to the southernmost tip of South America.

NAME THAT BIRD

Hirundo rustica (Barn Swallow): *Hirundo* is Latin for "swallow," and *rustica,* similar in meaning to "rustic," refers to anything suited to the country or farm. Its common name refers to this bird's preference for nesting inside farm structures, like barns.

The first arrival each spring is cause for a notation in my little record book. They may not get the same celebration as the Cliff Swallows that return to San Juan Capistrano, but in my heart, they're just as worthy of celebration.

Their first babies fledged this year the last week of May, so they'll likely raise a second brood. Still, it's risky business, going for a second brood, because fall migration takes its toll and demands strength and endurance. Females laying a second clutch of eggs obviously commit to a significant energy loss. And babies that hatch late may not be ready for the trip when it's time to go.

NEST NOTES

Nest Site: originally inside cave entrances and rocky niches but now adapting to human habitation inside barns, garages, or other buildings with exposed rafters or beams but also under bridges, wharfs, and inside culverts

Nest Construction: a nest cup, about 3 in. by 2 in., made of mud and grass pellets, glued to vertical surface (forming a half cup) or horizontal surface; lined with grasses and then feathers

Eggs: 3–7 eggs, 1–2 broods, incubated 12–17 days

Fledge: 15–27 days after hatch

For the short time they're here, Barn Swallows entertain me, twittering, swooping gracefully, only a few feet above the ground, across pastures and hayfields, darting through morning and evening skies, and along with our other avian friends, keeping us relatively bug free. They accept us humans as part of the landscape and nest in our structures.

BIRD TALK: WHO'S CALLING?
Barn Swallows sing a *twitter-warble* song, especially notice-able in flight.

In fact, Barn Swallows have lined every ceiling beam inside our neighbor's barn with their remarkable mud nests, each clearly an architectural miracle, made of row upon row of spitball sized mud-and-grass wads, each scooped up from the farm-pond banks, carried one at a time by the swallow pair, stuck together, forming a tight, half-cup nest, snug for mom and the kids.

Competition, however, sometimes creates an avian soap opera, complete with murder as bachelor Barn Swallows do the dastardly deed to nestlings. If the babies are dead, the previously mated female accepts a new mate (in the form of the murderer) and lays a new set of eggs. The bad guy has it made—the overwhelming task of nest building and its necessary accompanying spit and energy is done. So the murderer, free of a guilty verdict, moves in rent free.

SPOTTING THE SPECTACULAR
Myth Makers and the Conservation Movement

The Barn Swallow's close association with humans for over 2,000 years, especially in Europe, built the basis for multiple myths and legends. For instance, Barn Swallows nesting on your property supposedly bring you and your family good luck. But if the swallows leave the farm, cows will go dry or give bloody milk. Another legend proclaims that Barn Swallows consoled Christ on the cross. Even the bird's forked tail has a legendary explanation: Trying to help its people, the Barn Swallow stole fire from the gods. Angered by the theft, the gods threw a fireball at the bird, and the hot blast burned away the bird's central tail feathers.

It's also a myth that Barn Swallows eat huge numbers of mosquitoes. Not so. Mosquitoes come out of hiding at dusk and through the night, seeking blood sources that walk the ground—like us. By contrast, Barn Swallows feed until just before dusk and snag airborne bugs—big bugs—above tree-top level.

While the myths and legends create interest, the facts give the bird even more credit. According to Birds of North America Online, "These swallows—not the more famous egrets—have the distinction of having indirectly led to the founding of the conservation movement in the United States: the destruction of Barn Swallows for the millinery trade apparently prompted George Bird Grinnell's 1886 editorial in *Forest and Stream* that led to the founding of the first Audubon Society."

It's a bird with quite a tale to tell—in both fact and fiction!

ID CHECK
While males are more boldly colored than females, in general Barn Swallows can be distinguished by the following traits:
  • Long forked tails, obvious both perched and in flight
  • Long pointed wings
  • Steely blue-black head, back, wings, and tail
  • Cinnamon orange forehead and chin
  • Tawny orange breast and belly
  • White spots edging the tail, often visible in flight

SPECIES PROFILE

EASTERN TOWHEE

VITAL STATS
Length: 6.8–8.2 in.
Wingspan: 7.9–11 in.
Weight: 1.1–1.8 oz.

Left: *Eastern Towhee, male;* right: *Eastern Towhee, female*

The Eastern Towhee's claim to fame: It's our largest sparrow. The claim seems odd, though, because I don't usually think of the towhee as a sparrow at all. After all, it lacks the brown streaky back and wings I've come to expect most sparrows to have. But it is, indeed, big. And pretty.

In my opinion, the towhee steps out as one strikingly handsome, formally clad songster, all-black head and bib, black wings and tail, orangey brown sides, and white belly. To me, though, the male's most stunning feature is that fantabulous pair of red eyes. The female wears brown, a lovely, more delicately feminine form of the male's bold outfit—including the red eyes. Together, they make a lovely portrait pair.

But they're not readily seen. In fact, I hear far more of them than I see. Spring and summer choruses inevitably include towhee song from several directions, each proclaiming respective home turfs. Always ground lovers, they hide out in tangles, dense underbrush, and thickets. Only when the male hops out to sing, perhaps on a low branch or shrub, does he readily—or clearly—show himself. The female is even shier.

In winter, however, when thick leaves no longer conceal them, I get my best views of these pretty birds. Because they love to double-foot scratch for dinner in leaf litter, they show up regularly in my wintertime backyard, under shrubs and low-hanging hemlock branches under which I'd raked leaves in the fall. What a great reward for leaving the leaves!

Now, in July, they've fledged their babies, and I hear them talking along the woodland edge. Soon, I'll see the youngsters, overall drab and unlovely, checking out the bubble rock for a drink and a bath. All those pin feathers—how they must itch—so they seem to truly enjoy a long splash-splash bath.

NAME THAT BIRD
Pipilo erythrophthalmus (Eastern Towhee): *Pipilo* means "to chirp or twitter" while *erythrophthalmus* means "red eyed," referring to the bird's red eyes. (A white-eyed form of the Eastern Towhee ranges across parts of the Southeast.) Its common name refers to the bird's range and its two-syllable song, although the song varies.

FOOD FARE
Eastern Towhees eat a varied diet, from insects to berries to seeds, including weeds like ragweed and smartweeds. In the garden, find them foraging on the ground for bugs. At the feeder, they will forage among spilled seeds not only for the grain but also for insects that might be among them.

NEST NOTES
Nest Site: usually on the ground, sunk into a bed of last fall's leaf litter
Nest Construction: in leaf-litter hollow, lined with cypress or grapevine bark, dead leaves or grass stems, about 4 in. diameter; inner cup, about 2 in. by 1.5 in., lined with fine plant fibers, rootlets, and sometimes hair
Eggs: 2–6 eggs, 1–3 broods, incubating 12–13 days
Fledge: 10–12 days after hatch

But with this year's early spring, I'm betting they'll raise a second brood. Given the ground-nesting habit of towhees, and given snakes as the primary known nest predators, how towhees manage to successfully raise babies boggles my mind. I wish them well and hope the broad band of dense, thorny tangles I've left at the woodland edge helps protect them and their babies.

Beyond the obvious predators, however, a fellow bird probably causes more family problems for towhee parents than anything else. The parasitic Brown-headed Cowbird depends regularly on towhees for child support, family service, and foster care—all to the detriment of the towhees' own kids. Apparently towhees—like many other birds—can't recognize the difference between cowbird eggs and their own. Or, maybe they can but make a conscious decision to accept them. But why would they do that if it's to the detriment of their own breeding success? Well, it's like this: If an intended host, like the towhee, tosses out a cowbird egg, cowbirds are known to "punish" the hosts by completely destroying the nest. So, whether or not they recognize the foreign egg, towhees incubate the cowbird eggs and raise the young as their own. Sometimes Mother Nature's ways test my mettle, leaving me sad, even frustrated, knowing I can do nothing about the parasitism.

SPOTTING THE SPECTACULAR
Questionable Social Skills

Eastern Towhees prefer solitude. Not even in winter, when breeding territories need no defense, do towhees mingle with a crowd or with a few friends. Come spring, male towhees, set in their solitary ways, actually chase females from their territories. But the females persist, fleeing only when absolutely necessary—and even then, scooting away only a short distance. Then they return. Over the course of a day or so, the male finally figures out what's what, allows the patiently persistent female to stay, and finally, guards her, keeping vigil over his domain.

Daily, the male takes a foray away from his territory, apparently to keep an eye on neighbors and potential threats or competition.

ID CHECK
Males are readily identified by the following characteristics:
- Black head, bib, back, wings, and tail
- Orangey brown sides
- White belly
- Bright red eyes (except in parts of the Southeast where some have white eyes)
- Black conical bill
- Sparrow shape
- Ground-loving behavior, including the two-foot backward scratch in search of leaf-litter food
- Females look like males whose black plumage has softened to a leaf-brown color

August

*Have you ever observed a hummingbird
moving about in an aerial dance among the flowers—
a living prismatic gem . . . it is a creature of
such fairy-like loveliness as to mock all description.*

W. H. HUDSON

An American Goldfinch feeds on spent Mexican sunflower.

Ah, August. Heavy with heat. Bloomed out. Gone to seed. Dry. The final month of summer.

We cram last-minute activities into an already busy month. Weeks speed past. Days grow hectic. By month's end, it's back from vacation, back to school, back to work, following our own cycle, one governed by the Gregorian calendar rather than by the orbiting earth's length of day.

Birds in August, on the other hand, sensing the shortening days, slow the pace. Instinctively, they know to quit breeding. With no reason, then, to guard nest territories or protect eggs, broods, or fledglings, birds relax their aggressiveness, disperse for broader feeding options—sometimes taking offspring along, sometimes leaving them behind, sometimes chasing them off. And late this month, they begin to molt.

WHY DO BIRDS DO THAT?

Why Do Some Feed High and Others Feed Low?

Different birds feed at different levels, and they don't usually change their habits. You've seen it: Some backyard birds pick fallen seed from the ground; others prefer to hang from a feeder; still others regularly perch on a platform. Certain birds, especially migrants like warblers, vireos, and tanagers, feed not at feeders but in the tree canopy, sometimes really high in the canopy.

Birds that prefer bugs generally feed mid to high. After all, that's where many bugs hang out. Seed eaters feed low. That's where the seeds grow. So it's just plain logic: Birds habitually forage where they find their favorite menus.

The extension of that logic, however, reminds us that there's more to attracting birds than feeders and feed. If the backyard habitat doesn't support plants that support bugs, bug-eating birds like Scarlet and Summer Tanagers, all those gorgeous warblers and vireos, and sky birds like swallows and swifts will never show up in the yard.

So, think like a bird. Plant accordingly. You'll gain new avian friends in your yard.

A stray feather lying in the grass or caught in a tangle of vines reveals evidence: Birds are turning more and more ragged. With parenting demands complete, birds gobble down bugs solely for self-preservation, gorging on protein to build all-new wardrobes of strong, warm feathers. No empty-nest syndrome here. In short, spiffy is in the making. Wait till next month; you'll see.

End-of-Season Behavior

Perhaps hummingbirds display the most noticeable end-of-breeding-season behavior. The feeder swarms grow. Finally, the ferocious territorial battles over, they feed together peacefully, bulking up for journeys south. Second broods, newly fledged, find themselves in the company of more northerly nesters and their young, all moving south, all joining the local fray. I'm buying sugar in 50-pound lots, mixing syrup by the gallons. The little guys tank up, this year's drought having left them few options in the wild.

FEEDER FOCUS
Keeping a Clean House amid Heat and Humidity

Summer's heat and humidity challenge backyard birdfeeder hosts to keep a clean café. Mold, rot, rancid seed, spoiled suet—all create potential health hazards for birds and humans alike. Here's the best advice:

- Serve only the amount of seed/feed that birds will consume in three days. Fresh seed/feed is healthy seed/feed.
- Wash feeders with one part bleach and nine parts water and rinse, rinse, rinse. A once-a-month scrubbing keeps mold at bay.
- Avoid allowing aging seed to remain in the bottom of a feeder. Empty feeders completely at least once a week, making sure bottom seed/feed doesn't rot or turn rancid.
- Store seed in closed containers in a cool place. If heat in your storage area hits 85°F, expect seed/feed to turn rancid and buggy.
- Serve only rendered suet. It won't melt or turn rancid in the heat.

Cruise some country roads this month, and you'll note more behavior changes. You'll think you're seeing the gathering of the clans. And you are. Flocks of same-species birds hang out together, lining utility wires like so many pegged clothespins awaiting a big laundry. You'll likely see Barn, Tree, and Bank Swallows perched by the hundreds, maybe even by the thousands, massing for migration. In parts farther south, I've seen more than three hundred Purple Martins roosting in communal trees, readying themselves somehow for the journey. Called "staging," the gathering reminds me a bit of crazed teens at a music fest, all shouting,

Small groups of Tree Swallows merge with other groups, forming massive flocks for migration.

BIOLOGY BITS   **Bugs Eat Birds**

We know that birds need bugs to survive—lots of bugs—for themselves and their babies. But bugs also need birds—to eat. In short, the dietary demands run both ways. Here's the scoop.

- Chewing lice attack birds, eating feathers and debris found in plumage. Ultimately, lice weaken their host bird because the bird must exert significant energy to replace chewed feathers. Until feathers are replaced, the bird also faces less efficient flight and thermoregulation, further weakening it. So, logically, a louse-infested bird doesn't make a good mate. Some studies show, in fact, that birds select mates based on bright plumage, and a louse-infested bird tends toward dull plumage.
- Many different mites attack birds, some living in nests and eating nest debris and others living on birds, feeding on their blood or feathers. Mites can cause disease among birds. Ticks, which are blood-sucking mites, also attack birds.
- Various flies, including louse flies, midges, black flies, nest flies, and mosquitoes, feed birds by day but feed on birds by night, attacking feather-free areas like those around eyes. Mosquitoes can infect birds with West Nile Virus, some forms of malaria, and encephalitis.

- Fleas, cooperative ant groups, and praying mantises also eat—and are eaten by— birds.
- But birds fight back against the bugs. Some twenty-five or more species of birds, including cardinals, grackles, Indigo Buntings, and robins, rub their feathers with "medicinal" items to ward off bugs. In fact, to ward off bugs, they sometimes use other bugs: ants, earwigs, grasshoppers, true bugs, or wasps—all of which emit a smelly, repellent chemical. Ants, for instance, give off formic acid. Other birds rub themselves with oddities like walnut husks, mothballs, citrus fruits, onions, and marigold blossoms. Together, using any of these substances is called "anting," since among all the items listed, ants are most common.

"Black-headed" cardinals have lost their feathers to mites, exposing black skin. While unattractive, rarely does the condition lead to dire circumstances—although attraction to the opposite sex will be limited. At next molt, the feathers will grow back.

- In addition, to battle bugs, birds bathe, dust, preen, oil, scratch and sun themselves. Watch. You'll see.

all active, all ready to boogie. Daily, more and more birds of the same species gather until inner instinct says, "Everybody's here. Let's roll." And they go. Together. En masse. It's mind-boggling togetherness well worth witnessing. And then they're gone. Until next spring.

You've heard the cliché: "Birds of a feather flock together." Now, in August, at season's end, starlings, cowbirds, and Red-winged Blackbirds form their own massive flocks, joining ranks with their kind, not for migration but for upcoming winter foraging. Their flocking behavior plays big time in the air. Watch the sunrise or sunset skies for miles-long undulating ribbons of birds in flight. I've seen bands stretch from horizon to horizon, millions of birds on the wing, moving toward some unseen destination, taking twenty minutes, even a half hour to flow past my vantage point.

Starlings, especially, perform magnificent mass flight displays that surge and swirl, dipping and soaring across the skies, the flocks flying as if in sheer exaltation, until first one, then hundreds, then thousands drop out of formation and into communal nighttime roosts. How birds fly in these spectacularly close formations mystifies scientists, but it's an awesome display—only now, at season's end.

In a less spectacular manner, other birds demonstrate their understanding of the ongoing annual cycle. Some birds turn season's end into family time. Carolina Chickadees, who snatched seed from early summer feeders in ones and twos, now in late summer feed in families of five or six. Mourning Doves, resisting intrusive relatives all summer, now gather in groups of dozens, gleaning and feeding along roadsides and in grain fields. Compact Blue Jay families forage as extended groups of a dozen or so.

Other behavioral changes echo through the forests as Pileated Woodpeckers stake out or chisel out winter roosts, never deigning to use summer nest cavities for roosting. Goldfinches, soon to be olive finches, the last to breed, still hunt with a purpose. Hawks sit atop fence and utility posts, hunting leisurely, no longer stressed by screeching babes. Hundreds of Indigo Buntings, fattening up for departure, feed in grain fields.

FEEDER FOCUS
Frozen Berries for a Winter Day

By collecting and freezing autumn berries this month, like those from mountain ash and other bushes and trees, you can offer them in winter as part of your feeder buffet.

But there's one more noteworthy post-breeding behavior: Mother owls are sending their offspring off, alone and whining. Since the female nests repeatedly in her long-standing territory, her owlets must move out and establish their own home place. Maybe you'll hear them, typical adolescents, hooting, yowling, complaining. But not the mothers. Pressure's off for them—until late winter.

A male Indigo Bunting, grain in his beak, feeds to fatten up for his impending migration.

Shrubs, Hedgerows, and Thorny Thickets

When planting this fall for birds, skip routine azaleas and forsythia and choose instead native serviceberry (*Amelanchier arborea*), flowering or gray dogwood (*Cornus florida* or *C. racemosa*), viburnums (*Viburnum* spp.) and other natives. For thickets, look to hawthorn (*Crataegus* spp.), wild rose (*Rosa carolina*), juniper (*Juniperus* spp.), and raspberry or blackberry canes (*Rubus* spp.). Then plant in dense hedgerows for safe roost sites, nest sites, and weather-protection sites—and for your personal privacy from neighbors. To check which plants are native to your area, see http://plants.USDA.gov.

As another sure sign of season's end, the confusing fall warblers begin wandering through the area this month. Young warblers tend to resemble their mothers, and some warbler males have molted into plumage not quite female, not quite juvenile, but certainly not the male we saw last spring. Yikes! Who are these strangers in my yard? Sometimes I just have to be satisfied that they're here—whoever they are.

So August, marked as much by changing birds as by soon-to-be-changing leaves, continues to hurdle the year's cycle—and my backyard habitat—toward winter.

NOTABLE BEHAVIOR
Dust Bathing Routine

Doves, some sparrows—especially House Sparrows—grackles, wrens, and some other songbirds love to bathe in the dust. Ah, so refreshing! Yes, really—especially if summer days have left them itchy and miserable. Dust helps rid them of excess oils and some parasites, including lice. So save a bare spot of soft dusty earth for birds to take the baths they love.

Hummingbird Peak

More than any other bird, hummingbirds announce spring for backyard birders. Now, in August, more than any other bird, hummingbirds announce autumn. In southern Indiana, hummer populations peak in late August and early September—earlier or later in your yard, depending on where you live. The little buzz-bombs hog the feeders, drain them fast, swarm like gnats, refraining from the earlier battle mode, and fatten up for the journey.

PROBLEM SOLVER   **Ants in the Nectar**

Ants, of course, love sugar, including the sugar water you serve your hummingbirds. The entire ant colony will run a highway up to unprotected feeders. The solution, however, is simple. Water. In a moat. Ants can't swim, so your feeders are safe.

- Do *not* use pesticide-filled ant guards. If the label says "Keep away from children," why would you hang your hummingbird feeders from it?
- Do *not* use grease, Vaseline, or other sticky substances on or around the feeder or feeder pole. Hummers will eventually touch the substance and contaminate their feathers, most likely leading to their demise.
- Do *not* use any kind of pesticide in or around the feeder, on the ground nearby, or on the feeder pole. Hummers, after all, aren't much bigger than some bugs; and their incredibly high metabolism cannot tolerate pesticides.

Instead:
- Choose a nectar feeder with a built-in ant moat, and keep the moat filled with clean water.

A female Ruby-throated Hummingbird nectars on a nearly-spent zinnia.

- Or, hang the feeder from an ant moat, and keep it filled with clean water. (Then, watch little guys like goldfinches and chickadees consider it their personal drinking fountain.)

I watch these tiny ferocious creatures this month, zipping about in our flower gardens and at our feeders, and try to get my mind wrapped around the fact that they're going to fly to Costa Rica. Alone. At night. Across the Gulf of Mexico. More than 1,000 miles to their destination. And I can't quite manage to fathom all that.

FEEDER FOCUS   **Hummer Feeding**

While more folks feed hummingbirds than feed all other birds combined, understanding hummer feeding habits helps hosts offer the best buffet. Think along the lines of a hummingbird "trap-line." Ruby-throated Hummingbirds run a route, visiting widely spaced flowers but not defending them. So trap-lining saves energy, allowing them to forage over a larger area. Your nectar feeder is part of the trap-line. Offering nectar-producing flowers nearby saves the bird energy in its search.

But maybe their migration story serves as just one more measure of how tough these miniscule creatures really are. You've probably watched in amazement their willingness to take on almost anything they find threatening, sometimes critters fifty times their

Top, right: *Nectar feeders suspended from ant moats will be ant-free.* Bottom, right: *Ant moats, which last for many years, need only water to function and so provide pesticide-free feeders for sensitive hummingbirds. Some feeders have built-in ant moats.*

size. Ironically, though, these naturally aggressive feisty fighters find themselves lunch for frogs and praying mantises—Asian praying mantises, that is, not our native insects. In fact, the Asian praying mantises, which are more slender, larger, and longer than our natives, are considered the hummer's number-one predator. Maybe these foreign insects that have invaded our shores should be called "preying" mantises. In my yard, they'd better pray for protection: I whack them any time I find them. Beware: They bite. And you really don't want to know how they devour hummingbirds. It's a gruesome scene.

NOTABLE BEHAVIOR   **Hummingbird Habits**

Mighty mites, hummingbirds display rather brazen—and amazing—behavior. Tiny though they are, they will readily chase hawks and eagles, and usually win. While every hummer host knows these little jewels fly really fast, they change direction at seemingly warp speed in blurred maneuvers. They metabolize about 98 percent of the nectar and insects they consume—the highest rate of any bird. They eat their weight or more in nectar daily and defend nectar territory against intruders. In short, they're ferocious warriors. We can be glad they aren't the size of eagles.

Such amazing birds, these hummers! Surely nothing more about them could have any greater "wow" factor, right? Well, how about this: Folks who band hummingbirds have documented that hummers migrate on a to-the-day schedule. Exactly how this uncanny built-in schedule works is anybody's guess, but banders have frequently captured the same bird on the same day for four years in a row. Never a day earlier. Never a day later. The birds stop at the same feeders, at the same nectaring spots, at the same stopover sites on the same day year after year. When my mom was no longer physically able to maintain her hummer feeders, she was brokenhearted that for at least five years afterward, hummingbirds hovered where her feeders once hung. Always in August. Always the last two weeks. She couldn't bear to look.

Banding studies show that, during migration, the same individual Ruby-throated Humming-birds visit the same feeders on the same days every year.

While I'm awestruck at such clockwork behavior, I also sense some ramifications. If hummers are loyal to previous feeding sites, think about the difficulty of luring hummers to other backyard feeders for the first time. It's an uphill effort. Creatures of habit, hummers go where they know to go. Only the youngsters will likely be lured to new sites—because they don't have "old" sites already mapped into their internal GPS.

Thus, now, in August, if you're a new host, aim to attract your first hummers. It's prime time. Youngsters in your neighborhood are running the trap-line, and youngsters on the move south are establishing stopover sites, mapping the route and feeder sites into their incredible memories. Lure them in this month and next, and they're yours for life!

Memorable Moments: Chimney Swifts Swooping in Chimneys

Chimney Swifts, so named for their penchant for using chimneys, rightfully earn their "flying cigar" moniker. They fly recklessly fast, wings quivering more than flapping, as they snatch insects from the air. Without swifts, we'd be overrun by bugs.

Strictly aerialists, Chimney Swifts do everything in the air except nest and sleep. They hang in chimneys to do that, using strong claws on little feet that otherwise basically don't function. They can barely walk. They can't perch. They can only cling. So they hunt, eat, drink, bathe, court, gather nest material, and yes, mate on the wing. Tricky, huh? That's gotta earn 'em some sort of award. Okay, they also supposedly sometimes mate at the nest site, but these little flying cigars still win the prize for aerialist acrobatics.

Although they once nested in huge hollow trees, Chimney Swifts adapted to human habitation and now seek out urban areas for the old chimneys often found there. But witnessing their real attraction is like watching a high-speed, thrill-a-minute amusement park ride. The nightly extravaganza of their descent into their preferred chimney roost never fails to astonish first-time viewers—and keep the rest of us in awe. In a chimney near us, these birds have given me memorable moments for many years. Beginning about 8:00 p.m., just at dusk, thirty or so swifts gather, circling the area, attracting attention to themselves by their calls. Ten minutes later, the circling flock swells to three hundred—maybe four hundred, maybe more. Who can count? Their swirling forms a blur.

Then the show truly begins. Imagine black smoke pouring from a chimney, forming a cloud above. Only picture now the reverse: black smoke being sucked in. Or think of water swirling down a drain. So the birds pour into the chimney, aligning themselves on the chimney's inside walls, clinging in a colony, shingle-like, down the stack.

Within minutes, the sky empties, suddenly silent, all three hundred or four hundred or more swifts now within the chimney. Fifteen minutes after show time, it's over. Dramatic. Astonishing. Memorable.

HABITAT—YOURS AND THEIRS   **Nursery Needs**

Chimney Swifts, miniature bug-eating aerialists, face a serious problem: Many people cap their chimneys, depriving the birds of a place to roost or nest. By leaving your chimneys uncapped, removing caps from existing chimneys, or even building habitat for these long-distance travelers, the birds will reward you by eating your bugs.

Brainy Birds

Call someone "birdbrain," and you'll likely earn no hugs or kisses. But if you watch bird behavior carefully enough, you'll surely come to question the term's disparaging connotation. Watch this month for clues to birdbrain behavior.

For instance, some birds apparently talk to one another, especially about food. Toss out a handful of whole peanuts and await the first Blue Jay's arrival. Its raucous *Jay! Jay!* surely broadcasts news of treats, for multiple jays join posthaste, depleting shells and all.

NOTABLE BEHAVIOR   **Gangs in the Airways**

They don't carry knives or paint graffiti on railroad cars, but lots of smart birds form gangs and fight over territory. Still, the battle may not be what you think. Imagine multiple species ganging up together to fight a common enemy. And imagine the common enemy as larger than all the gang members together.

So it is when titmice, chickadees, kinglets, and gnatcatchers join forces to take on an owl, hawk, or snake that dared to invade their homeland. When one bird sounds the alarm, scolding, the others take note and dash to the defense, yelling their loudest—which, of course, may not be very loud at all. They'll likely also dive and peck at the intruder, targeting especially its back where a ready mouth can't catch them. There's no training for this army gang; the soldiers just know.

Most birds communicate danger, both to their own species and to others. Watch the Red-shouldered Hawk inadvertently land atop the Tree Swallows' nest box and hear the racket break loose. Barn and Rough-winged Swallows join the Tree Swallows in dive-bombing the hawk, amplifying their usual mild twitters into full-blown alarm. Or witness songbirds that discover an owl's day-time slumber spot. Diving, pecking, squawking, they may ultimately drive the owl to flight.

You may argue these are only survival traits, instinctual in wild creatures. Could be.

But some birds seem to figure out cause and effect. When our lawnmower roars to life, Barn Swallows appear, knowing, it seems, that the mower stirs up a gourmet buffet of bugs. Last year Barn Swallows showed other signs of intelligence, nesting, ironically, inside a Home Depot store, gaining access by flying in front of the electronic eye that automatically opens the doors—for people as well as for birds.

Some birds also seem to understand process. I've watched eagles chip the ice to get at fish frozen just below the surface; and I've seen gulls snatch clams from the shore, fly up and drop them on rocks or paved surfaces (or, alas, car tops), thus cracking the shells and exposing the seafood feast.

Corvids, however, the family including crows and jays, rank as the whiz kids of the bird world. Their northern cousins, ravens, steal fish by hauling in anglers' untended lines. One researcher has observed an American Crow pulling a sliver of wood off a fencepost and using it to probe for bugs hiding in a small hole. So birds can't use tools?

Crows Get Crackin'

One fascinating report of corvids' problem-solving skill comes from a Japanese university where Carrion Crows enjoy feasting on walnuts. Unfortunately, crows can't crack the tough walnut shells, so they sit at traffic intersections and patiently wait for the light to change. When it does, they dash down, place walnuts in front of automobile tires, and fly up to wait. When the light turns again, crows join pedestrians and walk into the street to gather the now-cracked walnuts.

Scientists have argued for years over whether birds—or other wild creatures, for that matter—show real intelligence. A few might still argue that bird behavior results from instinct, "knowledge" programmed into birds' genes. But to plan when and where to put those walnuts—well, doesn't that take some thought?

Just call me birdbrain. I think I'm flattered.

Barn Swallows show keen understanding of certain human behaviors.

Smelly Issues

You've watched your yard birds. Do you think they have a sense of smell? Are all birds created equal when it comes to olfactory perception?

Scientists have solved parts of the puzzle and discovered that, surprisingly, most birds have little or no sense of smell. The olfactory section of an avian brain is, for the most part, poorly developed.

PROBLEM SOLVER   **Don't Touch That Nest!**

Since birds have a poorly developed sense of smell, it's a myth that to touch a bird's nest and leave one's scent will send the incubating adults fleeing, abandoning the nest. But that doesn't mean it's okay to handle nests or their contents.

Indeed, the larger problem seems to be that when we leave our rich human scent at a nest site, predators like snakes and raccoons detect the scent and follow their highly developed noses to rob the eggs or nestlings. So the nest goes empty, although perhaps for a reason different than we might have assumed. Touching the nest, thus leaving human scent, attracts predators.

But wouldn't hummingbirds, for instance, have to use scent to find nectar? Apparently not. In fact, they seem generally to prefer flowers with little or no scent, leaving the sweetest to the bees. And therein lies a clue. Bees indeed find sweet scents attractive and flock to those food sources. Hummers, hoping to avoid the aggression and competition bees create, choose the flowers less traveled by. Over eons, flowers evolved to take advantage of the hummers' pollination services, forming long trumpets inaccessible to bees. Indeed, Mother Nature creates incredible checks and balances, both for the birds and bees as well as for the flowers.

One area bird, however, has a finely tuned olfactory sense, most likely because it considers ripe carrion delectable. Since other critters also relish carrion, however, whoever finds roadkill first reaps the harvest. Turkey Vultures, with their acute sense of smell, frequently win the feast.

BIOLOGY BITS   **Smelly Champion**

The Turkey Vulture's sense of smell is so keen that the bird's very presence has been used to signal danger. After the installation of a remote gas line, authorities needed some means of detecting leaks. By incorporating an additive in the gas that smelled like carrion, they could assure themselves that any leaks would attract vultures. Thus, the circling big birds signal a need for inspection.

Some birds apparently use their sense of smell to navigate, in some cases even to migrate. Homing pigeons likely return to their roost somewhat by the same means as salmon return to their ancestral hatch site: They follow a down-home aroma, traveling the direction in which the scent concentrates.

Turkey Vultures display a keen sense of smell, the primary means by which they find carrion, the riper the better.

But what scent would lead homing pigeons home? No, it's not steak grilling, onions frying, or garlic roasting. Rather, it's a continuum of odors, the scent of river or mountain, desert or marsh, pine forest or pasture, or as the pigeons' destination nears, one building versus another that houses their roost.

Birds in other parts of the world may also use scent more than we understand. Pelagic birds, those that spend their lives over and in water except to nest, seem to have a well-developed olfactory sense. A Storm Petrel apparently uses scent to single out its nest burrow from among the thousands of neighboring colony burrows. In fact, tubenoses in general, a pelagic family of birds, apparently sniff out schools of fish, thus efficiently locating food across thousands of square miles of water.

So if birds detect scent at all, it's likely about home and food.

Summer Drought

As climate changes, more and more of us witness weather extremes, including record-high summertime temperatures and record-high river levels followed by record-low rainfall. Severe drought ensues. Now, in late summer, we're most likely to witness these severe weather conditions. If this year has brought the disastrous blistering-hot and bone-dry combination to your neighborhood, what's the one most beneficial thing you can do for our feathered friends?

Let's let the scenario play out.

Year-round residents like chickadees, titmice, and cardinals; migrant summer-nesters like hummingbirds, House Wrens, and Indigo Buntings; and spring and fall migrating visitors like Rose-breasted Grosbeaks and the whole array of warblers—all face survival challenges in extreme heat and drought marked by dry, cracked ground and parched vegetation. Some native grasses and flowers might have produced seed before succumbing to drought; and goldfinches, in August, still feeding insistent fledglings, will likely feast on the early seed production, preferring vegetarian diets for themselves and their young.

Black-eyed susan, close up.

HOW DOES YOUR GARDEN GROW
Native Plants to Survive Drought

August's parched garden proves once again that native plants better survive the crazy whims of varying weather than do hybrids. After all, they've had tens of thousands of years to adapt and still remain tough and resilient. When gardeners plant native in all or at least in large portions of a garden, the garden grows nearly carefree. My kind of garden! Natives need no fertilizers, no pesticides, and for the most part, no additional water. Some of my favorite Indiana native landscape plants, especially for birds, include those in the chart on the following page.

To find a list of similar plants for your area, check with your local or state native plant society.

Favorite Drought-tolerant Native Plants

Common Name	Scientific Name	Benefits for Birds
Flowers for Shade or Part Shade		
Aromatic aster	*Symphyotrichum oblingifolium*	nectar
Sweet Joe-pye weed	*Eupatorium purpureum*	nectar; attracts butterflies
Stiff goldenrod	*Oligoneuron rigidum*	nectar, seed, cover (in masses)
Zigzag goldenrod	*Solidago flexicaulis*	nectar, seed, cover (in masses)
Flowers for Sun		
Autumn goldenrod	*Solidago sphacelata*	nectar, seed, cover
Black-eyed Susan	*Rudbeckia hirta*	seed
Butterfly weed	*Asclepias tuberosa*	nectar; attracts butterflies
New England aster	*Symphyotrichum novae-angliae*	nectar, seed, cover (in masses); attracts butterflies
Pale-purple coneflower	*Echinacea pallida*	nectar, seed, cover (in masses)
Prairie dock	*Silphium terebinthinaceum*	seed
Sneezeweed	*Helenium autumnale*	nectar, seed, cover (in masses)
Tall coreopsis	*Coreopsis tripteris*	seed
Wild bergamot/beebalm	*Monarda fistulosa*	nectar, seed, cover (in masses)
Grasses		
Big bluestem	*Andropogon gerardii*	seed, cover
Indian grass	*Sorghastrum nutans*	seed, cover
Little bluestem	*Schizachyrium scoparium*	seed, cover
Northern sea oats (part shade)	*Chasmanthium latifolium*	seed, cover
Switch grass	*Panicum virgatum*	seed, cover
Shrubs for Shade or Part Shade		
Arrowwood viburnum	*Viburnum dentatum*	nectar, berries, cover
Black chokeberry	*Photinia melanocarpa*	berries, cover
Eastern arborvitae	*Thuja occidentalis*	cone-berries, cover
Elderberry	*Sambucus canadensis*	nectar, berries, cover
Fragrant sumac (erosion control)	*Rhus aromatica*	berries, low cover
Nannyberry	*Viburnum lentago*	nectar, berries
Ninebark	*Physocarpus opulifolius*	nectar, berries, cover
Smooth hydrangea (spreads)	*Hydrangea arborescens*	nectar, cover
Spicebush	*Lindera benzoin*	nectar, berries, cover
Winterberry holly	*Ilex verticillata*	berries, cover
Witchhazel	*Hamamelis virginiana*	nectar, cover
Shrubs for Sun		
Hawthorn	*Crateagus viridis*	nectar, berries, cover
Serviceberry	*Amelanchier laevis*	nectar, berries, cover
Winged sumac	*Rhus copallinum*	berries, cover

WATER WAYS   **Drought Delights**

Nothing will delight birds more in parched landscapes than fresh, clear water. But if it's dripping, bubbling, or running, your proffered water attracts even distant birds by its attention-getting noise. Our yard includes a couple of standard bird baths, no more than an inch deep. More than that and it's neck-deep for the birds. We also maintain a little water feature with a mini waterfall and small pool, planted with cover adored by lots of happy little fish. Another small yard pond offers shallow water flowing into a 2-foot-deep basin. But our homemade bubbling rock sees the real action. (See page 289 for a diagram.) Who knows what birds will show up.

Hummingbirds, on the other hand, are migrating now, flying through what to them must seem a wasteland. Native flowers have either quit blooming altogether or produce few blooms with little or no nectar, leaving hummers stressed during high-energy-needs times. Without putting on weight, they'll have too little fat reserves to journey south. Gardeners who watered faithfully may still offer nectar-bearing blossoms to hungry hummers. But hummer feeder hosts find record numbers of birds at their feeders, demanding refills at unheard-of rates. During one drought-stressed year, I fed 30 pounds of sugar in twelve days, a rate matched and even surpassed by many of my neighbors.

Below: *Our small backyard water feature includes moving water with an inch-deep bathing area.* Bottom: *Our homemade bubbling rock draws birds by the dozens to its always-flowing water.*

From late August into the middle of September is the hummingbird peak in our yard. During a year of drought, hummers flock more heavily than usual to nectar feeders.

Other birds, however, snub both seed and nectar, favoring a feast of bugs. While from a human perspective, we seem to have ample bugs, I'm almost certain that during this year's hot drought, the supply diminished dramatically. Migrating warblers, most of which dine exclusively on bugs, will find slim pickings to nourish them; and hungry birds can't fly the distance. I worry about them, knowing there's little—probably nothing—I can do about the bug supply.

But the one thing that will bring more avian activity to backyards in drought-stricken August is water. Birds need water to drink. Birds need water to bathe. Clean, healthy feathers mean efficient flight, and efficient flight means, so to speak, more miles to the gallon.

BOTANY FOR BIRDS   **Thorns and Brambles**

What's to love about thorny bushes, shrubs, and brambles? Who wants to risk being raked and pierced?

Birds, that's who! Watch birds dash into the thickest, thorniest patch of dense vegetation, and you'll see them dodge and dart, tucking in for safety. That's the clue: safety. Little birds can nest, hide, roost, escape, and otherwise find secure lodging amid dense thorns where hawks can't venture, cats can't pounce, and raccoons and possums won't wander. Only snakes will wriggle through, undeterred. Still, the bramble patch ranks as the top-prize part of my habitat, where towhees and cardinals nest, where Carolina Wrens take their babies, where catbirds hang out during migration, and where fall warblers busy themselves bugging.

Depending on the thorny species, that safe-haven bramble patch may also serve up quite a lovely berry buffet—for both you and the birds. Blackberry cobbler, anyone?

Summer's End

As August shrivels to a close, as the annual cycle puts birds on the move, as the calendar tracks our ongoing march to year's end, the backyard begins to ease its way toward winter. Watching the changes—among both birds and the botanical array to which they are irrevocably tied—overwhelms me with a sense of wonder.

These birds I love go about the annual cycle routinely, as a matter of fact, preparing instinctively for what's to come. They know. They prepare. They do what their ancestors have done for tens of thousands of years before them.

They seem so much smarter than I.

Conservation Corner: Pesticides Attack Birds as Sitting Ducks

According to the Smithsonian Migratory Bird Center (SMBC), birds can be exposed to pesticides in numerous ways, and like sitting ducks, they have no means by which to avoid the exposure. Here's a summary from the Center's website, http://nationalzaa.si.edu: "Ingestion is probably the most common way that birds are exposed to pesticides. Birds can swallow the pesticide directly, such as when a bird mistakes a pesticide granule for a seed, or indirectly, by consuming contaminated prey. They may also ingest pesticide residues off feathers while preening, or they may drink or bathe in tainted water. Pesticides can also be absorbed through the skin, or inhaled when pesticides are applied aerially."

Even if pesticides don't kill birds directly, serious effects can result in indirect fatalities. SMBC lists the following effects from pesticides:

- Eggshell thinning
- Deformed embryos
- Slower nestling growth rates
- Decreased parental attentiveness
- Reduced territorial defense
- Lack of appetite and weight loss
- Lethargic behavior (expressed in terms of less time spent flying, foraging, singing)
- Suppressed immune system response
- Greater vulnerability to predation
- Interference with body temperature regulation
- Disruption of normal hormonal functioning
- Inability to orient in the proper direction for migration

SMBC concludes, "Each of the above sub-lethal effects can ultimately reduce populations as effectively as immediate death, since they lower birds' chances of surviving or reproducing successfully, or both."

But there's more. Indirect effects from pesticide applications further threaten birds. When pesticide applications kill off the bugs, birds face a sudden loss of food supply. When herbicide applications kill off weeds, the bugs that feed on those weeds die, too, hitting birds with a double whammy: a reduced bug supply and a loss of seed supply. And herbicides applied in nest areas eliminate cover for ground nesters and protection for ground foragers, leaving birds, their eggs, and their young wide open to predation.

Given the effect on birds, shouldn't we also worry about the effect of pesticides on us?

In short, SMBC recommends that we "educate [ourselves] and others about the effects of pesticides and [use] alternate pest control." Further, we should "buy organically grown products, and support organizations working to reduce society's dependence on pesticides."

Things to Do in August

- Make sure seed/feed stays fresh by serving no more than a three-day supply at once.
- Wash feeders monthly to deter mold and disease.
- Maintain healthy, clean hummingbird feeders in hot weather by changing syrup every other day.
- With each fill-up, wash nectar feeders using really hot water and a bottle mop.
- Keep birdbath waters fresh and sparkling clean.
- To challenge your ID skills, study juvenile birds.
- Avoid pesticides, and ask your neighbors to do the same.

---

46 Yard Birds in August

Canada Goose	Hairy Woodpecker	American Robin
Northern Bobwhite	Northern Flicker	European Starling
Great Blue Heron	Pileated Woodpecker	Cedar Waxwing
Turkey Vulture	Eastern Wood-pewee	Yellow-throated Warbler
Cooper's Hawk	Great Crested Flycatcher	Eastern Towhee
Red-shouldered Hawk	Eastern Kingbird	Chipping Sparrow
Red-tailed Hawk	Blue Jay	Song Sparrow
Mourning Dove	American Crow	Summer Tanager
Yellow-billed Cuckoo	Barn Swallow	Northern Cardinal
Barred Owl	Carolina Chickadee	Blue Grosbeak
Chimney Swift	Tufted Titmouse	Indigo Bunting
Ruby-throated	White-breasted Nuthatch	Brown-headed Cowbird
Hummingbird	Carolina Wren	House Finch
Red-headed Woodpecker	House Wren	American Goldfinch
Red-bellied Woodpecker	Blue-gray Gnatcatcher	House Sparrow
Downy Woodpecker	Eastern Bluebird	

SPECIES PROFILE

RED-TAILED HAWK or RED-SHOULDERED HAWK?

Left: *Red-tailed Hawk, in flight;* right: *Red-tailed Hawks, at nest*

We dashed to a vantage point and stood watching, transfixed. On this particular crystal clear but windy afternoon, three Red-tailed Hawks rode the thermals. Were they playing? Do birds play? These three, one a juvenile, soared effortlessly, never flapping a wing. Too high to be hunting, they dipped and turned, twisting their heads, probably watching us watching them. No wonder we mere humans have struggled for centuries to imitate their flight, envious of the apparent sheer joy of gliding cross country. Even now I could feel the pull to be airborne.

NAME THAT BIRD

Buteo jamaicensis (Red-tailed Hawk): *Buteo* is Latin for "hawk," and *jamaicensis* refers
  to Jamaica where the first was collected. Its common name, "hawk," comes from the
  Anglo-Saxon word for this kind of bird while "red-tailed" describes adult plumage.

Buteo lineatus (Red-shouldered Hawk): *Lineatus* means "striped," for the bird's tail bands.
  Its common name describes adult plumage, most obvious when perched.

Our partially forested southern Indiana neighborhood is surrounded by cropland, pastures, and hayfields, perfect habitat for open-country-loving red-tails, the most common of our buteos, not just locally but nationwide. This past summer, a pair nested in the woodlot across our neighbor's hayfield, and we've enjoyed their antics all season.

Left: *Red-shouldered Hawk, in flight, carrying mouse in talon;* right: *Red-shouldered Hawk*

VITAL STATS
Red-tailed Hawk (females larger)
Length: 17–25 in.
Wingspan: 45–52 in.
Weight: 24–51 oz.
Red-shouldered Hawk (females larger)
Length: 16–21 in.
Wingspan: 37–44 in.
Weight: 16–27 oz.

An invisible line somewhere through the pasture's middle apparently delineates the Red-tailed Hawk's territory from that of its somewhat smaller cousin and competitor, the Red-shouldered Hawk. They don't like each other. So the red-tail stays north of the invisible boundary; the red-shoulder, south. I'd like to add, "and never the twain shall meet"; but occasionally one crosses into the other's territory and an aerial battle ensues, each screeching, diving, and clashing until boundaries are reaffirmed.

But to the south, regularly this summer, I've heard a female Red-shouldered Hawk, calling *keer-keer-keer* as she skims the treetops. I catch myself smiling, just knowing the magnificent bird remains in the neighborhood. But one early afternoon, interrupting her call, shots rang out, three in quick succession, from somewhere in her direction. And the sky went silent.

Scanning the steel gray clouds, I saw nothing. Could the shots have been aimed at the female red-shoulder, this wonderful mouse-catching creature that has nested here for the past two years, strutting for her mate within our camera's eye, teaching her offspring to hunt from our tulip poplar tree, soaring across the pasture to post vigil from the pecan tree?

Was someone target shooting? Or purposely trying to scare the hawk away? Or kill it?

Fretting over the possibilities, I walked the woods, checked the ravines, searched the creek banks, afraid I'd find her body. Or afraid I wouldn't, in case the hawk lay wounded. The feeble calls that seemed to emanate from just over the hill—were they the weakened cries of the injured red-shoulder or a Blue Jay playing its Academy Award–winning score of a hawk mimic?

I never saw a sign of the hawk, but two days later I saw her smaller mate, gliding silently over the same woods where I last saw the female. Now, a week later, I still strain to hear her call. Nothing.

BIRD TALK: WHO'S CALLING?

Red-tailed Hawks call mostly in flight, a long drawn-out descending *keeeeeeerrrrrrrr*. Red-shouldered Hawks have a similar descending *keerrr*, but it's of short duration and repeated, sometimes five or more times, both in flight and while perched.

FOOD FARE

Both of these buteo hawks eat mostly small mammals, red-tails taking some weighing up to 5 pounds, preferring voles, rabbits, and squirrels; but both hawks also take large birds, especially pheasants, bobwhites, blackbirds, and starlings. Occasionally they eat reptiles, and red-tails occasionally eat carrion.

I'll never know what happened, of course. But I'm angry all the same. It's true that when I was a kid, lots of folks shot "chicken hawks." And a chicken hawk was any hawk that showed up near the farm lot, threatening, we thought, our Sunday fried-chicken dinner. And some folks still carry the misinformation with them that hawks— hawks of any kind—are threats that must be stifled.

ID CHECK

Study the following comparisons to separate Red-tailed from Red-shouldered Hawks.

Comparison of Red-tailed Hawk and Red-shouldered Hawk

Red-tailed Hawk	Red-shouldered Hawk
Bird of open country	Bird of deciduous woodlands, often near water
Nests in crown of tall tree	Nests in crotch of large tree
Shows overall rich brown above, creamy below	Brown on back, heavy reddish barring on breast
Red tail above (mature bird only), pale below	Black tail with narrow light bands
In flight, shows black bar at "wrist"	In flight, shows narrow pale crescents at wing tips
Very common, quite large	Less common, smaller than red-tailed
Call is prolonged descending *keeeeerrrrrrr*	Call is short *keer*, repeated quickly 5–8 times

NEST NOTES

Red-tailed Hawk

Nest Site: located high, typically in the crown of the tallest tree around or occasionally on cliff shelf

Nest Construction: huge pile of sticks, usually about 2.5 ft. in diameter, but as nest is reused and refurbished, can become 3.5 ft. high and 6 ft. across; lined with dry vegetation, fresh leaves and twigs as well as corn husks, whole songbird nests, stalks, and other surprises

Eggs: 1–5 eggs, 1 brood, incubated 28–35 days

Fledge: 42–46 days after hatch

Red-shouldered Hawk

Nest Site: in main crotch of tree, usually close to trunk, often near water, like pond, stream, swamp

Nest Construction: built of twigs, dried leaves, and (in South) Spanish moss, 20 in. by 10 in., lined with bark shreds, moss, sometimes human trash, and always live springs of evergreen, often hemlock and (in Wisconsin) white birch; green leaves added during nestling phase

Eggs: 2–4 eggs, 1 brood, incubated 33 days

Fledge: 35 days after hatch

But most of us know better. Our large hawks—the red-shouldered and red-tailed varieties—prefer mice, voles, bunnies, even a squirrel or two. The Cooper's and Sharp-shinned Hawks, while they do snatch an occasional yard bird, manage to snag only the weak or slow, Mother Nature's way of strengthening the gene pool.

But let's put it another way: Taking a bird is a federal crime punishable by up to a $15,000 fine and six months in prison. According to the Migratory Bird Treaty Act of 1918, all migratory birds and their parts (including eggs, nests, and feathers) are fully protected. The Act refers to "taking" as "pursuing, hunting, shooting, poisoning, wounding, killing, capturing, trapping, or collecting." Hawks included.

SPOTTING THE SPECTACULAR   **Color on the Wing**

Not all Red-tailed Hawks have red tails, especially the young. And red-tails, famous for their dramatic color variations, range from almost black (Harlan's subspecies) to almost white (Krider's subspecies), all quite lovely and readily distinguished, even in the air, from their somewhat smaller cousin, the Red-shouldered Hawk.

To separate the two species when they're sky high, first note tail bands, broad and distinct on red-shouldered, thin and indistinct on red-tailed. Note wing patterns, with translucent crescents near wingtips on red-shouldered and dark "wrists" on red-tailed. And then note breast patterns, unmarked on red-shouldered but a clearly streaked belly band on red-tailed.

SPECIES PROFILE

COOPER'S HAWK or SHARP-SHINNED HAWK?

VITAL STATS
Cooper's Hawk
Length: m. = 15 in., f. = 17 in.
Wingspan: m. = 30 in., f. = 32 in.
Weight: m. = 11 oz., f. = 18 oz.
Sharp-shinned Hawk
Length: 9.4–13.4 in.
Wingspan: 17–22 in.
Weight: 3.1–7.7 oz.

Above: *Cooper's Hawk, immature;* below, left: *Cooper's Hawk;* below, right: *Sharp-shinned Hawk*

Movement caught my eye. Feathers erupted from some unseen source ten feet above ground and now drifted, swaying, downward.

Then I saw it. A Cooper's Hawk gripped a female cardinal in its talons as it flapped awkwardly, struggling to drag its catch toward an evergreen's drooping branches. It may have startled the cardinal from its perch or snatched it from midair; I did not see the attack. But its demise was instantaneous from the Cooper's crushing talons.

NAME THAT BIRD

Accipiter cooperii (Cooper's Hawk): *Accipiter* translates roughly as "bird of prey," and *cooperii* honors William C. Cooper, founder of the New York Lyceum of Natural History. The bird's common name likewise honors the man, and "hawk" is the Anglo-Saxon word for this kind of bird.

Accipiter striatus (Sharp-shinned Hawk): *Striatus* means "striped or striated," referring to the bird's striped breast. Its common name refers to a raised ridge on the bird's leg, an area that equates to a human shin. Other birds lack this ridge.

Why couldn't the hawk snare a European Starling or House Sparrow? Or a frog or mouse? Why a beautiful cardinal? Struggling to keep my helpless rage under control, I came to grips with the cold, brutal balance between predator and prey. Mother Nature, in spite of our respect for her, could never serve as a role model for our children. She's brutal and bloody, never shies from a do-or-die battle for survival. Everything eats something else. In this case, a raptor survived another day because it was cunning enough and fast enough to snare a meal.

And the cardinal did not survive another day because it was too slow, too unobservant, perhaps too old or weak to escape the attack. Thanks to the Cooper's meal, the cardinal gene pool remains strong. In science class, we called that survival of the fittest.

But the story continues. As I watched, the Cooper's began a methodical meal, pausing after every bite to make sure that he, the predator, would not become prey. Shrill cries from a soaring Red-shouldered Hawk effected long pauses in the Cooper's meal; the Cooper's, its head cocked, watching skyward, edging backward, dragged its prey farther under the protective boughs.

FOOD FARE

Cooper's Hawks eat medium-sized birds, especially starlings, doves, and pigeons, although they will also take robins and flickers as well as some others. They will also eat mice, voles, squirrels, and chipmunks. Sharp-shinned Hawks, being smaller than Cooper's, take smaller prey, but they still prefer birds. In addition, they take large insects and a few small mammals.

An hour later, the Cooper's quit its meal. Still perched on the remains of its prey, it fluffed its feathers, settled down, and seemed to doze, looking every bit the after-dinner couch potato. After twenty minutes, it resumed its meal. Surrounding leaf litter prevented my seeing all the details (surely just as well), but the hawk pulled and tugged, ate and watched, finishing its feast.

Two hours later, it lifted off in labored flight. After all, it had just eaten one-sixth of its weight—the equivalent of a 150-pound person downing 25 pounds of food. The hawk will unlikely feed again for several days.

Afterward, I checked its dining spot. Only a few feathers remained. No feet, no bones, no skin, no head, no beak. It had eaten every shred.

While I hurt for the loss of the cardinal, I have to realize the implications of my pain. Who am I to say that one bird is more important, more valuable, more worthy of living than another?

Come winter, however, the Cooper's may be joined by its cousin, the Sharp-shinned Hawk. Last year, in spite of our larger resident hawks, a young sharpie sashayed in for a visit. Wintering sharpies eagerly trade elusiveness for good hunting. And for them, a yard full of feeder birds defines good hunting. Plucked songbird comprises their favorite meal—much to my consternation.

In years past, I thought my backyard habitat, lacking a sharpie, was somehow deficient. But last winter's visit changed my perspective. The Blue Jay–sized creature can blast through the yard with incredible agility and rip birds from their perches before they even see it coming. Awesome. Startling. And sometimes heart-wrenching.

A sharpie could well have made an earlier backyard appearance but went unrecognized. After all, a Sharp-shinned Hawk is almost indistinguishable from a Cooper's Hawk; the species are similar in color and have similar tail bands and overall appearance.

BIRD TALK: WHO'S CALLING?
Both hawks are mostly silent except during breeding season when male and female Cooper's Hawks do a loud *kak, kak, kak* that lasts up to five seconds or so, while Sharp-shinned Hawks do a less piercing *kik, kik, kik.*

ID CHECK
Study the following comparisons to separate the common Cooper's Hawk from the more secretive, elusive, and (where I live) winter-season Sharp-shinned Hawk.

Comparison of Cooper's Hawk and Sharp-shinned Hawk

Cooper's Hawk	Sharp-shinned Hawk
Year-round resident	Only in winter (check your area's range map)
Common; commonly seen; suburbanized	Common but secretive
14–20 in. long; about size of crow	10–14 in. long; about size of jay or flicker
Lanky, more robust than Sharp-shinned	Bowling-pin shaped; seems to have no neck
Appears larger headed	Appears smaller headed
Strong contrast between dark head and light-colored face	Little contrast between color on back and that on crown
Has larger bill, made prominent by longer neck	Appears to have a smaller bill
Head slightly more square with slight peak at back	Head appears rounded
Longer neck makes head more prominent	Shorter neck makes bird look "hunched"
Pale eyebrow sweeps up toward back	Dark crown curves down behind eye
Tail longer; tip slightly rounded	Tail shorter, tip squared
Sturdy legs	Thin, "pencil" legs
Call: Rapid *kek, kek, kek* similar to flicker; also a mewing call; more vocal than sharp-shinned	Call: Like Cooper's but shriller; less vocal than Cooper's
Hunts in forests but, unlike sharp-shinned, also commonly seen in open areas	Hunts in forested areas; tends to avoid open areas

Since the females of both species are larger than their counterpart males, the female Cooper's and the male sharpie might be easy enough to separate when they are side by side. You're unlikely, however, to see them side by side.

To add to the identity confusion, consider that a male Cooper's and a female sharpie are virtually the same size. Separating them often creates an argument among even the best birders.

NEST NOTES

Cooper's Hawk

Nest Site: about two-thirds up a tree, in deep crotch against the trunk or on horizontal limb, usually 25–30 ft. high in a variety of tree species

Nest Construction: crude pile of sticks about 2 ft. in diameter with 8 in. by 4 in. cup lined with flakes of bark and twigs

Eggs: 2–6 eggs, 1 brood, incubated 30–36 days

Fledge: 27–34 days after hatch

Sharp-shinned Hawk

Nest Site: usually 20–60 ft. high against the trunk of mature trees, often conifer, in dense forest

Nest Construction: large pile of conifer twigs, about 20 in. diameter, cup lined with bark chips

Eggs: 3–8 eggs, 1 brood, incubated 30–32 days

Fledge: 24–28 days after hatch

The Cooper's hawk regularly stands sentry in the front-yard oak causing birds to melt away, "freezing" in position or dissolving into the landscape. It sits and waits. Sharpies, on the other hand, terrorize with speed, jetting in and out, snaring prey in fractional seconds, scattering feathers on the fly. On its off time, it huddles in the pines, quietly surveying the backyard feeders and planning its next attack. But birds aren't stupid. At least not those that survive to pass on their genes. I console myself that the sharpie's role keeps the goldfinch gene pool strong. Still, I no longer perceive my backyard habitat as deficient without a sharpie. Quieter, less dramatic—but not deficient.

SPOTTING THE SPECTACULAR   **Careful Courting**

Male Cooper's Hawks court potential mates with care. Like most accipiters, buteos, and owls, a male Cooper's is smaller than a female. So why is that a problem for the Cooper's male when it seems not to be a problem for other male hawks? Well, it's all about lunch. Female Cooper's Hawks really like to dine on medium-sized birds. And the male Cooper's? Well, he's a medium-sized bird. Needless to say, a male Cooper's approaches this blind-date situation with care, waiting for a reassuring message before venturing into risky territory. Then, to assure his safety, he builds a nest and feeds the female during incubation, a three-month commitment. Job security, I think it's called—or maybe life insurance.

September

*Those who dwell among the beauty
and mysteries of the earth
are never alone or weary of life.*

RACHEL CARSON

Seplember marks the autumnal equinox, that single day halfway between summer and winter, when day and night each last twelve hours. It's a month in which summer fades—literally and figuratively—into autumn.

September also marks the peak of autumn's version of that magnificent twice-a-year phenomenon called migration. Many long-distance shorebird migrants left the Arctic and began their southward journeys in July, and some northernmost nesting songbirds began venturing southward in August; September, however, marks departures of the bird friends we've treasured, those nesting right in our own backyards.

Migration doesn't begin on a given date, an occasion we can mark on the calendar. Instead, after weeks of full-time preparation, beginning long before seeds and berries disappear or frost sends insects into hiding, birds slip away, a few here, a few there. No goodbyes. No announcements. No last-minute flings. No mass exodus. But on many days, come dawn, the yard holds fewer birds. They left in the night. Quietly. Alone. Flying with the setting sun into the darkness and out of our lives until spring.

Length of day triggers birds to start packing—packing on the fat, that is, storing extra energy to flap those tiny wings often enough to make, in some cases, a several-thousand-mile trip. And birds that have the farthest to fly leave the earliest, so Purple Martins left last month. Eastern Phoebes won't leave until next month. But the biggest wave of departures south occurs now, in September.

HOW DOES YOUR GARDEN GROW?
Garden Trash or Treasure?

You've heard the cliché that what's one person's trash is another person's treasure. And so it is in our gardens. The gardener's trash and debris are likely the birds' bounty and treasure.

If we deadhead all the flowers, pitching seed heads in the trash, we destroy the birds' best buy—an abundant seed supply, ripe for the picking. If we insist on cleaning the fall garden—pruning, snipping, cutting, raking, discarding all the drooping dead stems and now-lackluster annuals—we destroy birds' cover and wintertime shelter. So leave the treasures, those seed heads. Birds will enjoy them all winter. And wait until early spring to tidy up.

Memorable Moments: Mourning Warbler Stopover

In September, given the excitement of fall migration, I've come to expect unusual yard birds. But not in my wildest dreams did I expect a Mourning Warbler. Oh, yes, they do migrate through our part of the world, that's true. But they're truly elusive, secretive, ground-loving birds, related to equally elusive, secretive, ground-loving Connecticut Warbler and Kentucky Warbler. They skulk in dense vegetation, foraging low, darting from one hidden habitat to the next in maddeningly brief flashes. We have only that moment's flash in which to make an ID. The male Mourning Warbler's soft gray hood worn over pale yellow breast and delicate brown back boasts one tell-tale accessory: a distinct, black bib.

That mid-September early evening, I was peering carefully into trees, bushes, vines, and ground cover for movement, inching along at a speed my husband calls standing. Hoping to spot a migrant or two lurking in the vegetation, I dreamed especially of seeing warblers, maybe a Black-throated Green Warbler or American Redstart, maybe a Yellow-throated Warbler or Common Yellowthroat.

Top, left: *American Redstart;* top, right: *Black-throated Green Warbler;* bottom: *Common Yellowthroat*

Banks of goldenrod lining our yard path hides wonderful birds, including, one September early evening, a Mourning Warbler foraging low for bugs.

Along a lower path curving through the far back of the yard, I inched toward a chest-high stand of blooming goldenrod. Suddenly, I drew up short. Something moved in the golden patch to my right. Something low. Just a shake of a stalk. Then a shake of the next stalk. I could see nothing moving within, only the stalks themselves, one by one, each shiver moving one stalk closer to the edge where I trained my binocular.

I held my breath. Probably just a Carolina Wren, feeling quite at home in the cover, I guessed. But, still, I waited, watched, unmoving.

Then, there it was! In plain sight, hopping, not walking, it bugged along the edge. In only seconds, it flew across the path, not ten feet from me, as I followed with binoculars. Yes! The black bib. Then it hopped on, bugging deeper into the blackberry thicket to my left, and disappeared. I never saw it fly, but my heart rate finally slowed.

It was a first in my yard. And it was a first record for our southwestern Indiana county.

September Migration Flies On

Unfortunately, migration carries with it a staggering cost. Millions of birds die. It's a long, dangerous journey battling obstacles and sheer distance. Imagine getting yourself to South America without an auto, boat, or plane; without roads, maps, or GPS; without protection from the elements; without ready or even reliable food and water; without an assured safe place to rest. You must arrive within weeks. You return six months later. And you thought your AAA-planned 800-mile auto trip was long on endurance and short on fun.

PROBLEM SOLVER   **Feral Cats on the Prowl**

When we invite birds to the yard, either during migration stopovers or for year-round habitat, we owe them safety while they dine, drink, bathe, roost, and nest. Cats, feral or otherwise, deny that safety. While it's impossible to know exactly how many birds cats kill in a year, scientists estimate the number in the hundreds of millions, perhaps over a billion. Among urban and residential areas, cats are by far the most common predator. What to do?

Assuming the cat preying in your yard is not your neighbor's household pet, you can carefully and safely trap it and take it to your local humane society for adoption into a loving home. If your community has an ordinance against roaming animals, you can file a complaint and have animal control officers trap and remove the cat, again for possible adoption.

But what if the intruder is, in fact, your neighbor's household pet? No one wants to believe that his or her cuddly kitty will kill a bird. But it's a cat's nature. As a life-long cat lover and owner of many cuddly kitties over the years, I know. So, begin a conversation with your neighbor gently, reminding him or her of local ordinances. Lacking ordinances, recommend that, for the cat's own safety, health, and long life, it be kept in an enclosure, either indoors or out, especially at night when most cats do the most damage.

If the cat continues to prey in your backyard, consider a "three strikes and you're out" plan. Tell your neighbor each time the cat appears in your yard. Take pictures if you can. And explain that on the third count, you'll resort to filing a complaint or trapping the pet. In most communities, law enforcement will support you.

As you might suspect, thousands of air miles take their toll on migrants. Weakened birds die from exhaustion or starvation. Night fliers frequently crash into tall buildings. Millions die flying into microwave-tower guy wires. Storms and strong headwinds zap birds' strength. Typically, birds lose one-fourth to one-half of their body weight during migration across large bodies of water, and millions fall to a watery death. Predators, hunters, pollutants, and habitat destruction kill more. Scientists estimate that about half of all migrants don't survive to make the return trip. Watching September movement, then, always shrouds me with a mixture of emotion—thrilled to see these gorgeous flights of feathered creatures but fearful for their journey. Some won't return. I wish them well.

HABITAT—YOURS AND THEIRS   **Stopover Sites**

On their long migratory journeys, birds count on "stopover sites," rather like mega gas-station stops along our Interstates. They need plenty of food (mostly bugs), fresh water (preferably moving), and safe resting places (in dense vegetation). You can help migrants by designing your yard as a stopover site. Plant evergreens. Include native grasses and fruit-bearing trees and shrubs. Offer fresh water. Keep sunflower and nectar feeders filled and clean. And skip the pesticides to conserve the bugs these birds need.

Worn plumage on a Carolina Wren attests to a season of hard work raising babies.

Changing Seasons, Changing Clothes

September is also the month for new clothes. Who doesn't enjoy a new outfit? And a new wardrobe is doubly welcome if it's the primary line of defense against upcoming snow, sleet, and blasting frigid winds. And so it is with birds.

Early last month, most birds looked a bit ratty, as if they'd suddenly become homeless, wearing ill-fitting clothes in need of mending, washing, and pressing. But nothing can repair broken, worn, and ragged feathers; they're "dead," like fingernails. Only replacement does the fix. Feathers exposed to the brutal elements 24/7 for 365 days obviously weather tough times, including raking in and out of cavities or hidden nests in thorny thickets fifty times a day for weeks. No wonder birds look ratty.

True, those feathers kept the bird warm last winter, made it gorgeous for breeding this spring, and protected it through rain and searing sun this summer.

Now, in preparation for another winter, though, birds are working full time on their molt, replacing old feathers with new, barbs tightly zipped for the best insulation Nature knows. Furthermore, birds wear more feathers in winter than in summer—sometimes half again as many. Think about your own goose-down comforter or goose-down coat or jacket. Ooh, so snuggly in bitter cold.

BIOLOGY BIT   **Feathers—More than Fluff**

Birds wear an astonishingly huge number of feathers. Hummingbirds sport about one thousand while swans dress in twenty-five thousand. To put this feather-clad business in perspective, think about it this way: A bird's feathers generally weigh more than its entire hollow-boned skeleton.

To replace a full body of feathers, however, birds expend big-time energy. Thus, they wait until other energy-demanding jobs—like nest building, breeding, feeding and protecting young—have finished. Fortunately, foliage remains dense in September; so birds can hide, protected, resting and preserving energy while they molt.

Molt is complicated by the fact that birds can't grow feather replacements in a matter of days—or even a couple of weeks. Instead, they shed and grow replacement feathers in symmetrical patterns across their bodies and tails and along their wings, a symmetrical change completed, at least among most passerines, over five to twelve weeks.

BIOLOGY BITS   **Who's Crested?**

Birds like Northern Cardinals, Blue Jays, and Tufted Titmice have obvious feathery crests, right? Well, no, not always. Both birds can flatten their crests so that they appear round-headed. Other birds, like White-crowned Sparrows and Downy Woodpeckers, usually round-headed, can show what looks like a crest, especially when they're displaying an atti-tude. So how's a bird-watcher to know if the subject in view is crested or not? Given the fact that a bird can raise or lower head feathers at will, it's a tricky call. Watch for unusually long feathers on the head; those are true crests.

Here's how it works. A bird loses one primary feather at a time, from the same spot on each wing. As the two flight feathers regrow, the bird loses the next primary feather on each wing. The symmetrical loss and replacement allows the bird to continue flight in order to feed and protect itself from predators.

Molting ducks, however, take a different tack. They shed most flight feathers simultane-ously and, during that interval, as you might guess, find themselves flightless. In what's called

Crested birds can raise and lower their head feathers. When feeding, most crested birds, like this Northern Cardinal, relax their head feathers.

their "eclipse phase," they huddle in water deep enough to keep them safe from predators and in places remote enough to avoid threats that would otherwise force them to flee on the wing. Why undergo molt under such dangerous conditions? Even a few lost feathers hinder heavy birds like ducks, impeding their agile self-preservation flight. So, Mother Nature developed the plan for ducks to undergo a quick makeover, accepting the serious short-term risk in lieu of long-term hampered flight.

WATER WAYS   **Yard-pond Water Hole**

Molting birds, especially those also stressed by drought, love water—but not too much water. Think 1 inch deep. For the little guys, 1 inch deep is belly deep. For the big guys, an inch deep is still deep enough to bathe.

But inch-deep water evaporates quickly or gets splashed out quickly. So plan for a daily fill-up, maybe twice daily on scorching windy days.

Some birds, including American Goldfinches, molt twice a year. In winter, after a full-body fall molt, they wear olive drab. Come spring, after a partial molt, replacing only contour feathers but not wing and tail feathers, they regain their namesake golden plumage, able to expend the twice-annual energy because, unlike other birds, they nest in late summer. September, then, sees them dressed in half-and-half gold-olive ratty plumage. Within a few weeks, though, they've molted into sleek olive-drab, a natty camouflage.

By month's end, across your entire backyard, ratty turns to spiffy, and once again birds will be attired for winter—well-tailored, warm, and safe for the season.

Songbirds Head South

If you were a tropical bird having come here for summer nesting, right now, in September, you'd be eating. Well, no, not just eating—rather, you'd be gorging, stuffing yourself, gobbling down everything in sight, on a month-long effort to double your weight. Then, in human equivalency, you'd take off running, nonstop, for about one thousand miles. Think you might tire? Not a good idea. If you stop to rest, you'll die. There's no place to rest on your way across the waters of the Gulf of Mexico.

HABITAT—YOURS AND THEIRS
Frequent Fliers in the Yard

Last night's skies twittered with calls of thrushes, flying high, flying south, flying persistently onward, pushed ahead by a cold front, upper-level winds ushering birds along their way. On quiet nights this time of year, calls from wave after wave of migrating birds reach our land-bound ears, as most migrants travel at night, dropping down to feed and rest at early morning light, taking to the skies again at dusk.

One of those thrushes, a Swainson's Thrush, spent its daylight hours today foraging under our pines, bathing in the yard pond, loafing in the thicket. Since we've not seen this handsome thrush since April, how I wish it could tell me where it's been, what its trip was like, how the family fared, and where it's headed next.

Swainson's Thrushes wander through our yard in spring and fall but nest farther north, maybe where you live.

Fall migration, dramatically more immense than spring migration, mushroomed by this year's crop of babies, gets into full swing this month with the bulk of migrants hitting the sky-roads.

About half of the birds that breed in North America migrate. Not all migrations, however, are equal. Some birds migrate one hundred miles south or merely drop down several thousand feet to lower elevations. A few long-distance travelers rack up eight thousand frequent flier miles one way. According to experts who tally numbers, 338 of "our" bird species migrate south of the Tropic of Cancer, designated by an imaginary line circling the world, running through Mexico north of the Yucatan and south of Florida.

BIOLOGY BITS **Feathers Tell Travel Tales**

Stable isotopes. That's what biogeochemistry folks look for in feathers. These certain atoms, found in all feathers, can identify the location in which the feathers were grown. Isotopes vary by environment—by temperature, annual precipitation, altitude, and latitude. Analysis of these stable isotopes identifies where the bird was eating and living when it grew its current set of feathers, sort of a "flying fingerprint." So, plucking and analyzing a single feather gives a "world" of information, fine tuning scientists' understanding of who went where during migration.

Of course, Ruby-throated Hummingbirds have taken to the skies as well, their ranks thinning significantly since their late-August/early September peak. Once they double their weight to start moving, they, too, will fly at night, stopping to tank up wherever they find nectar. Keeping feeders fresh helps them on their way.

Believe it or not, keeping a feeder fresh until December's end helps late migrants. Even more exciting, however, that feeder may also lure a rare hummer to your yard. Most winters, through late December, someone somewhere in Indiana hosts Rufous Hummingbirds, sometimes more than one. Last winter, in Indiana, a Rufous Hummingbird and a state-record Calliope Hummingbird entertained hosts for the entire winter, leaving only when we were anticipating the Ruby-throated Hummingbirds' return. One year a Black-chinned Hummingbird made a short, early winter visit. Who knows how many of these delightful little creatures wandered through that no one saw—because folks take their feeders in too early. Maybe at your house, too?

Fall migrating Ruby-throated Hummingbirds love nectaring at my hyacinth-bean vine blossoms.

Hummingbird feeders in my yard see peak activity the second week of September but host few mature male ruby-throats like this one, most of which left earlier in the season.

BIOLOGY BITS   **Hummingbird Myths**

Myth: Hummingbirds migrate on the backs of geese.

Reality: Hummingbirds migrate on their own, from wherever they nest to their winter-time home, perhaps as far south as Costa Rica. They never ride on a goose's back, nor do geese migrate to the same places where hummingbirds winter.

Myth: Hummingbirds drink nothing but nectar.

Reality: About 60 to 80 percent of a hummingbird's diet is protein—in the form of tiny bugs. Hummers snap them out of the air or glean them off leaves.

Myth: Hummingbirds won't migrate if I leave my feeders out past Labor Day.

Reality: Hummingbirds migrate according to length of day. And they need feeders more desperately in drought-stricken September than in early summer when profuse flowering offers ample nectar. Keep feeders out until December to help late migrants and the occasional rare hummingbird species.

Myth: Baby hummingbirds come to my flower garden.

Reality: When hummingbirds leave the nest, they look like mom. Those "babies" at your flowers are likely hummingbird moths, more properly named "snowberry clearwing moth," and look very much like miniature hummers. Baby hummingbirds can't fly.

Myth: If my hummingbird feeders go dry while I'm on vacation, the hummers will die.

Reality: Hummingbirds may prefer the leisure of finding fast food at your feeders, but your feeders aren't the only place they feed. They won't die in your absence. Although they may quit checking empty feeders regularly, as soon as you refill feeders upon your return, hummers will, one by one, eventually discover the return of fast food.

Hummingbird moths, more properly called snowberry clearwing moths, are sometimes mistaken for young hummingbirds; but in fact, young hummingbirds are barely distinguishable from adult hummers at the feeders.

Weather Fronts Blow 'Em In—Or Out

Meteorologists predict the temperatures and rain chances, those details that affect our travel to work or school and the kids' football games. For birds, however, the more significant part of the prediction concerns the upcoming movement of highs and lows, the fronts and their directions, especially this month, during migration.

Spring migrants waited for southerly winds to give them a tail-wind boost, generating more miles per gallon, so to speak, on their long trek north. Now, fall migrants ride the northerly winds. While migratory birds wander south in dribs and drabs all through late summer and fall, and significant numbers of warblers began moving through early this month, dramatic bird movement coincides with dramatic seasonal changes, especially in late September. Then, a cold front's northerly winds often punch through with an accompanying wave of migrating birds. In short, birds take advantage of the wind's extra push to travel farther on less energy and effort. So bird-watchers watch the weather, hoping for a wave of warblers.

HABITAT—YOURS AND THEIRS
Gather Ye Tree Limbs While Ye May

The second stormiest time of the year falls during the autumn months. Gathering downed limbs and finding a way to discard them sometimes becomes a challenge. Here's a suggestion: save them. In fact, gather those from your neighbors as well. Then use them to build a brush pile for wintering birds. Over one hundred species are serious brush-pile candidates. But one word of warning: Avoid bringing wood to your yard from outside your area. You risk introducing unwanted pests and disease. Gather ye tree limbs locally. (See pages 302–303 for building plans.)

Last fall, a stagnant air mass perched over Canada for five weeks, dumping torrents of rain to the south but offering no supporting winds for migrants. Although many birds began their usual trek south in spite of little or no help from upper level winds, we saw only wavelets, not waves, of migrants. Then the weather broke, the front moved, and the jet stream sitting in Canada surged across Lake Michigan, pushing in cool, sunny weather. What came with it? Birds. Lots and lots of birds.

Migration is, indeed, a twice-a-year extravaganza that changes the complexion of the yard. Set in the changing botany of spring and fall, the birds that show themselves only as they pass through to and from their breeding grounds give us rare glimpses of their brilliant tropical colors. So the long-awaited cold front gave a boost to the travelers and brought 'em in. What a warbler fest we had—not to mention all the other migrant species foraging in the yard.

NOTABLE BEHAVIOR   **Caught in the Eye of the Storm**

For migrating birds caught in a storm, effects can be devastating. The worse the storm, of course, the worse the effects. In October 2005, Hurricane Wilma plowed up the East Coast during the heart of fall migration. Millions of birds on the wing were caught in her path. When the storm passed, 727 Chimney Swifts were found dead, and who knows how many weren't found at all. Nesting populations the next year barely reached half of that in previous years.

Most likely, birds, including vast numbers of Chimney Swifts, caught in the eye of the hurricane were carried with it, unable to escape—or feed. They died. And many that did escape sought refuge in chimneys. Sadly, because of the already cold weather, the chimneys were active, carrying significant heat. These birds, too, died.

Most of us probably don't think about the devastation serious storms inflict on birds. But severe storms wreak severe tolls.

Birding Fest

After the late-September cold front passed through, at least a dozen Rose-breasted Grosbeaks literally shook the tree branches, their sneaker-on-the-gym-floor screeches marking their progress. Six Black-throated Green Warblers picked bugs from the front-yard sugar maple, their characteristic yellow faces divulging their identity even in fall plumage. A Tennessee Warbler turned from bugs to berries, bouncing through the beautyberry bush, its fall plumage a perfect match with the yellow-green leaves in which it fed. A Nashville Warbler bugged in the weed patch, among the panicle asters, its eye ring distinctive.

In the pin oak, a Northern Parula, its yellow breast and bright wing bars distinctive, offered a decorator's dream color combination among the autumn gold and brown. A Wilson's Warbler lingered only briefly, its little black cap dignifying its style. Some sort of Blue-winged Warbler hybrid eluded my identification skills. A female American Redstart, the flick of her yellow banded tail tracing its path, zipped from the oak to the bubbling rock, posing briefly on a nearby perch.

Behind the house and down the hill, where twenty or so years ago we quit mowing anything other than paths and borders, the dense brush attracted a Gray Catbird, its quiet mimic song revealing its presence. And surprise! Two more snatched berries from the pokeweed.

A Nashville Warbler bugs among the native white panicle asters in the weed patch.

Left: *A female American Redstart, drawn to our bubbling rock, paused long enough for me to enjoy the flash of her yellow-trimmed tail. Right: Gray Catbirds, drawn to our backyard habitat, forage secretively among the tangles, affording me only occasional glimpses of them and their surprising russet undertail feathers.*

Our yard offered all these avian charmers the perfect stopover site, a place to feed and fatten up, a safe haven among the brambles for resting. So when bird-watchers watch the weather, sometimes we catch the wave—of migrants, that is.

Bird Feeding Beginnings

If you're not already feeding birds, fall makes the perfect time to start. Resident birds visiting your yard—like Northern Cardinals, Black-capped or Carolina Chickadees, Tufted Titmice, Blue Jays, Carolina Wrens, and American Goldfinches—will find your offerings early. In turn, their activity will attract soon-to-arrive winter visitors, like Dark-eyed Juncos, White-throated and White-crowned Sparrows, Red-breasted Nuthatches, maybe even Pine Siskins—depending on where you live. By the time snow flies and ice turns the world crystal, you'll have a score or more species dining while you watch.

FEEDER FOCUS   **Choosing Feeders**

In January, we talked about what makes a quality feeder. Now, as another winter approaches and you need to replace, add, or even choose your first feeder, let's add some details. Choose a bird feeder with the following qualities:

- Designed and made for birds, not people; functional, not fancy
- Dispenses seed evenly without spilling, maybe with a catch-tray attached to the bottom
- Keeps seed as dry as possible during fall and winter precipitation
- Includes adequate drainage
- Includes a bottom baffle that distributes seed to feeder ports, preventing spoilage
- Is sturdy, durable
- Is large enough to avoid constant refilling
- Fills easily
- Eliminates sharp edges harmful to birds
- Disassembles easily for cleaning (plastic and metal clean easier than wood)

If you want more than one feeder, choose different styles—hopper, tube, or platform—to accommodate a variety of birds and bird feeds.

In short, then, your theater ticket to Nature gives you a front-row seat to birds gathering around the bar—buffet bar, that is. Add water, be it a simple bird bath or something more elaborate, and some cozy nest boxes that double as winter roost boxes, and you'll have a stage beyond compare. Your theater reviews will be five-star.

But be warned: Backyard bird feeding is not without its quandaries, including who's feeding now, who's coming later, and who's eating what. Let's start with now, in September.

NOTABLE BEHAVIOR   **Hummer Departures**

Not all hummingbirds depart at the same time. Male hummers leave first—and early—and why not? Males don't help build nests, don't incubate, don't feed nestlings. When the female starts her second nest in mid-July, males have no further breeding opportunities. Their business is done; the tropics beckon; off they go.

Simultaneously, females, still incubating eggs, have no similar option for early departure. But once eggs hatch and nestlings fledge by late August, females, too, find themselves footloose and fancy free. They feed heavily, fatten up, and drift south in September.

Juveniles, some having fledged in late August, leave even later than adult females, perhaps not until next month, spending those extra weeks feeding, growing stronger, gaining weight. Finally, as autumn's shortening days trigger their instincts, they lift off, beginning their unguided journey. Alone.

The iridescent plumage of a Ruby-throated Hummingbird blends with the golden-green of pin oak leaves, both of which will soon be gone.

Feeding on the Cheap

You can spend almost any amount you want to feed backyard birds. Feeders can cost up to several hundred dollars or more; fancy foods can be equally pricey. But penny-pincher that I am, I cut corners—without cutting the birds' nutrition. For instance, economical feeders, can be made from the following:

- Home-grown gourds, dried and carved
- Recycled liter cola bottles
- Screen-wire-bottomed platforms

You'll find things that might otherwise go to the landfill that will work just fine for distributing bird feed. To keep price under control for feed:

- Comparison shop
- Buy in bulk (split with friends or neighbors if necessary)
- Watch for sales, online specials, store-wide and senior-citizen discounts

Where I live, swarms of ravenous hummingbirds hit their usual seasonal peak the first two weeks of September. Over the next five weeks or so, populations will slowly dwindle.

When hummer numbers finally drop, like most folks, I switch gears and exchange nectar feeders for seed feeders, preparing for winter birds' arrival. At the moment, of course, in late September, ample native seeds offer ready buffets, and likely will for another month or so. Pokeberries dangle clusters of lush purple tidbits. Grass stems hang heavy with seed. Spent garden flowers hold promise of tasty treats.

With bird feeding being the big business it is, many places carry bird seed and bird-

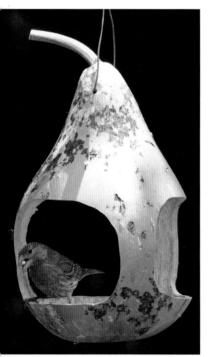

feeding supplies—places ranging from the biggest big box stores to the smallest specialty shops. Prices for everything vary as much as merchants selling them. When it comes to bird feed, be sure to compare apples with apples, so to speak. Read labels. Not all bird feed is created equal. Some has far more nutrition than others. Some has far more "grain products" than others, a term that rather loosely translates as "floor sweepings."

Read Those Labels

In the eastern United States, avoid mixes with milo, sometimes called sorghum (*Sorghum vulgare*), little round red seeds. Nothing here eats it. Skip wheat (*Triticum aestivum*), buckwheat (*Fagopyrum esculentum*), and oats (*Avena sativa*). Few birds like these seeds. Ditto canary seed (*Phalaris canariensis*), flax (*Linum berlandieri*), rapeseed (*Brassicanapus*), and rice (*Oryza sativa*)—all really

Many little birds, like this male House Finch, enjoy seed offerings in small private feeders like this little gourd, grown in the garden, dried, carved out, and hung for feeding on the cheap.

low on the preference scale for most birds. Instead, look for black-oil sunflower seed or kernels (*Helianthus annuus*), safflower (*Carthamus tinctor*), niger (*Guizotyia absyssinica*), and peanuts (*Arachis hypogaea*). In short, some seed is a better buy than others—at any price.

Autumn Migration on the Wing

In April, during spring migration, we talked about why birds fly thousands of miles to nest. Now, they fly more thousands to return to their winter quarters, an instinct-driven behavior—both direction and destination—hard-wired in their brains. Scientists squabble about reasons for migration, and perhaps birds make the epic journey for multiple valid reasons.

Today, we witness the ongoing evolution of migratory routes, some expanding, some shrinking, some edging east or west.

Regardless of the route, migration holds tough challenges. As relaxing and lovely as winter in the tropics sounds, believe it or not, life there for wintering birds is anything but relaxing and lovely. In fact, they come closer to facing starvation in the tropics than they do here on their breeding grounds. Here's why: When warblers and other migrants reach their tropical destinations, their numbers may double the local bird population. Double the bird population means double the food competition. And, depending on their final destination, wintering birds may arrive in September, the general onset of the tropical dry season, when insect populations there tend to be at their lowest.

Generally, wintering migrants bunk down in tropical habitat similar to their breeding habitat. Some birds even maintain a winter territory, protecting it much the way they protected their breeding territory. Other birds, however, hang out in loose flocks, joining their fellow species from across the United States, even flocking with resident tropical birds, foraging together but on different foods.

At one time researchers assumed that birds migrate in order to maintain their bug-lover diet. Some birds, however, dramatically change diets. Bug eaters here may eat tropical fruits there. For instance, our summering, bug-eating Cape May Warblers spend tropical winter days sipping nectar from flowers while White-eyed Vireos feast on gumbo limbo berries.

BOTANY FOR BIRDS
Berry-to-Bird-to-Berry Cycle

As avian migrants wing through this month and next, it's no coincidence that many berries ripen now. In an interesting twist of botany, foliage for those same berry-producing plants also now turns purple and crimson. Mother Nature has a reason: Bright leaves attract birds to bright—but tiny—berries. Birds eat nutrient-rich berries. Berries pass through birds. New shrubs show up a few miles away. Awesome plan!

WHY DO BIRDS DO THAT?
Why Hop When You Can Walk?

Whether birds walk or hop isn't a matter of personality. It's practicality—depending on where they live, and in direct connection, what they eat. Those that spend most of their time in trees, like cardinals, hop from branch to twig, limb to leaf. It's a habit hard to break, so even if they're on the ground, they hop. On the other hand, birds that live almost exclusively on the ground, like Ovenbirds, walk. After all, it takes more energy to hop, so why hop when you can walk? A few birds, like crows and robins, both hop and walk; other birds, like hummingbirds and Chimney Swifts can't do either; they can move only by flying.

Ovenbirds, critters that feed almost entirely on the ground, tend to walk, rather than hop.

If not for a continuous diet of bugs, why risk the horrendously arduous trip? Apparently, the rewards of migration merit the risks—of starvation, predation, heat exhaustion, and human-induced hurdles—and the premier reward is propagation of the species. Migratory songbirds produce nearly twice as many offspring as do birds that remain to breed in the tropics. And for good reason. There, no spring season bursts forth with everything popping blossoms at once—trees, bushes, vines, wildflowers. Thus, the "bloom" of bugs that accompanies the burst of blossoms also never happens in the tropics. Instead, seasonal change there means moving from dry to wet. So our spring profusion offers a veritable endless bug-lovers' buffet. What parents could want more for their babies—and themselves?

FEEDER FOCUS   ## Suet—Pure vs. Additives

Planning for winter feeding means planning for suet blocks. But have you noticed? Surely, at least a dozen varieties of rendered beef fat stock merchants' shelves. Some suet cakes include berries; some, nuts; some, cracked corn; some, sunflower seed; some, mostly white millet; some, a variety of seeds. Some come plain: "pure suet," they're labeled. So which to choose?

Most birds that eat wintertime suet are birds that ate bugs all summer. When bugs leave, suet serves them as a satisfactory substitute. Suet cakes that include seed, however, lure birds that want only the seed. Since seed also makes the block less stable, more easily broken and crumbled, seed-eating birds tend to shred the block, scattering rodent-attractive morsels on the ground.

Frankly, I'd rather skip the rats and feed the birds. That's why I personally prefer pure suet as opposed to suet blocks with additives.

Northern climes offer another critical reward: prolonged daylight hours, as much as eighteen hours at summer solstice. That added daylight, a 50 percent increase over the year-round twelve-hour days in the equatorial tropics, gives breeding birds more time to feed their offspring. Combine the bug bloom with daylight boom—more food and more time to feed—and babies grow robust.

In reality, then, migratory songbirds aren't "our" birds that leave for the winter; rather they're tropical birds that come for the summer, making the journey only to breed, relishing our long days of blooms and bugs.

PROBLEM SOLVER

Connecting with Fellow Birders

Most backyard bird hosts sooner or later like to connect with fellow hosts, comparing notes about what works and what doesn't, who's visiting and who's not, which plants thrive and which don't.

So how do birders connect? Check with the local Chamber of Commerce for bird clubs or nature groups. Visit nature centers and ask staff about bird hikes or field trips. Check online for area Audubon clubs. Ask among biology or ornithology department members at a local university. Inquire at bird-feeding specialty stores about groups or informal meetings and classes. Find out if an area community college offers birding classes. Ask at your local library about classes, clubs, or regular meetings for birders.

And if you hit a blank wall? Organize a group yourself and ask your local news media to get out the word. Remind them that bird watching is the second most popular spectator sport in the country. You'll enjoy meeting some really fun folks!

Commercial suet blocks impregnated with multiple seeds and fruits tend to crumble, chunks littering the ground below and leading to the possibility of attracting rodents and other animals to the site.

Conservation Corner: Important Birding Areas (IBAs) in Your Area

In a program begun in 1995 and spearheaded in the United States by the American Bird Conservancy (ABC) and the National Audubon Society (NAS), the Important Birding Area (IBA) designation is designed to "direct protection and management efforts towards these sites [that are deemed] crucial if viable populations of many species are to survive in the long-term."

The program began in Europe in the 1980s and has proven successful. At last count, more than 3,500 sites worldwide have been named IBAs, including 500 in the United States.

ABC explains the designation this way: "Using objective scientific information and relying on the recommendations of experts throughout the U.S., ABC has developed a list and set of descriptions of 500 of these internationally significant sites. For a site to be included, it must, during at least some part of the year, contain critical habitat that supports (1) a significant population of an endangered or threatened species, (2) a significant population of a U.S. WatchList species, (3) a significant population of a species with a limited range, or (4) a significantly large concentration of breeding, migrating or wintering birds, including waterfowl, seabirds, wading birds, raptors, or landbirds."

Check for IBAs in your area. As you expand your interests beyond your own backyard, these may be some of the first places you'll want to visit. And while you're there, study the habitat. What elements can you replicate in your own backyard?

Things to Do in September

- Check local nurseries for fall sales specials on perennials, shrubs, and trees—especially natives—that will enhance your backyard habitat.
- Avoid deadheading flowers, leaving seed heads for the birds.
- Step outside on quiet nights and listen for migrating birds high overhead.
- In early morning, check treetops, thickets, and water features for migrants that stop for the day to feed but don't visit feeders.
- If you don't find migrants in your yard this month, consider how you might alter your habitat in order to provide a better stopover site.
- If you're a beginning backyard host, September marks the perfect month to begin your efforts, introducing birds to your upcoming winter buffet.

63 Yard Birds in September

Temperatures moderated from August but now we have drought conditions; then record heat at month's end; everything crackling dry.

Canada Goose
Turkey Vulture
Cooper's Hawk
Red-shouldered Hawk
Killdeer
Mourning Dove
Barred Owl
Common Nighthawk
Chimney Swift
Ruby-throated
   Hummingbird
Belted Kingfisher
Red-bellied Woodpecker
Yellow-bellied Sapsucker
Downy Woodpecker
Hairy Woodpecker
Northern Flicker
Pileated Woodpecker
Eastern Wood-pewee
Acadian Flycatcher
Least Flycatcher
Eastern Phoebe

Great Crested Flycatcher
Eastern Kingbird
White-eyed Vireo
Yellow-throated Vireo
Red-eyed Vireo
Blue Jay
American Crow
Carolina Chickadee
Tufted Titmouse
White-breasted Nuthatch
Carolina Wren
House Wren
Ruby-crowned Kinglet
Blue-gray Gnatcatcher
Eastern Bluebird
Swainson's Thrush
American Robin
Gray Catbird
Northern Mockingbird
European Starling
Tennessee Warbler

Nashville Warbler
Chestnut-sided Warbler
Magnolia Warbler
Yellow-rumped Warbler
Black-throated Green
   Warbler
Black-and-white Warbler
American Redstart
Ovenbird
Common Yellowthroat
Eastern Towhee
Chipping Sparrow
Summer Tanager
Northern Cardinal
Rose-breasted Grosbeak
Blue Grosbeak
Brown-headed Cowbird
House Finch
Pine Siskin
American Goldfinch
House Sparrow

SPECIES PROFILE

BLUE JAY

VITAL STATS
Length: 9.8–11.8 in.
Wingspan: 13.4–16.9 in.
Weight: 2.5–3.5 oz.

Blue Jay

Blue Jays are Jekyll-and-Hyde birds with an attitude. Maybe even a temper, one always just below boiling, ready to blow. No one misses their backyard arrival, and that's surely intentional on the jay's part. Brilliant blue-and-white plumage and boisterous, bouncing behavior announce the haughty, even impudent 10-inch-long birds.

But just in case the minions of the backyard court ignore the 3-ounce king's lawless arrival, the jay's screaming Red-shoulder-Hawk imitation clears the yard of all other birds. What a clever way to garner feeders for oneself. Then, relaxing in its competition-free domain, the jay lowers its crest, its most visible sign of aggression now signaling a bird at ease.

But in breeding season, the other side of Jekyll-and-Hyde kicks in. Jays turn quiet, secretive, stealthy, perhaps nesting right in your yard but never revealing the site, entering from different directions and then slipping through foliage to a nest so well concealed you may never know it's there.

NEST NOTES
Nest Site: in a variety of tree species, 10–25 ft. high, in crotch of heavy branches
Nest Construction: outer portion, 7–8 in. diameter and 4 in. deep, made of twigs from live trees; inside cup of grass lined with rootlets, sometimes gathered from some distance; when near humans, may include "trash"
Eggs: 2–7 eggs, 1 brood, incubated 17–18 days
Fledge: 17–21 days after hatch

Although some writers describe the jay as an oddly shaped creature, one seemingly made up of leftover parts, I don't see it that way at all. In fact, this king of the backyard strikes me as markedly beautiful, a reminder of bright clear sky dashed with white clouds.

But jays bear the burden of a reputation for stealing other birds' eggs and babies in order to feed their own offspring, providing a high-protein diet only such thievery permits. In spite of the reputation, however, a study of the contents of 292 Blue Jay stomachs over the course of twelve months revealed only three with evidence of eggshells. So I have to wonder, especially about a bird whose fondness for acorns is credited with the spread of oak forests after the last ice age.

FOOD FARE

Blue Jay diet relies heavily on many kinds of nuts and seeds, some of which are cached for later dining. About 20 to 25 percent of its diet includes a variety of insects. Contrary to popular belief, jays almost never eat other birds' babies or eggs, but they do raid nests to feed their own nestlings. Because jays consume more than twice as much calcium as do other birds, offering eggshells will supplement their winter diets and prevent them from chipping calcium-rich paint from your house.

NAME THAT BIRD

Cyanocitta cristata (Blue Jay): The full name translates as "a dark blue chattering bird with a crest (*cristata*)." Its common name refers to its color and the French word for this bird, possibly a word coined to describe the bird's call.

BIRD TALK: WHO'S CALLING?

Its namesake call of a loud, raucous *jay, jay, jay* is only one of many of its calls. Blue Jays also imitate hawk calls and do multiple gurgling and whistling calls.

Among our most intelligent birds, Blue Jays have adapted to join humans even as we destroyed their original woodland homes. Their complex social life, tight family ties, and monogamous lifetime mating surely add merit to their otherwise lawless reputation.

Blue Jays' year-round presence in area backyards can be misleading, for they do migrate—just not out of North America, and mostly not out of the eastern half of the United States. Having said that, however, I must clarify that not all Blue Jays migrate; therein lies one of the pieces to the puzzle of why some jays wear a different shade of blue. No, they're not old and faded. Rather, three geographic subspecies roam the United States. The irregular migratory habits, added to the crossbreeding of some subspecies, account for color differences, especially in late winter. A northerner may have joined the local Blue Jay flock that chose to stay the winter.

As strong, healthy-looking birds, Blue Jays display apparent independence. When they cross open areas, they fly singly, perhaps for safety. But even in migration, flying quietly in long strings, they usually move in small groups, no more than five to fifteen together, seemingly independent even in migratory masses.

In spite of the jay's Jekyll-and-Hyde personality—or maybe because of it—I'm thrilled to have Blue Jays back in my yard. West Nile Virus hit the entire Corvid bird family hard, for they have no resistance to the disease. But their populations seem to have stabilized, and I celebrate the little family that stayed with us last winter.

Smart, sassy, boisterous, and lawless, or quiet, stealthy, and faithful to family—both Blue Jay personalities garner my affection.

SPOTTING THE SPECTACULAR   Caching in for Food

Blue Jays cache food for their wintertime enjoyment—and survival. During autumn's harvest, each bird may stash three thousand to five thousand acorns. Thus, if you offer peanuts in the shell, a small family of jays can ferry them off in a matter of minutes—not because they pig out but because they carry off. Among our smartest birds, jays also remember where they've stashed all those thousands of morsels. Ah, to have such a memory!

At your feeders, jays readily display a pecking order. Watch to see the head honcho get the prime feeding spots while the underlings take what's left. Those little flocks that feed together, however, tend to be extended families. So, as members of close-knit families, the underlings get the protection of the higher-ups. Eventually, of course, the underlings will replace the departed head honchos, but the family structure stays.

ID CHECK

Blue Jays are unmistakable yard birds. Identify either male or female by the following markings:

- Bright sky-blue head, back, wings, and tail
- Distinct bright-blue crest (lowered when feeding or with family)
- Gray-white breast and belly
- Black border on face, through eyes and above bill (distinctive enough to mark individual birds)
- Bright white and bold black pattern on wings and tail
- Black bill

SPECIES PROFILE

CEDAR WAXWING

VITAL STATS
Length: 5.5–6.7 in.
Wingspan: 8.7–11.8 in.
Weight: 1.1 oz.

Cedar Waxwing

Funny name for a bird, Cedar Waxwing. But a little red spot on the tip of the adults' wing feathers looks very much like a dab of old-fashioned sealing wax. The "cedar" part comes from the bird's affinity for cedar cone-berries. Still, they could just as well be called cherry waxwings. They'll strip a cherry tree of its entire fruit crop in a matter of a day or so. Or holly waxwings—for the same reason.

Actually, cedar waxwings don't show up just when cherries ripen; they're year-round residents here in southern Indiana. But they're more obvious when they arrive in flocks to enjoy fruit-bearing trees, like hawthorn, red mulberry, wild black cherry, American holly—whichever sweet berry or fruit is in season.

These handsome little birds sometimes display a charming and seemingly courteous behavior. I'm sure "courtesy" has nothing to do with avian behavior, but I sometimes add my own anthropomorphic slant to observations. And this Cedar Waxwing behavior tugs at me to think of courtesy, kindness, and sharing. Here's the story.

Cedar Waxwings hang out in flocks—from a half dozen to hundreds—so it's not uncommon for multiple birds to perch in a row along a single branch. It's likely a matter of convenience rather than any intent to be cozy. But when the time is right (and we mere humans don't have a clue about what triggers this behavior), one of the clan plucks a fruit and passes it along the branch to the next waxwing, rubbing bills in the process. That waxwing in turn passes the fruit along to its neighbor. Sometimes the tidbit reaches the end of the row only to have the last bird start it back. Somewhere along the way, somebody chooses to eat the fruit—perhaps when it's so mashed up from passing beak to beak that little remains to pass on. Rather sweet, don't you think?

In fact, their love of fruit not only defines these birds, it also defines their whereabouts. They're nomads, wandering wherever fruiting trees draw them. Hundreds of waxwings may dine on fruit in your yard today, but when the tree goes bare of berries tomorrow, it also goes bare of waxwings.

Waxwings prefer berries year round and even feed their babies fruit. Well, okay, yes, they do eat insects, and they do also feed their babies insects. But since they depend so heavily on fruit and berry production, waxwings tend to start nesting later than other songbirds and, thus, tend to continue nesting later into the season. Because of the waxwing's preference for feeding their babies berries, cowbird babies in parasitized Cedar Waxwing nests rarely survive. They can't develop properly on the berry diet. I say, "Hurray for waxwings!"

NAME THAT BIRD

Bombycilla cedrorum (Cedar Waxwing): *Bombycilla* translates roughly as "silk-tail" and *cedrorum* refers to cedar or juniper tree. Its common name comes from the bird's preference for eating cedar "berries" (actually tiny cones) and from the red waxy droplet-looking spots on the secondary feathers of each wing.

FOOD FARE

Mostly fruit eaters, Cedar Waxwings supplement their diet during breeding season with insects and feed their babies both fruit and insects. Favorite fruits in summer include serviceberry, dogwood berries, mulberries, and raspberries. In winter, they love mistletoe, hawthorn, honeysuckle, and as their name suggests, juniper cones. They do not come to feeders.

SPOTTING THE SPECTACULAR You Are What You Eat

Beginning about 1960, observers, particularly those in the Northeast, started noticing Cedar Waxwings with orange-tipped rather than yellow-tipped tails. Since then, orange coloration sightings have noticeably increased. Why would a bird's color change?

Scientists have traced the novel coloration to the bird's diet. Cedar Waxwings' tail tips turn orange if they eat the non-native Morrow's honeysuckle when they are simultaneously growing new feathers. The phenomenon came about when, in the late 1950s, folks intent on providing good wildlife food and cover planted Morrow's honeysuckle. The plant fruits about the same time as Cedar Waxwings molt and form new feathers, and the birds relish the fruits. Carotenoids in the fruits cause the orange pigmentation in the tips of waxwings' tails.

BIRD TALK: WHO'S CALLING?
Most often heard in flight, Cedar Waxwings have a very high-pitched *zeeee* call.

NEST NOTES
Nest Site: on fork of horizontal limb, in many tree species, anywhere from 3–50 ft. high
Nest Construction: twigs, cattail down, string, and similar material woven into bulky nest with tree catkins around outside, as if for decoration; about 5 in. by 3 in., lined with fine rootlets, grasses, and pine needles; some materials stolen from other birds' nests
Eggs: 2–6 eggs, 1–2 broods, incubated 11–13 days
Fledge: 14–18 days after hatch

Sometimes the birds' berry addiction turns problematic. In late winter, when fruits of any kind fall in short supply, any morsels still clinging to twigs are sure to lure these birds. Of course, late-winter fruits are overripe to rotten. Think fermented. When the hungry flocks descend, gobbling up scarce fruits with relish, the fermentation kicks in. Birds get drunk. While the birds' ensuing behavior may give bird-watchers a few chuckles, the birds' condition can result in serious injury or death. Falling-down drunk, they are at the mercy of cats, cars, window crashes, and other dangers. Because they tend to play "follow the leader," a window strike can kill an entire flock. As well, they can die as a result of the alcohol toxicity. John James Audubon reported catching drunken waxwings by hand.

To my eye, Cedar Waxwings have plumage so silky perfect that the birds look artificial, perhaps like a matte-painted ceramic piece. Their crest, which they sometimes lay down so that it droops down their shoulders, otherwise gives them a sporty look.

Generally, though, their flocking behavior defines waxwings during nonbreeding season. When they're roaming in sizeable groups, they take turns sharing the buffet or the bath. One group feeds, drinks, or baths until satisfied, leaves, and another group takes it place. No squabbling here!

ID CHECK
Because Cedar Waxwings tend to hang out as high up as they can and still feed, you can first identify them by their high-pitched calls. Then look for a bird that shows the following field marks:
- Silky brown back and upper chest
- Silky soft gray on wings
- Silky lemon-yellow and white underneath
- Narrow black face mask outlined in white
- Crest (which can be flattened)
- Gray tail with bright yellow tip (or, occasionally, orange)
- Red waxy tips on ends of wings' secondary feathers, although not always visible

The male tends to have a more extensive black chin than the female, but such plumages are highly variable.

SPECIES PROFILE

TREE SWALLOW

VITAL STATS
Length: 4.7–5.9 in.
Wingspan: 11.8–13.8 in.
Weight: 0.6–0.9 oz.

Tree Swallow pair at nest; the adult sexes often nearly indistinguishable

No doubt about it, they're control freaks. They control insects. Tree Swallows eat on the wing, snapping bugs and aerial plankton from the skies, eating bugs, bugs, and more bugs. Many people forget that birds are the number one means of insect control, and Tree Swallows live up to the claim.

Unlike other swallows, and unlike most other bird species, Tree Swallows can dine on wax myrtle berries. Because the birds have the unusual ability to digest the berries' waxy coating, they can adapt their wintertime diets to these berries, enjoy them as a primary food source when bugs grow scarce, and thus save the exertion of an extended migration. As a result, Tree Swallows winter farther north than any other swallows—a real boon when it comes to competition over natural resources.

FOOD FARE
Swallows eat primarily flying insects on the wing but will occasionally take berries. They do not visit traditional feeders.

NAME THAT BIRD
Tachycineta bicolor (Tree Swallow): *Tachycineta* means "swift mover," referring to the bird's fast flight. *Bicolor* refers to its strongly contrasting dark-light color combination. Its common name acknowledges the bird's penchant for nesting in tree cavities, while "swallow" comes from the Anglo-Saxon word for this kind of bird.

Their berry appetites also guarantee them an alternative food source when cold and/or wet weather minimizes bugs during breeding season—a scenario that brings about the demise of other swallows, including Purple Martins, and their babies.

Male Tree Swallows flaunt a rather formal appearance, their iridescent blue-green heads, backs, wings, and tails in stark contrast to their snow-white chins, breasts, and bellies. Young

Young female Tree Swallows show more brown than blue, but older females are nearly indistinguishable from males.

females are more brown than blue, but older females are nearly indistinguishable from males. The pair would surely win a best-dressed award at the prom.

During migration, Tree Swallows may linger along the southern U.S. coast or wing their way into Mexico, but they rarely travel beyond Central America. So, given their minimal migration, it's no surprise that Tree Swallows return fairly early each spring.

As soon as they arrive, however, the battle is on. Even though the swallows are early arrivals, prime nest box sites have already been commandeered by bluebirds and chickadees. After all, year-round residents get first dibs on real estate, and most bluebirds and chickadees are well into incubation, perhaps even feeding nestlings, by the time Tree Swallows wing in. So Tree Swallows, longing for the same accommodations, often face slim pickings.

NEST NOTES
Nest Site: cavity, either natural, as in standing dead tree, or man-made nest box, near or
    over water
Nest Construction: open cup of grasses, well-lined with overarching feathers, often those
    of waterfowl
Eggs: 2–8 eggs, 1–2 broods, incubated 13–14 days
Fledge: 18–22 days from hatch

Tree Swallows construct their nests with grasses and feathers—lots of feathers—that help keep babies warm. I've tossed fluffy white craft-store feathers out for them to ease their fervent search, and they grab up every one, most before they hit the ground!

Away from man-made nest boxes, however, Tree Swallows depend on old woodpecker cavities or natural cavities in decaying trees. But we humans, most of us unknowingly so, have put a serious limit on those natural cavities. Let a tree die, and posthaste, considering it unsightly, we chop it down. We whack off any dead tree limbs that might offer a swallow-sized cavity. And we've mostly done away with wooden fence posts. Granted, dead or decaying trees that create a safety hazard need attention, but trees away from homes and other structures can do what Mother Nature intended—provide a nursery and grocery store for wildlife.

Thus, as a result of human love for tidiness, the seriously limited number of cavities available puts life on a competitive edge for Tree Swallows. When they can't find a suitable nesting cavity, they can't breed. Nest boxes in your yard will likely attract their attention.

BIRD TALK: WHO'S CALLING?
Tree Swallows have ten different defined sounds, including bill snapping, but their common "song" is a series of chirps, whines, twitters, and gurgles.

SPOTTING THE SPECTACULAR

Flocks of Thousands

Every year, the Tree Swallows' habit of migrating in multitudes attracts attention, with flocks of thousands lining utility wires. As the fall migration escalates, however, flocks of thousands—growing to flocks of hundreds of thousands—swirl and undulate about an hour before sunset, forming a dense tornado-like cloud at roost sites, then, at each pass, dropping by the hundreds into marsh grasses or scrubby trees until the flock has all tucked in for the night.

Every fall, video posts to YouTube document the astonishing flocks. Of course, the farther south the activity, the larger the flocks, as they join masses and move in ever larger assemblages. Depending on where you live, you can expect to see the varying sizes of congregations.

ID CHECK

While young females wear more brown than blue, older females and male Tree Swallows can be distinguished by the following characteristics:
- Overall greenish-blue head, back, wings, and tail
- Clear white chin, breast, and belly
- Small bill
- Black eyes
- Short legs
- Wings and tail of about the same length

SPECIES PROFILE

EUROPEAN STARLING
and HOUSE SPARROW

VITAL STATS
European Starling
Length: 7.9–9.1 in.
Wingspan: 12.2–15.7 in.
Weight: 2.1–3.4 oz.

Above: *European Starling, summer plumage;* below: *European Starling, winter plumage*

Pairing European Starling and House Sparrow into a single profile may seem strange, but these two birds have more in common than being overly abundant and generally rude at backyard feeders: neither bird belongs here.

Above: *House Sparrow, male;* below: *House Sparrow, female*

VITAL STATS
House Sparrow
Length: 5.9–6.7 in.
Wingspan: 7.5–9.8 in.
Weight: 1.0 oz.

NAME THAT BIRD

Sturnus vulgaris (European Starling): The scientific name means "commonly found (*vulgaris*) starling." Its common name refers to the bird's native range combined with the Old English word for this bird.

Passer domesticus (House Sparrow): *Passer* is Latin for "small bird," and *domesticus,* like our word "domestic," means "belonging to the house," referring to the bird's preference for nesting near human housing. Its common name refers to the same preference while "sparrow" means "a flutterer."

Introduced by Shakespearean aficionados who wanted each of the birds mentioned in the Bard's plays to be with them in the New World, starlings (in the mid-1890s) and House Sparrows (in 1851) were released in New York's Central Park. In short time, they invaded the entire North American continent. Indeed, House Sparrows are now the most widely distributed bird in the world, inhabiting every continent except Antarctica. Similarly but in a less world-wide fashion, European Starlings have crossed the North American continent, recently reaching Alaska's western shores.

So what? Both birds nest in cavities. Thus, they rob our native cavity nesters—more than eighty-five species—of nest sites. No nest site, no babies. No babies, populations plummet. So these two non-native, aggressive, and territorially defensive birds have dramatically affected this nation's avian world. In fact, one scientific study recorded House Sparrows alone attacking seventy different bird species.

In my own yard, I've witnessed a House Sparrow piercing Eastern Bluebird eggs and tossing them out of a nest cavity it wanted as its own. I've discovered dead female bluebirds, eyes poked out, babies dead under their bellies, killed by a competitive House Sparrow pair that then built their own nest right on top of the carcasses.

BIRD TALK: WHO'S CALLING?

European Starlings sing a variety of songs, many of them warbles, whistles, and rattles, including many mimics of other birds; both sexes have about twenty different calls. Females also sing, especially in fall.

Male and female House Sparrows give an unmusical *cheep* call.

I've seen starlings fight off Red-bellied Woodpeckers to take over the cavity that the woodpeckers have spent weeks hammering out, one woodchip at a time. I've seen starlings fight off Great Crested Flycatchers to lay claim to a natural cavity. Red-headed Woodpeckers, Downy Woodpeckers, Hairy Woodpeckers—all suffer from the onslaught of these invaders. Even Wood Ducks have lost nest-cavity battles to starlings.

These are not scenarios that any of us like to see or even want to think about, especially when we know the blame falls squarely on our shoulders. We humans brought these birds to our nation's shores and turned them loose. On purpose. How tragic.

NEST NOTES
European Starling

Nest Site: in a cavity, either natural or man-made, including nooks in buildings, streetlights, and traffic signal posts, usually 10–25 ft. high

Nest Construction: cavity filled with grass, pine needles, trash; cup near back lined with soft fibers, feathers, and leaves; fresh green plant material added during nestling stage

Eggs: 3–6 eggs, 1–2 broods, incubated 12 days

Fledge: 21–23 days after hatch

House Sparrow

Nest Site: cavities, either natural or man-made, including nest boxes, where they will drive out and even kill bluebirds and tree swallows; also in building nooks, street lights, vines, gutters, downspouts

Nest Construction: messy nests of stiff grasses, trash, and feathers; sometimes sharing wall with adjoining nest; will reuse nests

Eggs: 1–8 eggs, 1–4 broods, incubated 10–14 days, one of the shortest incubation periods of any bird; single female can lay 25 viable eggs per season

Fledge: 10–14 days after hatch

But of course, it's not the House Sparrow's fault, nor the European Starling's fault. Because of their non-native status, however, these two birds, along with non-native Rock Pigeons, are the only three wild birds not federally protected. In fact, according to the National Audubon Society, nests, eggs, young, and adults of all three species can be legally destroyed in most places. Furthermore, the National Wildlife Federation, in their guidelines for certifying wildlife backyard habitat, insists that a certified wildlife backyard host must control exotics— not just plants but also exotic birds, including House Sparrows and European Starlings. In other words, a responsible backyard host does not allow these non-native species to breed in their yards, a commitment accomplished by regularly and persistently monitoring nest boxes in your habitat.

FOOD FARE

European Starlings eat almost anything, but they prefer insects when available. At feeders, they wolf down grain and small birdseed.

House Sparrows eat grain and seed, including weed seed, and discarded food, garbage. At feeders, they thrive on any seed small enough to eat whole, including milo, millet, wheat, sunflower hearts, and cracked corn.

In order to monitor nest boxes and be sure who's taking up residence there, study the nest, the eggs, and then verify who's coming and going from the box.

First, learn to recognize nests. Both birds build a trashy nest—literally. It includes trash like feathers, cigarette butts, plastic or cellophane wrappers, shredded bits of paper, string, and other refuse, as well as a messy array of grasses, leaves, and twigs. Starlings add greenery to their nests during the incubation period.

Then, if you've missed the nest-building cycle, check the eggs. Recognize House Sparrow eggs as white with brown speckles; starling eggs, larger than those of most cavity nesters, range from white to pale blue, minus speckles.

Finally, verify your suspicions by tracking adults into the nests, and then, once verified, remove House Sparrow and starling nests.

By monitoring nest boxes, you guarantee rightful—native—owners residency, and the dollars you spent on nest boxes will earn the highest interest at the best rates.

SPOTTING THE SPECTACULAR

Fancy Pants

Both House Sparrows and European Starlings wear certain fancy duds, but for quite different reasons.

Male House Sparrows wear black bibs, but not all bibs look alike. Some seem a bit bedraggled; some lack distinct coloration; some show indistinct borders. The bib's color variation marks the male's status. The larger, brighter, and more distinct the black throat patch—or bib—the older and more sexy the House Sparrow. The big-bibbed guys get the best girls—the girls' choice, not his—and they also reign supreme in the pecking order, including best feeding sites, best roost sites, and best winter shelters.

Starlings, on the other hand, undergo a whole-body transformation from winter to summer plumage that earns them the nickname "rice bird." After their fall molt, starlings wear white-specked plumage. As the winter wears on, the white spots wear off and the bird takes on an amazingly pretty iridescence. And their bills turn from black to bright yellow.

ID CHECK

House Sparrows blend in with the crowd of LBJs (little brown jobs) in the yard and at the feeders, and the female takes on total anonymity. Although males are usually brightly colored, in urban settings, House Sparrows can look scruffy, dull, and dirty. To make a certain identification, look for males that show the following markings:
- Brown back streaked with rufous, black, and white
- Gray top of head
- Bright white cheek patches
- Rufous above and behind eyes
- Whitish breast and belly
- Black bib, less distinct on young birds
- Black bill on mature birds; yellow at base on immature birds

Female House Sparrows show the following markings:
- Overall buffy brown
- Streaked backs and wings
- Buffy brown face with indistinct eye stripe
- Grayish brown breast and belly
- Yellow bill

European Starlings, males and females indistinguishable, are recognizable from other generally black-colored birds by these characteristics
- Overall chunky look
- Short tails
- Long, slender bills, black in winter, bright yellow in summer
- Brown early winter plumage covered with bright white spots
- Iridescent purple-green breeding plumage, black at a distance

October

*I realized that if I had to choose,
I would rather have birds than airplanes.*

CHARLES LINDBERGH

October marks harvest's end. Only stubble stands in area agricultural fields, corn shelled, beans cut. In the yard, though, harvest continues, as reapers labor dawn to dusk. Some cache crops; some eat all they gather. Some harvesters are immigrants—very much legal—the rest are locals. And crop preferences vary.

Some gravitate to our mini orchard, clinging to apples, dangling, now mostly rotten, hole-bored or shredded, pecked apart and gobbled down by Red-bellied and Downy Woodpeckers, the remainder moldering on the ground. Northern Cardinals work the orchard as well, alongside migrants hunting bugs.

Crabapples hang overripe in late October on leaf-bare trees. So it's easy to watch goldfinches, vegetarians that they are, gleefully harvesting fruit, clinging upside down, bobbing on slender twig tips. House Finches, occasional Downy Woodpeckers, and mockingbirds pick, too. As mockers stake out winter food territories, they surely measure crabapple potential—and then, instinctively smart, seek other, more lasting buffets.

Memorable Moments: Harvesters in the Dogwoods

But among the many harvesters, darlings of the dogwoods have been this fall's top reward. Dogwoods in our yard are—well, at least they were—limb-drooping berry laden. Locals zoomed in: goldfinches, Blue Jays, starlings. Beginning a few weeks ago, though, when summer visitors finished nesting duties and began packing on fat for the long journey south, dogwood berries started disappearing fast.

Among the first, a Summer Tanager made the tree home every morning and evening for more than a week. Soon, a Scarlet Tanager joined the banquet. Seeing both tanagers in one tree at one time surely rewards any backyard birder. Rose-breasted Grosbeaks also foraged through the tree, sometimes eight or ten at a time, grabbing berries in contortionists' moves of long reaches and sharp snatches, sometimes upside down.

American Goldfinches feast on dogwood berries, blending well, in winter plumage, with the tree's autumn foliage.

A female Summer Tanager blends so well with a dogwood's autumn foliage that she's difficult to see.

BOTANY FOR BIRDS   ## Plant Dogwood Trees

With sixteen bird species gorging in our trees this fall, it's a no-brainer that flowering dogwood wins autumn's first-place ribbon in the Luscious Berry category among hungry, harvesting birds. And fall's bounty doesn't take into account the dogwood's spring profusion of blooms and the bugs—and birds—they draw. Choose native white flowering dogwood (*Cornus florida*), and plant it where the tree gets partial shade. Typically, flowering dogwoods are not feature trees and don't like standing alone in the middle of an otherwise sun-drenched yard. In the wild, they are "edge" trees, growing along forest boundaries. Avoid planting them under maple trees, however, as they'll struggle to compete with the maple's thirsty, vigorous root system.

Or choose gray dogwood (*Cornus racemosa*), native in the upper two-thirds of the eastern United States, named for its whitish berries. More sun tolerant than flowering dogwood, its lipid-rich fruits serve migrants well.

A week later, three catbirds bounced through the shadows. Joining them, a Brown Thrasher, not a rarity but always a treat, ate its fill. A mockingbird, which abandons us every summer to nest elsewhere in the neighborhood, returned right on schedule this fall, scolding its way through the berries.

Then one day last week—just one day—the migrating thrushes took over the dogwood: Swainson's and Hermit Thrushes joined their local cousins, robins and bluebirds. It was the thrush family reunion, a delightful autumnal magical moment.

But this week, flickers arrived. Never anywhere have I seen more than three flickers at once, usually a pair, maybe feeding offspring. In the dogwood, however, they numbered seven and kept the tree in motion.

Bubbling Rock

If autumn in your yard is as dry as it typically is in mine, resident yard birds, arriving winter visitors, and migrants alike will visit water—even if they are not feeder friendly. A bubbling rock, a large stone with a hole bored through and set over a reservoir, creates a recirculating water flow that birds can't resist. Hummingbirds hover to drink from the edge,

Six American Robins, one partially hidden, enjoy a refreshing stop at a bubbling rock.

Besides flickers, four other woodpeckers joined the roster: downy, hairy, red-bellied, and—biggest surprise of all—a pileated, sagging the branch with its weight.

Memorable October moments, indeed!

Harvesters Harvesting

But crop harvests by other birds continue all through October. This year, our pin oaks produced ample mast crops. While squirrels stash acorns where they will, eight raucous Blue Jays surely win the acorn-harvesting prize. They've winged a path between the oaks and the badly ice-damaged Scotch pine behind the shed where they find myriad stashing places among the broken branches, secreting away a harvest against bad times. As pecans pop from hulls and fall, jays add them to their caches as well.

Even crabgrass gone to seed draws harvesters. Two dozen Chipping Sparrows worked the short grasses, popping up to snare 6-inch stems, pulling them down with their weight, methodically harvesting the seeds. Shortly, Song, White-throated, White-crowned, and Lin-

bluebirds jostle with goldfinches for position near the "bubble," robins arrive in families to sip and splash, and juncos bathe in leisure, freshening up after their travels. The hubbub sometimes gives me a chuckle as I watch the little guys vying for a drink or a bath, lining up in pecking order to await their turn, or pushing their faces into the bubble.

Closer Look at a Bubble Rock

Water pumped from reservoir up through stone spills over stone back into reservoir

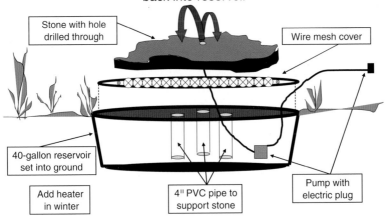

Stone with hole drilled through

Wire mesh cover

40-gallon reservoir set into ground

Add heater in winter

4" PVC pipe to support stone

Pump with electric plug

coln's Sparrows joined the picking crew. The Lincoln's won't stay, so I watch them more closely than the others, soaking up the pleasure of their visit.

The short grasses edge my weed patch. Granted, not every yard has the capacity—nor, for that matter, every backyard-feeder host has the desire—to permit a weed patch. But wait until you hear what happened in mine. Shoulder-high vegetation there attracts still more harvesters. In August, the tallest weeds, in the form of native wild prickly lettuce, began blooming, setting forth multitudes of flower heads with fifteen to twenty tiny dandelion-like white flowers that soon turned to seed. By September, seed heads began to mature.

Now, in early October, the weed-patch, ripe with seed, finds harvest in full swing.

Seed eaters like goldfinches scavenge the patch in flocks of twenty or more. A pair of Song Sparrows flicks among the lower leaves. A family of cardinals scolds its way through the patch. An occasional Chipping Sparrow ducks in and out among the bushy heads. A dozen House Finches bounce through the weed tops, gathering gourmet munchies. House Sparrows show up, too, but they don't please me.

Why Do Birds Eat Different Foods?

While goldfinches gobble seeds and warblers look for bugs, hawks seek meat from grasshoppers to rabbits. Hummingbirds drink nectar and snare bugs on the wing. Herons prefer fish. Vultures relish road kill. Gulls eat almost anything, including garbage. Why?

You already know that food preferences can be predicted by, and are associated with, bill size and shape. But here's the ultimate question: Which came first—the bill or the food? Did the bill shape evolve to allow the bird to eat the foods that evolved with it? The generally accepted theory is that available foods and competition for them determines who eats what—but only after tens of thousands of generations of adaptations.

Now, migrating warblers have arrived in the weed patch! For three days last week they feasted, not on seeds, but on bugs the seeds and late blossoms attracted. They darted from stalk to stem, porking up for the remainder of their journey south.

The first to catch my eye were Prairie Warblers—four of them! Darting among flower heads, they flashed bright yellow breasts. But then I spied two other olive-and-yellowish birds: Nashville and Tennessee Warblers—five altogether. A Yellow-rumped Warbler wandered through to see what all the fuss was about. A pair of not-so-common Common Yellowthroats popped through, letting me include them in the tally. All bug hunting; all surely happy. At least that was my anthropomorphic take on their busyness.

Then I spotted the little brown birds, the ones that always send me scurrying to my field guide to identify: female Indigo Buntings—eight of them, also soon heading south. Seed eaters extraordinaire, they, too, gorged on the bounty.

A Bird-magnet Plant

You can see in your yard only what the habitat attracts. So, what plant is this bird magnet in my weed patch? Native wildflower guides name it prickly lettuce (*Lactuca scariola*). How does it happen to be growing in my weed patch? I didn't plant it or sow the seed for it. But native plants, their seeds long dormant in the soil, await the chance to burst into bloom. Allow native grasses and wildflowers to grow in your yard, and you'll have a bird magnet. To birds, habitat is everything, and they love what they've grown up with for the past thousands of generations.

Unfortunately, however, the term "weed patch" carries an annoying connotation. After all, nobody wants a yard full of weeds. Or do you? Just what is a weed? Technically, a weed is "any native plant." By definition, then, that means purple coneflowers, daisies, violets, clover, butterfly weed, Joe-Pye weed, columbine—all great wildlife magnets, many perhaps already growing in your garden—they're all technically weeds.

So that wild lettuce—is it weed, wildflower, or wildlife habitat? As we know now, a great weed/wildflower patch is great habitat is a great bird magnet—at least for the sixty hungry diners that I tallied in mine. You know what—that's a bunch of birds. So the joy of a weed patch is all in the eye of the beholder, especially if yours is the eye of a savvy backyard bird-watcher.

In Praise of Goldenrod

Among the most bird-attracting plants elsewhere in my weed patch are the many spires of feathery goldenrod. Singing the praises of goldenrod may sound like sour notes to some. But the four-foot-tall plants topped with yellow-gold plumes put the pizzazz in this year's otherwise lackluster autumn colors dulled by drought.

HABITAT—YOURS AND THEIRS
In Praise of Native Plants

Almost any yard can boast goldenrod. Native plants host native bugs. And of course, to feed the birds, we must first feed the bugs. Bugs, beetles, and insects—more than twenty-five species—use goldenrod for food or shelter. Some come for the nectar or pollen; others come to munch on leaves or other insects; a few come to lay eggs. So goldenrod and birds make perfect partners.

But goldenrod or not, think native when you're adding or replacing plants. You'll add more than greenery; you'll add bird magnets to the yard. But there's more: Native tends to be carefree.

While over fifty species of goldenrod grow in North America, it's the one called showy goldenrod (*Solidago erecta*) that splashes its spectacular blooms across our yard, an aptly named standard of native autumn flowers. Goldenrod, however, gets an undeserved bad rap. Allergy sufferers blame it for their sniffles and sneezes, but they've misidentified the culprit. Ragweed, which blooms simultaneously with—and often alongside—many goldenrod species, correctly deserves the blame.

Watching for birds in goldenrod, however, calls for patience. Stand still, wait, and watch, letting birds grow accustomed to your presence, seeing you as an inanimate, or at least as a nonthreatening, lump in the landscape. Eventually, deep within the patch, a single stalk wiggles, a signal that something unheard and unseen is inching along, well below the top-most blossoms, down where bugs hide amid the remaining foliage.

An adjoining stalk bobs, almost imperceptibly, then shivers noticeably. Another stalk sways, even as the rest of the patch stands motionless. At some time, someplace in the patch, a warbler pops up, snags a bug, and dives back into cover. Another scoots out from the edge and darts across the path to other buggy sites.

Besides our resident Carolina Wrens, chickadees, and titmice, multiple migrants graze the yellow-blossomed oasis. Hummingbirds cruise through for nectar (as native plants provide the most nectar). Eastern Phoebes and Eastern Wood-pewees fly-catch from above. Cardinals, Song Sparrows, and goldfinches glean seeds while just-arrived wintering White-throated Sparrows and Dark-eyed Juncos take refuge in the tangle, foraging in leaf litter below.

HOW DOES YOUR GARDEN GROW?
Goldenrod Choices

Almost any yard can boast goldenrod. In addition to the natives that grow in my weed patch, I've added to my flower garden several other varieties I discovered at local native nurseries. Plant catalogs carry multiple species of goldenrod, and perhaps your local native-plant nursery carries locally appropriate choices. Select those native to your area to guarantee success. Native plants need virtually no attention once established, and a patch of goldenrod tends to slowly expand, welcoming even more birds.

Because it's native, goldenrod is a beacon to migrating birds and arriving winter residents like this Yellow-rumped Warbler.

Even the highly elusive Mourning Warbler and a seldom-seen Lincoln's Sparrow have flitted through, bugging the patch, both birds prized additions to our yard list—all because of native goldenrod.

Add to the virtues of native goldenrod the tendency of certain gall-forming insects like gall gnats or gall wasps to target the plant. In turn, chickadees and Downy Woodpeckers target the galls for quick, easy wintertime meaty treats.

So singing the praises of goldenrod, especially as it's sung by the birds, is hardly a solo event. In fact, given all the birds that enjoy goldenrods' bugs, nectar, and seeds, it's more like a full chorus, mixed voices singing music for the bird-lover's soul—and praises for these native plants.

Garden Seed Harvest

Let's move now beyond the native weed patch and on to the spent flower garden. There again, I watch a harvesters' parade. Goldfinches pluck seeds from past-prime Mexican sunflower (*Tithonia* spp.), shaking eight-foot stalks as they glean their way down the row. Cardinals show half-hearted interest among the zinnia stalks, but assorted sparrows forage actively for scattered seeds below. Butterfly bushes droop heavily with seed. Adding variety to their diets, goldfinches flit from zinnias to butterfly bushes and back. Song Sparrows, though, give the bushes their singular attention, as if in pickers' paradise.

HOW DOES YOUR GARDEN GROW?
To Deadhead—or Not?

Most gardeners deadhead plants like daisies, coneflowers, coreopsis, and bee balm, removing seed heads to keep flowers blooming, maintaining tidy appearances. But birds power up on those seeds, so to deadhead is to destroy the bird buffet. Depending on your level of tolerance, avoid deadheading altogether, or top only a portion of the seed crop. Then, near season's end, leave the garden alone, allowing seeds and tangle to remain until early spring. You'll provide both a food source and an added layer of sheltering habitat for wintering birds.

Native beautyberry bushes, laden with clusters of lavender berries, draw a nice range of immigrant harvesters, including Tennessee Warblers and, earlier, Rose-breasted Grosbeaks, as well as robins, cardinals, and mockingbirds.

Pokeberries, even shriveled from dry weather, still draw an array of harvesters, and purple droppings around water features attest to the berries' popularity.

While banks of sumac turn October highway rights-of-way scarlet, I know not to look for harvesters there. Sumac berries, rock hard now, need several freeze-thaw cycles to soften even a little and become palpable as winter food. And even then, sumac berries contain so little nutrition that birds need about six sumac berries to equal a single dogwood berry. So the sumacs hold their berries, untouched, until the dregs of winter and the dearth of other, richer berries force hungry birds to feed.

But even as apples, crabapples, dogwood, goldenrod, garden flowers, pokeberries, and other fall crops disappear, more are yet to come. After freezing temperatures soften the fruits, holly berries will turn into the prime crop. So, the harvest will continue.

How I love watching the harvesters.

American Goldfinches eat both seed and blossom of many garden flowers, including butterfly bush.

Native beautyberries attract berry lovers, including Northern Cardinals.

Leave the Leaves

In anticipation of winter and the dwindling seed harvest, make a concession this October as you tidy up the yard. Leave your leaves. At least some of them. That's the plea from your avian friends who struggle to survive the winter. So what's with leaves and birds?

By now you know how birds love bugs. After the first hard freeze, though, bugs mostly disappear. We cheer; but birds surely must despair when cold kills off their protein-rich foodstuff.

But, wait. Does a freeze really kill the bugs? Hardly. Bugs disappear, but most don't die. Many burrow into shallow ground or hide in the depths of matted leaves, turn inactive, only to pop out on the first warm days of spring—or even on an unseasonably warm winter day. Those bugs that do die leave behind eggs and larvae, safely stored, many amid leaf litter. By necessity, birds forage all winter, flipping leaves for bugs, bug eggs, and larvae—turning up life-supporting meals.

Some folks, however, proud of tidy yards, and others, fearing a few bugs, chase every leaf, armed with vacuum, blower, rake, and bag. Of course, raking and bagging defeats Mother Nature's inherent checks and balances. Above all, the clean-up destroys habitat.

Thus, neat-yard folks find themselves amid an avian desert, the birds having left for better buffets—and environs. Wintering White-throated and White-crowned Sparrows look else-where to forage. Fox Sparrows and Hermit Thrushes check desert-yards and flee posthaste. Brown Thrashers skip past the neat and tidy, desperately searching to flip leaves for food.

NOTABLE BEHAVIOR   ## Leaf Lovers

Leaf lovers are many. Just watch!

Throughout the winter, towhees rustle among leaves for eggs and larvae; Song Sparrows two-foot scratch for bugs; Carolina Wrens pick through the litter for morsels; flickers poke under leaves for ants; even robins check for grub. Sometimes Brown Thrashers disappear, scooting under the leaves, a spooky undulation the only clue they're at work, foraging for lunch.

Come spring, more ground feeders sift through the leaves: migrating Ovenbirds, returning Chipping Sparrows, all the passing thrushes, even certain warblers, like Nashville, Kentucky, and Mourning Warblers. Some bill-flip, some foot-scratch, some scoot under.

In all, 122 species nationwide thrive—and survive—on foods foraged from backyard leaf litter. Thus, if your leaves are gone, your bugs are gone—and so are the birds.

Of course you'll use common sense when you leave your leaves. In my own yard, leaves piled under shrubs, along borders, next to fences, under dogwoods out to the drip line, and under low-hanging evergreens, all offer a fancy feast for ground-feeding birds.

Can't leave all those leaves and keep peace in the neighborhood? How about a compromise? Instead of raking and bagging, run the lawnmower over the leaves, mulching them. Then, either leave the mulch as it falls for fertilizer, or rake it under bushes, along a back fence, or around tree bases. Birds will love your good deed. And your yard will still look neat and tidy.

BOTANY FOR BIRDS   ## Leaf Mulch

Leaves funneled through a shredder and left to overwinter, in a bin or even in a pile out back, make magnificent mulch. In turn, a well-mulched flower garden needs little or no weeding. While the mulch remains a site for foraging, the added nutrients and moisture retention in the garden will provide even better production of flowers and, therefore, seeds—all of which make for happy birds—and happy gardeners.

But wait. Mustn't you worry about bugs in your garden? In spite of conventional wisdom, the answer is no. In our yard, we never use pesticides; we leave all our leaves, some whole and some mulched; and the bugs don't eat our garden. There's a simple reason: The birds, here in abundance, eat the bugs—in abundance. It's Nature's balance. What's more, 96 percent of birds feed their babies bugs. No bugs, no babies.

In spite of this advice, though, I know there will be bags and bags of leaves sitting curbside throughout the city, awaiting transport to the landfill. That's convenient for us, though, because we drive past those curbs, load our truck, and haul leaves home. We put them through a shredder, pile them in compost bins, and use them to mulch flower beds next spring. Or add them to our own leafy piles under the shrubs, dogwood trees, and low-spreading hemlocks. Either way, as the leaves enrich the soil, the birds enrich our lives.

Dining In or Carry Out?

By October's end, winter can't be far behind. Some folks recognize approaching winter by the multitudes of harvest festivals. Others know winter nears when football fever kicks up a notch. Some wait for falling leaves and the roar of leaf blowers. Probably a preponderance of folks test air temperatures, judging the day that summer heat and humidity finally creep south.

The rest of us, however, recognize the autumn-to-winter passage because of the backyard's changing bird populations.

This week, changes flew off the charts. Bunches of birds came—and went—with the wind. Big wind. On October 3, a weather front blew through, dropping temperatures from 85°F Thursday afternoon to 55° Friday morning. The front carried with it 25-mile-per-hour northwesterly winds and triggered mass bird movement across the entire Midwest.

While migratory birds wander south in dribs and drabs all through late summer and fall, and significant numbers of warblers have moved through since mid-September, the really dramatic fall migrations—just like the really dramatic spring migrations—coincide with dramatic weather changes. By dramatic, we're talking a cold front with brisk north winds, significantly dropping temps, a rising barometer, and clearing skies.

Then the rush is on! Thursday night, birds took to the skies in flights massive enough for radar detection. By Friday morning, the backyard revealed an eye-popping parade of newcomers—and absentees.

Hummingbirds, already on the cusp of migration, blew out in droves that night, leaving Thursday's swarming feeders all but empty Friday morning. The few remaining hummers likely came from the north, here to recharge their batteries a day or so before moving on. By Saturday, even more were gone, likely riding the remaining breezes from the slowly moving front.

Goldfinches, having completed their molt into now-sleek winter drab, fed here in hordes over past weeks, emptying feeders daily and foraging in flocks through spent flowerbeds. By Saturday, they thinned to a handful, one flock moving on before another arrived.

While hummer and goldfinch numbers dropped, other numbers rose. A flock of 140 Yellow-rumped Warblers was reported in a community nearby. In my own yard, a flock of twenty or twenty-five Chipping Sparrows swept in with the front. Using the crabapple tree as home base, they flew out and back like yo-yos, harvesting weed seeds.

FEEDER FOCUS   **Ground Feeders**

Juncos, White-throated Sparrows, American Tree Sparrows, and Fox Sparrows typically feed on the ground, so look for them scratching under evergreen boughs, searching for wintering bugs, or beneath feeders, foraging for spilled seeds. A ground-level platform mixed-seed feeder under low branches may lure these visitors to your yard. You may choose to avoid, however, seed mixes that include cracked corn, grain that attracts birds some folks consider undesirable, like starlings, House Sparrows, grackles, and blackbirds.

By Friday afternoon, the first-of-the-season Dark-eyed Juncos made their debut. My grandma always called the junco "snowbird," because, she said, its arrival means snow is on the way. But juncos also often usher in the first of other winter visitors. And sure enough! By Sunday morning, we had a yard full of White-throated Sparrows.

This isn't to say, of course, that fall migration is over. We'll see migrants through most of October. But when a dramatic seasonal weather change sweeps through, we can expect birds to sweep in—or out—with it.

Stay tuned to the meteorologists.

End of the Rush

The crazy, early October rush complete, White-throated Sparrows now tie with juncos for first place in our yard as most common winter-visitor feeder birds. In fact, to my ears, one of October's most welcome sounds is the junco's one-pitch musical trill in chorus with the white-throat's sweet *Oh, Sam Peabody, Peabody, Peabody.* Two other sparrows—American Tree Sparrows and Fox Sparrows— are also likely yard birds, at least where I live. On a good day, the big brush pile near the back property line draws other sparrows as well. Swamp Sparrow, Lincoln's Sparrow, and Chipping Sparrow join the others, flitting through the tangle.

Occasionally, October brings an irruption of Red-breasted Nuthatches to join our resident White-breasted Nuthatches. October also brings Yellow-bellied Sapsuckers to join our six resident woodpeckers. Uncommon yard birds, sapsuckers enjoy suet when sap no longer runs. Look for a red forehead, red bib (white on female), messy white wing patches and yellowish underparts.

Yellow-bellied Sapsuckers migrate farther than any other North American woodpecker.

If you're lucky and your habitat offers lots of brushy hideaways, a Winter Wren may pop in, its perky appearance and melodious trill a welcome substitute for our now-departed House Wren.

Other regular winter visitors include Ruby-crowned and Golden-crowned Kinglets, neither common yard birds but both found regularly in woodlands and thickets.

So keep seed feeders filled and a sharp eye out. Winter visitors are pouring in this month. And snow or no snow, they're hungry!

FEEDER FOCUS **Fresh Seed or Buggy?**

By October, when you're readying winter bird buffets, check the birdseed. While birdfeed bags carry no expiration date, hot summer months could have rendered the seed useless. If nothing eats your offerings, here's the probable cause: Seed stored in summer-hot garages or vendor's warehouses will likely have gone buggy. Because many birdfeed bags are no-see-through paper, ask your vendor if seed is fresh. Then, if it isn't, return the bag for replacement—of product or money.

BIOLOGY BITS   **Tracking Then and Now, Near and Far**

The fall migration phenomenon gives wing to questions. Where do birds go, and what route do they fly? Where do they forage and rest; what habitat do they need to survive? Above all, how do we know? From pencil and paper to global positioning systems, migratory tracking has flown a long way. Here's more:

Historically, crude tracking methods prevailed: dedicated bird-watchers noted species' arrival and departure dates at a given location. The simple method, however, evolved into huge citizen-science data-gathering projects, like International Migratory Bird Day counts, the Great Backyard Bird Count, and the summer North American Breeding Bird Survey.

To expand their tracking database, bird biologists began systematic banding, the process of attaching a tiny metal band to a bird's leg. The first banding record dates to 1595 when, in a twenty-four-hour span, Henry IV's banded peregrine falcon flew 1,350 miles to Malta; but this country first witnessed banding in 1803 when John James Audubon tied silver cords on the legs of baby Eastern Phoebes, thus verifying that phoebes return to their ancestral nest site the following spring.

The true pioneer in American banding studies, however, was Jack Miner who, between 1909 and 1939, banded twenty thousand Canada geese. In the midst of his studies, in 1923, the U.S. Department of the Interior and the Canadian Wildlife Service jointly instituted the North American Bird Banding program that now, nearly a century later, still oversees banding activities worldwide.

But the problem with banding is that while geese are frequently harvested by hunters and their bands recovered, song birds are rarely recaptured or their remains found. In fact, the band-return rate for non-game birds is about 1 percent. Scientists needed better data returns.

Banding birds, like this Tufted Titmouse, helps scientists understand local and migratory movements, life spans, and breeding habits so that we can better protect birds and their habitats.

Scientists know from various studies that many birds, like Chestnut-sided Warblers, leave our southern coast and fly directly across the Gulf of Mexico to the Yucatan Peninsula in an extraordinary eighteen-hour flight—non-stop by necessity. From there, they continue into South America.

In the 1950s, moonwatching gained popularity when four-night watches at 265 sites provided the first continental snapshot of nighttime migration. But only for a few nights each month—assuming clear weather—is the moon large enough to silhouette birds passing before it. So, based on the moonwatching idea, scientists developed a ceilometer, a device projecting a strong beam of light straight up into the sky, and counted birds as they flew through the artificial moonlight.

About the same time, scientists first recognized that radar could detect migrant flocks. As technology developed, analysts could distinguish species by their uniquely shaped blip and determine speed, altitude, and flight direction. In 1990, the Radar Ornithology laboratory at Clemson University began gathering and analyzing radar data about migratory birds. Today, anyone can check NEXRAD sites on the Internet and watch fall migrants flood southward.

Other technology also helps ornithologists track migrants. Infrared imaging devices detect passing birds by registering their body heat. Audio devices record, identify, and tabulate flight calls of nocturnal migrants. Analyses of birds' feathers reveal stable-isotope patterns created by weather and plants, patterns that, in turn, identify the locale where a bird produced new-feather growth. Radio tagging attaches tiny antennas to birds so that scientists, using transmitter receivers, can chase a bird by car, plane, or helicopter, tracking its route, an expensive process that at best provides data for a single bird.

Enter miniaturized electronics. Today, scientists outfit birds with minute solar-powered satellite transmitters. Lasting two years, the transmitters allow biologists to sit at their office computers, access satellite global positioning data, and determine the bird's altitude, body temperature and heart rate, and relay to colleagues hundreds or thousands of miles away where, within a fraction of a yard, they can find the bird—any day, any time, during any part of the breeding or migration season.

Preparing the Yard for Winter Arrivals

The migrants arriving in October are, for the most part, birds that breed in the boreal forests of Canada and have sailed in to winter here. They hope your welcome mat is out, because your backyard may be their version of a Caribbean destination.

What should your welcome mat look like?

One year on vacation in early August, I witnessed Dark-eyed Juncos, White-throated Sparrows, and White-crowned Sparrows on their breeding grounds in Newfoundland and Labrador, near their northern nesting limits. Watching them, chuckling at their scrappy youngsters, hearing their reedy, high-pitched warning chips—all yielded better understanding of what they'd like when they visit my wintertime yard.

Four ingredients dominate much of the Newfoundland-Labrador landscape: water (salt, brackish, and fresh), rock, bog, and tuckamore (spruce trees stunted by vicious, stinging, howling, icy, wind-driven salt spray). Inland, scanty clumps of wildflowers cling to whatever thin soil they find in glacial-scribed cracks, and sparrows forage and find protection there. Bog vegetation, low, dense, and springy, hides birds that fly up and, in a flash, back down, concealed instantly, without even a trembling leaf.

PROBLEM SOLVER   **Hawks Hawking Your Yard**

Depending on where you live, Sharp-shinned Hawks may swoop in for the winter as early as October, joining year-round resident Cooper's Hawks. Sharpies, not much bigger than robins, and Cooper's, their larger cousin, feed on small birds. Their forays through the yard scatter songsters. When birds sit motionless, tight against tree trunks, or disappear entirely, either hawk may be nearby, on the hunt.

While you may not like their presence, neighborhood hawks are only doing what comes naturally. In reality, as they hunt, they pick off the sick, weak, old, feeble, and inattentive, thus keeping gene pools strong. Take time to watch. Appreciate them for what they are. Perhaps unappealing to your senses, in the natural world, including that in your backyard habitat, most creatures are either feeders or food.

Well inland, the still-rocky terrain supports miniature tree clumps the locals call forests, but they show little trace of the majesty most of us expect in the name. Trees, mostly spruce and fir, stand a scant ten feet tall. Along the coast, though, trees are smaller still; tuckamore rules the rock.

Even in midsummer, cold winds tear at trees that seem to have hunkered down, trunks the diameter of dinner plates but branches no higher than my shoulder, their limbs tightly, impenetrably interlaced. It's here that the sparrows—white-crowned and the more abundant white-throated—fly in, shelter, and for all practical purposes, disappear.

Birds that spend their summers in northerly climates will, if they winter in your backyard, look for dense, impenetrable coniferous vegetation similar to the tuckamore of Newfoundland, seen here in the foreground.

BOTANY FOR BIRDS   **Imitating the Boreal Forest**

In our backyards, evergreen trees, especially with branches to the ground, come close to replicating boreal forest habitat. Aim for evergreens that will survive your climate, recognizing that not all conifers tolerate hot weather or drought. Think juniper, spruce, hemlock, and cedar; and then seek the advice of a trusted local nursery for what grows well in your spot of the world.

So their chosen summer abode reflects their habitat preference: dense anything, like dense weeds, dense brush, dense trees, dense as in impenetrable by hawks, dense to the ground.

And now they're here in the yard. Only recently have we hosted White-crowned Sparrows all winter, new company for their numerous cousins the White-throated Sparrows. What invited them in? Almost twenty years ago, we dedicated part of our once-manicured lawn to dense sparrow habitat—uncut gone-to-seed grasses, weed stems twined among brambles, thorny-thicket protection for sparrows fleeing hungry hawks, with already mature juniper, spruce, and hemlock replicating as best we could their summer-home tuckamore.

How can you, too, roll out the welcome mat? While October is too late to plant evergreens for maturity this winter, and while it's too late for dense ground vegetation to form matted safety and winter-wind barriers, it's not too late to provide other attractive habitat as you plant for better years ahead.

When it comes to brush piles, bigger is better, offering protection for little birds fleeing predators as well as seeking protection from wind and rain.

HABITAT—YOURS AND THEIRS
Building a Brush-pile Teepee

Given adequate space in your yard, offer birds a winter-refuge brush pile. Choose a site preferably near feeders, near your water source, or along a backyard fence so that birds can flee to nearby safety while feeding or bathing. Start by stacking large limbs on the bottom, teepee style, and build up with smaller branches and twigs. A brush pile about shoulder high will offer adequate protection from hawks and other predators and offer overnight roosts for some species. For brush piles, bigger is better.

Add a brush pile in a back corner. Accustomed to diving into impenetrable tuckamore, sparrows will feel snug in the tangle. Below evergreens, especially those whose limbs reach to or near the ground, offer mixed wild birdseed in ground feeders under the lowest branches. Your popularity will soar.

Next spring, plan ahead: Mow less, plant more, save storm-torn branches, rebuild the brush pile. You'll transform your yard into a luxury Caribbean resort—all in preparation for following Novembers and winter months to come.

Conservation Corner: Habitat Loss and Your Backyard

For birds, life is all about habitat. So habitat loss has put some birds in dire straits, their very survival in jeopardy. In general, three kinds of habitat loss put birds at risk: 1) out-and-out habitat destruction (bulldozed and/or paved), 2) habitat fragmentation (roads and other human interferences that break up large habitat tracts), and 3) habitat degradation (habitat deteriorated from pollution, invasive species, and other ruinous conditions).

According to the National Wildlife Federation (NWF), habitat loss is caused by agriculture (grasslands and forest cleared for crops), development (housing, roads, parking lots, strip malls, industrial sites), water development (dams and other water diversions), pollution (sewage, mining waste, acid rain, fertilizers, pesticides), and climate change (eliminating cool habitats required by some species and powering rising seas levels).

NWF clarifies, however, that each of us can make a difference by creating wildlife habitat in our own yards. According to NWF, "Plant native plants and put out a water source so that you can provide the food, water, cover, and places to raise young that wildlife need to survive."

Conservationist and former president Theodore Roosevelt initiated numerous federal programs to protect habitat for wildlife as well as for mankind. In 1916 he wrote, "Birds should be saved for utilitarian reasons; and, moreover, they should be saved because of reasons unconnected with dollars and cents. . . . The extermination of the Passenger Pigeon meant that mankind was just so much poorer. . . . And to lose the chance to see frigate-birds soaring in circles above the storm, or a file of pelicans winging their way homeward across the crimson afterglow of the sunset, or a myriad of terns flashing in the bright light of midday as they hover in a shifting maze above the beach—why, the loss is like the loss of a gallery of the masterpieces of the artists of old time."

Each of us can contribute toward protecting the gallery by developing and protecting backyard habitats.

Things to Do in October

- Leave some leaves, especially under shrubs, next to fences, or under low-hanging branches to offer birds a natural food source.
- Build a brush pile to give birds a safe haven from marauding hawks.
- Prepare ground feeding stations using platform feeders with heavily perforated bottoms for quick drainage and place them under low-hanging branches for wintering sparrows.
- Avoid the urge for an excessively tidy yard and garden, leaving flower and grass seed heads for autumn bird food.
- Leave an area unmowed, perhaps along a back fence or adjoining a clump of trees, to offer cover for wintering sparrows.
- Watch for arriving winter visitors, especially White-crowned and White-throated Sparrows, Dark-eyed Juncos, and irruptive species like Purple Finches and Red-breasted Nuthatches.
- Check sales fliers for special bird seed prices, but avoid buying seed stored during summer months in hot warehouses, a situation that makes seed go buggy. Look instead for new seed crops.

65 Yard Birds in October

Drought continues; cooler with strong winds and very scattered frost near month's end.

Canada Goose	American Crow	Palm Warbler
Wood Duck	Carolina Chickadee	Common Yellowthroat
Turkey Vulture	Tufted Titmouse	Swamp Sparrow
Cooper's Hawk	Red-breasted Nuthatch	Eastern Towhee
Red-shouldered Hawk	White-breasted Nuthatch	American Tree Sparrow
Red-tailed Hawk	Winter Wren	Chipping Sparrow
Killdeer	Carolina Wren	Field Sparrow
Mourning Dove	House Wren	Song Sparrow
Chimney Swift	Golden-crowned Kinglet	Lincoln's Sparrow
Ruby-throated	Ruby-crowned Kinglet	White-throated Sparrow
Hummingbird	Eastern Bluebird	White-crowned Sparrow
Belted Kingfisher	Hermit Thrush	Dark-eyed Junco
Red-bellied Woodpecker	American Robin	Summer Tanager
Yellow-bellied Sapsucker	Gray Catbird	Northern Cardinal
Downy Woodpecker	Northern Mockingbird	Rose-breasted Grosbeak
Hairy Woodpecker	European Starling	Blue Grosbeak
Northern Flicker	Cedar Waxwing	Red-winged Blackbird
Pileated Woodpecker	Tennessee Warbler	Common Grackle
Eastern Wood-pewee	Nashville Warbler	Brown-headed Cowbird
Eastern Phoebe	Yellow-rumped Warbler	House Finch
Great Crested Flycatcher	Black-throated Green	American Goldfinch
Blue-headed Vireo	Warbler	House Sparrow
Blue Jay		

WHITE-THROATED SPARROW
and WHITE-CROWNED SPARROW

VITAL STATS
White-crowned Sparrow
Length: 5.9–6.3 in.
Wingspan: 8.3–9.4 in.
Weight: 0.9–1.0 oz.

Above: *White-crowned Sparrow, adult;* middle: *White-throated Sparrow, white-striped;* bottom: *White-throated Sparrow, tan-striped*

VITAL STATS
White-throated Sparrow
Length: 6.3–7.1 in.
Wingspan: 7.9–9.1in.
Weight: 0.8–1.1 oz.

Octyober brings the return of White-throated and White-crowned Sparrows to my yard. While I know deep down that they're bringing winter with them, I'm in awe of the fact that they found their way north, raised their babies, and have now found their way back to my yard. That a 1-ounce bundle of feathers can survive such a journey causes me to catch my breath when I spy the first one each fall.

NAME THAT BIRD

Zonotrichia albicollis (White-throated Sparrow): *Zonotrichia* means "banded song thrush," referring to the bands, or stripes, on its head, while *albicollis,* meaning "white necked," refers to the bird's white throat. The common name refers to the bird's plumage.

Zonotrichia leucophrys (White-crowned Sparrow): The name *leucophrys,* meaning "white eyebrow," refers to the white band that runs above and just beyond the eye. The common name refers to the bird's plumage.

White-crowned and White-throated Sparrows nest mostly in the Canadian boreal forests. And they share enough general features—appearance, behavior, and habitat—that some folks find them difficult to distinguish.

So how do you tell these close cousins apart? Think of it this way: The white-crown looks spiffy, well groomed, crisp and clean, freshly starched and pressed. By comparison, the white-throat seems a bit dowdy, certainly less fashion conscious, even a bit rumpled.

White-throated Sparrows wear their name, a white bib, set against a mostly gray, slightly streaked breast. A long-tailed, somewhat chunky sparrow, it sports the usual sparrow-streaked back and wings.

To put it more precisely, however, the differences between the two are all about makeup and hair-do.

The hair-do for both includes head stripes. But for the white-crown, the head stripes come first for identification. Contrasting with its satiny gray breast, the crisp bold white crown stripes alongside alternating bold black stripes, sometimes raised like a starched top-knot, readily identify this sparrow. I have to smile when I see its raised head feathers, empha-sizing its fancy stripes, especially when it has an attitude. Gotta love that attitude!

White-throats, on the other hand, wear more muted stripes, brown and white or brown and tan, never raised. And yes, of course, the white-throat wears a white bib at its throat. But check out the face. Except for first-winter birds not yet old enough for makeup, white-throats wear a bright yellow spot between their eyes and the base of their bills (the body location referred to as lores), as if their blush makeup turned golden. With all due respect, I think this bundle of winter cheer should be called the Golden-lored Sparrow.

So, for these two winter sparrows, separate them by makeup and hair-do.

FOOD FARE

Both sparrows prefer small seeds, like weed seeds, but will take millet and sunflower seed from ground feeders and forage for spilled seed under elevated feeders.

Both birds typically prefer to forage on or low to the ground amid tangles and dense brush, occasionally venturing into adjoining open areas but quick to dive back into cover. Both will perch, even roost overnight, in brush piles and spent flower-bed tangles, and both delight in feeding on weed seeds. Fortunately for backyard birders, both species also enjoy ground-feeder buffets.

Like virtually all other birds, they also find water features attractive. If I don't find these two sparrows in the brush pile or amid the brambles, I am likely to find them at our home-made bubbling rock. Every day they visit the water to drink and to bathe. It's fun to watch the pecking order to see who gets choice bathing spots.

My yard hosts far more white-throats than white-crowns, most likely because white-crowns tend to hang out close to watery places; but, I can count on seeing white-crowns during both fall and spring migrations.

BIRD TALK: WHO'S CALLING?

Sweet-singing winter visitors, White-throated Sparrows sing *Oh, Sam Peabody, Peabody, Peabody.* Or, as some prefer, *Oh, sweet Canada, Canada, Canada,* as if longing for their summer home. At dusk, they exchange quiet chip notes, as if checking everyone in for the night.

White-crowned Sparrows have little to say in winter, but come spring, you may hear a sweet, thin whistle as they tune up for breeding season.

When the troops arrive in October, youngsters look somewhat different from their parents. White-crowned youngsters have not yet achieved their name and wear instead a drab brown-striped crown. Even so, they seem nattily dressed. By spring departure, though, they're in full regalia.

White-throated Sparrow youngsters, on the other hand, just seem scruffier than their parents, their head pattern poorly defined, their breast more streaked. I have to acknowledge, however, that even the adults don't all look alike.

White-crowned Sparrow, immature

SPOTTING THE SPECTACULAR   **White Stripe or Tan?**

Here's a surprise: White-throated Sparrows come in two models, white striped and tan striped.

The two forms do not depict sex or age, just a difference. And the quirky part? Tan-striped girls prefer white-striped boys, and white-striped girls prefer tan-striped boys. And even more strangely, white striped birds—male or female—generally show more aggression.

Watch your feeders and you'll see who gets first dibs on the choice morsels.

NEST NOTES

White-throated Sparrow

Nest site: on or just above ground, under cover of shrubs or grasses

Nest construction: ground depression lined with mosses; nest sides built of woven grasses, twigs, and pine needles; nest lined with fine rootlets, grasses, or animal hair; 3–5 in. across, 1–2.5 in. deep

Eggs: 1–6 eggs, 1–2 broods, incubated 11–14 days

Fledge: 7–12 days after hatch

White-crowned Sparrow

Nest site: nest on tundra on ground hidden among mosses, lichens, and low shrubs

Nest construction: twigs, heavy grasses, dead leaves, pine needles; lined with fine grasses and animal hair; 5 in. across, 2 in. deep

Eggs: 3–7 eggs, 1–3 broods, incubated 10–14 days

Fledge: 8–10 days after hatch

ID CHECK

While white-throats and white-crowns can be confused with each other, they can also be confused with other sparrows. Use these field marks to check identity:

- WC—bold black and wide white stripes on their heads; WT—brown and white or brown and tan stripes on their heads
- WC—orange or yellowish bills; WT—mostly dark bills
- WC—white throats that fade into grayish breasts; WT—distinct white bib clearly delineated (Some other sparrows, like Swamp Sparrows, have white throats, so look for other distinctive markings.)
- WC—no yellow on their faces; WT—in maturity, wear bright yellow on the lores, the areas between the eyes and the bill
- WC—clear unmarked gray check, nape, and breast; WT—streaked napes and dull, dark mottling on gray breasts

SPECIES PROFILE

DARK-EYED JUNCO

VITAL STATS
Length: 5.5–6.3 in.
Wingspan: 7.1–9.8 in.
Weight: 0.6–1.1 oz.

Above: *Dark-eyed Junco, male;* below: *Dark-eyed Junco, female*

Dark-eyed Juncos, the ones my grandma called "snow birds," have arrived right on schedule this October, here in anticipation of generous winter hospitality. Neat, flashy little sparrows, they've arrived from their breeding grounds in the boreal forests of Canada (or, depending on your location, from the upper elevations of the Appalachians). While our yard usually hosts two or three dozen juncos, this year they've apparently brought all their friends and their friends' extended families. At least fifty or sixty juncos feeding across the backyard give the dizzying appearance of a yard in undulation—enough to make me suspect my morning's coffee.

These abundantly common but jazzy little sparrows easily catch my eye, even without my morning coffee. When they flit from ground cover to trailing branch or zip low across an open space to the next set of tangles, those long bright-white tail feathers flash like beacons. No, the full tail isn't white—only the outer feathers. And they show a nattily sharp contrast with the remaining dark gray. Then, in flight, the junco opens and closes its tail like a fan but with such rapidity that the fan flashes. And bingo! The bird's identity clearly shows.

NAME THAT BIRD

Junco hyemalis (Dark-eyed Junco): *Junco* comes from a Medieval Latin word that means "reed bunting," because our little bird resembles this European species. *Hyemalis* refers to winter. We use the common term "dark-eyed" to separate our eastern bird from Yellow-eyed Juncos, found in Arizona and New Mexico.

I like to think of the junco as dressed in a full hooded cape and decked out in white under-pinnings. No matter how they're described, though, juncos earn their "snow bird" moniker—not only because they seem to bring winter's snow with them when they arrive for the winter but also because they seem to have brushed their bellies white with snow. And when we really do have snow and the world turns black and white, juncos skitter under the lowest hemlock branches like scurrying little charcoal smudges against the gray-white shadows.

SPOTTING THE SPECTACULAR
Leaden Skies Above; Snow Below

Snow birds, our common Dark-eye Juncos, tend to return to the same wintering spots each year, hang out with the same flock, and roost in the same spots each night. Flocks maintain a pecking order, with the dominant bird threatening others by lunging toward them or squaring off and doing a head-dance, bobbing their heads up and down. Rarely does the power play come to blows. Mostly the less dominant birds back off and feed peacefully in quieter quarters. Watch for the pecking order at your feeders.

Their color variation, however, can tease a backyard bird-watcher's ID skills. Some juncos, especially fresh males, show rich charcoal gray against crisp white. Others, including most females, take on a softer gray or even brownish gray against white. A few show pinkish casts on their sides. Across the United States, however, six forms of this little guy account for several pages of junco variations in field guides.

All juncos, though, wear small pinkish bills, adding a rather delicate look to an already charming face. Bill size and shape, of course, determines diet, so don't look for juncos to tackle tough seeds.

BIRD TALK: WHO'S CALLING?
The male's long rapid musical trill (sometimes up to two minutes) reminds me of a chipping sparrow, but I don't hear it much in winter. More likely, I'll hear the males and females chipping quietly to one another, keeping track, staying together. Think brittle twitter.

FOOD FARE

Winter-visiting juncos forage for native seeds like chickweed, lamb's quarters, and wood sorrel, which make up about 75 percent of their diet. While they take insects when available (especially during breeding season to feed their babies), they also visit winter ground feeders to dine on millet. In general, although black-oil sunflower seeds are too large for their dainty bills to crack, sunflower hearts, on the other hand, provide suitable sustenance.

To attract juncos to the yard, cultivate a weedy area with seedy plants. A woodlot's tangled edges offer a safe haven and secure night roost. Evergreens like pine, juniper, or hemlock, reflect their preferred summer home and render protection against howling winter wind, snow, and sleet.

NEST NOTES

Nest site: in depression, directly on ground or on platform of twigs, also favoring sloped thick grasses so overhanging grasses cover nests; sometimes in upturned tree roots; in human-inhabited areas, under buildings or even in hanging pots; one of most common birds found along trails with soil or root banks

Nest construction: quite variable, depending on available materials; lined with fine grasses, pine needles, ferns, hair, mosses; 3–5 in. across, 1.5–2.5 in. deep

Eggs: 3–6 eggs, 1–3 broods, incubated 12–13 days

Fledge: 10–13 days after hatch

ID CHECK

Dark-eyed Juncos are readily identified by the following traits:

- Overall gray hoods, backs, and tails, without wing bars or streaking
- Crisp charcoal gray of male and soft pale gray of female
- White breast
- White outer tail feathers that seem to flash when birds fly

Each spring, I try to remember to watch for the final junco of the season. Then I forget. One day, though, it hits me: They're gone. Without thinking, I still watch for them, looking for little guys hopping (not walking), bursting sometimes almost straight up on takeoff, or dodging with lightning-speed agility into cover when a Cooper's Hawk sails through the yard. I wish them Godspeed on their journey north.

Now, though, they're back, having migrated to Canada and spent their summer building nests and raising babies. After their long journey up and back, they deserve a rest. And I hope they enjoy it in my yard—and yours!

SPECIES PROFILE

WHITE-BREASTED NUTHATCH and RED-BREASTED NUTHATCH

VITAL STATS
White-breasted Nuthatch
Length: 5.1–5.5 in.
Wingspan: 7.9–10.6 in.
Weight: 0.6–1.1 oz.

Above: *White-breasted Nuthatch;* below: *Red-breasted Nuthatch*

VITAL STATS
Red-breasted Nuthatch
Length: 4.3 in.
Wingspan: 7.1–7.9 in.
Weight: 0.3–0.5 oz.

Last year, because drought extended far to our north, many backyard birders hosted an infrequent visitor, so infrequent that this perky little upside-down bird had been absent from my yard for over five years.

We're talking about Red-breasted Nuthatches, those roughly half-size cousins to our year-round White-breasted Nuthatches. They zip about like miniature masked bandits, snatching peanut pieces and sunflower hearts, darting off, stashing their goods in some safe cache. I'm thrilled to see them, but not at all thrilled about what it means.

NAME THAT BIRD

Sitta carolinensis (White-breasted Nuthatch): From the Latin, *sitta* means "tiny" or "very small." *Carolinensis,* or Carolina, refers to the generally southeastern location where the bird was first discovered. Its common name "nuthatch," originally "nuthack," comes from the bird's habit of hacking nuts apart in order to feed. "White-breasted" describes its plumage.

Sitta canadensis (Red-breasted Nuthatch): *Canadensis* refers to its year-round range, generally Canada. Its common name suggests plumage color.

The Red-breasted Nuthatch visitors are demonstrating something called "irruptions," meaning that the birds show up only rarely and only when their dwindling winter food supplies force them to migrate beyond their usual territories. For whatever reason, though, Red-breasted Nuthatches tend to wander south earlier than other irruptive species, so that's likely why early October has brought these irregular visitors to our yards.

FOOD FARE

Nuthatches hitch along tree trunks in typical upside-down fashion, poking about for bugs and bug eggs hidden in tree bark. They will also take shelled peanuts, unsalted preferred, and peanut butter, crunchy preferred. In the absence of first-choice foods, they will dine on black-oil sunflower seeds.

Unlike most other birds, nuthatches will cache seeds, usually in tree bark. Watch for birds sailing off, laden with seed, far too often to be eating it all themselves; they're storing seed against bad times.

The Red-breasted Nuthatch can be distinguished from the white-breasted by its namesake reddish brown underparts. But since the white-breasted can also show a blush of rusty red on its sides, it's the little bandit-like eye mask that truly sets the red-breasted apart. Its smaller size is also diagnostic, but unless the two are side by side, that's a tricky call.

While Red-breasted Nuthatches nest in the coniferous forests of Canada, White-breasted Nuthatches prefer our area's mature deciduous woodlands. Fairly common and widespread, White-breasted Nuthatches nest in our neighborhood. So I watch for them at the peanut or peanut butter feeders year round. Sleek, well groomed, with slightly uplifted bills, they're busy, busy, busy, to the point of being hyper little beings.

BIRD TALK: WHO'S CALLING?

Both nuthatches sound as if they're playing little tin horns, a nasal monotone *yank, yank*. White-breasted song is faster, more nervous than that of red-breasted which sounds more evenly paced, more deliberate.

SPOTTING THE SPECTACULAR
Head-first Birds

Nuthatches are the only birds that can go head-first down trees. Unlike woodpeckers, they don't have a stiff tail by which to prop themselves against a tree. Thus, they have adapted. Watch carefully. When they move down—or up or sideways—along a tree trunk, they keep one foot ahead and one foot back, both clinging to the bark. And what does the nuthatch gain by its unique locomotion? It spots bugs, bug eggs, and larva in bark crevices that other birds, looking from the opposite direction, never find.

Both cousins give the impression that they're breathlessly in a hurry, ducking here, dodging there, zipping off with a single seed, returning for more in a rush-rush fashion. Bright-eyed and intense, they should, it seems, need an occasional respite. But I've never seen them napping or even quietly roosting (although surely they do somewhere sometime).

NEST NOTES

White-breasted Nuthatch

Nest site: in cavity, either natural or woodpecker-made; in future years will reuse cavities; occasionally use man-made nest boxes

Nest construction: female lines cavity with fur or bark; adds final layer of fine grasses or feathers, other soft materials; size dependent on cavity; seems not to mind large cavities

Eggs: 5–9 eggs, 1 brood, incubated 13–14 days

Fledge: 26 days after hatch

Red-breasted Nuthatch

Nest site: in self-excavated cavity 2–8 in. deep; may choose existing natural cavity; will reuse cavity in future years; not known to accept man-made nest boxes

Nest construction: grass, bark strips, and pine needles; lined with soft grasses, fur, feathers; both sexes apply conifer resin to cavity entrance, sometimes displaying tool use by using bark pieces to apply resin

Eggs: 2–8 eggs, 1 brood, incubated 12–13 days

Fledge: 18–21 days after hatch

While our White-breasted Nuthatches entertain us year round, they change behavior by season. In summer, of course, they're dutifully raising babies and protecting territory from predators and invaders. Come winter, though, they and their now-mature youngsters typically join chickadees and titmice in feeding and foraging flocks. Whether more eyes help the flock to find more food or whether more eyes help the flock to spot predators more quickly is open to debate. Some research suggests that flocking increases the odds that a predator will snatch some other bird, thus offering any one individual increased odds of survival. However we look at it, one interesting study showed that when titmice were removed from the flock, nuthatches were more wary and less willing to visit backyard feeders.

So watch feeders not only for seed-carrying gray, black, and white bark climbers, but keep an eye on flocks of chickadees and titmice for nuthatches among them.

ID CHECK

Unless you live in the far north or at higher elevations, season will help separate white-breasted from red-breasted. Most of us see only White-breast Nuthatches except during irruption years. Nuthatches are most readily noticed by these characteristics:

- Upside-down travel along tree trunks and tree limbs
- Bandit-like face mask and orangey sides of Red-breasted Nuthatch
- Black cap, gray back, and white breast of White-breasted Nuthatch
- Year-round calls that sound like toy tin horns

SPECIES PROFILE

HOUSE FINCH or PURPLE FINCH?

Above: *House Finch, male;* below: *House Finch, female*

VITAL STATS
House Finch
Length: 5.1–5.5 in.
Wingspan: 7.9–9.8 in.
Weight: 0.6–1.0 oz.

Think you'd more likely have a purple cow in the yard than a Purple Finch? Depending on how far south you live and how this year's northerly seed crops fared, you could be right. But Purple Finches—which, by the way, are not purple—can make backyard appearances throughout the Midwest, South, and East. They're unpredictable, always a pleasant surprise, sometimes popping in for a day or a week, and then they're gone. This October, I had a female Purple Finch that hung around for several weeks, but it was the first I'd seen at my feeders in seven years. That's a long time. I've missed them.

Easily confused with our year-round, widespread House Finches, Purple Finches come south only in winter and only when food shortages send them south.

VITAL STATS
Purple Finch
Length: 4.7–6.3 in.
Wingspan: 8.7–10.2 in.
Weight: 0.6–1.1 oz.

Above: *Purple Finch, male;* below: *Purple Finch, female*

NAME THAT BIRD

Carpodacus mexicanus (House Finch): *Carpodacus* refers to a fruit biter, a word from the early Greek, that zeros in on the bird's vegetarian diet, including fruit and berries. *Mexicanus,* of course, references the region in which the house finch originates. Its common name refers to its preference for living among humans while "finch" comes from the Anglo-Saxon word for this bird, reflecting its call.

Carpodacus purpureus (Purple Finch): References the bird's color.

In order to appreciate the uncommon Purple Finches, let's first take a peek at the far more common House Finch. While House Finches originated in the Southwest (see Spotting the Spectacular on page 319), their subsequent expansion eastward suggests that, at least in the minds of some scientists, it was inevitable that the species would ultimately wing its way into Midwestern, Southern, and Eastern backyards. Likewise, it was probably inevitable that competition with established native species would change backyard composition, and discussion ensues about good versus bad results.

One bird with which the House Finch competes is the introduced House Sparrow, a bird originally from England and at one time called English Sparrow, a bird not really a sparrow at all. (See more on page 280.)

As recently as 2007, however, researchers found an inverse relationship between populations of House Sparrows and House Finches. The results have tantalized backyard feeder hosts, reminding them to keep an eye out, watching, sharing citizen-science observations with researchers who continue efforts to get to the bottom of the competition issue. For whatever reason, when House Sparrows thrive, House Finches decline, and conversely, when House Finches thrive, House Sparrows decline. What we don't know? How and why.

In spite of their name, House Finches do not prefer cavities for nesting as do House Sparrows. So, where is the competition? Food. Food for themselves and for their babies. Both birds prefer a diet of seed. But whether one species can out-eat the other or whether one species ultimately prefers quieter quarters and seeks alternative habitat to the other—these issues remain for some PhD candidate to research and report. Meanwhile, keep an eye open for competitive signs in your yard.

HOUSE FINCH EYE DISEASE
Mycoplasmal Conjunctivitis

One reason for House Finch decline is a respiratory infection affecting the eye, called mycoplasmal conjunctivitis, caused by a parasitic bacterium once believed to infect only poultry. If you've spotted a House Finch with red, swollen, or crusty eyes, you've witnessed the condition. When the disease progresses, one or both eyes swell shut or crust over. Infected birds usually die, not of the disease but, as the result of blindness, from starvation or predation. Infected birds can carry the disease to other finches, including goldfinches.

If you see infected birds in your yard, immediately empty feeders and clean with a 10 percent bleach solution (one part bleach to nine parts water), dry thoroughly, and rehang. Rake below feeders to remove droppings and old, molded seeds and hulls. Space feeders well apart to reduce concentrations of birds.

Separating the LBJs

Separating the little brown jobs (LBJs) snatching seeds from your feeders can offer a challenge. In summer, only LBJs like female House Finches, House Sparrows, and perhaps a Song Sparrow or two forage feeder offerings. Depending on your habitat, an occasional nesting Chipping Sparrow may join the throng. (Male House Finches wear enough red to never be mistaken as an LBJ.) In winter, however, beginning in October, multitudes of LBJs abound around the buffet. They all look fairly similar: brown backs, maybe with some white spots, beige breasts, maybe with some streaks. Sorting them out sometimes seems a fruitless effort.

FOOD FARE

Both finches are primarily vegetarian, eating seeds, fruits, berries, and buds. Purple Finches prefer tree seeds (coniferous cones as well as seed from elm, tulip poplar, and maple), but will take some insects, especially during breeding season. Both accept black-oil sunflower seeds and millet.

Over the next month, LBJ numbers will likely explode. White-throated Sparrows, White-crowned Sparrows, and American Tree Sparrows all move here from the far north where they summer. Again, depending on your habitat, Field Sparrows may congregate, too. Maybe a Fox Sparrow. Even winter-visiting Pine Siskins join the fray, birds that at first glance seem nothing more than striped LBJs, especially among equally drab winter-plumaged goldfinches with whom they usually hang out.

BIRD TALK: WHO'S CALLING?

Both finches sing a lovely musical trill often lasting several seconds, but House Finches sing a slower, somewhat more choppy melody than do Purple Finches, an aria typically ending in a slur, either up or down. Females of both species also sing, but their rendition is a shorter, less complicated version of that of the males.

Any of these wintering LBJs may show up at feeders, expanding the summer mobs to demanding winter throngs.

Surprisingly, distinctly colored, chunky, big-beaked Purple Finches can also melt into a mob of LBJs—if they're females. All these possible species give reason to check out the little nondescripts feeding on and under feeders. And the possibility of visiting Purple Finches may be the most exciting reason of all.

Just as many sparrows are winter-only visitors, Purple Finches also visit my yard only in winter, sometimes as early as late October. But unlike winter-only sparrows that sail in, clockwork-like, every winter, Purple Finches arrive only in winters when dwindling northern conifer cone supplies leave them hungry enough to venture our way, typically every other year, corresponding to cone production cycles. The phenomenon is called an irruption.

Male Purple Finches, which look like sparrows dipped in raspberry juice, can be confused with our common year-round slimmer and more streaked male House Finches. On the other hand, female Purple Finches show a snazzy facial pattern that attracts attention and should prevent confusing them with female House Finches—or even with other LBJs.

NEST NOTES

House Finch

Nest site: in variety of trees, also in and on buildings as in vents and hanging planters; occasionally in other birds' abandoned nests

Nest construction: stems, rootlets, feathers, found human materials; lined with similar but smaller and softer materials; 3–7 in. wide, 2 in. deep

Eggs: 2–6 eggs, 1–6 broods, incubated 13–14 days

Fledge: 12–19 days after hatch

Purple Finch

Nest site: out on limb protected by overhanging branches, usually coniferous but in
  southern part of range, also deciduous trees
Nest construction: twigs, roots, grasses; lined with fine grasses, animal hair; 7 in. wide,
  4 in. deep
Eggs: 2–7 eggs, 1–2 broods, incubated 12–13 days
Fledge: 13–16 days after hatch

Many other LBJs wear rather indistinct faces, vaguely striped or generally overall brown. But a female Purple Finch wears a Hollywood face, beauty marks including a bold dark-brown ear patch, deep-brown jaw stripe, contrastingly crisp white streak behind the eye, and a bright white stripe from bill's base to neck.

To my eye, female Purple Finches stand out in other ways among the crowd of LBJs. They're perky, maybe even a bit feisty, often raising their head feathers almost as if they have crests. It's as if they're strutting their stuff, maybe showing an attitude. Whichever the case, few feeder fellows can boss these girls around, not even larger cardinals. You gotta love 'em for that.

SPOTTING THE SPECTACULAR
Competition between Finches

In the 1940s, House Finches were captured illegally in their native Southwest and transported to the East Coast where they were sold as caged birds, jazzed up with the fancy name "Hollywood Finches," and sought after for both their color and their song. Then, just ahead of law enforcement officers, the birds were released to the wild.

I remember the thrill we all had when the first House Finches reached the Midwest, giving certain backyard bird-watchers bragging rights that the Hollywood birds had arrived in their very own yards. Excitement ensued! Sightings recorded!

Today, of course, excitement has waned. The released eastern population has expanded westward, meeting the western population spreading east, giving the House Finch a coast-to-coast range across the United States The result, of course, is that the House Finch range now overlaps that of the Purple Finch. Unfortunately, where the House Finch has encroached on the Purple Finch, the Purple Finch is losing ground, according to one reference, 95 percent of the time.

Most years at my feeders—years when irruptions do occur—I see far more female than male Purple Finches. And there are several good reasons. First, female and immature males look identical. Not even the experts can distinguish between them unless they hold the birds in hand. Probably, then, not every "female" I see is actually a female; it could be an immature male.

Then add two other little twists: Immatures—whether males or females—migrate earlier than adults, so they show up earlier at area feeders. And males return to breeding grounds before females, disappearing from area feeders earlier than females. So the limited timeframe for seeing mature male Purple Finches in my yard presupposes I'll see fewer males than females—even in good irruption years.

Which Finch Is Which?

House Finch	Purple Finch
Male highly variable in amount of red but only on head and chest	Male washed all over in a raspberry tint, including entire head, back, wings, and rump
White belly and flanks, streaked brown on both male and female	White belly and flanks, no streaking
Female plain-Jane; streaked brown	Female has distinctly bold facial pattern
Flanks on male and female are streaked brown	Flanks on male reddish washed with underlying darker streaks
Wings on male lack red	Wings on male show two raspberry wing bars
Tail squared off	Tail forked
Sings vibrant bubbly song	Sings lazy warbled song
Side by side with purple finch, house finch is slightly smaller	Side by side with house finch, purple finch is slightly larger; head appears larger, more rounded

That's all the more reason to study the throngs of LBJs at your wintertime feeders. They've come from central Canada to enjoy your buffet. You wouldn't want to miss them.

ID CHECK
Use the chart above to distinguish between House Finch and Purple Finch. Watch your feeders at different times:
- House Finches visit year round
- Purple Finches visit only in winter (unless you live in the far north)

November

"What kind of bird are you, if you can't fly?" said he.
To this the duck replied, "What kind of bird are you
if you can't swim?" and dived into the pond.

SERGEI PROKOFIEV

November brings a chill to the air and, in my yard, usually the first hard freeze. Heavy frost has already quelled the bugs, but occasional 70°F days confuse violets. They're blooming—way out of season—so I pluck a few, tuck them in a tiny vase, perch them on my kitchen windowsill.

Four mostly gray months of short days and long nights will drag by before violets bloom again. Depending on where you live, by November's end, lingering leaves of scarlet and gold turn the color of fine leather and waft to the ground. Trees stand bare armed, leaning against late autumn's deepening blue skies, resigned to winter's ways.

But what surprises those bare limbs hold! Often, I'm left wide-eyed and slack-jawed at the summer secrets they now reveal. Can you believe—not twenty feet from our backdoor, a Cooper's Hawk nest sits snug in a fork in the old oak tree. We had no idea. And the Indigo Bunting nest tucked tightly in a goldenrod stalk? Gosh, I'd walked past it dozens of times, right along the edge of my weed patch, never knowing. An Eastern Towhee nest at the base of a clump of blackberry canes stayed hidden from my eyes all spring. And a White-eyed Vireo nest, hanging delicately between a sapling's two twigs, obvious if I'd looked in just the right spot. But I'd missed it, too. Like feathered phantoms, they'd all raised their families, well hidden, secreted away, safe, protected. It's what birds do. November lets me in on the secret.

Nests like that of the White-eyed Vireo show astonishing workmanship, causing me to wonder how the birds know to suspend their nests between two twigs and how to weave them sufficiently strong to support both mother and babies—and last the rigors of wind and rain.

Season's Slide to Winter

November blurs late fall into early winter. Another month rolls by, my backyard habitat and its birds transform themselves—dramatically so—but by month's end, the curtain rises on yet another annual drama. You'll see!

HABITAT—YOURS AND THEIRS
Measuring Habitat: Nests Unveiled

You know, of course, that good backyard habitat provides food, water, shelter—and places to raise young. Now, November's barrenness reveals what leaves concealed. Where and how did each bird tuck its nest, secure in wind and rain, safe from predators and prying eyes? In grass clump, shrub, bush, or tree? High or low? Deciduous or coniferous? A field guide to nests can identify your find. But, wait! No nests unveiled? Something's missing in your habitat. Plan next spring's backyard updates accordingly.

But leave the nests you find. The International Migratory Bird Act makes collecting them illegal. Unless you hold state and federal salvage licenses, owning any part of any bird—like feather, egg, or nest—can result in fines, or worse.

Winter visitors that burst into the yard on wild October weather fronts have now sorted out their differences with our full-time residents, each having garnered a habitat niche of its own for feasting, sheltering, roosting. Constants remain: Carolina Wrens still awaken me at first light, singing out their locations. Cardinals still beat everyone else to feeders at dawn and outlast all others at dusk. Our tiny heated bubbling rock still offers sip-and-splash for all.

Another quartet keeps up routines. Chickadees, ever busy, select one feeder seed at a time, scurry off to hull it, and return, repeating the routine more times than I can count. Goldfinches cling upside down on now-spent zinnia heads, checking diminishing returns, plucking remaining morsels. Titmice, topknots erect, hammer peanuts clamped between toes. A bluebird pair, in year-round routine, guards its nest/roost box.

WATER WAYS
Leaves in the Water

As blustery winds blow leaves across the landscape, some may accumulate in your water feature. Since wet leaves rot, emitting tannins, keep leaves cleared from bird baths, bubbling rocks, and yard ponds. Tannins turn water brown, bitter, and ultimately, smelly.

Cover large water features with netting, available at most garden-supply centers. To allow birds ongoing access, drop netting to the bottom along a shallow side and anchor with stones or bricks to prevent birds from getting tangled or trapped.

But November's changes alter routine. Now, year-round residents sing half-hearted solos and duets merged, as if in much-needed rehearsal, with weakened choruses of winter-only White-throated Sparrows, their song whistled from junipers, announcing who's here. Juvenile white-throats, not yet masters of song, make me chuckle at their off-key, notes-missing efforts. By spring, though, when hormones kick in, they'll get it right. Then they'll leave. Meanwhile, they're flipping through leaf mulch, bugging.

BOTANY FOR BIRDS   ## Buffet in the Leaves

Autumn's fallen leaves, now wind-whisked into winter corners, harbor a virtual bird-buffet, an array of invertebrates, insect eggs, and larvae. For birds, flipping leaf litter equates with a do-or-die food search. For females, however, leaf litter equates with breeding success. How so? To produce egg shells, their bodies demand a super calcium-rich diet. And where do our feathered friends find calcium? Primarily in land snails, little critters that overwinter in—guess where—fallen leaves. If you rid your yard of leaves, you also rid your yard of snails—and the calcium for next spring's egg-laying birds.

Gone are waves of juncos that swept in last month. Now, a couple dozen remain, murmuring their even, monotone trill or, more frequently, their measured, staccato, soft chip call. The remainder, though, continued on, farther south. I wonder how they decide who stays and who goes. Did some of them winter with us last year and so have dibs on the yard? Somehow they figure out exactly how many of their kind our backyard habitat will support.

HOW DOES YOUR GARDEN GROW?
Spent Flowers Repay in Seed

By November, my garden earns no awards for beauty—only for bounty. Since I don't deadhead anything, spent flowers, gone to seed, naked of leaves, now hang their bounty-borne heads. Garden flowers vary by geography, but in my garden, zinnias, coneflowers, Indian grass, and goldenrod win winter fare awards among goldfinches, white-throats, juncos, cardinals, chickadees, and titmice. They've already stripped monarda, coreopsis, and brown-eyed Susans.

Birds love a seedy garden. I'll trade beauty for bounty any day.

My mid-November garden serves up spent flower seed heads and tangles of protection—all attractive to wintering birds.

Some winters, when diminishing food supplies chase them south, Pine Siskins visit our feeders.

Here Today? Or Here to Stay?

Among the newly arrived this month, feisty Pine Siskins join the feeder fray, hogging sunflower hearts or blending with goldfinches at or under the thistle feeder, high-pitched flight calls tracing their coming and going. We've not had siskins in our yard in three years, but we could predict their arrival. A widespread drought decimated wild seed and berry crops. These cute little yellow-tinged finches don't want to fly this far south, but it's all about food. They're looking, and most habitat north of here is lacking.

Another exciting seasonal change flew in: a Blue Jay family, announced via raucous *jay, jay* calls. How good to hear the five of them, the first little flock in two years to return to our yard after West Nile Virus did a number on their numbers.

BIOLOGY BITS   **West Nile Virus: Its Effect on Birds**

Identified in the West Nile District of Uganda in 1937, West Nile Virus (WNV) was first detected in the Western Hemisphere in New York in May 1999. By testing dead birds, the U.S. Geological Survey followed the mosquito-borne virus across the continent.

Like humans, birds contract the virus from mosquitoes; but unlike humans, birds serve as hosts, infecting other mosquitoes. Tragically, people do die from WNV; however, the virus primarily affects birds, killing hundreds of thousands. In 1999, crows, which suffer a 100 percent mortality rate from WNV, and jays, members of the same family, were first to succumb. In three years, crow populations plummeted 81 percent; jays, 66 percent. Mortality among hawks and owls followed suit.

To complicate the problem, pesticides used to eradicate virus-carrying mosquitoes further deteriorate bird populations that feed on mosquitoes: swallows, swifts, and a wide variety of flycatchers. It's a catch-22.

Blue Jays, having suffered dramatic losses as a result of West Nile Virus, have returned to the yard.

While people can wear long sleeves and long pants, use mosquito repellants, or simply stay indoors to protect against WNV, birds have no such options. Human globalization transported the virus to North America where native birds have no immunity. We must shoulder the blame.

Now, in their return, the jays' blue seems more vibrant, their calls more exuberant than before. Is it because absence makes the heart grow fonder?

And the Northern Mockingbird is back. The little scamp fed on our holly berries all last winter, and we cheered it on as it protected its one berried branch from hordes of hungry robins. In spring, it left, taking its song with it. Now it's returned, stripped the dogwood, and nearly finished the beautyberries. Like others of its appetite, it faces a tough winter if holly berry crops fail.

HOW DOES YOUR GARDEN GROW?
Beautyberries for Thanksgiving

Native beautyberry (*Callicarpa* spp.), a graceful understory shrub, produces bunches of lavender berry clusters. Varieties adapted for multiple hardiness zones make it an easy choice no matter where you live. Berries attract mockingbirds, cardinals, robins, and grosbeaks. November finds earlier berry producers, like pokeberry and dogwood, past prime, fruits long since gobbled up by hungry birds. Thus, beautyberry, with its Thanksgiving bounty, fills the gap between early berries and late. Most remaining berries, like holly and sumac, must undergo several freeze-thaw softening cycles to become palatable to birds.

Hoping to help the mockingbird stay strong, I hung another peanut butter feeder between the kitchen window and the mockingbird's holly tree. So far, the bird has snubbed its nose at my offering, still content with berries. But Downy Woodpeckers found it and have made it their own.

A homemade peanut butter feeder draws a busy lunchtime crowd, including, here, a Downy Woodpecker. In addition, cardinals, wrens, titmice, chickadees, mockingbirds, and other woodpeckers enjoy the high-fat offering.

FEEDER FOCUS
Serving Up Suet and Peanut Butter

Offer suet and peanut butter (preferably salt free) to birds that, in summer, prefer bugs to seeds: woodpeckers, wrens, bluebirds, chickadees, and others. Rich in fat, these spreads help birds keep warm. Homemade feeders save dollars, but you can also smear peanut butter and softened suet directly on tree bark. Or cut a fallen branch to length and hang it on a shepherd hook or tree limb. Or drill holes in anything wooden—scrap lumber, firewood piece—and hang. Birds that don't like to eat clinging vertically, including cardinals and mockingbirds, will appreciate the same menu offered horizontally.

Raiders of Last Night

Changing seasons also change other critters' routines. Raccoons now waddle in nightly to steal the mocker's apple, scoop out suet, and rob the jays' peanuts. Last night a skunk, disturbed as it rooted among spilled seeds, left its scented calling card. It, too, wants to fatten up for winter. Thus, the price of bird feed being what it is, my routine has changed, too. Nightly, we'll haul the feeders in until the masked and striped bandits move on.

PROBLEM SOLVER   **Raiding Raccoons**

Raccoons live everywhere and eat almost anything, including expensive birdseed. Although they seem not to like safflower or thistle seeds, I've caught them draining my summertime hummingbird nectar. They also wreck feeders, even drag them off. To trap and remove these bandits is only to move the problem to someone else's yard. The only humane solution—although no easy one—is to remove feed and feeders from the yard each evening, storing them securely overnight, perhaps in a garage, and returning them for hungry birds at dawn.

Raccoons frequently raid feeders, sometimes destroying them, causing backyard birdfeeder hosts frustration.

Birds'-eye View

Have you noticed, now that autumn blurs into winter, how certain of our resident birds congregate on utility wires? Thousands of pigeons and starlings and dozens of Mourning Doves line up, evenly spaced, stretching along miles of wires. Why do they do that? Why now?

BIOLOGY BITS   **Pigeon Lore**

Pigeons and people have coexisted for so many dozens of centuries that the birds' origins blur into uncertainty. Early Turkish troglodyte homes included painstakingly carved niches to attract roosting and nesting pigeons so that residents could gather the nitrogen-rich bird droppings to fertilize crops. Today, our vocabulary speaks to our coexistence: Desks have pigeonholes. We categorize by pigeonholing. We think poorly of stool pigeons. Some people walk pigeon toed.

Partly, the congregating has to do with extra time on their hands—er, wings. By November, they have no reason to sing to mates, mark or defend breeding territory, or protect nests or nestlings, or manage the delivery of baby food. The utility-wire crowd gathers, especially in late afternoon, primarily to socialize. But the thousands of birds must, by necessity, choose multiple roost sites. And maybe that's what they're talking about—who's going to go where with whom for the night.

When Invasives Invade

Neither starlings nor pigeons belong in North America. When either species finds backyard feeders, they bring their noisy, bustling flocks of friends. Songbirds flee. Watch what you feed and what starlings and pigeons eat. Then adjust your buffet. Avoid cracked corn to solve much of the problem. Then eliminate small grains like millet and wheat, "fillers" that enable retailers to sell mixed birdfeed cheap. Unfortunately, birds that eat fillers are likely undesirables, including non-native House Sparrows.

But here's an even better trick. Since pigeons and starlings prefer feeding on the ground, spilled seed and ground-level feeders draw them in like magnets. Using tube feeders will restrict access to these two; but given no other alternative, starlings will cling by whichever toehold possible to steal a meal from tubes. Still, at best, a hanging tube feeder or two accommodates only a few starlings as opposed to the hordes that congregate on the ground.

Something odd happens, though, when multitudes of birds gather along utility wires. Have you noticed? They all face the same direction. But tomorrow they may all face the opposite direction. How do they know? Who decides?

Like airplanes, birds take off and land into the wind—and face the wind when perching. Only on perfectly calm days do birds perch facing opposite directions.

HABITAT—YOURS AND THEIRS
Not Guilty but Facing Electrocution

Given their wire-roosting habits, up to 175 million birds die each year of electrocution, especially eagles, owls, and hawks. Collisions with power lines kill hundreds of thousands more. When a bird touches two wires simultaneously, or comes in contact with a wire while perched on a metal post or cross arm, it is, unfortunately, electrocuted. Small birds, whose short wingspans make it unlikely they'll simultaneously touch two wires, typically enjoy a safe perch.

Improved regulations will better protect birds, including those rules calling for wooden rather than metal poles and requiring wire spirals on lines to increase their visibility.

Birding the Third Dimension

Near month's end, depending on where you live, the yard opens to new drama, one played out in the third dimension. Not something mystical, but definitely magical. Let me explain.

Myopic views limit yard habitat to two dimensions, front to back, side to side. But the third dimension spectacularly extends the playbook—from ground up. Way up. Soaring raptors, a solitary eagle, wintertime flocks at dawn and dusk, migrating waterfowl—all likely pass through your yard at high altitudes. Backyard feeders rarely draw ducks, but I'm betting a skein of Mallards trace a beeline through your air space. Backyard feeders rarely draw geese either, but I'm betting a chevron cuts through your yard's third dimension.

In my area, November logs thousands of waterfowl on the move, splashing down in wetlands, lakes, and rivers. Wintering geese forage in harvested grain fields or newly emerged

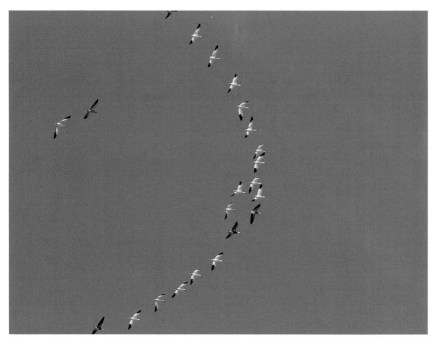

Snow Geese, as well as pelicans, cormorants, and some other species, frequently fly in V formations.

wheat fields, seeking the safety of water for resting. Wintering ducks, on the other hand, forage and loaf in inches-deep waters. I'm guessing some such areas might be within flight of your backyard.

WHY DO BIRDS DO THAT?
Why Do Some Migrants Fly in V Formations?

Nothing marks waterfowl migration more visibly in most people's eyes than the V flight formations of Canada Geese. Other birds also migrate in chevrons. Some say V patterns create a current of air, easing flight for birds along the ever-widening line. Others debunk the idea, claiming air currents don't flow that well that far. Instead, formations likely aid communication. Have you noticed? Sky-high honking sends your eyes searching, squadrons heard long before seen. Ornithologists identify more than a dozen communicating goose calls, used mostly in flight, perhaps qualifying them as one of the planet's most talkative creatures.

Any yard can tout waterfowl, albeit some yards more than others. Our neighbor's farm pond, the only body of water within sight of our yard, expands opportune habitat in the first and second dimensions. Its small size precludes flocks, but occasional migrants like Hooded Merganser and Blue-winged Teal splash down or wing over. Once, a Common Goldeneye startled me from lethargy, sending me scurrying for binocs. Along with Mallards, I also see an occasional gaggle of Canada Geese.

But the third dimension can increase anyone's list, no water necessary. In fact, Snow Geese and White-fronted Geese both appear on my yard list. Neither would ever sit down in my yard or anywhere near here, but there, up in the third dimension, they're regulars.

Listen. And look up!

My favorite waterfowl, though, differs dramatically from typical ducks. The Wood Duck is one of only a couple of ducks that nest in trees. Not in a sticks-and-grass affair wedged in a tree fork, but inside a tree, in a cavity. Given the right habitat, this duck may nest in your yard. And an artificial tree cavity in the form of a nest box near water may bring it to your doorstep—as it did mine. They whistle their comings and goings early morning and late evening during breeding seasons, but in November I hear them only when I've startled them from their secretive winter hangouts.

NOTABLE BEHAVIOR **Brutal Beginnings**

Within twenty-four hours of hatching, baby Wood Ducks heed mom's call and jump to the ground. Since woodies can't chisel out their own nest cavities, they must accept "found" cavities that may be forty feet up. Since ducks don't feed their babies, ducklings must feed on their own—immediately. So, down they must come, plop. When mom calls, ducklings jump, one by one, stubby wings useless, bouncing where they land, tumbling over and over. But they appear unhurt, right themselves immediately, and scurry to mom's calls.

Wood Ducks tend to disappear in early summer, having hatched their broods and waddled off with them somewhere elusive. They like our nest boxes, designed just for them, mounted in the shallows of the neighbor's pond. Woodies have nested there year after year.

Drake Wood Ducks surely win the prize for most handsome bird.

One year I counted twenty-one ducklings—surely the result of multiple females, perhaps unable to find nest cavities of their own, "dumping" all their eggs in one box. But the momma who led the just-hatched crowd into the willows that sunny June morning herded them carefully away from another watchful female. Maybe some ducklings were hers. Maybe not.

HABITAT—YOURS AND THEIRS
Nest Boxes Bring 'Em Home

Wood Duck nest boxes mounted only a few feet above water make ducklings' introduction to the world a bit less brutal. Given the shortage of usable natural cavities, Wood Ducks readily accept man-made boxes. (See page 49 for specifications.)

Goose, Goose, Duck

But back to the third dimension and the magnificent migrant waterfowl masses in your sky-high yard.

November's rising overhead drama leaves me mouth agape, in awe of the vast numbers and the breathtaking spectacle of migration. But not everyone sees it that way. Among many, Canada Geese get a bad rap. Throughout much of the country, resident goose numbers have exploded, populating—yes, overpopulating—local parks, golf courses, residential lakes, and perhaps your lakeside yard. Many of these nonmigratory "urban geese," however, are supersized subspecies of common Canada Geese. Called Giant Canada Geese, they were once presumed extinct. A tiny population discovered in the 1960s brought numbers back, and giants were reintroduced in urban areas.

Feeding ducks can be detrimental to the health of both humans and ducks, including this Mallard drake (top) and his mate.

For protection, a Canada Goose pair keeps its flightless goslings between them.

FEEDER FOCUS   **Breadcrumbs for Ducks in the Park**

Some folks take kids to the park to feed ducks and geese. Don't. It's bad for people; it's bad for ducks and geese. Here's why. Waterfowl poop. A lot. Runoff washes waste into nearby ponds creeks, or rivers. Feces promote algae blooms and starve aquatic plants of oxygen. Worse, feces contain high levels of bacteria, such as E. coli, a cause of serious human illness. If ducks or geese leave food, the scraps mold, posing yet another disease threat.

But here's the nitty-gritty: No bird has a digestive system that can process bakery goods. Sugar, salt, and additives cause birds' eggshells to crack. Even if you avoid stale cookies and bread, feeding anything—even healthy grain—causes waterfowl to congregate, increasing the risk for disease—yours and theirs.

Skip feeding wild ducks or geese.

Here's what happened next. Larger and lazier than their smaller cousins, giant Canadas prefer not to migrate. And mostly don't. If adults don't migrate and teach their offspring the route, however, youngsters become permanent homebodies.

Now do the math. Most geese lay five or six eggs. Within three years after the first pair mates, 128 geese could easily be strutting through that single urban setting. Extrapolate the number over each pair's typical thirty-year lifetime. Add the other pairs that likely flocked with the first pair. And . . . oh, my.

Of course, not all adults raise six goslings. Some die or don't mate. And not all goslings survive. Predators thin the brood. Still, the potential for troublesome overpopulation of non-migratory geese boggles the mind—and stymies golf course and park caretakers as well as homeowners along lakefronts.

Holding ponds, the housing-development contractor's alternatives to storm sewer systems, often exceed ten acres and typically remain open long after outlying bodies of water freeze. You may live on or near such a body of water, lake-front lots priced at a premium. Your habitat is perfect goose habitat.

Withdrawing the All-Goose Welcome Mat

If your yard adjoins water, nonmigratory Giant Canada Geese may wander your yard, making more of a mess than you'd like. Your mowed yard, however, creates perfect goose habitat. They love grazing in short grasses, loafing along the way. So prevention is obvious: Don't mow to water's edge. Maintain a 6-foot-wide strip of taller grasses or other vegetation between your yard and the low-water level. Geese will unlikely cross the border.

In short, the wild, migratory Canada Goose is not the same being as the nonmigratory urban goose, the waterfowl that fouls. Instead, the splendid, elegant Canada Goose, the grand wild creature of northern breeding grounds—these are the impressive winged creatures that leave me mouth agape, in awe of the vast numbers and the breathtaking spectacle of migration through my sky-high yard this month.

Scene Changes

Wetland restoration has changed the landscape—and the birds. For instance, certain waterfowl sightings have now lost their "gee whiz" factor. Forty years ago, I never saw Snow Geese or White-fronted Geese in southern Indiana. Last winter, given wetlands restoration, twenty-four thousand snows and twelve thousand white-fronts loafed in a single local marsh. Until recently, a Tundra Swan sighting would have been attributed to faulty vision—or imbibing. Now, each winter, more settle here, until last winter, one thousand arrived in mid-November. I wonder how many will overwinter here this year.

The results of wetland restoration reiterate an important principle: If we restore habitat, birds will come. For birds, it's always about habitat. Always. Even in your yard.

Watching (Unusual) Waterfowl

During a warm, sunny, late-autumn day, a walk in your closest city or county park may treat you to great birds. And if there's water, the treat may include some unusual waterfowl, well beyond the typical ducks and geese. On one particularly euphoric November day, we walked the circuitous paths around and over the hills and along the lake at our local park. Along the way, of course, I watched birds flying wild and free within the park's natural habitat, a habitat I strive to imitate in my yard.

Blue Jays, Wild Turkeys, Deer, and the Future of Oak Forests

Vast oak forests that early this month turned from green to scarlet, then bronze and leather-brown, took root years ago, planted by unsuspecting farmers: Blue Jays. Their practice of caching seeds and nuts—including acorns—for winter feeding "planted" thousands of acorns. Watch a jay tend its "crop." It carries an acorn (several, if they're small enough to stuff multiples into its craw) to a likely safe spot, drops it to the ground, furtively watches for another jay that might spy on its endeavors, beak-rakes open a suitable hole, drops the acorn, and covers it neatly—securely, it hopes.

Wild Turkeys eat an enormous number of acorns as part of their regular diet.

As winter wanes, the jay, having remembered most of its caches, dines in abundance. But sometimes, it forgets a safely stored morsel. Or maybe it stored an excess. The neglected acorn, carefully "planted," takes root, grows. The forest begins.

Enter Wild Turkeys. Now that reintroduction numbers have mushroomed, more and more turkeys forage forest hillsides for food. Their favorite? Acorns. Scratching deeply, they scour clean viable acorns that might produce the next oak forest.

But assume both the jays and turkeys miss a few acorns. Enter the now-overabundant reintroduced white-tailed deer. Nothing tastes more scrumptious to them than succulent oak saplings. Nipped to the ground, the sapling is no more.

Mother Nature's balance, now imbalanced by human intervention and reintroductions, may ultimately result in oak forests being only a vague memory.

On the big lake, a squadron of Canada Geese patrolled open water while Northern Shovelers, Mallards, and Ring-necked Ducks dozed along the far shore, camouflaged by shady steep banks, fallen trees, and mats of floating leaves. Two American Coots flashed white bills against slate-gray bodies, bobbing cork-like between fishing dives. The resident (but non-native) Mute Swan added a splash of pizzazz floating by.

Then, odd movement caught my eye. Something dove, disappeared, and didn't come up. We stopped. Waited. Finally, 30 feet away, a small tawny-brown bird popped up from the deep. Southern Indiana marks the northern edge of Pied-billed Grebe winter range, but they grace our waters more frequently in fall than during winter's depths. And here they were in November—two of them.

The species name, *Podiceps*, means, appropriately, "rump footed," because when grebes swim, their feet seem to sprout from their rumps. These stocky little foot-long grebes wear white chicken-like bills encircled in black, thus the name "pied-billed."

Pied-billed Grebes have an amazing ability to sink like tiny submarines.

As we watched, stock still, one grebe went under. It didn't dive; it dropped straight down, submarine-like, a defense unique among grebes. By squeezing air from lungs and feathers, they sink, submerging 12-ounce bodies, eyes at water level, appearing every bit like some miniature mystical sea serpent lurking in the deep.

Or they dive, headfirst. And they stay down for what seems like too long, swimming surprising distances, fishing along the way, before resurfacing.

Pied-bills, odd little birds that they are, intrigue me. Common and widespread, they hide by being avian hermits. Clumsy on land, they rarely haul out. But they're equally clumsy in air and rarely fly. Becoming airborne takes great effort, sprinting great distances across water, finally lifting off, flying low, rowing with weak, labored wing beats. So they prefer water, rarely leaving, not even to nest, instead building floating nests, anchored to reeds near open water.

In spite of their clumsiness on land and in air, grebes live the fine life on and in water— floating, sinking, diving, fishing, and long-distance underwater swimming. Watching them adds a spark of delight to any November walk in the park.

PROBLEM SOLVER   **Who's Who in the Books**

The dandy little book you hold in your hands has introduced you to about one hundred birds, especially those common to many backyards. Depending on where you live, however, you may have different birds frequenting your backyard. And no matter where you live, eventually you'll likely expand your horizons from birds in your yard to those in your area, state, even the entire continent. Thus, you'll do well to invest in a field guide to birds, commonly called a "bird book."

More than twenty field guides to U.S. birds line bookstore shelves. How to choose? Consider these suggestions.

- Depending on how much you travel, choose either a regional guide (eastern or western United States) or a North American guide. State guides tend to shortchange birders watching migrants.
- Consider the book's size and portability. If you use the book only at your kitchen table, you might choose a different book than you if you plan to use the book in the field.
- Field guides use one of two styles: photographs or artists' illustrations. The advantage of illustrations is consistency—in position and light. Compare before you choose.
- A good field guide shows all plumages: male, female, immature bird, and where applicable, winter versus summer plumages. Check before you buy.
- Look for range maps that make sense and show summer, winter, and migratory ranges for each species.
- Evaluate text. Some guides offer little or no narrative to identify a bird's habitat or describe its behavior.
- Finally, pick three birds, ones you know well, and compare how each guide treats them. The comparisons should help you choose the guide best for you.
- Your local library may have multiple guides available to borrow. Consider using several for a period of weeks before you make your final choice.

When Things Go "Hoo" in the Night

Sometimes, late-autumn backyard birding turns auditory, with not even a glimpse of the singer of song. Especially at night. And North America's most talkative November nighttime singer belts a song more yowl than aria.

Given the tendency of this common, widespread singer to hoot from the bowels of dark woodlands, it's no wonder Barred Owls carry an aura of mystery and suspense. Amid November's chill during a starry, shadow-filled night, the singer may be a benign wise old owl; but it can scare the blue lightning out of a first-time witness. Like last night.

A full moon crept through bare-armed trees. Clear skies promised brittle temps—a brisk night, quiet, peaceful, star-bright. Outside, I lingered among strong moon-cast shadows, listening to the quiet, peering through bare branches at the North Star, enjoying the faint smell of fireplace wood smoke.

HABITAT—YOURS AND THEIRS
Owl Food in Your Yard

Owls eat live critters. Think mice, voles, frogs, other small reptiles and mammals. To attract owls, your habitat must harbor their preferred foods. Tall grasses and brushy tangles offer habitat for the small critters, and adjoining short-grass areas give owls the space to snare them.

Suddenly, a startling yowling, screaming duet shattered the quiet. Two of them. Barred Owls. Just across the garden in the woods. The crescendo exceeded their recent quiet late-afternoon chit-chat. A serious discussion, this—maybe even an argument. Loud. Rising and falling. Then, slowing from allegro, growing quiet, finally silent. They made me smile.

The duet having ended, I checked the full moon once more and returned indoors, happier for the glimpse into another being's life.

Memorable Moments: Sandhills in My Third Dimension

I'm stepping back now, forty years back, to another memorable crisp November day. Sunny and bright, the day welcomed late fall yard work. Jeans and sweatshirt weather. Calm winds. I remember exactly where I stood, the direction I faced. The memory replays in my mind as clearly as the day I first heard them, long rolling trumpets, sky-high birds calling to one another, the eleven of them. When I saw them, up in our yard's third dimension, they were nothing I recognized. Big. Really big. Long necks leading; long legs trailing. Gray. And trumpeting.

I watched. They wheeled, made a U-turn, disappeared, still trumpeting, dropping out of sight beyond the southern tree line. An eerie feeling made me believe they'd made that U-turn in my third-dimension just to introduce themselves. My field guide said Sandhill Crane. A life bird. Right in my own sky-high yard. Since then, I've seen thousands, but none so awesome—or so memorable—as those first eleven.

BIOLOGY BITS   **Sandhills on the Move**

In migration, Sandhill Cranes fly in loose V formations, at 5,000 to 12,000 feet, 15 to 50 miles per hour. Impressive birds, sandhills migrate to Tennessee and south from summer breeding grounds in the northern fringes of Minnesota, Wisconsin, Michigan, Idaho, and Montana, as well as Canada and into the Arctic Circle. There, they seek out rolling marshy tundra devoid of anything more than scrubby trees. Here, they seek corn stubble (for foraging) surrounding wetlands (for safe roosting).

Sandhill Cranes mate for life and can live twenty years or more. Based on DNA testing and their nearly 3-million-year-old fossils, scientists estimate sandhills to be among the

Sandhill Cranes in flight joined my yard list by virtue of my birding the third-dimension.

world's oldest living birds, a species that has witnessed the earth's evolution. Like most birds, however, today these stately creatures face threats of habitat destruction, particularly of migratory staging areas. May we have sense enough to protect these ancient dignitaries, may our progeny thrill to their dance, and may they grace your third dimension.

In flight, of course, I missed their charming bushy tails, reminiscent of a Victorian lady's bustle, a feature defining an unmistakable profile. Only the adult's red "cap," actually a featherless forecrown, accents the gray. Statuesque, they stand over 4 feet tall and walk, grazing, with a stately tread, moving slowly with the group. Rarely alone, they instead feed in family groups of three to five or in colonial groups of up to several hundred. They typically roost, standing in shallow water, in groups of thousands or even tens of thousands.

In flight, their seven-foot wingspans make them a formidable sight. They fly short distances in single file but long distances in V-formation, their in-flight calls, constant resonant bugling trills, carrying a mile. Oh, how I remember!

To birds, windows reflecting the great outdoors appear to be passageways to safety, shelter, or additional feeding grounds.

Killing Window Kills

Dreary gray days of winter become the norm here by late November—maybe earlier or later where you live. On overcast days of any season, human habitat becomes charged with danger for birds. I'm talking about windows. Every backyard birder's heart sinks at that *thunk* against glass, the unmistakable sound of a bird flying full tilt into a window. We dash to check. Did the bird strike only a glancing blow and fly on? Is it in a heap on the ground, dazed, a target for predators? Or, fear of all fears, is it dead?

Birds don't see houses as buildings with windows. They see obstructions with passageways. Of course they recognize a solid wall for what it is. But that window, reflecting foliage and clouds, looks like a passageway through the wall—an avenue to another feeding territory or a means of escape from predators. And so, *thunk* into the "passageway" they go.

HABITAT—YOURS AND THEIRS   **Operation Rescue**

If a bird crashes into your window, respond to the emergency. A stunned bird makes easy lunch for predators. Rescue the victim; place it in a small cloth-lined box, maybe shoebox sized, lid in place. Bring the box indoors; keep the bird warm; give it time for quiet recuperation. After several hours, if it's still daylight, take the box outside, lid in place, and slowly open it. If the bird has recuperated, it will take immediate flight. If not, but it's still alive, check with a local wildlife rehabilitator for advice. Contact a veterinary office, zoo, or nature preserve for area licensed rehabbers.

Reports tell the story. Hundreds of species suffer fatalities at our windows, totaling a staggering 900 million North American birds each year. Imagine our world with 900 million more birds alive, singing, sharing backyard habitats with us all.

The crisis extends beyond our backyards. Migratory birds crash into tall buildings during night flights, and a single skyscraper can kill two hundred birds in a single night—indiscriminately, including threatened and endangered species. In fact, only habitat destruction kills more birds than do windows.

NOTABLE BEHAVIOR   **Titmouse at the Window**

Last week, a titmouse lit on my kitchen windowsill. I feared for it. Dense spider webs cut a diagonal across the window's bottom corner, and already the web snared moths and flies. Spider egg sacks clung amid tightly woven strands. Tougher than iron, these spider webs— or so I've always heard. What if the titmouse, too, became snared, wings tangled, preventing its safe flight? Oh, how I wished I'd cleaned the window. I had good intentions.

But then the titmouse yanked free a captive moth, flew off, pecked apart lunch. Then it returned for an egg sack, tugging and fluttering until the sack, too, broke loose. Methodically, the titmouse cleaned the web of every shred organic, a tasty selection, easily had. Ah, there's more to life than clean windows—especially to a bird's life.

The windows in our homes, however, kill vast numbers of birds simply because there are vast numbers of houses that feature vast expanses of glass—and vast reflections of the great outdoors. Any of our favorite yard birds, startled by a cat, hawk, or other danger provoking frantic flight, can flee headlong, smack into the reflection. In full flight, a bird strikes glass with fatal force, breaking wings, beak, and/or neck.

Experts agree: Any solution to window kills involves breaking up reflections, eliminating passageways.

HABITAT—YOURS AND THEIRS
Decals Deter Window Kills—Not

Eliminating window kills by sticking hawk-shaped decals on the glass simply does not work. Birds don't look at decals and think, "Hawk." It's only a small obstacle in the passageway through your window, an obstacle that they must fly around. In fact, my neighbor reported that a dove crashed into her window precisely between two hawk decals.

In order to break up reflections, decals of any shape—hawks, dots, butterflies or stars— will work, but only if spaced uniformly, two to four inches apart, over the window's entire outer surface, thus transforming the window into an obstacle birds will see and avoid. That's a bunch of decals and probably not what you want on your windows.

While experts agree there's no perfect solution for homeowners, the best solution is covering the entire window surface with netting. A reasonable substitute, probably less obstructive, is regular window screen. Other suggestions include the following:

- Place feeders and birdbaths within 3 feet of windows so that, should birds fly into the window, they will be moving too slowly to cause serious harm.

- Conversely, place feeders and baths a safe distance from windows so that departing birds have adequate space to avoid windows.
- Try vertical exterior tape strips placed about 12 inches apart.
- Hang obstacles like tree limbs, strips of cloth, or strings of feathers in front of the glass.
- Arrange interior vertical blinds with the slats half open.
- For those of us who don't like to do windows . . . dirty windows don't reflect. Excuse enough for me!

Conservation Corner: Everyday Ways to Help Birds

Today and every day, according to The Nature Conservancy, you can help protect birds. Perhaps at this point, the following suggestions seem redundant. Still, knowing that yet another major conservation group offers these words of wisdom makes them all the more authentic.

At home, practice the following:

- Put up a bird house.
- Add a year-round water source.
- Put out, fill with appropriate food, and maintain bird feeders, placed safely to avoid predation.
- Skip the lawn chemicals and other pesticides.
- Take action to eliminate window kills.
- Plant native plants.
- Think "lights out" in your high-rise office or apartment by turning off lights or closing blinds, especially during migratory months.

Away from home, do the following:

- Stay on trails and away from restricted areas, especially during nesting season, and keep dogs on leashes.
- Buy shade-grown "bird friendly" coffee.
- Identify neighborhood birds and teach young people their value.
- Help local nature preserves and/or parks improve wildlife habitat.
- Get involved with local and backyard monitoring projects and clubs.

Things to Do in November

- Add feather strings, netting, or other protection against window kills.
- To discourage non-native birds at feeders, choose seed mixes without cracked corn.
- Check yard and neighborhood for berries and plan spring plantings to add number and variety.
- Check the yard's third dimension to witness migrating waterfowl.
- Add a nest box or two to backyard habitat for cavity nesters to use as winter roost boxes.
- Keep leaves cleared from water features to avoid sour water.
- Evaluate your backyard's nesting suitability by surveying abandoned birds' nests (but leave them where they are).

39 Yard Birds in November

First hard freeze, then Indian Summer; almost no rain since July; during month's last week, three inches of rain, then 24°F.

Turkey Vulture
Cooper's Hawk
Red-shouldered Hawk
Red-tailed Hawk
Killdeer
Mourning Dove
Red-bellied Woodpecker
Downy Woodpecker
Hairy Woodpecker
Northern Flicker
Pileated Woodpecker
Blue Jay
American Crow

Carolina Chickadee
Tufted Titmouse
White-breasted Nuthatch
Carolina Wren
Eastern Bluebird
Hermit Thrush
American Robin
Northern Mockingbird
European Starling
Cedar Waxwing
Yellow-rumped Warbler
Eastern Towhee
Fox Sparrow

Song Sparrow
White-throated Sparrow
White-crowned Sparrow
Dark-eyed Junco
Northern Cardinal
Red-winged Blackbird
Common Grackle
Brown-headed Cowbird
Purple Finch
House Finch
Pine Siskin
American Goldfinch
House Sparrow

SPECIES PROFILE

MOURNING DOVE

VITAL STATS
Length: 12 in.
Wingspan: 17–19 in.
Weight: 4.3 oz.

Mourning Dove

Found nearly everywhere except in deep woods, they fly fast and bullet straight but can dart, dip, and wheel like drunkards. They're also the most frequently hunted nonwaterfowl bird species in North America.

Named for their soulful, lamenting song, Mourning Doves, the Rodney Dangerfields of the backyard, don't get much respect. Folks seem either to love 'em or hate 'em, without much middle ground.

NAME THAT BIRD

Zenaida macroura (Mourning Dove): The dove family name honors a princess. Princess Zenaide was the wife of Prince Charles Lucien Jules Laurent Bonaparte, a French ornithologist. *Macroura* comes from the Greek and means "long tailed," as the Mourning Dove's tail is much longer than that of other doves. Its common name, "mourning," refers to the bird's sad song.

Now, in late November, they've mostly abandoned our rural yard. During spring, summer, and fall, multiple pairs have cuddled, cooed, and snoozed on sunny perches across the yard, sometimes basking ill-advisedly below the arching branches of the beautyberry bush. There they were targets for an ever-vigilant Cooper's Hawk that would power-fly through, aiming for lunch. As relaxed, sleepy, and sun-soaked as they seemed, however, the doves rarely fell to the Cooper's aim.

BIRD TALK: WHO'S CALLING?

Male Mourning Doves "sing" a sad song sometimes confused with an owl's call. Described as *cooah-coo-coo-coo*, the second syllable rises in tone while the first and last three syllables are consistently monotone.

FOOD FARE

FOOD FARE

Unlike many birds that relish a fine fat bug, vegetarian doves choose grain year round—agricultural grain, weed, and grass seeds—and occasional berries. The lesson? If you wish to limit doves at your feeder, avoid small grains, like millet or millet mixes. Because of their bill structure, doves can't crack sunflower seeds, and they typically don't swallow them whole.

Finally, snooze time over, as if at some secret signal, one after another, they'd stretch one wing and then the other, and take their signature head-bobbing walk from the bushes to seed spills under the feeders to search out and scarf down lunch. Youngsters followed, bobbing along behind.

As ground feeders, doves instinctively recognize their dinnertime exposure to predators. So they stuff themselves quickly, cramming vast quantities of seeds into an enlarged portion of the esophagus called the crop. Then they retreat to a safe perch, hunker down, pushing their heads back against their shoulders, and snooze, couch potato–like, digesting the feast. One study found 17,200 bluegrass seeds in a single crop.

As a result of their having crops, doves and their pigeon cousins are the only birds that feed their babies "milk"—a substance both males and females create within their seed-filled crops. Now there's a bit of trivia for backyard birders!

Now that winter has set in, however, doves have moved out of the yard, flocking where abundant food awaits. Rather than search among the slim pickings in my yard, where I've kept the spilled seeds cleaned up in an effort to protect avian health, they've moved to the fields. When I drive by, they lift up, fifty or one hundred together, their crops no doubt bulging with spilled soybeans and corn.

I miss them. Oh, I know they'll return to the yard come spring, setting up housekeeping, or when snow covers the fields. But right now, I miss them.

NEST NOTES

Nest Site: in wide variety of habitats, usually in bushes, shrubs, or brushy trees, 10–25 ft. up; may nest atop another bird's abandoned nest; depending on climate, may nest year round

Nest Construction: flimsy platform of twigs, lined with grasses, often see-through construction

Eggs: 2 eggs, 1–6 broods, incubated 14 days

Fledge: 14 days after hatch; parents feed fledglings additional 4 weeks

They're pretty birds, I think. Their silky brown-gray frocks look prim, proper, neatly pressed; their glowing blue eye rings merit the avian award for best eye makeup, and a breeding male's pink iridescent neck spots would be a hard match among fine jewels.

Perhaps my dad taught me to love the birds. He never thought they should be hunted, and he lovingly fed them the shelled corn they adore. I remember his keeping count of the birds, sharing his delight from time to time that he'd lost count somewhere around three hundred or so. In his yard, during deep snows, he'd shovel a path from the grain shed to a feeding area outside the kitchen window. Every day, he'd scatter a 5-gallon bucket of shelled corn, and every day the doves would clean it up. His diaries record the counts.

Eurasian Collared Dove

SPOTTING THE SPECTACULAR   **Hunter's Target**

Annually, about 1 million hunters take 20 million doves nationwide, representing about 7 percent of the fall population. One of the ten most abundant birds in the United States, the Mourning Dove population likely exceeds 350 million birds, and it is the third most frequently reported bird in many states during the annual Great Backyard Bird Count.

Because Mourning Doves dart and frequently fly a zigzag pattern, they're a difficult target for hunters, a challenge that makes the birds more enticing game. Regardless of personal opinion about hunting in general or hunting doves in particular, there's no cause for concern about doves' conservation status. Hunting is carefully controlled, hunters licensed, and bag limits enforced.

ID CHECK   **Mourning Dove**

Unless you live in the southern tier of states, any dove in your yard is likely a Mourning Dove. Look for these characteristics:
- A foot-long gray-beige bird with long, pointed tail
- Ground feeder and vegetarian
- *Cooah-coo-coo-coo* call during breeding season

Because the Eurasian Collared Dove (*Streptopelia decaocto*) is expanding ever northward, however, check for two important differences between it and the Mourning Dove. First, the Eurasian Collared Dove is about another 5 inches longer than a Mourning Dove. And a Eurasian Collared Dove wears a black "half moon" band on the back of its neck.

SPECIES PROFILE

CANADA GOOSE

VITAL STATS
Length: 29.9–43.3 in.
Wingspan: 50–66.9 in.
Weight: 106–317 oz.

Canada Goose

In spite of the apparent grammar glitch, they're Canada Geese, not Canadian Geese. In spite of the "Christmas Goose" reference to fine dining, they're muscular, brawny guys, powerful fliers who can withstand the rigors of migration. And in spite of the pesky behavior of nonmigratory golf-course geese, I'm enamored of wild geese, the magnificent, migratory flocks. Majestic. Loyal to family. Keen eyed. Stalwart. Protective. Sleek. And beautiful.

But not everyone agrees. The story goes back to 1962 in Minnesota. In the early 1900s, Giant Canada Geese were thought to be extinct or nearly so, populations decimated by over-hunting and habitat loss. Then, a small flock found in Minnesota allowed officials to reintro-duce the birds to parks and cities. Big mistake. Since no one taught these geese to migrate, they didn't. And don't. And never will.

Those are the bad guys, the ones that have become pests on golf courses. And, tragically, at airports. Our fault, not the birds'.

NAME THAT BIRD
Branta canadensis (Canada Goose): *Branta* refers to the dark, or burnt, color of the bird's plumage, and *canadensis* refers to Canada, where the wild birds breed. The bird's common name, "goose," comes from the Anglo-Saxon word for these birds.

But the truly wild Canada Geese, those native to the lands where they still live, the ones that migrate as Mother Nature intended—ah, those are elegant birds.

A spring visit to a northerly wetland finds Canadas pairing, scouting nest sites, and claim-ing territory. Mated twosomes eye me through cattails and sedges, the female settled on her nest, neck crooked back against her shoulder, while her partner stands tall, neck stretched, ever vigilant, gauging my proximity and my potential threat. If I get too close, the male will hiss, neck extended, parallel to the ground, and threaten me, bill wide open. It can bite, hard, so I'll certainly respect its territorial boundaries. So will others of its kind.

NEST NOTES
Nest Site: on the ground on an elevated spot near water
Nest Construction: grasses and other vegetation from immediate area, lined with down
    from female's breast
Eggs: 2–8 eggs, 1 brood, incubated 25–28 days
Fledge: leave nest immediately but fly 42–50 days after hatch

Humans could do worse than take lessons from Canada Goose families. Male and female protect their goslings both on land and in water. On land, one adult serves as sentinel while others feed, keeping youngsters corralled using quiet little grunts and clucks. On water, one adult swims ahead and the other behind as youngsters follow the lead, all in line. Unfortunately, turtles can clamp onto a gosling's foot and pull it under until it drowns, while adults remain helpless—circling, calling, frantic, frustrated, but helpless. It's more than I can stand to watch.

BIRD TALK: WHO'S CALLING?
One of the most "talkative" of birds, Canada Geese emit more than what we hear as honks. Nevertheless, that is their signature call, both on land and in flight. They hiss when they or their goslings are threatened.

The Canada Goose's molt occurs with remarkable timing to further support family togetherness. Adults molt their flight feathers during the time they're raising young, so the entire family is grounded. By the time the youngsters mature sufficiently for flight, the adults have their new flight feathers. Everyone lifts to the skies together—mom, dad, and all the kids.

SPOTTING THE SPECTACULAR
Homebodies in Action

While Canada Geese don't breed until they're about three years old, females ready to lay eggs lead their mates back to the area where they were born. With few exceptions, females will return to the same nest site year after year.

Monogamous birds, Canada Geese remain loyal, even in injury, until death. If a hunter's shot wounds a Canada and brings the bird down, its mate drops from the flock to attend and stays behind until the wound heals or the mate dies—tender but heart-wrenching to watch. I am certain, in spite of my being accused of carrying too much human emotional baggage, that these two gorgeous creatures feel a caring if not loving bond for one another. Nothing will convince me otherwise.

And those huge flocks? Surprisingly, many if not most birds within the flock are related to one another. Geese live a long time, the oldest recorded at over thirty years, and goslings stay with their parents a full year. The extended family unit, then, can be quite large and perhaps accounts for why individuals within a flock demonstrate such social behavior. They're brothers and sisters, aunts and uncles, kids and grandkids, first and second cousins. Think family reunion in the wetlands.

About 2.6 million Canada Geese fall annually to hunters throughout the United States and Canada. While the total seems astronomical, the bag limits apparently have no effect on goose populations. Numbers remain constant, perhaps slightly increasing.

ID CHECK
Even though Canada Geese include about 11 different subspecies, they differ primarily in size. So look for the following traits:
- Large body, long neck, and webbed feet
- Black neck and head with white cheeks and chin strap, brown back, beige breast
- Loafing near or on water, typically with a mate or, outside breeding season, in large flocks
- Producing honking calls in flight, female's honk higher pitched than male's, thus sounding like a single, two-note call

SPECIES PROFILE

MALLARD

VITAL STATS
Length: 19.7–25.6 in.
Wingspan: 32.3–37.4 in.
Weight: 35.3–45.9 oz.

Mallards, drake (left) *and hen* (right)

If it walks like a duck and quacks like a duck, it must be—a female Mallard, a hen. True! Drakes, or males, don't quack. And other duck species don't quack, either. So, as common and familiar as they are, Mallards throw us a few surprises.

For instance, virtually every domestic duck in the United States traces its ancestry to Mallards, including all-white ducks that paddle across farm ponds and urban lakes. Even domestic ducks that closely resemble wild Mallards differ in size, the domestics being somewhat larger than their truly wild ancestors. In fact, the only current threat to vast Mallard populations lies in their willing and ready hybridizing.

Another surprise comes from Mallards' off-kilter breeding. While most birds gain their breeding plumage in time for spring pursuits, Mallard drakes transform to gorgeous in the fall. That's when Mallard pairs join. For these commoners, courtship lasts all winter. Even though they nest and lay eggs in spring like most other birds, including other waterfowl, Mallards surprise us with their handsome wintertime courtship wardrobe.

NAME THAT BIRD
Anas platyrhynchos (Mallard): *Anas* is the Latin name for duck, and *platyrhynchos* refers to having a broad beak. The common name, Mallard, is an Anglicized Old French word that means "wild drake."

BIRD TALK: WHO'S CALLING?
The female Mallard is the only duck that truly *quacks*. The drake's call is a softer, raspy, *rab*.

Mallards, along with some other birds, also have the ability to sleep with one eye open—literally. And here's an even bigger surprise: These birds have two-part brains that control their two eyes, one part for each eye, so they can sleep with one eye and keep a lookout for potential predators with the other. And I thought being ambidextrous was clever.

Another Mallard surprise greets us in late summer. Then, after breeding season, when their youngsters are all grown up and independent, drakes and hens undergo a complete body molt. For a period of three to four weeks, males cannot fly—at all—because, unlike the

FOOD FARE

Mallards prefer aquatic invertebrates and vegetation, "nodding" as they poke around underwater. They also take grain, seeds, and insects.

NEST NOTES

Nest Site: depression scraped in ground within walking distance of water

Nest Construction: lined with vegetation from immediate area and down from female's breast

Eggs: 6–13 eggs (12 average), 1 brood, incubated 23–30 days

Fledge: leave nest less than a day after hatch; independent 52–70 days after hatch

hens (and most other birds of all species), they molt all flight feathers simultaneously. During that dangerous period, they cower in protected waters, perhaps among cattails, brush, or other vegetation, as far from shore as possible, seeking cover as a protective alternative to flying. While they must feed in shallow water, nodding or doing their humorous bottoms-up maneuver, they typically venture into unprotected shallows only briefly to forage.

Mallards surprise us again when they change their bill color. That's the equivalent of ladies changing fingernail color but without using nail polish. Drakes sport bright yellow bills along with their handsome breeding duds, and hens wear yellow to orange. In other seasons, their bills look greenish to yellowish olive.

Year round, however, adults wear leg and foot color that makes quite a fashion statement. Watch them waddle out of water and you'll get an eyeful of those outrageous orange-red legs and feet.

And a final surprise is the Mallard's stable populations—in spite of apparent threats to their numbers. As the most sought-after and harvested duck in North America with hunters sometimes taking 20 to 25 percent of the fall populations, Mallards still manage to maintain their masses. But they're also threatened by mercury poisoning from treated seeds, by lead poisoning from ingested shot, by habitat degradation, and by oil spills that destroy their feathers' waterproofing and insulating properties.

SPOTTING THE SPECTACULAR

Courtship on the Water

This winter, take time to watch courting Mallards. Maybe you'll catch drakes and hens performing their ritualized courtship. The two face each other, jerk their heads down, the female lowering her head closer and closer to the water. If the "dance" reaches adequate intensity, the drake steps on her back, grabs the back of her head, and mates. Then, he swims around her, nodding, as she baths. Quite a show!

The North American Waterfowl Management Plan, however, implemented in 1986 by United States and Canadian federal governments, set goals for Mallard populations and established restoration, maintenance, and rehabilitation of wetland habitat. The goal was to achieve an autumn flight of 8.7 million Mallards by the year 2000. It happened—with population estimates that year topping 9.5 million. They're in good hands in every state.

ID CHECK

The Mallard, a large dabbling duck believed to be the world's most common and wide-ranging duck, wears distinctive plumage in fall and winter:

- Iridescent green head on fall-winter males
- Central tail feathers that curl up toward back of males
- Brown back and chestnut breast; black rump and under tail
- All-over brownish females

December

I hope you love birds too.
It is economical.
It saves going to heaven.

EMILY DICKINSON

Decenber rings with celebrations, festivities, gift-giving, and all other manner of holiday sights and sounds. For birds, however, this month typically heralds the first serious cold and wind-blown snows, clarification that winter wields its brutality without favoritism. My backyard goes brittle. And birds grow even busier than before.

They must eat more to stay warm, but they have fewer daylight hours to forage. This month measures their endurance with the longest nights of the year. Dark. Numbing cold. Brutal. Mean.

BOTANY FOR BIRDS   ## Cones, Conifers, and Evergreens

Good backyard habitat requires good cover. "Cover" equates with "shelter" in the Big Four of stellar backyard habitat: food, water, shelter, and places to raise young. But cover assumes different shapes and sizes, each serving a different purpose. Think nesting cover, escape cover, thermal cover, roosting cover, storm cover, wind cover, rain cover—and you get the picture.

As cover, evergreens—like pine, cedar, hemlock, holly, juniper, fir—should stand as staples in every backyard bird habitat. Tall or dwarf, round or conical, they fit any yard and stand ready to shelter winter birds against weather and predators. Even in mild winter areas, conifers serve great food—tiny seeds inside cones, berry-cones on red cedar, and berries on holly. Watch for waxwings, robins, cardinals, mockingbirds, and bluebirds in these always-green bed-and-breakfast trees.

Beyond food and shelter, evergreens embrace secure nest sites. Early season nesters find the best protection in evergreens. Later, for a second brood, those same birds can—and usually do—move house and home to then-leafed-out deciduous trees.

Beyond the yard, check the neighborhood. Do public lands, rights-of-way, office or industrial parks, school campuses, nursing homes, your place of worship, or other lands offer a site on which you—or a group of you—can plant a range of evergreens? The birds will thank you.

Many conifers serve as bed-and-breakfast trees, offering not just shelter but also food, including our red cedar trees that produce berries (actually tiny cones) that Cedar Waxwings love.

No backyard bird habitat should be without evergreens to offer shelter from storms of wind, rain, ice, or snow. Favorites in my yard include eastern white pine, Scotch pine, eastern red cedar, shrub juniper, and, pictured here, eastern hemlock, offering shelter to a male Purple Finch.

Yesterday, in early morning's brittle air, I trudged sleepy-eyed through the season's first snow dust, on my way to retrieve the morning paper. Yeah, I'm old-fashioned that way. I still like to hold a newspaper in my hands rather than peer over my coffee at a computer screen. So, off I went. When I approached our little grove of forty-year-old pines, skirted by bushy junipers, activity in the evergreens popped my eyes open. I heard them first—mostly juncos and white-throats. Then, more: the *dee-dee-dee* of two chickadees, the clear bell-like *deeter-deeter-deeter* of a titmouse, and a carol of *hickory, dickory, dickory, dock* from a Carolina Wren. For an instant, I glimpsed flashes of red—two cardinals—then a jay, and a Downy Woodpecker. All busied themselves amid the evergreen boughs, sheltered there from the cold. Nowhere else in the yard was there so much activity—except in the cedars and hemlocks in the lower backyard where winter-visiting Purple Finches have been tucking in to roost.

Had I been reading the morning news online, I would have missed the show!

PROBLEM SOLVER   **Where Are My Birds?**

"What's happened to my birds?" the caller asks, incredulous. "I've always had all these birds, but now I don't see them anymore." The common cry of concern is answered only with possibilities:

Yard changes. Even seemingly innocuous changes in your yard can affect bird populations. Maybe you cleared brush, pruned trees or shrubs, cleared vegetation from a fence, added a patio, widened the driveway. Any of these, especially an accumulation of these, affect habitat.

Neighborhood changes. Birds roam. Your yard is only one stop along a bird's sometimes vast foraging route. So check a half mile in all directions from your house. Do you find new houses, bulldozed and paved lots, trees removed, grasslands destroyed, or brush, vines, or shrubs yanked out? Has someone doused the roadside, field, or yard with pesticides? Any such activity affects your yard's visitors.

Weather changes. Nationwide, weather extremes affect habitat, be it too much or too little rain, hotter or colder than usual temperatures, ice storms or blizzards, forest fires or floods, severe wind storms, tornadoes, or hurricanes. Any—or worse yet, a combination of these—will directly affect birds, their survival as well as their habitat.

Diseases. To reduce the risk of avian disease, feeders must be kept clean. While you may be diligent at this effort, your neighbors—even distant neighbors—may not. Their negligence also affects your birds.

That was yesterday. This morning, though, snow smothered the yard in powder white, temperatures turned all things solid, and wind whipped chill factors to indecent lows. And backyard birding changed.

Bird populations skyrocketed. Behavior dramatized the struggle to survive. Starlings and cowbirds, absent so far this winter, suddenly appeared, and then multiplied. Less obvious but more welcome, cardinals and goldfinches doubled their usual numbers, as did Downy Woodpeckers that gathered in small combative twosomes and foursomes, hitching up the utility pole to a high-mounted pulley-drawn suet basket. At day's end, for the first time, chickadees fed later than cardinals, pigging down another few kernels to help them survive through the night.

HABITAT—YOURS AND THEIRS
Tree Planting for Dollars and Sense

As you plant trees for birds, situate them to help you, too. Evergreens anywhere shelter birds, but those arrayed on the north and west sides of your house cut your heating and cooling bills, standing as windbreaks from prevailing northerly and westerly winter winds and offering shade against summer's heat. Likewise, deciduous trees anywhere feed and shelter birds in summer; but situated on the east and south sides of your house, they bestow shade, cutting air conditioning bills.

Among the snow-day's newly arrived, one mockingbird became three. Battles ensued. Aggressive when defending summer breeding territories, mockers maintain battle mode when defending winter feeding territories. In our yard, one has commandeered both peanut butter feeders and a suet feeder. Nothing else, not even starlings, can sneak through the mocker's line of defense.

A second mocker guards the holly tree with a clever tactical strategy. It lets a scolding flock of robins drive starlings and cowbirds away. Then, as robins tussle among themselves for berries, the mocker takes aim, its brutal bombardment scattering the robin flock. What ensues is a wicked free-for-all in the upper branches.

A third mocker, obviously low bird on the avian totem pole in this three-way life-and-death confrontation for food, defends the cedars. Fortunately, the berry-laden trees offer ample, if not a favorite, buffet.

NOTABLE BEHAVIOR **Cavity Huddles**

Cavity nesters—like chickadees, titmice, and bluebirds—often huddle, but we're not talking football. For birds, to huddle means to join same-bird species, overnight, in a cavity. We know why: Huddling keeps birds warm. But we don't know how: Birds on the bottom might smother, it seems, piling in together as they do.

Keen bird-watchers, however, detect signs of roost-box huddle. Watch for tails slightly curved left or right, bent from conforming to the confines of the cavity, all part of the drama unfolding in wintertime backyards.

While the holly battles rage, I'm drawn to clever little bluebirds. They slip into the holly tree quietly, ease among the berry clusters, and pluck their fill.

But when berrying ends and day turns to dusk, the real bluebird drama begins. One by one, calling along the way, they fly, undulating, to a nest box in our front garden, peer into the cavity, checking, and then, duck inside. Like other cavity nesters, they're also cavity roosters, huddling for warmth. One after another I counted them as eight—yes, eight!—entered, snuggled in, and presumably kept warm for the night. Talk about a family that stays together!

FEEDER FOCUS **Mealworms on the Dinner Plate**

To bluebirds, wiggling mealworms equate to a fine gourmet meal. The worms, actually larva of flightless darkling beetles, served live and squirming, rank high in protein, a boon for breeding birds. Backyard hosts addicted to the mealworm habit sometimes "train" bluebirds to accept regular handouts, increasing bird-watching pleasure. Feeding gourmet, however, costs gourmet bucks, so many hosts order mealworms in bulk online or raise their own.

Eastern Bluebirds, bug eaters during three seasons, turn to berries in winter and especially enjoy American holly berries, slipping in when other birds busy themselves jousting for the best feeding spots.

My personal decision not to offer these tasty treats springs from critics' concerns. They fear that offering a regular mealworm supply outside breeding season, like now, in December, misrepresents the true resources of a habitat, perhaps causing birds to breed where tough times will ensue for supporting a family.

Indeed, handouts can be a great service, perhaps preventing starvation, but it's never as sound as natural native bugs. Make sure your habitat supports lots of bugs, and handouts of mealworms become passé. But if you thrill to the pleasure of the expensive habit, then offer mealworms only when bluebirds are feeding young. Now we're talking dandy-fine supportive services.

December Hummingbirds

By December, most of us Midwestern and East Coast folks have only lingering memories of our beloved Ruby-throated Hummingbirds. I've never had a hummer in my yard past October 23. But while most folks are hanging holiday decorations and dreaming of a white winter wonderland, some folks faithfully continue tending nectar feeders, keeping them fresh, and dreaming of a rare hummer.

Agreed, talk of hummingbirds, frozen birdbaths, and December snow flurries seems incongruous. But sometimes hummingbirds make spectacular appearances this month—not our usual Ruby-throated Hummingbirds, but rather a Western species called Rufous Hummingbird.

Tolerant of cold, Rufous Hummingbirds breed farther north than any other hummingbird species, nesting from southern Oregon to southeastern Alaska. Conventional wisdom says they migrate 3,900 miles southward to winter in southern Mexico, one of the longest migratory journeys (as measured by body size) of any bird in the world. Recently, however, growing numbers of reports throughout the Midwest and along the East and Gulf Coasts have challenged conventional wisdom.

FEEDER FOCUS　　　　　　**Cafeteria Style**

Beyond maintaining nectar feeders for a vagrant hummer or two, consider offering other foods during winter's cold. The more variety your feeders offer, the more birds you'll have. So think "cafeteria" rather than short menu. And consider birds to be like picky kids—they eat only certain things, and they like those things served on their favorite plates. Picky, picky, picky.

In addition to seeds like sunflower, niger, and safflower, and add-ons like suet, nectar, unsalted raw peanuts, and natural unsalted peanut butter, consider offering fruit (apple and orange slices or halves, past-prime berries, rehydrated raisins or cranberries), shelled corn (preferably whole kernel, not cracked), past-prime ear corn, ground beef, cooked unsalted grits.

Also like kids, birds will eat things not good for them. So, avoid serving stale or leftover baked goods like bread, cookies, crackers, popcorn, and cereal. Not only are these foods loaded with salt and sugar, they're empty calories for birds. While birds willingly gobble down the goodies and likely feel full as a result, their systems cannot digest these foods. It's zero nutrition you're serving. You see where this is going. People foods do birds more harm than good.

The Rufous Hummingbird's typical fall migratory path, according to most field guides, stretches down the California Coast into Mexico; and the birds generally wander no farther east than Nevada or Arizona. Growing records, however, document increasing numbers of individuals crossing the high Rocky Mountains and cruising across the Central Plains so that the Southeast Coast notes an influx of these Western birds in early December.

From early fall into early winter, these wayward migrants occasionally show up at Indiana-area feeders—as well as sites closer to the East Coast, maybe including your yard. They're slightly bigger and much feistier than our usual ruby-throats. Part of the curiosity of rufous appearances, however, lies in the behavioral differences between the sexes. For whatever reason, males tend to zip through quickly, often in late summer, feeding only a few days or maybe a few weeks. Even when they show up in November or December, they don't linger.

NOTABLE BEHAVIOR   **Hummer with an Attitude**

The rufous is a hummingbird with an attitude, so much so that some folks label it the terrier of the bird world. Apparently oblivious to its own diminutive size (3 to 4 inches, including bill length), it will attack anything winged invading, or perceived to be invading, its food source. One host told me her visiting rufous cleared the yard of goldfinches. And hummingbird bander Cathie Hutcheson reports a rufous attacking—and winning the battle with—a red-tailed hawk, effectively chasing the hawk from the general area of the nectar feeder.

Females and juveniles, however, live a different lifestyle. Rufous females and juveniles look very much like our ruby-throated females and juveniles—except for the copper wash on their sides and rump. Unlike speedy eat-and-run male Rufous Hummingbirds, females, especially immature females, tend to dawdle, often through December and sometimes into

Female Rufous Hummingbirds closely resemble female Ruby-throated Hummingbirds, especially first-year birds; mature female rufouses like this one show a coppery wash on their sides.

spring. Since rufous hummers nest in the Northwest and upward into Alaska, they're accustomed to the cold. So Midwestern and Eastern early winter temperatures fall within their comfort zone.

Is the rufous changing its migratory pattern? Or has some small population of the species always migrated eastward but done so unheralded? Are there simply more observers, more hummer hosts covering more geography, who watch their feeders more diligently and thus take note of the otherwise obscure presence of a rufous? Are hosts leaving feeders out later and thereby attracting these sometimes late migrants?

No one knows the answers to these questions, but for whatever reason, we're seeing more of them now than in the past. And rufouses have even stayed the winter in snowy, blustery Indiana, departing in early April when the ruby-throats returned. If you play host to one or more rufouses, please report the activity to your state birding association, local Audubon Society, or someone otherwise connected so that scientists can start fitting the puzzle pieces together.

FEEDER FOCUS   **Late-season Hummingbird Feeding**

Because of the growing potential for later hummers, Indiana's DNR Nongame Bird Biologist Dr. John Castrale recommends keeping nectar feeders out until the end of December. So if this year you took your hummer feeder in early, consider next year following that suggested late-in-the-year take-in date; then you, too, may enjoy a beautiful copper-colored visitor to your holiday yard. Your feeders won't keep hummers from migrating, but your nectar might offer a direly needed source of survival for late or wayward migrants.

Raptor Rapture

Backyard changes occur in more places than in the conifers and at the feeders. Sounds change, too. In contrast to the robust dawn chorus of spring, December song soft-pedals to mere ensembles, trios, duets, and often, quiet solos. Blue Jays screech and chortle in a little family ensemble. Dark-eyed Juncos and native sparrows solo-call to one another with an occasional trio of comments. Wrens chatter and *chirr* to one another to stay in touch. And at night, the owls duet.

Ahhh, those owls! I bet you've heard them. They've been talking for some weeks, but the conversation is changing. For them, the heart of winter warms the heart of romance.

As raptors, owls garner the hapless award for most sedentary and territorial of our carnivorous birds. In spite of their habitual all-day naps, though, their nighttime pursuits generate an exclamatory "wow" factor. Part of the "wow" springs from the owls' acoustical ability. They can hear beyond our comprehension. I'm convinced they hear me tiptoeing inside my house, easing toward a door to peer out, hoping to spy them, hooting on location. When I touch the door, all hoots cease. Always.

Of course, if you hunt in the dark of night, when you can't see, then you must hear, and hear well. Keen hearing for owls comes built in. Ears set on the sides of the head, behind the eyes, align slightly asymmetrically, one a bit higher than the other. The asymmetry lets owls pinpoint a sound's source. In addition, the enormous concave circle of feathers called a "facial disk" serves as a parabolic reflector, gathering sounds and channeling them, funnel-like, toward the ears. Amazingly, owls can adjust the feathers in the circle to alter sound, and thus they focus—or refocus—their hearing to specific distances. In short, owls can zero in on a rustle and, in total darkness, dive on a mouse scurrying under leaf litter below undergrowth. The mouse never knows what hits him. And I never get my hand past the doorknob.

WHY DO BIRDS DO THAT?
Why Do Little Birds Get By with Ganging Up on Big Birds?

Little birds that attack owls at roost or hawks on a perch seem to risk their very lives. In an effort to drive away larger birds that have trespassed into their nests or foraging areas, little guys dive and peck with apparent sheer abandon. The larger birds duck but never attack, even though the big guys could easily snatch the little guys and down them in one gulp. So why don't big-guy birds fight back? It's all about conserving energy. Why chase a mere annoyance when a similar exertion, aimed at a different target, could yield a hefty dinner?

PROBLEM SOLVER   Bambi Wears Out His Welcome

White-tailed deer, also nocturnal foragers, regularly invade backyard habitats, but at least where I live, they're less welcome overnight visitors than our owls. In fact, the abundance of deer throughout the eastern United States causes widespread problems—to auto drivers, gardeners, park naturalists, and yes, backyard bird hosts. The critters chomp down favorite bushes, munch off expensive perennials, and trample beds of annuals. Fearing no enemy, they grow brazen, daring to visit yards in full daylight, guzzling birdseed right from feeders. What to do?

Many nurseries now label plants as deer resistant, so consider them if you're planting new or forced to replant. Certain deterrents, however, help keep deer at bay, most notably, in my garden at least, bars of strongly scented soap, cut in quarters, and hung either directly from the plants or from adjoining stakes. Certain other products available at garden centers promise to deter deer, but they usually need reapplication after every rain. Most recently, a friend gifted me with a garden stake topped by a vinyl stylized heron that bobs in the wind, providing enough motion to keep deer at least at arm's length from its action. Combining scent and motion seems to offer at least some deterrent.

Brazen, predator-free white-tailed deer not only eat and trample vegetation, they also raid bird feeders, sometimes in broad daylight.

BIOLOGY BITS   **The Better to See You**

Owls have some of the avian world's biggest eyes. Reason? The better to see in the dark. Nighttime hunters, owls see and hear better than most of their counterparts, and far, far better than humans.

Here's the scoop: Birds' eyes differ dramatically from humans' eyes. First, birds' retinas have about three times as many sensory cells as our human retinas have. Thus, like a camera with three times more pixels, birds enjoy much keener vision than do humans. Owls, specifically, have large retinas that give them not color, but maximum black-and-white vision in very low light.

Second, bird eyes don't move in their heads the way human eyes do. We can move our eyes left to right, up and down, all without moving our heads. Birds, on the other hand, with fixed eyes, must turn their heads. It's a myth, though, that owls can turn their heads 360 degrees. Rather, it's only 270 degrees—still, quite a swivel.

Left: *Unlike most other birds, owls, including this Great Horned Owl, have binocular vision like humans because their eyes face forward. Right: Most birds, including Northern Cardinals, have eyes on the sides of their heads, so they lack binocular vision. Instead, however, they have a broad field of side vision, including, especially among shorebirds, the ability to see behind themselves—a real benefit while feeding on the ground.*

Finally, because many bird eyes sit on the sides of their heads, birds lack binocular vision. Owls, on the other hand, are bestowed with front-facing eyes, like humans. While they lose the peripheral vision that some birds have, owls gain that all-important depth perception through their binocular vision—all the better by which to snare prey on silent wing.

Hearty meat eaters, owls swallow small prey whole, head first, gulping it down in a few swallows. After digesting dinner, they eliminate the indigestible parts—like bone and fur—by regurgitating pellets. Incidentally, as disgusting as it may sound, one of the best ways to get kids excited about birds is to let them dissect an owl pellet, identifying the contents of dinner. The irresistible "yuck" factor draws kids like a magnet.

But back to the wintertime romance. Some nights I hear them, our two resident hoot owls. No such critter named "hoot owl" exists, but the calls merit the moniker. The *hoo-hoo-hoo* kinds of calls belong to one of two big birds: Barred Owls or Great Horned Owls.

But hoot owls aren't our only owls. Others live here, too, hunting in dark of night in their characteristic silent-flight manner. Owls own silent flight. No other bird wears serrated edges on their outer flight feathers, serrations that permit air currents to pass whisper-quiet through, rather than around, feathers. But whisper-quiet doesn't equate with silent. So owls also wear a sound-absorbing velvety wing surface that smothers the whisper. The serration-velvet combination renders flight eerily silent, ghostly, stealthy. So owls also own the night.

These other owls, however, while they're also owners of night, don't earn the "hoot owl" moniker. They don't hoot. Eastern Screech-owls, little guys half the size of Barred Owls, manage a mere horse-like whinny. Short-eared Owls, gracing this area's grasslands only in winter, bark much like a dog. And Barn Owls, now extremely rare here (but maybe not where you live), only hiss or scream—sounds apropos for a haunting Halloween.

Beyond their haunting hoots, our two big owls live fascinating lives. In early fall, mostly monogamous owl pairs, both barred and great-horned, re-establish feeding territories, once and for all chasing away their now-self-sufficient offspring, sending them off to carve out their own life-long territories. Hooting helps owls define boundaries and warn off intruders, including other owls' offspring that might be sneaking through in search of their own new territory.

Short-eared Owls bark rather than hoot, but most of us see them only in winter when they filter south from their Arctic breeding grounds.

Now, in December, though, hooting marks more than territorial battles. It's the onset of mating season, and love is in the air. To find the lovers, look for whitewash on tree trunks and pellets on the ground, or listen for their bickering.

HOW DOES YOUR GARDEN GROW?
Measuring Backyard Success

Given year's end and the potential for New Year's resolutions, December may serve as a good time to take a judgmental look at your backyard habitat. What works? What doesn't? What should be improved? How should/could it be improved?

The following checklist may serve as a guide for your own evaluation.

Backyard Habitat Checklist

All birds, irrevocably tied to the vegetation around them, can live only where vegetation meets their needs for food, shelter, and nesting. The following checklist serves as a guide for creating as much habitat as practical for your space, soil type, and climate zone. Consider additions, replacements, or substitutions.

In general

• Are areas of mowed lawn limited to about 10% of my habitat?

• Are most plants in my yard native to the area?

• Is my yard free of all pesticides and other chemicals?

• Is vegetation varied, from short to sky-high and from dense to open?

• Have I left areas of leaf litter or leaf mulch to supply food for wintering and breeding birds?

Trees

• Does my habitat include one or more of the top five mature trees: native oak, black cherry, willow, birch, or tulip poplar, trees that provide the most food for birds?

• Does my habitat include a wide variety of other native deciduous trees?

• Are native coniferous trees included in my habitat, like pine, spruce, cedar, or fir?

• Does my habitat include native trees like American holly or red cedar that produce berries small enough for birds to swallow whole?

• Where safely possible, have I retained dead or dying trees and branches in order to provide natural cavities?

Bushes and shrubs

• Does my habitat include native shrubs or bushes that produce berries small enough for birds to swallow whole?

• Do some shrubs or bushes offer thorny protection, thickets, or brambles?

• Do shrubs drape to the ground to offer protection for ground feeders and nesters?

• Do most shrubs bloom profusely to offer nectar?

• Does my habitat eliminate exotic invasive bushes and shrubs like autumn olive or Russian olive?

Depending on where you live, owls, among the earliest breeding birds in North America, start nesting in January; thus, snow-covered owls incubating eggs is not an uncommon sight. So, as we humans approach what we think of as the dead of winter, the owls are thinking spring.

BIOLOGY BITS

Nest Recycling

Owls never build their own nests. Instead, they must find other birds' abandoned nests, most likely that of a hawk species. Some owls succeed in locating tree cavities large enough to serve their purposes, usually rotted-out portions that provide a cup adequate to house eggs and chicks.

Vines

- Do vines enhance my habitat's vegetative variety?
- Have I offered vines like wild grape or wisteria to provide nesting materials, food, and nest sites for birds?
- Do some vines' blossoms offer nectar for insects and birds?
- Do some vines provide bite-sized berries for birds?
- Have I eliminated invasive vines like winter creeper and Japanese honeysuckle?

Herbaceous plants

- Does my habitat offer the trio of top herbaceous food producers: native goldenrod, asters, and sunflowers?
- Does my habitat include other native flowering plants that provide nectar for insects and birds as well as seed for birds?
- For vegetative variety, have I included other nectar- or seed-producing perennials?
- Are my flowers planted in drifts and blankets rather than in small clumps or clusters?
- Do I leave the spent flower heads to serve as a food source for birds?

Grass

- Is most of my mowed lawn devoted to paths and borders?
- Where feasible, have I used native no-mow grasses instead of typical exotic lawn grasses?
- Are some grassy areas planted in native prairie or tall grasses and left unmowed?
- Does an out-of-the-way site include a native "weed patch" for food, shelter, and protection?
- Have I set apart unmowed areas with a low border or other designation in order to differentiate between "unmowed" and "untended" to maintain peace in the neighborhood?

And finally

- Have I encouraged my neighbors to join me in the effort to improve habitat, making it healthier for us—and for the birds?

Choose wisely. If an adjoining yard boasts several white pines, for instance, choose an alternate tree for your habitat. Perhaps your property abuts a forest. Consider, then, planting more shrubs and herbaceous plants rather than duplicate trees.

In short, monocultures never attract as many species as multicultures. Go for variety.

Memorable Moments: Habitat Yields "Big Year" in the Yard

Last year went down in my own backyard musings as Big Year in the Yard. Every week, for fifty-two weeks, I rousted myself from bed early and made dinner late, spending innumerable hours searching tree tops, drooping branches, weed patches, thorny brambles, flower gardens, woods edges, berry bushes, blooming vines, grassy spots, and third-dimensional skies, recording every species I saw or heard. Some birds flying high, some foraging low, some in ones and twos, some in noisy flocks, some for only a day, some year-round—I looked for them all. And learned.

WATER WAYS   **Helpful Heater Hints**

Keeping water thawed for winter birds can be simple. For a quick-to-fix heater, place a light bulb in a flower pot and set a shallow dish of water on top. Heat from the light bulb will prevent freezing unless temperatures are especially severe and long-lasting.

Avoid antifreeze or glycerin to prevent freezing. Both are toxic to birds. In fact, avoid any foreign substances. Just water, please. Fresh water.

The year-long exercise made one principle perfectly clear: We see in the yard only those birds that the habitat attracts.

Birds discovered lurking in dense blackberry tangles never foraged among towering bald cypress trees. Birds that bugged among the lofty bald cypress boughs never flipped through leaf litter. Species that scratched through leaf litter never nipped flower buds from black cherry trees. Migrants that chased bugs among the black cherry blossoms never visited feeders. Nectar lovers that fed daily among garden flowers never sought larva tucked in tree bark. Birds that hammered on tree bark never foraged in the weed patch for blossoms or seeds. Birds that scoured seeds from the weed patch never fluttered among treetops for insects. Birds in the deep woods' treetops never visited the flower garden.

WHY DO BIRDS DO THAT?
Why Do Birds Love Poison Ivy "Candy"?

Poison ivy berries (*Toxicodendron radicans*) equate to candy for birds: They love 'em for their rich nutrition. Unlike humans, birds and other wildlife don't suffer from the plant's toxicity. But the avian love of vine extends beyond the berries. The native vine tends to collect autumn leaves, and the resulting tangle houses spiders and other bugs. They, in turn, attract chickadees, titmice, and kinglets throughout the winter. Of course, because some folks suffer severe allergies from poison ivy, caution is in order. In our yard, we limit the vine to the woods and its edges.

Except for year-round residents, almost none of these birds visited feeders. So, what brought them to the yard? Habitat. It's always about habitat.

And the proof? My Big Year in the Yard yielded 114 bird species. Just in my yard. Just in one year. Not until we altered the habitat, however, could we have seen so many species. And so, once again, we come face to face with the undeniable maxim that there's more to attracting birds than feeders and feed.

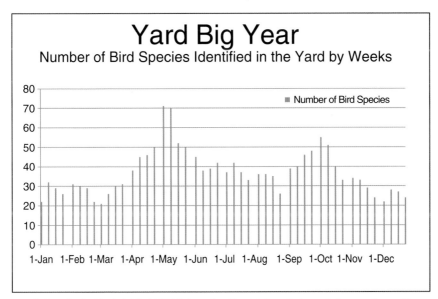

Yard Big Year
Number of Bird Species Identified in the Yard by Weeks

My Big Year in the Yard yielded 114 bird species. The totals varied month by month, peaking during spring and fall migrations.

FEEDER FOCUS   **Make-Your-Own Goop Ingredients**

Birds love suet and find much-needed fat calories in pure suet offerings. Some folks make their own "goop" substitute for suet, but depending on what you make it with, you may cause birds more harm than good. As you choose from among many ingredients, stick to pure lard (never other solid shortenings such as Crisco), avoid anything with salt or sugar, always choose natural and unprocessed ingredients, and select high-fat items. Choose responsibly.

In short, I find it easier—and safer and healthier for the birds—to offer pure suet from the butcher shop or the commercially prepared pure suet blocks.

As the weeks and seasons of the Big Year passed, I grew accustomed to finding certain birds in certain spots in the yard. The little family of Carolina Wrens was almost always scolding among the briars or chirring through the weed patch or low in branches just above the briars and weeds. During migration, I could count on warblers bugging among the cypress trees. In winter, Eastern Towhees kept to the woods' edge where they foraged in leaf litter. Eastern Meadowlarks sang from the tops of the white pines, their songs floating across the neighbor's adjoining hay field. Without the neighbor's farm pond, Great Blue Herons, Green Herons, or even Mallards would have been no-shows. The only time I saw a Scarlet Tanager, it had paused at our mulberry tree to feast on berries. But Summer Tanagers sang daily from the woods where they nested.

HABITAT—YOURS AND THEIRS

Records Tell the Story

Attracting birds to your backyard involves observation, planning, and action. After forty-some years, I'm still watching, learning, and altering the backyard habitat accordingly. But success is easily measured by the birds that visit. Begin recording the birds that visit your own backyard. Record-keeping need not be complicated. You can tick yard birds off in the margins of your field guide. For your convenience, some guides even include a checklist in the front or back.

You can keep a single yard list, a year list, a week list, and if you're truly dedicated, even a day list during busy seasons. I like to keep records of when I first see each of the spring and fall migrants. I'm always amazed that they show up nearly the same time every year, sometimes on the same date. Because of my records, I know when to look for them.

Given your efforts to improve backyard habitat, keeping a list of birds new to the yard helps reward you for your work and, if you're so inclined, lets you point out your successes to others, perhaps encouraging them to improve their own backyard habitats. My records show when I planted what and who came as a result—to visit, to eat, to bathe, to drink, to nest, or to stay.

Or just keep a list—handwritten or electronic—noting the dates on which you first saw a given bird in your yard. Computer software lets your organize lists and update them without writing—or rewriting—anything. Certain websites offer personalized lists that can, in turn, support national databases. Birder's journals give you ample pages for notes and details whether you use a commercially designed illustrated text or a generic spiral notebook.

So keeping records can be as simple or as complicated as you wish. Suit yourself. My own records have evolved over the years from notations in a tattered field guide of the date of a first sighting to the evolution of the book you hold in your hands. Just know that keeping records will make you a better observer, reward you for your efforts, and ultimately make you a more knowledgeable backyard host.

To put it more simply, everything lives somewhere. The corollary, however, is also simple. If I remove the "somewhere," if I eliminate the brush pile, cut down the tangles, mow the weed patch, chainsaw the dead tree, destroy the red cedars, and yank out the flower garden, the birds that lived there leave, too—probably foreshadowing their demise. You see, they likely have nowhere else to go simply because other nearby habitats suitable for their survival are already taken. And birds don't stack up on one another like humans in high-rise condos.

So, as you evaluate your habitat, compare the typical cookie-cutter landscape design with that of a truly bird-friendly habitat—one boasting someplace for everyone, high canopy and low, thorny dense shrubs and open edges, vines and cavities, water and wildflowers. Good backyard habitat is always a work in progress, but armed with an evaluation of present conditions and an image of the goal, you'll be well along with the progress. Indeed, what we do in our yards matters. And, oh my, what a difference we can make!

Creating a Bird-Friendly Yard

Before: Typical Landscape

KEY

 Deciduous tree or shrub

 Coniferous tree or shrub

 Berry-producing tree or shrub

 Tangle, weedy, thorny low vegetation

 Native vines

 Flowering nectar-producing bushes

 Flower beds

 Native perennial flowers

 Water source

 Dead tree snag

 Rotting log

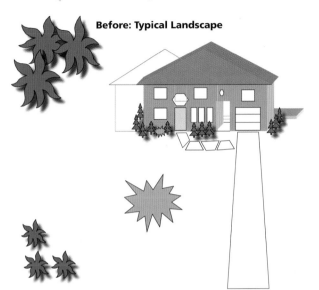

After: Bird-friendly Landscape

In Whose Place Do You Live?

Odd, isn't it, how we think of "our" property, "our" yards, and "our" landscaping? In fact, we're only borrowing this land from our grandchildren and their grandchildren. But the real owners are the birds and all other native wildlife.

In general, small nesting songbirds, like Indigo Buntings, chickadees, and sparrows, need between a half acre and two acres, depending on habitat quality, in order to successfully raise and fledge a brood. Medium-sized birds, like bluebirds and robins, need five to fifteen acres. Large birds, like eagles, sometimes depend on several hundred acres. Territory, however, varies by season, species, region, and habitat quality.

Christmas Bird Count

Across the continent, bird-watchers join forces in late December to report bird populations to the National Audubon Society's database, a citizen-science project that provides scientists with data they could never gather alone. This year's count in my area turned up an unusual Loggerhead Shrike. In other parts of the state, evidence of a Snowy Owl irruption flew into the picture. Rarities make for great fun, but much of the count's importance comes as data are compiled and evaluated for population trends of "regular" birds—how they're doing as an overall population, where they're hanging out, and how our lives are affecting their lives. Consider doing your part. Even if you're not inclined to participate in field counts, your backyard tallies matter. I'm betting no scientists come to your yard to count. Right? Then they need you to count for them—and for the birds.

Conservation Corner: Duck Stamps for Birders

Here's another way to make a difference. In 1929, the Migratory Bird Conservation Commission was established to manage wetlands conservation. A major source of funding for these activities comes from the sale of Migratory Bird Hunting and Conservation Stamps, commonly called Duck Stamps. All proceeds go to acquire vital habitat in the National Wildlife Refuge System. To date, virtually all Duck Stamps have been purchased by waterfowl hunters, but birders enjoy the results. Now, with waterfowl hunting in decline, birdwatchers need to step up to the plate, purchase a $15 duck stamp each year and display it proudly on binoculars, field guide, or auto windshield. Buy them online or at most U.S. Postal Service Offices—for yourself and as gifts for others. Stamps also grant free admission to any National Wildlife Refuge.

Things to Do in December

- Armed with information found here, use the checklist above to measure your backyard habitat's success and evaluate means to improve it.

- Plan your own Big Year in the Yard to learn who lives where and when—and who's missing—using improved understanding to improve habitat.

- Find satisfaction in the knowledge that your habitat improvements really do make a difference, for you, your neighborhood, and the birds.

- Support conservations efforts.

- Watch birds to soothe your soul.

31 Yard Birds in December

Sharp-shinned Hawk	Tufted Titmouse	White-throated Sparrow
Cooper's Hawk	White-breasted Nuthatch	Dark-eyed Junco
Mourning Dove	Carolina Wren	Northern Cardinal
Red-bellied Woodpecker	Eastern Bluebird	Red-winged Blackbird
Downy Woodpecker	American Robin	Common Grackle
Hairy Woodpecker	Northern Mockingbird	Brown-headed Cowbird
Northern Flicker	European Starling	Purple Finch
Pileated Woodpecker	Yellow-rumped Warbler	House Finch
Blue Jay	Eastern Towhee	American Goldfinch
American Crow	Song Sparrow	House Sparrow
Carolina Chickadee		

SPECIES PROFILE

GREAT HORNED OWL

Left: *Male Great Horned Owls typically roost near their nesting mates.* Above: *Great Horned Owls use "found" nests, in this case a last-year's hawk nest, now a bit crowded for mom and her three owlets.*

VITAL STATS
Length: 18.1–24.8 in.
Wingspan: 39.8–57.1 in.
Weight: 32–88 oz.

The largest, strongest, and fiercest of all our owls, the Great Horned Owl generates fear, even among its own kind; for a great horned will rip apart a Barred Owl for lunch and snack on a little screech owl for dessert. And it's the only animal—bird or otherwise—that regularly kills and eats skunk. So there you have it: a dinner companion you'd best respect but can readily do without.

Bully of the bird world, boasting a 4-foot wingspan and nearly 5 pounds of sinew and muscle, a Great Horned Owl new to the neighborhood finds no avian welcoming committee. In fact, to witness the not-in-my-backyard attitude, watch crows. Discovering a roosting great horned, they'll gather clan members from far and wide and mob the napping giant. Crows face their greatest threat from Great Horned Owls—as do baby Bald Eagles and Ospreys. So they're all eager to move it out of the neighborhood.

NAME THAT BIRD

Bubo virginianus (Great Horned Owl): The Latin word for horned owl is *bubo*, while *virginianus* references the region in which the bird was found. Our common name suggests its size (great) and its appearance (feather tufts, or "horns"). The word "owl" comes from Latin meaning "to cry out."

When it comes to hunting, Great Horned Owls take on a single killer focus. Relentless. Tireless. Tenacious. Unyielding. Even though they pursue a variety of prey, some surprisingly large, once the attack is on, there's no turning back. These so-called flying tigers kill their prey or, quite literally, die trying. Be assured, however, that they have ample strength to kill.

They go at it two ways. For larger prey, they attack with strong hooked bill, bite the neck, severing the spinal cord, taking quarry in a single snap. For smaller prey, owls attack with incredibly strong talons, able to exert 500 pounds of pressure per square inch, crushing victims. If owls' talons were big enough to reach around a man's arm, they'd crush his bones.

Given a great horned's penchant for hunting, how does its presence affect your backyard? A resident neighborhood Great Horned Owl will likely keep the rabbit and squirrel populations at bay, perhaps even geese and herons. Mice and vole numbers will decline. Large insects will diminish. More importantly, however, since furry rabbits and squirrels bear a striking similarity to furry domestic cats and small dogs—at least on owl radar—pet owners beware. Protect pets by keeping them indoors or staying with them outside, especially during owl nesting season.

Although Great Horned Owl's eyes are about the same size as ours, they can see ten times better, especially in extremely low light. They hear even better. In fact, that weaving, bobbing head movement common among owls is, in reality, a kind of radar at work. In pitch dark, an owl on its hunting perch near an open area can identify precisely the location of a mouse scurrying under leaf litter. It's dead meat.

FOOD FARE

Great Horned Owls eat mostly mammals but also reptiles and small amphibians, caught and consumed freshly killed.

SPOTTING THE SPECTACULAR
Flying Freight

If a Great Horned Owl kills prey too large for a one-gulp meal, it carries the kill to a safe perch to dine. In an awesome display of power, the great horned grips the hapless body in bone-crusher talons and lifts off on wings with the strength to carry three times its own weight.

BIRD TALK: WHO'S CALLING?

The call is best described as five-syllable *hoo-h'HOO-hoo-hoo,* or *You a-wake? Me, too.* Unlike the Barred Owl, which sometimes calls early and late in the day, the Great Horned Owl rarely vocalizes during daylight. Owls' low-frequency vocalizations allow them to communicate long distances, the sound carrying through the dark to unseen, silent-flying fellows. Males and females "duet," the male's voice identifiable by its lower pitch.

NEST NOTES

Nest Site: wider range of nest sites than any other North American bird, including in trees, snags, and tree hollows but also in cliffs, deserted buildings, sometimes on ground
Nest Construction: does not build nest but often reuses other birds' nests
Eggs: 1–4 eggs, 1 brood, incubated 30–37 days
Fledge: 44–49 days after hatch

ID CHECK

One of two "hoot" owls, a Great Horned Owl is best identified by its
- Five-syllable call of *You a-wake? Me, too.*
- "Horns," actually feather tufts resembling horns
- Large size, female noticeably larger than male
Compare this bird with the Barred Owl, the profile for which follows.

SPECIES PROFILE

BARRED OWL

VITAL STATS
Length: 16.9–19.7 in.
Wingspan: 39–43 in.
Weight: 17–37 oz.

Above: Barred Owls, like other owls, can turn their heads about 270 degrees; below: Barred Owl

Compared with a Great Horned Owl, a Barred Owl is a gentle soul, lunching on small mammals, frogs, and large insects. Although it carries only a quarter of the weight of a great horned, its wingspan generally equals that of the great horned's. The advantage: fast, nimble travel through dense forest, its preferred habitat. Given a feasting opportunity, however, a Barred Owl will visit wooded yards as well. In fact, we see more Barred Owls than Great Horned Owls in our yard, perhaps because, on one side, our property abuts woodlands.

We discovered, however, we shouldn't grow too comfortable with the "gentle soul" label. One summer several years ago on a midafternoon canoe venture, we wound our way through a wetland filled with dense bald cypress trees, a made-in-heaven haven for Barred Owls. While Barred Owls lack bad-boy meanness, they don't take kindly to wanderers in their territory. And by mistake, we wandered in. By day, owls sit quietly, seemingly asleep, eyes closed or barely slits. Motionless, quiet, a lump on a limb, they look like an extension of tree bark, camouflaged to nearly invisible.

And so it was that, unwittingly, we found ourselves near the base of their nest tree, easing the canoe through the massive stand of cypress trunks, gliding quietly, taking pleasure in the solitude. They, of course, heard us long before we arrived. And they were awake and ready. In silent swoop, the male, talons extended, raced past our heads. We ducked, instinctively, paddles smacking the canoe gunnels. Startled out of our wits, we beat a hasty retreat, owl swooping in pursuit, bill snapping—a distinctive threat needing no further interpretation.

Barred owls occasionally call in daylight hours, especially early and late. So it was no surprise that, as we neared the end of our canoe venture, when the sun was ready to set, we heard the two of them, probably recounting their success, dueting about the invaders they'd chased, saving their babies and protecting their territory. Somewhere in the conversation, they also probably talked about where the male would find the most success snaring food for their babies that night.

NAME THAT BIRD

Strix varia (Barred Owl): Both *strix* and *varia* mean "of many different (or variegated) colors," a reference to the bird's plumage. Our common name also suggests the bird's plumage, especially the pattern (barred) on its breast. "Owl" is Latin for "to cry out."

BIRD TALK: WHO'S CALLING?

Male and female Barred Owls duet using many variations of hoots, gurgles, and screams in addition to their best-known call, *Who-cooks-for-you, who-cooks-for-you-awwllll.*

FOOD FARE

Barred Owls eat small mammals, rabbits, reptiles, amphibians, some birds, and large invertebrates, all captured and eaten fresh-killed.

NEST NOTES

Nest Site: tree cavity or tree, using abandoned hawk or crow nest; will accept appropriate nest boxes or open platforms

Nest Construction: does not build own nest

Eggs: 1–5 eggs, 1 brood, incubated 28–33 days

Fledge: 35 days after hatch; fly 75 days after hatch

While Barred Owls and Great Horned Owls live in similar territories, barreds will avoid that part of the territory in which great horneds live. They flat out don't like each other—except that the great horned likes barreds for lunch. If you hear both species in your neighborhood, listen for territorial quarrels. They won't be just silly little spats.

SPOTTING THE SPECTACULAR   **Bird of the Baths**

Barred Owls love a good bath. And somehow, they seem to need one. They've been described as looking as if they're wearing a dirty shabby coat with a ragged scarf around their necks. Still, nothing could have surprised me more than seeing a fluffed up Barred Owl one morning at the edge of our little backyard water feature, apparently contemplating a good splash. Perhaps the shallows were too shallow and the deep water too heavily vegetated, because after some neck stretching, ducking, and dodging, it lifted up, effortlessly it seemed, and settled three limbs up near the trunk in our largest pine tree.

ID CHECK

A Barred Owl can be identified by the following characteristics:
- Lack of "horns," or ear tufts
- Large round head
- Short tail
- Whitish underparts with dark streaking

SPECIES PROFILE

YELLOW-RUMPED WARBLER

VITAL STATS
Length: 4.7–5.5 in.
Wingspan: 7.5–9.1 in.
Weight: 0.4–0.5 oz.

Above: *Yellow-rumped Warbler, male;* below: *Yellow-rumped Warbler, female/immature*

Nicknamed "butter butts," Yellow-rumped Warblers distinguish themselves by being the only warbler species that spends its winter with us in southern Indiana. Depending on where you live, they may be one of the most common warblers on your turf. In fact, their numbers so dramatically flood the continental United States in fall that sometimes birders make light of them as "just another yellow-rump." If winter turns brutal, of course, they wander farther south, seeking a ready source of seeds, bugs, and berries. So spring and fall really give Indiana backyard bird-watchers our best chances to enjoy these otherwise common warblers.

Like some of their cousins, and like other birds such as American Goldfinches, yellow-rumps wear an entirely different wardrobe in summer breeding season than they do in the other three seasons. We see them in winter as mousy brown, streaked, maybe with some pale yellow on the sides, their bright buttery rumps their only clearly identifying mark.

But, oh! What a gorgeous outfit they wear in summer. Breeding males sport an eye-popping golden head stripe and side patches, crisp white wing bars against charcoal wings and backs, white throat and belly, and a black face mask worthy of the best bandit. Only in spring will we Hoosiers see them gorgeous—maybe. Whether or not we see them in breeding plumage depends on how quickly they zip off to nest in the far Northeast and Canada, making house and home in coniferous or mixed coniferous-deciduous forests. In winter, though, their butter rumps set them apart from remaining flocks of little brown jobs—the sparrows and finches—scampering through backyard habitat. Knowing these fashion-glamour darlings wear camouflage now, I have to smile when I get a peek at that tell-tale buttery yellow, letting me pick them out of the crowds.

NAME THAT BIRD

Setophaga coronata (Yellow-rumped Warbler): *Setophaga* means "moth eater," referring to warblers' preference for bugs. *Coronata* translates roughly as "wearing a crown," a reference to the central golden stripe on the breeding male's head. Our common name refers to the yellow rump patch on both sexes.

NEST NOTES

Nest Site: in conifers on horizontal branch, 4–50 ft. high
Nest Construction: 3–4 in. diameter, 2 in. deep, of twigs, grasses, rootlets, lined with hair
    and feathers
Eggs: 1–6 eggs, 1–2 broods, incubated 12–13 days
Fledge: 10–14 days after hatch

In our yard, they hang out mostly in, around, and under our pine trees, plucking bugs (most likely larvae) from near the tips of branches or flipping fallen needles and other leaf litter as they forage below. Red cedar trees adjoin the pines, and little cedar berries (actually tiny cones) also attract yellow-rumps. Their preference for shrubby areas keeps them near the back of our property, and although they supposedly come to feeders, I've not seen any at mine. Maybe they see no reason to leave the buffet in the tangles and shrubs.

FOOD FARE

In summer, northerly nesting Yellow-rumped Warblers eat mostly insects, including the serious pest, spruce budworm, and dart out to snag flying insects. During fall and winter, they switch to seeds and fruits, the only warblers able to digest the waxy materials in wax myrtle and bayberry. They also devour juniper and dogwood berries, wild grapes, and poison ivy and Virginia creeper berries. They occasionally visit feeders for sunflower seed, raisins, peanut butter, and suet.

BIRD TALK: WHO'S CALLING?

Males sing a low, thin, bell-like warble, usually rising at the end. From a distance, the song sounds a bit like that of a junco.

Yellow-rumped Warblers range across the entire United States and are equally plentiful through most of their range. But eastern and western yellow-rumps dress differently. Eastern birds, the Myrtle subspecies, wear white throats. The western birds, those west of the Rocky Mountains, the Audubon's subspecies, wear a snazzy yellow throat patch. Their songs vary, too, with Myrtles singing a higher pitch, sounding more hurried and somewhat less musical than their western counterparts.

SPOTTING THE SPECTACULAR

Birds by the Number

Yellow-rumped Warblers easily rank as our most common and abundant warbler. Especially along the Eastern Seaboard, yellow-rumps migrate in huge numbers, so common they're often a beginning birder's first identified warbler. Unlike most other wood warblers, they often forage in sizeable flocks, sometimes by the score. Since they're wintertime berry lovers, look for them wherever berries hang ripe. Often, their busy activity draws your attention.

ID CHECK

In summer, in the Northeast, identify male Yellow-rumped Warblers by the following colorations:
- Bright yellow side patches
- Bright yellow crown stripe
- Well-defined black mask
- Crisp white wing bars
- Bright yellow rump, obvious in flight
- Duller plumage on females, a less crisp version of the males

In winter, use these keys to identify yellow-rumps:
- Pale, washed-out brown plumage
- Pale yellow side patches
- Bright yellow rump, obvious in flight

Habitat Counts

Final Good Words

When one tugs at a single thing in nature,
he finds it attached to the rest of the world.

JOHN MUIR

Where's the good news? Over the course of this book, I've frequently shared unsettling bad news about birds, especially news of habitat loss and ongoing population declines. News about air, water, and noise pollution and their negative effects on birds seems even more bleak when accompanied by sobering news about light pollution—nighttime illumination along city streets, in high buildings, in millions of backyards—and its negative effects on migration and breeding behavior. Climate change threatens already stressed birds.

During my grandmother's lifetime, two Indiana backyard birds went extinct. I never saw them, but she remembered them from her childhood. Passenger Pigeons, *Ectopistes migratorius,* went extinct from overhunting. Grandma talked about the dwindling migrations that, at peak, consisted of flocks reported to be a mile wide and 300 miles long, taking fourteen hours to pass a given point, an estimated population of that single flock at 3.5 billion. And that count likely represented only a small portion of the total population.

But they were tasty, and the market rich. Since they roosted in huge masses, they made easy targets for the greedy. They were shot, trapped, or netted, and shipped to the East Coast for elegant dining. Those birds too damaged for human consumption were fed to the hogs. While habitat loss surely had some impact, the birds were quite simply hunted to death. The last bird died in the Cincinnati Zoo in 1914.

In 1918, the last Carolina Parakeet (*Conuropsis carolinensis*) died. It once thrived along the banks of the Wabash River, only a few dozen miles from my yard; artwork housed in New Harmony, Indiana, illustrates an abundance of these colorful birds roosting among the riverbank sycamores. But the birds were considered pests. They ate crops, so farmers shot them. Other issues combined to finalize their demise: Habitat destruction no doubt played a role; introduced honeybees robbed them of their cavity nest sites; unknowing folks caged them for pets so the birds couldn't breed; Victorian women coveted them as decorations on their hats; and poultry disease apparently spread violently through the few remaining closely knit flocks. In short, the birds disappeared from the face of the earth. Forever. Worldwide, more than thirty species have gone extinct in recorded history.

Kirtland's Warbler, male, is red-listed as endangered.

Red-listed Birds of Eastern United States: Highest Concern

* = endangered

Mottled Duck	*Least Tern	Golden-winged Warbler
Magnificent Frigatebird	*Red-cockaded	*Kirtland's Warbler
Reddish Egret	Woodpecker	Henslow's Sparrow
Yellow Rail	*Bell's Vireo	Saltmarsh Sparrow
Black Rail	*Florida Scrub Jay	Seaside Sparrow
*Piping Plover	Bicknell's Thrush	

So, historically, we humans have done some really stupid things, things that affect our own well-being. Wouldn't I love to have a Carolina Parakeet or Passenger Pigeon as a yard bird? Quite feasibly, they were both backyard birds.

But surely we've learned from the experiences. Right? Maybe. Maybe not.

Today we're faced with a list of endangered and threatened birds right here in the eastern half of the United States. Another list, posted on page 51, reports those in serious decline. Granted, shorebirds and other wetlands species will never be a part of my yard—or most other folks' yards either, for that matter, unless of course, the backyard abuts the coast. But given the balance of nature and what happens in the food chain and overall habitat when a species goes extinct, we have to care—backyard bird or not. Believe it or not, some of the rare and declining birds *could* be yard birds—if they weren't so rare.

Allow me, please, to make this story even more personal, not from my grandma's recollections but from my own.

Beyond the endangered/threatened list and the declining/rare list you find here, other birds have declined that didn't make the critical list. In fact, more than a half dozen birds that I loved as a child and even as a young adult are now, at best, mostly rare sightings, at least where I live. At worst, they are only vague memories.

Consider the dramatic population changes since 1967, as documented by the U.S. Department of the Interior (www.fws.gov/migratorybirds). Here's what I remember from just the past forty years:

When I was a kid, Northern Bobwhites called their name across the fields from fence row to fence row every summer evening. Their numbers have since declined by 82 percent. Evening Grosbeaks used to squabble by the dozens at my feeders, but it's been thirty years since one has passed through the yard. Their populations crashed by 78 percent. Eastern Meadowlarks brightened our pastures, singing from fence posts, greeting the mornings and bidding goodnight in the evenings. Their numbers have dropped 72 percent. How well I remember Field Sparrows perched atop weed stalks, singing out their territorial rights. They've declined by 68 percent. Noisy Common Grackle populations, considered a nuisance in the neighborhood, have nevertheless deteriorated by 61 percent. Whip-poor-wills perched atop the roofline used to sing us to sleep. I've not heard one in years. They've declined by 57

Field Sparrow

percent. Horned Larks once skittered through the row crops by the dozens, twittering along the way. Fewer than half remain.

Bird population decline delivers a dramatic impact on those of us who have personally witnessed the many losses. It saddens my heart. It hurts my soul. But so it goes. Still, we are learning. Really, we are.

Yellow-listed Birds of Eastern United States: Declining or Rare

Swallow-tailed Kite	Stilt Sandpiper	Prairie Warbler
Clapper Rail	Roseate Tern	Cerulean Warbler
King Rail	Black Skimmer	Prothonotary Warbler
American Golden-plover	Mangrove Cuckoo	Swainson's Warbler
Snowy Plover	Short-eared Owl	Kentucky Warbler
Wilson's Plover	Red-headed Woodpecker	Canada Warbler
Marbled Godwit	Olive-sided Flycatcher	Le Conte's Sparrow
Red Knot	Willow Flycatcher	Nelson's Sharp-tailed
Sanderling	Wood Thrush	Sparrow
Semi-palmated Sandpiper	Blue-winged Warbler	Painted Bunting
Western Sandpiper	Bay-breasted Warbler	Rusty Blackbird
White-rumped Sandpiper		

Wood Thrush

Prothonotary Warbler

Now, at the end of the year, as you look forward to your own improved backyard habitat as the result of what this book has shared, let's focus on good news—the news that says we can save our birds. Each of us. One by one. Little by little.

While human behavior has caused the serious decline, even the demise, of many species, human intervention has also turned around some populations, bringing them back from the brink of extinction. In short, we *can* make a difference—both in our yards and in the larger community. The models are in place.

Conservation groups make a good suggestion: Think globally; act locally. All of us together can do more than any one of us alone, and as we act locally, by improving our own backyards and by supporting broader conservation projects, then collectively we can make a difference.

If your habitat has reached its pinnacle for the birds, look elsewhere for another project spot—school or college campus, business or industrial park, railroad right-of-way, nursing home campus, shopping center's edge, area park, intersection with a grassy spot. If you build it, birds, desperate for habitat, will come.

Think globally; act locally. Make a difference. Consider two examples: one of national significance with backyard implications and another of backyard importance with national implications.

Celebrating Comeback Kids: Bald Eagles

Let's begin with a headline newsmaker, the national emblem adopted by our forefathers on June 20, 1782.

Strong and majestic, Bald Eagles can fly 65 miles per hour in level flight, dive at speeds over 150 miles per hour, and soar at 10,000 feet. For hours, they can ride natural wind currents and thermal updrafts and then drop to water and use those same muscle-powered wings to paddle to shore if they catch a fish too heavy to lift up to their tree.

"Eagle eye," no meaningless expression here, helps these top-of-the-line hunters spot prey miles away. Experts maintain that if eagles could read, they would be able to read a newspaper from across a football field. On a clear day, they can see a fish from two miles away. You'll not likely sneak up on one.

Spectacularly beautiful and murderously muscular, an eagle earns recognition as a sky-high acrobat, fighting-mad defender, loyal mate, and majestic monarch—all phrases of adoration for our nation's beloved emblem. Thus, when the Bald Eagle approached extinction in the lower forty-eight states, it became the poster bird for the Endangered Species Act.

Bald Eagle in flight

Bald Eagle perched

We've engaged in a checkered history with these magnificent birds. Early North American explorers found the bird in abundance, but Alaska's territorial residents felt the bird was a bit too abundant, faulting the bird for taking vast numbers of salmon. In addition, sheep farmers blamed them for lost lambs; fox farmers, for lost pups. So in 1917, the federal government voted to impose a fifty-cent bounty on every eagle killed. Bring in a pair of talons, and the fifty cents was yours—not bad pay for easy hunting during the days of World War I.

While politicians battled over the issue, pro-eagle spokesmen were defeated at the ballot box. Fishery lobbies won out, and by 1923, the bounty doubled. In 1949, it doubled again. So a pair of talons hanging on a cabin wall represented two dollars—nothing to sneeze at in those hard times. Before the bounty was finally and forever repealed in 1952, the Alaskan Territorial Government had paid for 128,000 pairs of Bald Eagle talons.

In the remaining states, however, Bald Eagles were growing scarce. By 1963, although Alaskan eagle populations remained relatively stable, only 417 baldies flew the skies above the lower forty-eight states. What a pitifully poor number, given original populations in the tens of thousands. What was happening?

Two culprits worked jointly to bring down the incredible birds: humans, who continued to persecute eagles as vermin, and DDT (dichloro-diphenyl-trichloroethane), which was used in the agriculture business.

Very slow to decay, DDT washed from fields into streams and then into rivers and entered the food chain through absorption by plants and animals living in the water—including, of course, fish, many of which also ate the contaminated plants. As eagles ate more and more of the contaminated fish, the accumulating toxicity caused eggshells to thin. The eggshells then cracked from the incubating adult's weight, and nests failed. Within ten years, reproduction fell to near zero. By 1966, Bald Eagles were listed as endangered under the Endangered Species Preservation Act. By 1978, they were added to the endangered list under the Endangered Species Act of 1973.

Once they were declared officially endangered, Bald Eagles became the target of extensive protective measures, including the elimination of the pesticide DDT and the protection of nesting and foraging habitat. Implementing habitat protection measures demanded big-time efforts, for single eagle pairs need big-time territories—300 to 500 acres, even thousands of acres, depending on abundance of prey. But the efforts found success.

Although DDT was banned in 1972, declines in nesting success continued through the 1970s. Then, a slow turnaround began. By the 1980s, a population upturn helped stabilize the numbers, and by the 1990s, the magnificent creatures showed dramatic, clear signs of recovery.

The eagle's recovery, as a result of education and the elimination of DDT, is probably the country's most successful and most highly lauded conservation story. Human intervention determined the story's outcome.

Even now, some sources report that 40 percent of Bald Eagles don't survive their first flight and less than 10 percent reach maturity. Given the fact that young eagles take four to five years to gain an all-white head (hence the name "bald") and all-white tail, indications of sexual maturity, an adult bird seems almost a miracle. Given the species' return from the brink of extinction, it is, indeed, a miracle.

Still struggling with their number-one enemy—humans—Bald Eagles continue to face constant onslaught, primarily from mercury poisoning. Nevertheless, by 2008, the regal birds were removed from the Endangered Species List. And that's reason to celebrate.

Human intervention can—and definitely did—make a difference. What we learned through the nationwide effort to save these birds carries lessons to backyard habitat hosts. Skip the pesticides, protect the food supply, and conserve the habitat.

Bald Eagles build the largest nest of any North American bird, so massive that sometimes small birds nest within the structure. The largest on record weighed more than two tons when its support tree finally crashed from the weight.

Celebrating Comeback Kids: Eastern Bluebirds

Of course, few of us would ever have a Bald Eagle as a yard bird. On the other hand, many of us celebrate Eastern Bluebirds in our yards. So, let's consider this lovely little bird that carries the sky on its back. Its brilliant clear-blue plumage identifies it as a member of the thrush family, the object of widespread affection, sometimes termed the "bluebird of happiness." But a most telling phrase identifying the Eastern Bluebird is probably "comeback kid."

Top: *Eastern Bluebird, male;* bottom: *Eastern Bluebird, female*

Eastern Bluebird populations plummeted, declining by 90 percent after European immigrants introduced in the late 1800s two now-common avian species: House Sparrow and European Starling. Both of these exotics rob bluebirds of potential nest cavities, even killing incubating females, readily destroying their eggs and nestlings. By the 1960s, Eastern Bluebirds teetered on the point of near-extinction. As a kid, I never saw a bluebird.

But they have since rebounded, thanks to Dr. Lawrence Zeleny and his founding of the North American Bluebird Society (NABS). In 1978, NABS organized with the purpose of directing efforts to establish monitored bluebird "trails," clusters of man-made nest boxes. The plan aimed to help compensate bluebirds for their loss of natural nest cavities. Nationwide, folks built bluebird trails, some consisting of only one or two nest boxes, others, like those of Robert and Judy Peak, numbering nearly two hundred boxes posted over hundreds of acres. In fact, between 1990 and 2010, Peaks' boxes produced over twenty thousand bluebirds.

Yes, one or two people can make a difference. But thousands of other folks contributed to bluebird trails, too. Some built nest boxes, others mounted them in appropriate habitat, still others volunteered to monitor them. Together, acting locally, these caring individuals affected the total world's population of Eastern Bluebirds. Thus, while human behavior nearly destroyed the bluebirds, human intervention has also brought them back. Those of us who live in appropriate habitat can continue the work of the thousands, acting locally in our own backyards.

That's reason to celebrate. Once again we see that human intervention can make a difference. And applying what we've learned in the course of pulling the bluebird back from the brink of extinction helps us understand how to prevent other birds from nearing the edge. Control invasive species and implement the Big Four of good habitat: food, water, shelter, and especially, places to raise young.

An Eastern bluebird flies with nest material to one of our homemade nest cavities where he and his mate typically raise three broods every year.

Proactive Citizens

Thus, in spite of continuing broad habitat deterioration, good news for birds springs from proactive folks, genuinely alarmed by habitat decline, who are conserving land, insisting on legislation, contributing to citizen science, and supporting worthy organizations that fight for birds' protection. Nonprofit groups, like the American Bird Conservancy (www.abcbirds .org), the National Audubon Society (www.audubon.org), the American Birding Association (www.americanbirding.org), The Nature Conservancy (www.nature.org), and the National Wildlife Federation (www.nwf.org), promote birds and other wildlife and their habitat protection. Their strength comes from their members and contributors. Continued support of your favorite conservation organizations will further sustain ongoing habitat protection.

Meanwhile, still thinking globally but acting locally, we can all be proactive in our own backyard habitats, perhaps corralling others in the neighborhood to join the effort, creating one little patch of great habitat at a time, one after another after another. And every little patch of habitat counts when it comes to birds desperate to find a good home—yours included!

ACKNOWLEDGMENTS

When a book reflects a lifetime of experiences, where does one start the necessarily long thank-you list? My parents introduced me to birds as we watched from the kitchen window. We didn't have a field guide, so we made up our own names for the birds. By the time I was in high school, we had a homemade bird feeder, a highly unusual yard feature in those early days, and it was about that time that Mom bought a *Golden Guide to the Birds of North America*. That activity, taken for granted then, instilled my love of birds. So, thanks to Mom and Dad, now both long gone.

During my first twelve years of school, I don't remember any teacher talking to us about birds, although maybe my memory fails me. College was intense, but my work sent me into literary fields—writing, speaking, communicating—rather than biology. Mostly, then, I feel compelled to acknowledge those who supported my school-of-hard-knocks education—watching, reading, experimenting, and watching some more.

Field guides let me thumb my way toward gradually identifying birds, and my worn *Golden Guide*, kept mostly for nostalgia, its loose pages held in place with a rubber band, its margins scribbled with now seemingly naïve notes, attests to my early efforts. Presently, my bookshelves overflow with more than a dozen guides, most with nicked corners, bent covers, and ragged edges, some muddy from too many forays into wet wonderlands, a few still crisp and new, lovingly reserved as lap books for armchair dreaming. I'm grateful to all those authors, old and new, for works ranging from Roger Tory Peterson's pioneering guide to multiple state-of-the-art products.

Nowadays, of course, online resources also earn my thanks. Cornell Lab of Ornithology's site "All about Birds" and my subscription to *Birds of North America* online have served as invaluable resources, the final word for resolving conflicting bits of information, and my first-line authority for measurement details and other statistics for species profile segments labeled "Vital Stats." Joel Ellis Holloway's *Dictionary of Birds of the United States* became my go-to reference for those complicated scientific names, what they mean, and how they came to be. Thanks to these and every other author, all like ghostly mentors, whose works appear in the references pages at the end of this book.

The down-and-dirty thanks for getting this project off the ground, however, goes to my initial cheerleaders, Janice Zimmerman and Ann Moore. Jan and Ann became my support team, serving as sounding boards for early organizational plans, engaging in exciting brainstorming lunches, keeping me on track, steering my thoughts toward what has become this finished product, talking me through edits and revisions, and keeping my eye focused on the nebulous but intended audience.

Special thanks to my longtime mentor Patricia Goodaker. While she, too, cheered me on, her companionship as a devout reader of all things about the natural world shaped my understanding of bird habitat and its significance. She shoved books my way that I needed to read. But more than that, she modeled what the books said. Rarely does she post bird-feeders in her city yard because her garden, amid parking lots and power lines but profuse three seasons of the year, welcomes more than one hundred species of birds. A mecca for all things avian, Pat's yard testifies to her expertise as both birder and gardener. Everyone should have such a mentor.

Thanks, too, to Paul Bouseman, botanical curator for Mesker Park Zoo and Botanic Garden; Stephen Heeger, past president of the Evansville Audubon Society, and his wife Delores; and Jack Spruill, conservation activist, for teaching me about plants—from ferns to sedges, from annuals to perennials, from bushes to stately denizens of the forest. Surely, they understood best when I cried over storm-torn trees.

Over the years, a good many folks shared their yards, allowing me to peek in on their habitat and survey their birds—and I learned from them: Marilyn Swonder, Dr. Raymond and Cynthia Nicholson, Stephen and Delores Heeger, Dr. Richard and Sandra Mahrenholz, Jerry and Vera Kleek, Jerry and Ann Moore, John Knox, Albert and Janice Gmutza, Robert and Janice Zimmerman, Michael and Laverne Jankowski, Jack and Jenny Spruill, Dr. David and Melanie Powell, and the Turkey Run State Park Nature Center. Thanks to them and others who wrote about, talked about, and opened their yards for public tours. Together, they broadened my understanding of habitat.

Dr. Lee Sterrenburg, who almost single-handedly tracked the bird population changes in a massive wetland and prairie restoration, patiently expanded my horizons and guided my identification of new wetland species. Brad Feaster, wildlife biologist and property manager of Indiana's Goose Pond Fish and Wildlife Area; Mike Morton, wildlife biologist and property manager of the Sauerheber Unit of Kentucky's Sloughs Wildlife Management Area; and numerous officers, staff, and friends at the Indiana Chapter of The Nature Conservancy helped me understand habitat restoration and the inherent problems therein. Thanks to them for their patience with my never-ending queries.

Thanks, too, to my many mentors and supporters in the Indiana Audubon Society, Sycamore Audubon Society, Amos Butler Audubon Society, Evansville Audubon Society, Evansville Birding Club, and IN-BIRD, Indiana birders' online listserv. Field experiences, classes, and ongoing discussions with these fine folks taught me much.

A special thanks to Don Gorney, Indiana's Rare Birds Committee Chair and my longtime mentor, who taught me how to look at a bird—not for its color but for its shape and size, its bill structure and face pattern. He always answered patiently every time (oh, so many times) when I asked, "How do you know?"

Keeping a keen eye and ear on Cathie Hutcheson and Robert Scott Kramer as they banded birds taught me about avian waywardness. Thanks to Cathie, a licensed hummingbird bander, and Scott, a licensed general bird bander, who let me experience a bird in the hand and startled me into a whole new appreciation for tiny—and not so tiny—feathered creatures.

I'm grateful to three folks who opened doors for me to write about my passion for birds and test the waters for reader reaction. More than ten years ago, Linda Negro, then Lifestyles Editor for the *Evansville [Indiana] Courier and Press*, entertained my proposal for a biweekly "For the Birds" newspaper column. Today, she and Ryan Reynolds continue to accept my work, and readers have rewarded us by demonstrating their growing love for birds. Editor J. Bruce Baumann, in a serious vote of confidence, invited me to join the founding staff of the online *Posey Magazine*, thus exposing my work to an international audience.

When it comes to the nitty-gritty of getting this manuscript right, one person truly turned the pages on accuracy. Dr. Jill Jankowski, Assistant Professor of Zoology, University of British Columbia, Vancouver, focused her keen, practiced eye on myriad details, reining me in, demanding accuracy when I waxed anthropomorphic, and correcting my misconceptions. Her knowledge, outweighed only by her tireless willingness to work with this non-scientific literary writer, brings a level of authority to this work that would otherwise fall seriously short. May she reap many blessings for the hours she has contributed. My thanks go far beyond these words, and any errors that remain are mine.

Other manuscript readers brought their own respective areas of expertise to the project. For their hours of commitment and numerous suggestions, my thanks to Alan Gehret, wildlife biologist by degree and Curator of Collections and Naturalist by vocation at the John James Audubon Museum, Henderson, Kentucky; Carol Gehret, former President and Education Chairperson of South Mountain Audubon Society, Pennsylvania, and former English teacher; Marcia Onnybecker, retired English teacher and active Southwestern Indiana Master Gardener; and Patricia Goodaker, mentor, international birder, retired teacher, and habitat creator.

No writer survives without the support of family. My husband of almost fifty years, Charles has made all things possible for me, personally and professionally. He takes photos, too, and taught me how to do the same. Between us, for better or worse, we've illustrated these pages. Thanks is hardly the appropriate word, but it's the best I can offer in print.

To the many unnamed folks who propped me up, murmured words of encouragement, and humored me through grumpy times, my thanks to you all.

Finally, thanks to Stackpole Books for accepting my proposal and seeing it through to publication. Special thanks to Mark Allison for leading me through the editorial process and providing ongoing support.

Somehow I feel I'm only the mouthpiece for all these amazing people and that I have really nothing at all to do with whatever success this book may have. Thank you, all. May birds grace your every day.

BIBLIOGRAPHY

Abell, Jo Ann. "Catbird: The Bird in the Plain Gray Wrapper," *Bird Watcher's Digest.* May/June 2009, 22–29.

———. "Jack-of-All-Trades," *Bird Watcher's Digest.* Jan./Feb. 2009, 58–63.

Alderfer, Jonathan, ed. *National Geographic Complete Birds of North America.* Washington, DC: National Geographic, 2006.

Alderfer, Jonathan, and Jon L. Dunn. *Birding Essentials.* Washington, DC: National Geographic, 2007.

Allison, Sandy, ed. *100 Things to Know: Backyard Birds and Bird Feeding.* Mechanicsburg, PA: Stackpole Books, 2007.

Alsop, Fred J., III. *Smithsonian Handbook of Birds of North America, Eastern Region.* New York: DK Publishing, 2001.

American Bird Conservancy, "Bird of the Week" email, Oct. 28, 2011.

Arcese, Peter, Mark K. Sogge, Amy B. Marr, and Michael A. Patten. 2002. "Song Sparrow (*Melospiza melodia*)." *The Birds of North America Online* (A. Poole, ed.). Ithaca: Cornell Lab of Ornithology. Retrieved from the Birds of North America Online: http://bna.birds .cornell.edu.bnaproxy.birds.cornell.edu/bna/species/704doi:10.2173/bna.704.

Askins, Robert A. *Restoring North America's Birds: Lessons from Landscape Ecology,* 2nd ed. New Haven: Yale University Press, 2002.

Baicich, Paul J. "American Kestrels Continue to Slip," *Bird Watcher's Digest.* Mar./April 2009, 16–17.

———. "Power Line Rights-of-way and American Kestrels," *Bird Watcher's Digest.* Mar./April 2009, 17.

Baicich, Paul J., and Colin J. O. Harrison. *Nests, Eggs, and Nestlings of North American Birds,* 2nd ed. Princeton, NJ: Princeton University Press, 2005.

Barker, Margaret A., and Jack Griggs. *The Feeder Watcher's Guide to Bird Feeding: A Cornell Bird Library Guide.* New York: HarperResource, 2000.

Batt, Al. "Migration," *Bird Watcher's Digest.* Jan./Feb. 2009, 70–73.

Baughman, Mel. *National Geographic Reference Atlas to the Birds of North America.* Washington, DC: National Geographic, 2003.

Bent, Arthur Cleveland, et al. Patricia Query Newforth, ed. *Life Histories of Familiar North American Birds.* Online at http://birdsbybent.netfirms.com/index.html (1996–2012).

Bildstein, Keith L., and Ken Meyer. 2000. "Sharp-shinned Hawk (*Accipiter striatus*)." BNA Online.

Bird, David. "The Art of Mobbing," *Backyard Birds Newsletter.* June 2011, 8–9.

———. *The Bird Almanac: A Guide to Essential Facts and Figures of the World's Birds.* Buffalo: Firefly Books, 2004.

———. *Bird's Eye View: A Practical Compendium for Bird-lovers.* Quebec: Vehicule Press, 1999.

———. "Birds: 'Smarter' than We Know?" *Bird Watcher's Digest.* July/Aug. 2006, 112–115.

———. "How Much Wood Could a Woodpecker Peck?" *The Backyard Birds Newsletter.* Dec. 2009, 8–9.

———. "Never Underestimate the Intelligence," *Bird Watcher's Digest.* Sept./Oct. 2008, 108–113.

———. "Noise Pollution and Bird Song," *Bird Watcher's Digest.* Nov./Dec. 2006, 111–117.

———. "Quick Takes," *Bird Watcher's Digest.* July/Aug. 2006, 10–14.

———. "Strange Dangers," *Bird Watcher's Digest.* Nov./Dec. 2009, 96–99.

———. "The Turkey Vulture," *Bird Watcher's Digest.* Nov./Dec. 2008, pp. 108–113.

"Birding Briefs." *Birder's World.* June 2009, 12.

"Birding Briefs." *Birder's World.* Dec. 2008, 13.

Boldan, Mary. "Cultivating Nature's Bird Feeders," *Bird Watcher's Digest.* Sept./Oct. 2006, 70–79.

Bonta, Marcia. "Cardinals," *Bird Watcher's Digest.* Nov./Dec. 2008, 34–37.

Bradley, Fern Marshall, and editors of Yankee Magazine. *Projects for the Birder's Garden.* Emmaus, PA: Yankee Books, 2004.

Brown, Charles R. 1997. "Purple Martin (*Progne subis*)." BNA Online.

Brown, Charles R., and Mary Bomberger Brown. 1999. "Barn Swallow (*Hirundo rustica*)." BNA Online.

Buckley, Neil J. 1999. "Black Vulture (*Coragyps atratus*)." BNA Online.

Buehler, David A. 2000. "Bald Eagle (*Haliaeetus leucocephalus*)." BNA Online.

Bull, Evelyn L., and Jerome A. Jackson. 2011. "Pileated Woodpecker (*Dryocopus pileatus*)." BNA Online.

Cabe, Paul R. 1993. "European Starling (*Sturnus vulgaris*)." BNA Online.

Carey, Michael, M. Carey, D. E. Burhans, and D. A. Nelson. 2008. "Field Sparrow (*Spizella pusilla*)." BNA Online.

Cavitt, John F., and Carola A. Haas. 2000. "Brown Thrasher (*Toxostoma rufum*)." BNA Online.

"Chickadee," *BirdScope.* Winter 2011, 10.

Chilton, G., M. C. Baker, C. D. Barrentine and M. A. Cunningham. 1995. White-crowned Sparrow (*Zonotrichia leucophrys*). BNA Online.

Chu, Miyoko. *Songbird Journeys: Four Seasons in the Lives of Migratory Birds.* New York: Walker and Company, 2006.

Cink, Calvin L., and Charles T. Collins. 2002. Chimney Swift (*Chaetura pelagica*). BNA Online.

Conner, Jack. "Not All Sweetness and Light," *Living Bird.* Autumn 2010, 34–35.

———. "Vultures Riding North," *Living Bird.* Spring 2011, 36–37.

Cook, Kevin J. "The Backyard Question Box," *Bird Watcher's Digest.* July/Aug. 2008, 90–92.

———. "The Backyard Question Box," *Bird Watcher's Digest.* Mar./April 2009, 78–79.

———. "Summer Bird Questions," *The Backyard Birds Newsletter.* June 2011, 4.

Cooper, Caren B., Wesley M. Hochachka, and Andre A. Dhondt. "Contrasting Natural Experiments Confirm Competition between House Finches and House Sparrows," *Ecology* 88 (4), 2007, 864–870. Online at http://www.esajournals.org/doi/pdf/10.1890/06-0855.

Cornell Lab of Ornithology. *All about Birds: Bird Guide.* 2012. www.allaboutbirds.org.

———. *All about Birds: Birding Basics.* 2012. www.allaboutbirds.org.

Craves, Julie. "Since You Asked," *Birder's World.* April 2002, 10–12.

———. "Since You Asked," *Birder's World.* Dec. 2003, 12–13.

———. "Since You Asked," *Birder's World.* Feb. 2009, 10.

———. "Since You Asked," *Birder's World.* June 2009, 10.

———. "Since You Asked," *Birder's World.* Aug. 2009, 10.

———. "Since You Asked," *Birder's World.* Oct. 2009, 10–11.

———. "Since You Asked," *Birder's World.* Dec. 2009, 10.

———. "Since You Asked," *Birder's World.* Feb. 2010, 12.

———. "Since You Asked," *Birder's World*. April 2010, 12.

———. "Since You Asked," *Birder's World*. June 2010, 10.

———. "Since You Asked," *Birder's World*. Oct. 2010, 10.

———. "Since You Asked," *Birder's World*. Feb. 2011, 10.

Cunningham, Val. "Calls in the Night," *WildBird*. Sept./Oct. 2009, 21, citing 2008 Queen's University study in "Behavioral Ecology and Sociobiology" (Sept. 2008, 62:1769–1777).

———. "The Migration Season," *WildBird*. Sept./Oct. 2008, 20–21.

———. "A World of Watchers," *WildBird*. Mar./April 2008, 28–29.

Curtis, Odette E., R. N. Rosenfield, and J. Bielefeldt. 2006. "Cooper's Hawk (*Accipiter cooperii*)." BNA Online.

Day, Susan. "Create a Habitat: Think Like a Bird," *WildBird*. Nov./Dec. 2003, 20–25.

———. "A Feast for All Seasons," *WildBird*. Sept./Oct. 2003, 19–23.

Day, Susan, Ron Rovansek, and Jack Griggs. *The Wildlife Gardener's Guide to Hummingbirds and Songbirds from the Tropics*. New York: Harper Collins, 2003.

DeArmond, R. N. "Shoot the Damned Things! Alaska's War Against the American Bald Eagle," http://raptors.hancockwildlife.org/BEIA/PAGES/Section-30.pdf.

Deinlein, Mary. *Neotropical Migratory Bird Basics*. Washington, DC: Smithsonian Institute Migratory Bird Center, 2011. Online at http://nationalzoo.si.edu/scbi/migratorybirds/.

Donnelly, David B. *Creating Your Backyard Bird Garden*. Marietta, OH: Pardson Corporation, 2008.

"Don't Use Cypress Mulch," *INPAWS Journal*. Autumn 2010, 16.

Drilling, Nancy, Rodger Titman and Frank Mckinney. 2002. "Mallard (*Anas platyrhynchos*)." BNA Online.

Ducks Unlimited Canada. "Facts on Canada Geese." 2012. http://www.ducks.ca/resource/general/wetland/geese.html.

Dunn, Jon L., and Jonathan Alderfer. *National Geographic Field Guide to the Birds of North America*, 6th ed. Washington, DC: National Geographic, 2011.

Dunne, Pete. *The Art of Bird Finding: Before You ID Them, You Have to See Them*. Mechanicsburg, PA: Stackpole Books, 2011.

———. "Bodies in Motion," *Birder's World*. April 2002, 24–27.

———. *Essential Field Guide Companion,* Boston: Houghton, Mifflin, 2006.

———. "Protecting Their Nest Eggs," *WildBird*. Mar./April 2008, pp. 30–33.

———. *The Wind Masters: The Lives of North American Birds of Prey*. Boston: Houghton Mifflin, 2003.

Dykstra, Cheryl R., Jeffrey L. Hays, and Scott T. Crocoll. 2008. "Red-shouldered Hawk (*Buteo lineatus*)." BNA Online.

Eaton, Stephen W. 1992. "Wild Turkey (*Meleagris gallopavo*)." BNA Online.

Eckles, Joanna, dir. *Bird-Safe Building Guidelines*. St. Paul: Audubon Minnesota, 2010.

Edwards, Scott. "Beginner's Guide to Water Features," *WildBird*. May/June 2004, 20–25.

Ehrlich, Paul R., David S. Dobkin, and Darryl Wheye. *The Birder's Handbook: A Field Guide to the Natural History of North American Birds*. New York: Simon and Schuster, 1988.

Elliott, Lang, with Donald Stokes and Lillian Stokes. *Stokes Field Guide to Bird Songs, Eastern Region*. 3 compact disks. New York: Time Warmer Audio Books, 1997.

Ellison, Walter G. 1992. "Blue-gray Gnatcatcher (*Polioptila caerulea*)." BNA Online.

Erickson, Laura. *The Bird Watching Answer Book*. North Adams, MA: Storey Publishing, 2009.

———. "Listen to the Mockingbird," *BirdScope*. Summer 2009, 1.

———. "Snow Birds," *Birder's World*. December 2003, 68–69.

Falls, J. B., and J. G. Kopachena. 2010. "White-throated Sparrow (*Zonotrichia albicollis*)." BNA Online.

Ferrari, James B. "All Around the Mulberry Bush," *Bird Watcher's Digest.* July/Aug. 2001, 88–93.

Foote, Jennifer R., Daniel J. Mennill, Laurene M. Ratcliffe, and Susan M. Smith. 2010. Black-capped Chickadee (*Poecile atricapillus*). BNA Online.

Freiday, Don. "Avian Larder: Birds Save Their Seeds in the Pantry," *WildBird.* Nov./Dec. 2011, 24–25.

———. "Backyard Safari," *WildBird.* Sept./Oct. 2010, 6–9.

———. "Brush Up," *WildBird.* Mar./April 2011, 26–27.

———. "Eggshells in the Yard," *WildBird.* May/June 2010, 22–23.

———. "Go Fruity for Fall Migrants," *WildBird.* Sept./Oct. 2011, 36–37.

———. "Whose Territory Do You Live In?" *WildBird.* July/Aug. 2011, 24–25.

———. "Where Are They Now?" *WildBird.* Jan./Feb. 2010, 24–27.

———. "Winter Warmth," *WildBird.* Jan./Feb. 2011, 24–25.

Friebele, Elaine. "Chickadees," *Bird Watcher's Digest.* Nov./Dec . 2008, 53–55.

Funk, William H. "In the Forests of the Night," *Bird Watcher's Digest.* Nov./Dec. 2010, 36–41.

Geis, Aelred D. "Relative Attractiveness of Different Foods at Wild Bird Feeders." U.S. Fish & Wildlife Service Special Scientific Report No. 233; 1980.

Geis, Aelred D., and Donald B. Hyde Jr. "Wild Bird Feeding Preferences." Washington, DC: National Wildlife Federation, 1983.

Ghalambor, Cameron K., and Thomas E. Martin. 1999. "Red-breasted Nuthatch (*Sitta canadensis*)." BNA Online.

Gordon, Jeffrey. "Cooper's Hawk: The Perfect Backyard Dinosaur," *Bird Watcher's Digest.* Nov./Dec, 2010, 22–29.

Gowaty, Patricia Adair, and Jonathan H. Plissner. 1998. Eastern Bluebird (*Sialia sialis*). BNA Online.

Greij, Eldon. "Amazing Hummingbirds," *Birder's World.* June 2010, 44–46.

———. "Distance Champion," *Birder's World.* Feb. 2009, 50–52.

———. "Dual Pipes," *Birder's World.* Dec. 2009, 44–45.

———. "The Eyes Have It," *Birder's World.* April 1998, 50–52.

———. "Flight with a Twist," *Birder's World.* April 2002, 58–60.

———. "Water Carriers," *Birder's World.* June 2009, 50–52.

Greenlaw, Jon S. 1996. "Eastern Towhee (*Pipilo erythrophthalmus*)." BNA Online.

Grubb, T. C., Jr., and V. V. Pravasudov. 1994. "Tufted Titmouse (*Baeolophus bicolor*)." BNA Online.

———. 2008. "White-breasted Nuthatch (*Sitta carolinensis*)." BNA Online.

Guzy, Michael J., and Gary Ritchison. 1999. "Common Yellowthroat (*Geothlypis trichas*)." BNA Online.

Haggerty, Thomas M., and Eugene S. Morton. 1995. "Carolina Wren (*Thryothorus ludovicianus*)." BNA Online.

Halkin, Sylvia L., and Susan U. Linville. 1999. "Northern Cardinal (*Cardinalis cardinalis*)." BNA Online.

Hall, George A. 1996. "Yellow-throated Warbler (*Setophaga dominica*)." BNA Online.

Hannisian, Mike. "Cedar Waxwing, Nationwide Wanderer," *WildBird.* July/Aug. 2009, 32.

Hanson, Thor. *Feathers: The Evolution of a Natural Miracle.* New York: Basic Books, 2011.

Harrison, George H. "America's Red-breasted Thrush," *Birder's World.* April 2002, 49–51.

———. "Big Red and His Lady," *Birder's World.* Dec. 2003, 32–35.

———. "Southern Charmer," *Birder's World.* April 2003, 48–51.

———. *Squirrel Wars: Backyard Wildlife Battles and How to Win Them.* Minocqua, WI: Willow Creek Press, 2006.

Harrison, Hal H. *A Field Guide to the Birds' Nests: Eastern.* Boston: Houghton Mifflin, 1975.

Harstad, Carolyn. *Go Native!* Bloomington: Indiana University Press, 1999.

Hassler, Lynn. "The Birds Gardener: Jumpin' Junipers," *The Backyard Birds Newsletter*. Dec. 2009, 1, 9.

Heinrich, Bernd. *The Nesting Season*. Cambridge: Harvard University Press, 2010.

Hill, Geoffrey E. 1993. "House Finch (*Carpodacus mexicanus*)." BNA Online.

Hill, James R., III. "Martin Mania," *Birder's World*. April 1998, 32–36.

Hilton, Bill Jr. "Operation RubyThroat," www.rubythroat.org. York, SC: Hilton Pond Center for Piedmont Natural History, 2012.

Holloway, Joel Ellis. *Dictionary of Birds of the United States*. Portland: Timber Press, 2003.

Houston, C. Stuart, Dwight G. Smith and Christoph Rohner. 1998. "Great Horned Owl (*Bubo virginianus*)." BNA Online.

Hunt, P. D., and David J. Flaspohler. 1998. "Yellow-rumped Warbler (*Setophaga coronata*)." BNA Online.

"Innovations in Reintroductions," *Bird Conservation*. Winter 2008–2009, 9–11.

Jackson, Bette J., and Jerome A. Jackson. 2000. "Killdeer (*Charadrius vociferus*)." BNA Online.

Jackson, Jerome A., and Henri R. Ouellet. 2002. "Downy Woodpecker (*Picoides pubescens*)." BNA Online.

Jackson, Jerome A., Henri R. Ouellet and Bette J. Jackson. 2002. "Hairy Woodpecker (*Picoides villosus*)." BNA Online.

Janetatos, Mary. "A History of the North American Bluebird Society." 1996. Bloomington, IN. Last updated October 5, 2011, www.nabluebirdsociety.org.

Jaramillo, Alvaro. "Backyard Rarities: When to Sound a 'Rare Bird Alert'," *Bird Watcher's Digest*, Nov./Dec. 2009, 29–31.

———. "Hollywood Finches," *Bird Watcher's Digest*. Jan.–Feb. 2011, 26–30.

———. "Not Like in the Book," *Bird Watcher's Digest*. Sept./Oct. 2008, 32–37.

Jobes, William. "David vs. Goliath," *Bird Watching*. Oct. 2011, 36–38.

Johnson, Anne Marie. "Windows Can Be a Threat to the Birds at Our Feeders," *Focus on Citizen Science*, p. 16, supplement to *Living Bird's Winter Bird Highlights* from Project Feederwatch 2008–09.

Johnson, Catherine J., Susan McDiarmid, and Edward R. Turner. *Welcoming Wildlife to the Garden*. Point Roberts, WA: Hartley and Marks, n.d.

Johnson, L. Scott. 1998. "House Wren (*Troglodytes aedon*)." BNA Online.

Karlson, Kevin T. "Cheerful Chatter," *WildBird*. Jan./Feb. 2010, 28–29.

———. "The Magic of Migration," *WildBird*. Sept./Oct. 2003, 50–55.

———. "Northern Flicker: Wary but Welcome Woodpecker," *WildBird*. Sept./Oct. 2008, 28–31.

Kaufman, Kenn. *Field Guide to Advanced Birding*. Boston: Houghton Mifflin Harcourt, 2011.

———. *Lives of North American Birds*. Boston: Houghton Mifflin, 1996.

———. "Magee: Anatomy of a Migrant Hotspot," *Birding*. Jan. 2010, 38–45.

———. "Pushing the Season," *Bird Watcher's Digest*. Mar./April 2006, 16–29.

Kerlinger, Paul. *How Birds Migrate*. Mechanicsburg, PA: Stackpole Books, 1995.

———. "Leapfrog Migrant," *Birder's World*. June 2010, 48–50.

———. "Maybe Bird," *Birder's World*. Dec. 2009, 48–50.

———. "Similar, Yet Different," *Bird Watcher's Digest*. April 2002, 64–66.

———. "Taking the Long Way," *Birder's World*. April 2009, 52–53.

Kight, Caitlin. "Nest Building in the Material World," *Bird Watcher's Digest*. Mar./April 2010, 58–63.

———. "Reconsidering the House Sparrow," *Bird Watcher's Digest*. Mar./April 2009, 56–61.

Kirk, David A., and Michael J. Mossman. 1998. "Turkey Vulture (*Cathartes aura*)." BNA Online.

Klem, David, Jr. "Birding Briefs," *Birder's World.* Oct. 2009, 12.

———. "Preventing Avian Mortality at Windows by Angling Glass and Feeder Placement," Papers Session, 73rd Annual Meeting of the Wilson Ornithological Society, April 9–12, 1992.

Kress, Stephen W. *The Bird Garden.* New York: Dorling Kindersley, 1995.

Kroodsma, Donald. *The Singing Life of Birds.* Boston: Houghton Mifflin, 2008.

Lanyon, Wesley E. 1995. "Eastern Meadowlark (*Sturnella magna*)." BNA Online.

Leahy, Christopher W. *The Birdwatcher's Companion to North American Birdlife.* Princeton, NJ: Princeton University Press, 2004.

Lincoln, Frederick C., revised by Steven R. Peterson (1979) and John L. Zimmerman (1998). *U.S. Fish and Wildlife Circular 16: Migration of Birds.* Reston, VA: U.S. Geological Survey, Aug. 2006. Available online at http://www.npwrc.usgs.gov/resource/birds/migratio.

Lowther, Peter E. 1993. "Brown-headed Cowbird (*Molothrus ater*)." BNA Online.

Lowther, Peter E., C. Celada, N. K. Klein, C. C. Rimmer, and D. A. Spector. 1999. "Yellow Warbler (*Setophaga petechia*)." BNA Online.

Lowther, Peter E., and Calvin L. Cink. 2006. "House Sparrow (*Passer domesticus*)." BNA Online.

Lynch, Wayne. *Owls of the United States and Canada: A Complete Guide to Their Biology and Behavior.* Baltimore: The Johns Hopkins University Press, 2007.

Manville, Albert M., II. "Bird Strikes and Electrocutions at Power Lines, Communication Towers, and Wind Turbines: State of the Art and State of the Science—Next Steps toward Mitigation." Online at http://www.fs.fed.us/psw/publications/documents/psw_gtr191/Asilomar/pdfs/1051–1064.pdf.

Marsi, Rick. "Sexy Signals," *WildBird.* May/June 2009, 36–38.

Mazur, Kurt M., and Paul C. James. 2000. "Barred Owl (*Strix varia*)." BNA Online.

McCarty, John P. 1996. "Eastern Wood-Pewee (*Contopus virens*)." BNA Online.

McGowan, Kevin J. 2001. "Fish Crow (*Corvus ossifragus*)." BNA Online.

McGraw, Kevin J., and Alex L. Middleton. 2009. "American Goldfinch (*Spinus tristis*)." BNA Online.

Michael, Edwin D. "Backyard Turkeys, Stuffing Themselves at Your Feeders," *Bird Watcher's Digest.* Nov./Dec. 2009, 67–73.

Middleton, Alex L. 1998. "Chipping Sparrow (*Spizella passerina*)." BNA Online.

"Migration of Birds: Influence of Weather," Northern Prairie Wildlife Research Center, http://www.npwrc.usgs.gov/resource/birds/migratio/weather.htm, Aug. 3, 2006, Sioux Falls, SD.

Mizrahi, David. "Avian Development," *WildBird.* May/June 2004, 58–60.

———. "Meterology ABCs for Birders—Part 2: Weather Maps," *WildBird.* Nov./Dec. 2003, 58–61.

Moss, Stephen. *The Birder's Companion.* Buffalo, NY: Firefly Books, 2007.

Mostrom, Alison M., Robert L. Curry, and Bernard Lohr. 2002. "Carolina Chickadee (*Poecile carolinensis*)." BNA Online.

Mowbray, Thomas B., Craig R. Ely, James S. Sedinger and Robert E. Trost. 2002. "Canada Goose (*Branta canadensis*)." BNA Online.

Murphy, Michael T. 1996. "Eastern Kingbird (*Tyrannus tyrannus*)." BNA Online.

National Audubon Society. "Audubon at Home: A Healthy Yard." 2012. http://athome.audubon.org/.

———. "Audubon at Home: Helping Birds." 2012. http://athome.audubon.org/.

National Wildlife Federation. "Garden for Wildlife: Making Wildlife Habitat at Home." 2012. www.nwf.org/backyard.

———. "Wildlife Conservation: Threats to Wildlife—Habitat Loss." 2012. www.nwf.org/ Wildlife/Wildlife-Conservation/Threats-to-Wildlife/Habitat-Loss.aspx.

Nature Conservancy, The. "How to Help Bird Conservation." 2012. my.nature.org/ birds/engage/everyday.html.

"News and Notes: Tracking Songbirds' Travels," *Birding*. Sept. 2009, 30.

Nolan, V., Jr., E. D. Ketterson, D. A. Cristol, C. M. Rogers, E. D. Clotfelter, R. C. Titus, S. J. Schoech, and E. Snajdr. 2002. "Dark-eyed Junco (*Junco hyemalis*)." BNA Online.

North American Bird Conservation Initiative, U.S. Committee, 2009. *The State of the Birds, United States of America, 2009*. Washington, DC: U.S. Department of Interior, 2009.

Newfield, Nancy. *Enjoying Hummingbirds More*. Marietta, OH: Pardson Corporation, 2001.

O'Connor, Mike. *Why Don't Woodpeckers Get Headaches? And Other Bird Questions You Know You Want to Ask*. Boston: Beacon Press, 2007.

O'Connor, Rebecca I. "The Last Great Wilderness," *WildBird*. Nov./Dec. 2011, 30–33.

Osborne, June. "Back to Basics: Fruit," *WildBird*. July/Aug., 2003, 16.

———. "Back to Basics: Roosting Boxes," *WildBird*. Nov./Dec. 2003, 18.

Otis, David L., John H. Schulz, David Miller, R. E. Mirarchi, and T. S. Baskett. 2008. "Mourning Dove (*Zenaida macroura*)." BNA Online.

Payne, Robert B. 2006. "Indigo Bunting (*Passerina cyanea*)." BNA Online.

Peer, Brian D., and Eric K. Bollinger. 1997. "Common Grackle (*Quiscalus quiscula*)." BNA Online.

Peterson, Roger Tory. *Peterson Field Guide to Birds of North America*. Boston: Houghton Mifflin, 2008.

Podulka, Sandy, Ronald W. Rohrbaugh Jr., and Rick Bonney, eds. *Handbook of Bird Biology*, 2nd ed. Ithaca, NY: Cornell Lab of Ornithology in association with Princeton University Press, 2004.

Pollan, Michael. *Second Nature: A Gardener's Education*. New York: Dell Publishing, 1991.

Preston, C. R., and R. D. Beane. 2009. "Red-tailed Hawk (*Buteo jamaicensis*)." BNA Online.

Read, Marie. "Herald of Spring," *WildBird*. Jan,/Feb. 2009, 34–35.

———. "Music to Our Ears," *Birder's World*. April 2002, 29–33.

Riutta, John. "The Days of Christmas Wonder," *The Backyard Birds Newsletter*. Dec. 2009, 7.

Rising, James D., and Nancy J. Flood. 1998. "Baltimore Oriole (*Icterus galbula*)." BNA Online.

Robinson, T. R., R. R. Sargent, and M. B. Sargent. 1996. "Ruby-throated Hummingbird (*Archilochus colubris*)." BNA Online.

Roth, Sally. *Bird-by-Bird Gardening*. Emmaus, PA: Rodale Press, 2006.

Rothenberg, David. *Why Birds Sing*. New York: Basic Books, 2005.

Sallabanks, Rex, and Frances C. James. 1999. "American Robin (*Turdus migratorius*)." BNA Online.

Sargent, Robert. *Ruby-throated Hummingbird*. Mechanicsburg, PA: Stackpole Books, 1999.

Seidensticker, Mat. "Owl You Need to Know," *WildBird*. July/Aug. 2003, 42–46.

Shackelford, Clifford E., Raymond E. Brown and Richard N. Conner. 2000. "Red-bellied Woodpecker (*Melanerpes carolinus*)." BNA Online.

Shalaway, Scott. "Phoebe Fidelity," *Birder's World*. April 1998, 44–47.

Sibley, David Allen. "Crest or No Crest?" *Birder's World*. Feb. 2009, 66.

———. "ID Birds by Their Flight Style," *BirdWatching*. August 2011, 58.

———. "Identifying Hawks," *Birder's World*. June 2010, 58.

———. *The Sibley Guide to Birds*. New York: Alfred A. Knopf, 2000.

———. *The Sibley Guide to Bird Life and Behavior*. New York: Alfred A. Knopf, 2001.

———. "Singing Posture." *Birder's World*. April 2009, 66.

Simonds, Calvin. *Private Lives of Garden Birds*. North Adams, MA: Storey Books, 2002.

Skutch, Alexander F. *Birds Asleep.* Austin: University of Texas Press, 1989.

Smallwood, John A., and David M. Bird. 2002. "American Kestrel (*Falco sparverius*)." BNA Online.

Smith, Kimberly G., James H. Withgott, and Paul G. Rodewald. 2000. "Red-headed Woodpecker (*Melanerpes erythrocephalus*)." BNA Online.

Smith, Robert J., Margret I. Hatch, David A. Cimprich, and Frank R. Moore. 2011. "Gray Catbird (*Dumetella carolinensis*)." BNA Online.

Stokes, Donald and Lillian. *Stokes Nature Guide to Bird Behavior, Vol. 1–3.* New York: Little Brown and Company, 1979, 1983, 1989.

———. *The Bluebird Book: The Complete Guide to Attracting Bluebirds.* Boston: Little, Brown and Company, 1991.

Stokes, Lillian and Don. "Coping with Grackles," *Birder's World.* Aug. 2008, 40–41.

Stangel, Peter. "Plant Now for Fall Birds," *WildBird.* Mar./April 2011, 6–9.

———. "Safety First." *WildBird.* Jan./Feb. 2012, 10–13.

———. "Wet and Wild Birding," *WildBird.* May/June 2011, 6–9.

Stutchbury, Bridgett J. M. *Silence of the Songbirds: How We Are Losing the World's Songbirds and What We Can Do to Save Them.* New York: Walker and Company, 2007.

Sullivan, Brian L. "Any Shape and Size," *WildBird.* Nov./Dec. 2010, 16–19.

———. "Avian Safety Goggles," *WildBird.* July/Aug. 2011, 6–8.

———. "Hot, Cold, Aggressive, Alert: Behavior Can Change a Bird's Shape," *WildBird.* May/June 2011, 10–12.

———. "Winter Migration," *WildBird.* Nov./Dec. 2008, 16–19.

"Talking Turkey," *NestWatch eNewsletter.* Nov. 2011, Cornell University Lab of Ornithology.

Tallamy, Douglas M. "About Native Gardening." Online at http://bringingnaturehome.net.

———. *Bringing Nature Home: How You Can Sustain Wildlife with Native Plants,* 2nd ed. Portland, MA: Timber Press, 2009.

Tarvin, Keith A., and Glen E. Woolfenden. 1999. "Blue Jay (*Cyanocitta cristata*)." BNA Online.

Terres, John K. *The Audubon Society Encyclopedia of North American Birds.* New York: Wings Books, 1991.

Thompson, Bill, III. *Identify Yourself.* New York: Houghton Mifflin, 2005.

"Tools for Investigating Migration," *BirdScope.* Autumn, 2009, 1.

Toops, Connie. "Get Ready for Bluebirds," *Birder's World.* April 1998, 20–23.

———. "How Birds Sleep," *Birder's World.* Aug. 2008, 28–33.

———. "Winter Havens," *Birder's World.* Dec. 2003, 88–91.

Townsend, Andrea. "The Young and the Restless," *BirdScope.* Winter 2010, 7.

U.S. Army Corps of Engineers, St. Louis District. "Riverlands Migratory Bird Sanctuary Watchable Wildlife Bald Eagle." n.d.

U.S. Fish and Wildlife Service. "Birds of Conservation Concern 2008." Arlington, VA: U.S. Department of Interior, Fish and Wildlife Service, Division of Migratory Bird Management, 2008. Online at www.fws.gov/migratorybirds.

Vennesland, Ross G., and Robert W. Butler. 2011. "Great Blue Heron (*Ardea herodias*)." BNA Online.

Verbeek, N. A., and C. Caffrey. 2002. "American Crow (*Corvus brachyrhynchos*)." BNA Online.

Waldbauer, Gilbert. *The Birder's Bug Book.* Cambridge: Harvard University Press, 1998.

Walton, Richard K. and Robert W. Lawson. *Birding by Ear: A Guide to Bird-song Identification, Eastern/Central.* 3 compact disks. Boston: Houghton Mifflin, 1989.

———. *More Birding by Ear: A Guide to Bird-song Identification, Eastern/Central.* 3 compact disks. Boston: Houghton Mifflin, 1994.

Weckstein, Jason D., Donald E. Kroodsma, and Robert C. Faucett. 2002. "Fox Sparrow (*Passerella iliaca*)." BNA Online.

Weeks, Harmon P., Jr. 2011. "Eastern Phoebe (*Sayornis phoebe*)." BNA Online.

Weidensaul, Scott. *Living on the Wind: Across the Hemisphere with Migratory Birds.* New York: North Point Press, 2000.

———. *The Raptor Almanac: A Comprehensive Guide to Eagles, Hawks, Falcons, and Vultures.* Guilford, CT: The Lyons Press, 2004.

Wells, Diana. *100 Birds and How They Got Their Names.* Chapel Hill, NC: Algonquin Books, 2002.

Wiebe, Karen L., and William S. Moore. 2008. "Northern Flicker (*Colaptes auratus*)." BNA Online.

"Wild Turkey: An American Success Story," *Bird Conservation.* Winter 2008/2009, 24.

Williamson, Sheri. *Attracting and Feeding Hummingbirds.* Neptune City, NY: T. F. H. Publications, n.d.

———. "Rock On, Mockers," *WildBird.* Mar/April 2011, 24–25.

———. "Tiny Terrors," *WildBird.* May/June 2011, 22–23.

Winkler, David W., Kelly K. Hallinger, Daniel R. Ardia, R. J. Robertson, B. J. Stutchbury, and R. R. Cohen. 2011. "Tree Swallow (*Tachycineta bicolor*)." BNA Online.

Witmer, M. C., D. J. Mountjoy, and L. Elliot. 1997. "Cedar Waxwing (*Bombycilla cedrorum*)." BNA Online.

Wootton, J. Timothy. 1996. "Purple Finch (*Carpodacus purpureus*)." BNA Online.

Wyatt, Valerie E., and Charles M. Francis. 2002. "Rose-breasted Grosbeak (*Pheucticus ludovicianus*)." BNA Online.

Yasukawa, Ken, and William A. Searcy. 1995. "Red-winged Blackbird (*Agelaius phoeniceus*)." BNA Online.

Youth, Howard. "King of the Field," *Bird Watcher's Digest.* July/Aug. 2006, 28–35.

Zickefoose, Julie. "Birds Watch Us, Too," *Bird Watcher's Digest.* Nov./Dec. 2009, 82–87.

———. *Enjoying Bluebirds More.* Marietta, OH: Pardson Corporation, 1993.

———. "Mourning Dove," *Bird Watcher's Digest.* Jan./Feb. 2003, 30–37.

———. "A Solution to Window Strikes: Thinking about Thunking," *Bird Watcher's Digest.* Mar./April 2009, 80–85.

INDEX

Page numbers in italics indicates illustrations.